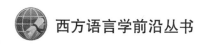
西方语言学前沿丛书

论辩话语中的策略操控
语用论辩学拓展
中文导读注释版

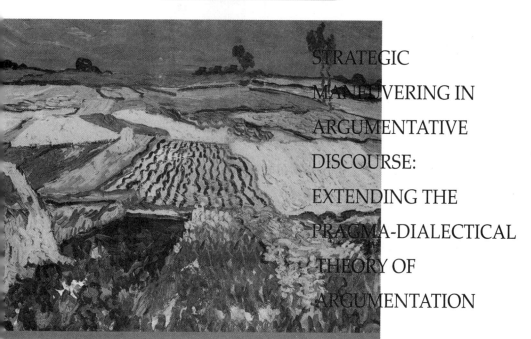

STRATEGIC
MANEUVERING IN
ARGUMENTATIVE
DISCOURSE:
EXTENDING THE
PRAGMA-DIALECTICAL
THEORY OF
ARGUMENTATION

〔荷〕弗兰斯·范爱默伦（Frans van Eemeren） 著
毛浩然 吴鹏 导读
高丽珍 注释

北京大学出版社
PEKING UNIVERSITY PRESS

著作权合同登记号　图字：01-2016-1058

图书在版编目(CIP)数据

论辩话语中的策略操控：语用论辩学拓展：中文导读注释版：英文 / (荷) 弗兰斯·范爱默伦 (Frans van Eemeren) 著. —北京：北京大学出版社, 2016.10
（西方语言学前沿丛书）
ISBN 978-7-301-27643-3

Ⅰ. ①论… Ⅱ. ①弗… Ⅲ. ①语用学-研究-英文 Ⅳ. ①H03

中国版本图书馆 CIP 数据核字 (2016) 第 237121 号

Original edition: "*Strategic Maneuvering In Argumentative Discourse*", by Eemeren, F. van.
©2010 John Benjamins Publishing Company, Amsterdam/Philadelphia.
Reprinted by permission for distribution in the People's Republic of China only.

书　　名	论辩话语中的策略操控——语用论辩学拓展（中文导读注释版） BIANLUN HUAYU ZHONG DE CELÜE CAOKONG
著作责任者	〔荷〕弗兰斯·范爱默伦 (Frans van Eemeren) 著
责任编辑	刘文静
标准书号	ISBN 978-7-301-27643-3
出版发行	北京大学出版社
地　　址	北京市海淀区成府路 205 号　100871
网　　址	http://www.pup.cn　新浪微博：@北京大学出版社
电子信箱	liuwenjing008@163.com
电　　话	邮购部 62752015　发行部 62750672　编辑部 62754382
印 刷 者	三河市北燕印装有限公司
经 销 者	新华书店
	650 毫米 ×980 毫米　16 开本　20.75 印张　350 千字 2016 年 10 月第 1 版　2016 年 10 月第 1 次印刷
定　　价	59.00 元

未经许可，不得以任何方式复制或抄袭本书之部分或全部内容。
版权所有，侵权必究
举报电话：010-62752024　电子信箱：fd@pup.pku.edu.cn
图书如有印装质量问题，请与出版部联系，电话：010-62756370

*Dedicated to the memory of
Peter Houtlosser,
My former student, co-author, and friend*

In the end, reasonableness prevails

专家委员会

陈新仁	程晓堂	丁建新	丁言仁
封宗信	高一虹	顾曰国	胡壮麟
黄国文	姜望琪	李　兵	李福印
李战子	廖美珍	刘世生	卢　植
马秋武	毛浩然	苗兴伟	彭宣维
齐振海	钱　军	冉永平	申　丹
史宝辉	田贵森	王初明	王克非
王立非	王　寅	王振华	文　军
文　旭	熊学亮	杨永林	张德禄
张　辉	张绍杰	张应林	赵蓉晖

总　序

马年甫始，喜讯频传。北京大学出版社自2012年起着手准备影印出版"西方语言学前沿丛书"，经过国内专家多方推荐和认真论证，并与国外出版社谈判版权，已取得很大进展，最近将陆续出版。就我所知悉的内容，这套丛书的选题涉及句法学、心理语言学、社会语言学、语用学、认知语言学、隐喻学、话语分析、文体学、多模态语言学等。"丛书"的出版无疑具有巨大的现实意义和深远意义。

就现实意义而言，我国外语教育界近年来不时受到种种骚扰，最典型的、危害最大的论调是有人不把高校的外语教育看作一个专业，以致我国高校的外语专业学生除了学习听、说、读、写四个技能外，被要求到外系学习专业课；也有人不能正确认识我国改革开放后在外语教育方面所取得的成就，不图进取，走新中国成立前老路的片面观点。在此关键时刻，"丛书"的出版，将有助于外语教育界的决策者和高校老师树立正确的全面的认识。

就深远意义而言，北京大学出版社继2011年出版"语言学论丛"系列论著外，再接再厉，如今又出版"西方语言学前沿丛书"，其用意无非是让国内高校和研究机构了解国际上在语言学研究方面的动向和进展。我认为此举还具有深层次的意义，就我国治学情况说，这将有利于扭转我国学术研究中不重视理论研究的陋习，如改革开放前我国外语界主要为编纂词典和教材；其次，这将帮助我们了解国外不同学派的出现和争鸣以推动学术创新；不仅如此，这也帮助我们了解国外学者如何注意把握理论与实践的关系，将理论应用于实践，在实践中发现问题和对理论不断修正。应该说，我们对实践还是一贯重视的，但对于如何以先进理论指导实践的认识有待提高。

这里，我还想就"西方语言学前沿丛书"的"前沿"二字谈一些看法。"前沿"的一层意思指"处于领先地位的"。我们平时常说要将我国外语教学和科研达到国际水平，就是要达到国际上的前沿水平。在这一点上，我们已取得很大进步。读者会发现本次出版的上下两集 *LANGAUGE AND STYLE* 的论文集中，就收录了我国北京大学学者申丹教授的论文，这表明我国已有学者达到"前沿"水平，与国外学者平起平坐了。我相信这一趋势将日益明显。"前沿"的另一层意思是"前部的边儿"，它隐含的意义是一个学科或一门专业必然与其他学科或专业有这样那样的相邻关系，从其他学科和专业获得营养，拓宽视野。这是反映学术发展的交叉学科得以出现的前提。因此本语言学丛书既有传统意义的句法学、词汇学、语音学等选题，也有心理语言学、认知语言学、文体学、隐喻学等选题，特别是与现代信息技术密切结合的多模态语言学。这便为我国学者指引了努力方向。

本套丛书采取英文原版影印，同时配有中文导读，并对目录主题等主要段落进行中文翻译的方式，以促进高校教师与学生更充分地汲取国内外语言学研究的最新理论和成果。这体现了"丛书"策划者和编者能为读者着想、为读者服务的敬业精神。

最后，我对各书导读作者的学术水平和辛勤劳动非常钦佩，导读作者们不仅帮助我们如何正确理解和掌握各书的内容和要点，而且能够勇于对一些问题或观点发表评论，引导读者批判学习，殊非易事。可见，"前沿"的丛书需要"前沿"的导读执笔者、"前沿"的编者，谨向各位"者"们致敬！

胡壮麟
北京大学外国语学院
2014 年 3 月

导 读

毛浩然 吴 鹏

论辩是人们为论证或反驳某一立场而展开的言语交际活动。它是社会生活的一种常见话语现象，大到国与国之间的外交争议，小到人与人之间的日常交流，随时随地都能看到论辩的身影。一场成功的论辩可以让旷日持久的摩擦化干戈为玉帛，而一场失败的论辩可能会使冲突火上浇油，甚至使战争一触即发。正是因为论辩的常态化和重要性，两千多年来，中西方先贤和学者均高度关注论辩话语的理论与实践探索。春秋战国时期，孟子、韩非子、墨子等先贤均擅长论辩，各家著述中均有关于诸子通过论辩说服各国君主权贵的记载。在西方，依据论辩的不同场景与用途，Aristotle 第一次系统提出了论辩研究的三个不同视角：分析学（analytic）、论辩术（dialectic）和修辞术（rhetoric）。这三个视角正是逻辑学（logic）、论辩学 (dialectic) 和修辞学 (rhetoric) 的雏形。遗憾的是，Aristotle 之后，这三条视角似乎正朝着各自为政的方向发展，未能协同突破。20 世纪 70 年代末，Frans van Eemeren 和 Rob Grootendorst 以论辩学和语用学为基础，综合话语分析（特别是会话分析）、言语交际理论（特别是言语行为理论和会话含义理论）、逻辑学等多学科知识，创立并发展了具有重要国际影响力的语用论辩学理论（Pragma-Dialectics）。该理论与北美以温莎大学为中心的非形式逻辑学共同推进了经典论辩学的复兴，开辟了不同于以往纯粹逻辑学或修辞学研究范式的另一种论辩研究范式。近十多年来，语用论辩理论在原有标准理论中加入修辞考量维度，提出了"策略操控"（strategic maneuvering）概念，试图以此整合论辩学和修辞学两种经典论辩分析与评价传统，再现现实论辩话语在辩证合理性（dialectical reasonableness）和修辞有效性（rhetorical effectiveness）两方面的微妙平衡。拓展后的语用论辩理论在理论解释力和实践意义上都得到很大提升。为了系统构建策略操控的概念体系及恢复其在整个语用论辩学理论中的地位，2010 年，Frans van Eemeren 在 John Benjamin 出版了专著《论辩话语中的策略操控——语用论辩学拓展》（*Strategic*

Maneuvering in Argumentative Discourse: Extending the Pragma-Dialectical Theory of Argumentation）。该书共十章，第一章系统介绍了语用论辩学标准理论，第二章至第六章介绍了策略操控概念框架下的论辩分析方法，第七章讨论了策略操控视角下的论辩谬误，第八章和第九章以两个具体实例论证了论辩话语中的策略操控分析与评价路径，第十章讨论了语用论辩学拓展理论的未来发展方向。接下来我们将简要述评各章的主要内容。

第一章"论辩话语分析"回顾了语用论辩学的标准理论。与逻辑学和修辞学对论辩的理解不同，语用论辩学对论辩和论辩研究的理解，一方面受到经典论辩学和形式论辩学的影响，另一方面又受到当代语用学理论（特别是言语行为理论和会话含义理论）的启发。基于论辩学，Frans van Eemeren 认为，论辩的本质是批判性讨论的一部分，其目的是消除双方（可能）存在的意见分歧。虽然有时参与论辩的双方可能并不是为了说服对方，而是为了赢得第三方的青睐（如政客间的电视辩论），但他们还是要通过（貌似）合理的方式来消除与目标受众之间的意见分歧。因此，在现实生活中论辩可能无处不在，因为无论是在家庭、课堂、法律还是政治领域，人们都有可能提出自己的立场，与他人产生意见分歧，并试图消除这些意见分歧。在明确了论辩的批判性本质与实现消除意见分歧的目的之后，Frans van Eemeren 指出，论辩研究的目的是"为了改善论辩话语的质量"。因此，单纯描述性的论辩研究（如描述语言学路径下的法国论辩研究学派）并不理想，研究者必须要有实证性和批判性两种研究导向：实证性导向指的是相对客观且完整地展现论辩的构成要件。不过，不同理论视角下论辩的构成要件也不尽相同。受语用学理论的启发，Frans van Eemeren 认为，作为言语交际的论辩是由论辩双方不同类型的言语行为组成的，这些言语行为在论辩的不同阶段或环节担负着不同的论辩功能。描述论辩要件实际上就是刻画和阐释其中发挥核心论辩功能的核心言语行为，即论辩话步（argumentative move）。批判性导向指的是对论辩话语的合理性进行评判，指出其中存在的谬误。毋庸置疑，对合理性的评判必须要有一套合理性评判标准，这也是语用论辩学的一项重要任务。Frans van Eemeren 指出，语用论辩学研究者必须在哲学、理论、实证、分析和实践五个层面上进行深入探究，才能保证论辩研究的实证性和批评性导向：哲学层面，主要探讨论辩合理性与可接受性的哲学内涵，语用论辩学中的"合理性"主要受到

Barth 和 Krabbe 的形式论辩术（formal dialectic）的影响，也与 Popper 的批判理性主义（critical rationalism）有关；理论层面，Frans van Eemeren 与 Grootendorst 在哲学内涵的基础上建构起一个批判性讨论模型，该模型为分析和评价论辩提供概念框架。此外，该模型还提供了论辩分析工具，即对论辩话步的"分析概览"（analytic overview）；实证层面，主要呈现、阐释和评估真实论辩实践，并依据理论模型考察各相关要素对论辩话语的影响；分析层面，根据理论模型中建构的理论框架，为重构真实论辩提供具体分析工具，目的是在理论模型和真实论辩话语之间架起互通的桥梁；实践层面，主要利用上述四个层面的研究结果，来解决真实论辩话语中出现的各种实际问题。

语用论辩学中建立的批判性讨论理想模型（或者说论辩理想模型）由冲突、开始、论辩和结论四个阶段组成。在冲突阶段，双方明确意见分歧及各自立场；在开始阶段，双方定位正、反两方角色，并就程序性和实质性出发点达成一致；在论辩阶段，正方为自己的观点辩护，反方可针对正方的立场和论证提出异议；在结论阶段，正反双方确定意见分歧是否被消除，或在多大程度上被消除。在现实论辩话语中，论辩各阶段在顺序上可能会出现跨越或颠倒，这就需要以上述四个阶段为模板对批判性讨论进行重构，其方法包括删除冗余信息、增添潜在信息、重排论辩顺序和替换模糊表达。重构的目标是形成完整清晰的分析概览，其中包含可供研究者进一步评析的六个关键性要素，即意见分歧、双方立场、出发点、论辩结构、论证图式和论辩结果。

重构形成的"分析概览"应该尽量满足经济性、有效性、连贯性等三大要求。经济性要求分析概览应该简明地呈现只与解决意见分歧相关的言语行为；有效性要求分析概览应该为实现公正评价而对所有话语要素进行功能性归类。连贯性要求建立最为连贯的分析概览。除此之外，分析概览还应该满足现实性要求和充分性要求。现实性要求分析概览尽可能地体现论辩的合理性和可信度，也就是说，分析概览应尽量忠于论辩现实，且能得到论辩双方的认同。充分性要求分析概览应能为实证观察所支撑。

Frans van Eemeren 认为，分析者可通过语用论辩学的标准理论对论辩话语进行重构，得出分析概览，以便进行批判性评价。但在现实生活中，仅使用标准理论对论辩话语进行分析是不够的。因为在现实中，论辩者的目的不仅是"合理"解决意见分歧,还要使得论辩结果向有利于自己的方向有效地发展。因此,为了拓展语用论辩学的分析范围,语用论辩学的拓展理论被提上了日程。该拓展理论为分析论辩话语提供了一个新的理论视角:在重构论辩话语时,分析者不仅要考虑标准理论所关注的论辩的合理性,还应展现论辩者为使他的对话更具有效性而做出的努力。

在第二章,Frans van Eemeren 着重引入了"拓展后的语用论辩学"中最重要的概念——"策略操控"(strategic maneuvering)。他阐释了语用论辩学中"论辩"被赋予的三个重要特征:(1)"论辩"一词不仅应包含论辩的"过程",也应包含论辩的"结果";(2)论辩的目的是为了合理地解决意见分歧,因而诸如吵架、斗嘴这些与"合理"相悖的语言行为不应包括在"论辩"之中;(3)论辩是为了维护立场,因而立场本身并不应被包含在论辩中。语用论辩理论认为论辩研究必须遵从四个基本理论出发点——功能化(functionalization)、社会化(socialization)、外显化(externalization)和论辩化(dialectification)。功能化指的是不把论辩视做结构化、静态的逻辑推演,而是要明确语言或者其他符号系统在论辩中实现了哪些特定的交际互动功能;社会化指的是将论辩视做正反双方两个或两个以上主体之间的显性或隐性对话;外显化指的是仅仅阐释正反双方通过言语行为而做出的承诺("接受"或者"不同意")及其对论辩过程的影响,而无需主观揣测论辩者内在的认知或心理状态;论辩化指的是将论辩视做一种受合理性标准约束、旨在解决意见分歧的批判性讨论,即对论辩话语采取一种"客位"而非"主位"的分析立场。

在"保持论辩话语的合理性"和"追求论辩话语的有效性"两节,Frans van Eemeren 分别对有效性和合理性的概念以及两者之间的联系进行了讨论。如前所述,如何通过批判性讨论使双方意见分歧得以合理消除是语用论辩标准理论的核心问题,合理性是其分析和评价论辩的出发点和落脚点。但是,在现实论辩话语中,论辩者不仅需要"合理"地解决意见分歧,还要尽力使论辩结果朝着有利于自己的方向"有效地"发展。语用论辩学中,"合理性"是指在完成论辩四个阶段所赋予的任务时,根据具体情况以恰当的方式运用理性,对合理性的评价主要从问题解决的有效性(是否有利于意见分歧的解决)和主体间性的有效性(是否能为正反双方所接受)出发。"有效性"不仅是指在论辩阶段说服对方,而且是贯穿于论辩的四个阶段的。

在真实的论辩话语中，论辩者在批判性讨论的四个阶段都要追求论辩的合理性和有效性。为了解释论辩话语的这个特征，Frans van Eemeren 提出了"策略操控"的概念。所谓"策略操控"指的是论辩者为了实现"合理性"和"有效性"之间的微妙平衡在论辩的四个阶段付出的"持续性努力"。"操控"指的是"视论辩的具体情形做出最好的选择"，而"策略"强调的是"技巧性的安排与规划"，意即论辩中的每个"操控"不是临时起意的，而是在平衡了论辩合理性和修辞有效性之后做出的整体策略安排。

为说明"论辩合理性"和"修辞有效性"概念的历史变迁，第三章接着探讨了"合理性"概念在古典论辩术以及现代论辩学中的发展，其后介绍了"有效性"概念在古典修辞学和现代修辞学研究路径下的理论发展。Frans van Eemeren 首先介绍了 Zeno 的论辩推理模型、Plato 对论辩术的看法以及 Aristotle 的论辩术系统理论。通过对这些古典论辩术的描述，Frans van Eemeren 归纳出了古典论辩术对论辩过程、论辩过程的结构以及理性标准的总体看法。其后，Frans van Eemeren 介绍了当代论辩学者（如 Barth & Krabbe、Walton 等人）从不同角度对古典论辩术的深入探索。本章第四节、第五节简要介绍了修辞学的历史变迁。在 Aristotle 那里，与逻辑学和论辩学的目的一致，修辞学也是为了指导人们更好地进行论辩，只不过修辞学服务的论辩话语主要是诸如政治演说、公开演讲等说服性论辩话语。古罗马时期的修辞学代表人物有 Cicero 和 Quintilian，他们提出的修辞教育思想（如修辞五艺）继承并发展了古希腊的修辞学，对修辞学的发展至关重要。古罗马衰落之后，修辞学渐渐变为专门研究文体和临场言说的学问，并一直处于受压抑的学科地位。现代修辞学研究的一个重要特点是研究范围的不断扩展，越来越多地被用于论辩及其他类型的话语分析中。

综合论辩学和修辞学的历史发展轨迹，Frans van Eemeren 提出了自己对修辞学和论辩学关系的看法：在当代论辩研究领域，论辩学和修辞学一直是两个相对分离的研究视角，两者之间存在较大的概念鸿沟。这不仅背离了 Aristotle 的论辩研究初衷，也在深层次上阻碍了论辩理论的全面发展。因此，对论辩的分析和评价必须将论辩学和修辞学有机融合，而"策略操控"就是使两者可以互通的论辩话语的分析框架。

第四章主要介绍论辩话语中策略操控实现方式。受西方古典修辞学三大研究范畴——话题（topoi）、受众（audience）和表达（presentation）——

的启发，语用论辩学认为策略操控主要体现在论辩者对"潜在话题"（topical potential）、"受众需求"（audience demand）和"表达手段"（presentational devices）的运筹帷幄。下面具体阐述这三个方面。

"潜在话题"指的是论辩者在不同阶段选择的谈论话题，即切入议题的角度。在冲突阶段，论辩者一般会首先界定"争议空间"（disagreement space），并通过对其中可用话题的选择使论辩焦点有利于己方论证或质疑；在开始阶段，论辩者会致力于创造"一致区域"（zone of agreement），使论辩的程序性和实质性出发点符合自己利益。通常论辩者会努力将对方的妥协之处确定为一致区域；在论辩阶段，论辩者会根据批判性讨论的具体情况选择最适合自己的论证或质疑话题；在结论阶段，论辩者会通过对"结论范畴"（scope of conclusiveness）的界定，尽力使论辩的结果与其理想方向相符，比如从自己的角度指出论辩结果的意义。

"受众需求"指的是论辩者将自己的论证或质疑与受众持有的观点或喜好相呼应，尽最大可能迎合受众的需求，以便使自己立场更容易被接受。为此，论辩者在冲突阶段可能会将意见分歧界定为更易论辩的非混合型分歧；在开始阶段，论辩者通常选择既能被受众认可、同时又符合自己利益的程序性和实质性起点；在论辩阶段，迎合受众需求表现为挑选能够最大程度迎合受众利益的论证；在结论阶段主要表现为尽力使受众相信论辩的结果不会给他们带来任何不利。

"表达手段"指的是利用言语表达的"语用空间"（pragmatic room，即同一言语表达可能具有的语境含义集合），通过对句式、词汇、修辞格等语言形式的选择，使论辩话语取得理想的交际与互动目的。比如，在论辩的冲突阶段，论辩者可能会在陈述立场时刻意隐藏自己的态度以使意见分歧不至于过早复杂化；在开始阶段，论辩者可能会借用能够引起受众共鸣的隐喻表达作为实质性出发点；在论辩阶段，论辩者可能会一口气提出全部论证并为论证加上序号，以使自己的立场显得严谨而充分；在结论阶段，论辩者会以控制、谦虚的方式用"事实"进行素描式表达，形成"理在我方，无需雄辩"的印象。

总之，策略操控的根本含义就是论辩者从潜在主题、受众需求和表达手段三个角度出发，在遵守批判性讨论准则的同时，综合运用多种修辞手段，对论辩话语的内容与形式进行策略性重组，努力使论辩话语兼具合理性和有效性。

第五章介绍了策略操控与宏观交际活动类型之间的关系。在拓展后的语用论辩学中，识别和评判策略操控不但要分析上下文语境和情景语境，更要对论辩的交际活动类型及其机构语境进行细致分析。所谓"交际活动类型"（communicative activity type），是指某一交际领域中的惯例化交际实践，它体现在具体的交际事件之中。根据交际语类的不同，Frans van Eemeren 将常见的交际活动类型大致划分为裁决、协商、调解、谈判、咨询、争议、推广、交流等八类。遗憾的是，这八类之间依然有相互重叠之嫌，且分类标准不明。

之所以要明晰论辩所处的交际活动类型，是因为不同交际活动类型中的制度语境约束着论辩的策略操控。但是不同的交际活动类型的特征千差万别，与其对应的机构语境构成要素也不尽相同。在这种情况下，从哪几个方面或角度分析制度语境对策略操控的约束就显得十分重要。对此，Frans van Eemeren 提供了一个较为简便的解决方案。他从四个方面解构不同交际活动类型的制度约束因素，这四个方面与批判性讨论的四个阶段一一对应：起始状态（冲突阶段）、程序性和实质性出发点（开始阶段）、论证方式与质疑（论辩阶段）和可能的结果（结论阶段）。在本章的最后部分，为了验证交际活动类型的制度语境分析能够使得整个论辩理论通往现实论辩，Frans van Eemeren 以政治领域冲突阶段中的策略操控为例进行了分析。

第六章主要介绍策略操控及其功能的四个分析维度。Frans van Eemeren 提出可以从结果（results）、路径（routes）、制约（constraints）、承诺（commitments）四个维度展开。"结果"指的是借助分析概览揭示某个策略操控在特定阶段可能达成的结果，即借助分析概览帮助我们厘清某种策略操控对其中某一阶段的实际影响。"路径"指的是通过论辩轮廓（dialectical profile）呈现该策略操控实现上述结果的具体路径。论辩轮廓指的是论辩者在批判性讨论中为实现某一阶段合理性目标而可能采取的话步序列。"制约"指的是通过对论辩所属交际活动类型及其特征的剖析，揭示制度语境对该策略操控的制约。对于不同交际活动类型的制度约束因素的分析，语用论辩学中采用的是与批判性讨论四个阶段一一对应的四个方面来解构，即起始状态、程序性和实质性出发点、论证方式与质疑、可能的结果。

"承诺"指的是剖析论辩者在策略操控发生时达成的承诺，以此揭示影响策略操控的论辩情境。Frans van Eemeren 认为，批判性讨论的任何一个节点上的论辩情境，都是由双方言语行为互动形成的一组承诺建构起来的。研究者可以从识别性条件（identity conditions）和正确性条件（correctness conditions）两个角度分析这些承诺的具体组成，然后进一步探讨论辩者是如何在策略操控中遵守并充分利用这些承诺的。

第七章从策略操控的角度探讨了论辩谬误的形成机制。Frans van Eemeren 指出，人们对谬误的研究源自改善论辩实践的需求，而对谬误处理方式的探讨也成了所有规范性论辩理论的重要组成部分。早在古希腊时期，Aristotle 就对可能出现在反驳观点时的谬误进行研究。自此之后，越来越多的谬误种类得以识别、分类，对各种谬误的处理方式也逐渐定型。20世纪 70 年代，Charles Hamblin 在其出版的《谬误》（*Fallacies*）一书中对当时逻辑学教科书中出现的谬误"标准处理方法"（Standard Treatment）提出了批评，激发了论辩研究者们对这一领域进一步探索。Hamblin 之后，加拿大逻辑学家 Woods 和 Warton 尝试对谬误的"标准处理方法"进行修补。与此同时，在欧洲，Barth 和 Krabbe 基于"批判理性主义"提出了"形式论辩术"（formal dialectic），Frans van Eemeren 和 Grootendorst 提出了语用论辩学，前者提出了批判性讨论的形式系统，并将谬误视为无法由该形式系统生成的话步，后者与前者有关联，但关注的是日常生活中的论辩话语，认为只从交际和互动过程中的语言使用角度来看，论辩话语中的出现谬误也可能被合理地理解。

语用论辩学将所有谬误系统地串联在批判性讨论的行为准则之中，认为谬误是违反批判性讨论行为准则的结果，这种违反阻碍了合理解决意见分歧的进程。语用论辩学理论提供了另一种行之有效的谬误处理方法，其不仅关注解决问题的有效性（problem-validity），也关注进行批判性讨论时符合惯例的有效性（conventional-validity）。如前文所述，论辩者会使用策略操控来达到"合理性"和"有效性"之间的微妙平衡，但这种平衡并不是绝对的平衡。为了更好地达到对其中某一方面的效果，论辩者可能在一定程度上会牺牲对另一方的诉求。但当论辩者过分注重有效性而忽略合理性时，策略操控就会"脱轨"（derail）。当一条或一条以上的批判性讨论行为准则被违背时，谬误就随之产生，因而，在"拓展后的语用论辩学"

中，谬误被视为策略操控的脱轨。每种谬误都对应着一种合理的策略操控，两者就如同滑行在合理性和有效性之间的两个点，区别是前者过于靠近有效性且距离合理性太远，而后者刚好处于平衡点。例如，与人身攻击谬误（ad hominem）对应的是合理的人身攻击（personal attack）；与诉诸权威谬误（ad verecundiam）相对的是合理的诉诸权威（ex autoritate）。

谬误具有欺诈性，一是因为谬误的偏离与合理的策略操控可能只有寸步之遥，二是由于谬误与合理策略操控之间的差别具有语境敏感性——某个交际活动类型中的合理策略操控在另外一种活动类型中可能就是谬误。因此，Frans van Eemeren 主张对谬误的识别必须同时具备两个标准：脱离语境的一般标准和针对语境的特别标准。在具体操作中，我们可以锁定某种策略操控类型，根据批判性讨论行为准则检视与此对应的谬误类型及其一般识别标准（脱离语境），然后在具体语境中结合制度语境考察该一般性识别标准的具体适用，对其细化、修正或补充，形成基于语境的策略操控类型的具体识别标准。在本章的最后，Frans van Eemeren 还举例展示了如何评价策略操控的合理性。

在第八章以对举证责任（burden of proof）的策略操控为例，讨论了在批判性讨论的开始阶段中，谬误性策略操控与合理策略操控之间的界限。在论辩中，举证责任被赋予重要的程序意义，举证责任指论辩中正方在面对反方提出的质疑或反对意见时，维护己方立场的责任。当面对质疑或反对时，正方只有基于双方在开始阶段达成的共同出发点，进一步提出论证才能履行其举证责任。对举证责任进行的策略操控可能是合理的，但当正方试图回避举证责任时，策略操控就出现了"脱轨"。

在论辩中，意见分歧可以是非混合型的（反方仅质疑正方立场），也可是混合型的（反方不仅质疑，且反对正方立场），在混合型意见分歧中，确定论辩双方的辩护顺序对于举证责任的分配至关重要，而辩护顺序主要是由语用原则（pragmatic rationale）决定。语用原则主要指双方在进行言语交际和互动时，彼此要遵守的规则或要履行的义务，这在 Searl 的言语行为理论、Grice 的合作原则中都有体现。除此之外，Frans van Eemeren 和 Grootendorst 还提出了"互动准则"（Interaction Principle），互动准则是凝练出一套不能被谈话对象所接受，说话者应避免做出的言语行为的准则。但与 Grice 的合作原则不同的是，对互动准则的违反不是要求说话者考虑对发言做进一步阐释，相反，这种违反阻碍了正常互动的发展，甚至导致言语行为无法被接受。只有遵守互动准则的言语行为才能被真正接受。此外，辩护顺序还受该言语行为是否违反了语用现状（pragmatic status quo）的影响。

策略操控的运用旨在尽可能地强化己方立场的劝服效力，对其运筹帷幄可能出现在论辩四个阶段的任一阶段，针对举证责任进行的不当策略操控也会导致谬误的产生。Walton指出，一些谬误"反映出了举证责任的轻微转移，可能造成很大的影响，却常常被人们所忽略"。事实上，对举证责任的策略操控可能出现在论辩的任何阶段中，并对论辩产生不同的效果。通过对广告话语实例的分析，Frans van Eemeren具体阐释了不同阶段针对举证责任可能出现的各种策略操控形式。

第九章主要关注如何使脱轨的策略操控"重回正轨"得以校正（re-rail）。在论辩中，一方常会攻击对方前后言语或行为上的不一致性，这种不一致可能是逻辑上的，也可能是语用上的。在策略操控层面上指出这种不一致性可能是合理的，也可能会"脱轨"并产生谬误。当反方质疑正方将一命题作为出发点，指出正方在不同时间或在不同场合下就此命题存在言行不一致行为时，就犯了一种可归为"你也是"（tu quoque）类型的谬误。判断攻击"前后不一"的策略操控是否合理，主要取决于三个方面：（1）正反双方在经过主体间推断（intersubjective inference procedure）后对命题在逻辑或语用上是否存在不一致所达成的共同观点；（2）正方所做的命题承诺是"公开的"（avowed）还是"语境化的"（contextual）；（3）前后不一致的言行是否出现在同一个批判性讨论之中。

Frans van Eemeren指出，在日常生活中，论辩中出现谬误是不可避免的，但并不是所有谬误的出现都会给意见分歧的解决带来灾难性影响。有时人们并没有注意到这些谬误（如该谬误无关紧要），受到"冒犯"的一方可能也不会意识到。有时人们会故意忽略谬误（如将其当成玩笑话），这也并没有给意见分歧的解决带来负面影响。谬误的产生并不一定意味着理性讨论的终结，正反双方也可能愿意在存在谬误的情况下继续将论辩进行下去。因而，只有在谬误严重违反了"合理性准则"（Principle of Reasonableness）的情况下，论辩才应该终止，因而修复尚存合理性的"脱轨"论辩很有意义。最佳的谬误处理方式应是将每一个可能存在谬误的话步看做次级讨论中的策略操控，在此期间，一方仍将对方视为努力合理地解决意见分歧的对象，并同时尽量让对方明白，他的策略操控脱轨了，且无益于意见分歧的解决。在使得脱轨的策略操控重回正轨得以校正的努力过程中，我们应重新考虑策略操控在"话题选择""受众需求"和"表达手段"三方面上的设计。

第十章论述了语用论辩学拓展理论的后续研究方向。以策略操控概念为核心的语用论辩拓展理论打通了论辩学、逻辑学与修辞学之间长期存在的人为隔阂，有力推动了论辩理论的多学科全面发展。但是，与成熟的标准理论相比，拓展理论的研究时间尚短，很多方面都应加以深化。Frans van Eemeren 对此有着十分清醒的认识，他认为拓展理论在哲学、理论、实证、分析和实践五个层面上都有很大提升空间。具体而言，哲学层面还需深入探讨论辩学和修辞学两大视角的兼容性和深入融合的路径；理论层面可以对策略操控进一步类型化，并为不同类型的策略操控制定合理性标准；实证层面，研究者还要通过实验、定量统计等实证方法验证关于策略操控的各种理论假设，包括合理性、有效性、影响谬误的各种因素，等等；分析层面的任务是重构论辩不同阶段的策略操控形式及其组合效应，并在此基础上勾勒具有普适性的冲突策略、开始策略、论辩策略和结论策略；实践层面的任务是需要继续挖掘和归纳各种交际活动类型，深入探讨不同交际活动类型对论辩话语的机构语境。

纵观全书，从对语用论辩学标准理论的回顾，到对拓展后的语用论辩学的理论剖析、应用示范和未来展望，Frans van Eemeren 尽力将语用论辩学数十年发展之大观完整地展现在读者面前。遗憾的是，本书存在如下两点不足：

（1）Frans van Eemeren 在本书中对谬误标准的介绍有所欠缺。语用论辩理论的前期标准理论为识别谬误制定了十条戒律，但是没有进一步明确适用这些戒律的具体标准。具体标准的缺失有时会使谬误识别成为另外一个谬误。拓展理论虽然明确了这一标准必须分成脱离语境的一般标准和语境敏感的特殊标准两大类，但仍未深入探讨一般标准到底是哪些，这应该成为未来的研究重点。

（2）拓展后的语用论辩学还应考虑进一步完善其语境分析。Frans van Eemeren 认为，论辩话语的生产和理解受到微观语境(上下文)、中观语境(即时情景）、宏观语境（制度约束）和互文语境等四种语境因素的制约。但是从目前的相关研究看来，互文语境尚未受到足够重视。将宏观语境简约为制度约束因素的做法也值得商榷。当然，与相对固定的制度约束因素相比，互文语境和更为宏观的社会、政治、历史和文化语境显然过于庞杂和不确定，研究者的确很难勾勒出基本分析框架，这也许是语用论辩学不愿过多涉及的重要原因之一。但是，在具体个案中，特别是涉及政治或社会的论辩话语，全面系统的宏观语境分析和互文语境分析可能同样十分重要。更加多维和更加系统的语境分析，有助于拓展理论真正与论辩实践真正接轨。

值得一提的是：层级分类是理论建构必不可少的重要环节，也是最具挑战性的要害之一。规范的分类须注意如下四点：①要有统一且科学的分类标准；②子类别之间要逻辑平行；③子类别相互之间不能有重叠；④新分类要进行客观规范的命名并给出新分类的定义。

参考文献

van Eemeren, F.H. van. 2013. Fallacies as Derailments of Argumentative Discourse: Acceptance based on understanding and critical assessment. *Journal of Pragmatics* 6: 141-152.

van Eemeren, F. H., Garssen, B.& Krabbe, E. C. 2014. *Handbook of Argumentation Theories.* Amsterdam: Springer.

van Eemeren, F. H. & Grootendorst, R. 2004. *A Systematic Theory of Argumentation. The pragma-dialectical approach.* Cambridge: Cambridge University Press.

van Eemeren, F. H., Grootendorst, R. & Snoeck Henkemans, 2000. A. F. *Argumentation: Analysis, Evaluation, Presentation.* Mahwah, NJ: Routledge/Lawrence Erlbaum.

吴鹏，熊明辉. 2015. 策略操控：语用论辩学之修辞拓展 [J].《福建师范大学学报》（哲学社会科学版）192 (3): 64-69.

Table of contents 目 录

Preface 前言   I

CHAPTER 1 第一章
Analyzing argumentative discourse 论辩话语分析   1
1.1 The scope of reason in argumentative discourse 论辩话语中的合理性范畴   1
1.2 Normative pragmatics as a theoretical perspective 作为一种理论视角的规约语用学   4
1.3 Reconstructing the process of resolving a difference of opinion 重构意见分歧的消除过程   8
1.4 Constructing an analytic overview of argumentative discourse 构建论辩话语的分析概览   12
1.5 Accounting for an analytic overview 解释论辩话语的分析概览   16
1.6 Getting a better grip on argumentative reality 论辩现实的更佳把握   19
1.7 An extended pragma-dialectical theory 语用论辩学的理论拓展   22

CHAPTER 2 第二章
Strategic maneuvering between effectiveness and reasonableness 有效性和合理性之间的策略操控   25
2.1 Defining argumentation theoretically 论辩的理论界定   25
2.2 Maintaining reasonableness in argumentative discourse 保持论辩话语的合理性   29
2.3 Aiming for effectiveness in argumentative discourse 追求论辩话语的有效性   36
2.4 The notion of strategic maneuvering as an analytic instrument 作为理论分析工具的策略操控概念   39
2.5 Strategic maneuvering in the various stages of the resolution process 分歧消除过程中的阶段性策略操控   43
2.6 Coordinated strategic maneuvering and discussion strategies 协同性策略操控与讨论策略   45
2.7 Accounting for strategic maneuvering in the analysis 在分析中阐释策略操控   47

CHAPTER 3 第三章
Dialectical and rhetorical perspectives on argumentative discourse 论辩话语的论辩学与修辞学视角   51
3.1 Diverging meta-theoretical outlooks on dialectic and rhetoric 论辩学与修辞学的不同原理论辩   51
3.2 Reasonable argumentative discourse in classical dialectical approaches 合理论辩话语的古典论辩术路径   55
3.3 Reasonable argumentative discourse in modern dialectical approaches 合理论辩话语的现代论辩学路径   59
3.4 Effective argumentative discourse in classical rhetorical approaches 有效论辩话语的古典修辞术路径   66
3.5 Effective argumentative discourse in modern rhetorical approaches 有效论辩话语的现代修辞学路径   72
3.6 Different views on the relationship between dialectic and rhetoric 对论辩学与修辞学之间关系的不同看法   81
3.7 Strategic maneuvering as a concept bridging dialectic and rhetoric 架构论辩学与修辞学桥梁的策略操控概念   87

2　Strategic Maneuvering in Argumentative Discourse

CHAPTER 4 第四章
Three inseparable aspects of strategic maneuvering 策略操控的三个有机组成部分　93
4.1　The strategic maneuvering triangle　策略操控"三角"　93
4.2　Topical selection in strategic maneuvering　策略操控中的话题选择　96
4.3　Theoretical contributions to the analysis of topical selection　话题选择分析的理论资源　101
4.4　Adaptation to audience demand in strategic maneuvering　策略操控中的受众需求调适　108
4.5　Theoretical contributions to the analysis of adjusting to audience demand　迎合受众需求分析的理论资源　113
4.6　Presentational choices in strategic maneuvering　策略操控的呈现方式选择　118
4.7　Theoretical contributions to the analysis of presentational choices　呈现方式分析的理论资源　122

CHAPTER 5 第五章
Strategic maneuvering in conventionalized communicative practices 惯例化交际实践中的策略操控　129
5.1　Argumentative discourse in different domains of communicative activity　不同交际活动领域中的论辩话题　129
5.2　The theoretical treatment of argumentation in context　语境中论辩理论分析　131
5.3　Distinguishing between communicative activity types　不同交际活动的类型区分　138
5.4　Communicative activity types and the model of a critical discussion　交际活动类型与批判性讨论模型　144
5.5　Characterizing the argumentative features of communicative activity types　不同交际活动类型的论辩特征描述　146
5.6　Institutional preconditions for strategic maneuvering　策略操控的机构性先决条件　152
5.7　A case of confrontational strategic maneuvering in the political domain　政治领域的冲突策略操控个案分析　159

CHAPTER 6 第六章
Determining the strategic function of argumentative moves 论辩话步策略功能的界定　163
6.1　Four factors serving as parameters　策略操控的四个分析维度　163
6.2　A case in point: Shell's advertorial about its role in Nigeria　社论式广告个案分析：壳牌公司在尼日利亚的角色　165
6.3　The analytic overview as a source for results aspired to　从分析概览中考察论辩的预期结果　168
6.4　Dialectical profiles as a source for available routes　从论辩轮廓中考察论辩的可选路径　171
6.5　Communicative activity types as a source for institutional constraints　从交际活动类型中考察论辩的机构性制约因素　174
6.6　The argumentative situation as a source for commitment sets　从论辩情境中考察论辩中形成的承诺集　178
6.7　Analyzing an argumentative move for its strategic function　论辩话步的策略功能分析　183

CHAPTER 7 第七章
Fallacies as derailments of strategic maneuvering 谬误：脱轨的策略操控　187
7.1　Hamblin's criticism of the logical standard treatment　汉布林对谬误逻辑学标准处理方法的批评　187
7.2　The need for a comprehensive approach to the fallacies　谬误综合研究路径的必要性　190
7.3　Fallacies as violations of rules for critical discussion　谬误：批判性讨论规则的违反　193
7.4　Strategic maneuvering and the deceptiveness of fallacies　策略操控与谬误的欺诈性　196
7.5　Context-independent criteria for judging fallaciousness　脱离语境的谬误识别标准　200
7.6　Context-dependent criteria for judging fallaciousness　基于语境的谬误识别标准　203
7.7　Evaluating the soundness of strategic maneuvers: An example　策略操控的合理性评判实例　207

CHAPTER 8 第八章
Strategic maneuvering with the burden of proof 对举证责任的策略操控 — 213

- 8.1 The burden of proof as a procedural concept 作为程序性概念的举证责任 — 213
- 8.2 Meeting the burden of proof by means of argumentation 通过论辩承担举证责任 — 216
- 8.3 The order of defense in a mixed difference of opinion 混合意见分歧中的辩护顺序 — 218
- 8.4 A pragmatic rationale for deciding on the order of defense 决定辩护顺序的语用原则 — 224
- 8.5 The pragmatic *status quo* and the order of defense 语用现状与辩护顺序 — 227
- 8.6 Stage-bound maneuvering with the burden of proof 基于举证责任的阶段性操控 — 230
- 8.7 A case of managing the burden of proof in advertisements 举证责任策略操控的广告案例 — 235

CHAPTER 9 第九章
Strategic maneuvering in response to presumed inconsistency or fallaciousness 回应"前后不一"或谬误指责中的策略操控 — 241

- 9.1 Logical and pragmatic inconsistencies in a party's avowed commitments 一方公开承诺中的逻辑与语用不一致 — 241
- 9.2 *Tu quoque* fallacies as derailments of pointing out inconsistencies "你也一样"谬误：脱轨的"前后不一"指责 — 244
- 9.3 An accusation of inconsistency case from Dutch politics 荷兰政坛"前后不一"指责的个案分析 — 249
- 9.4 The practical impact of the occurrence of fallacies 谬误出现的现实影响 — 252
- 9.5 Repairing derailments that do not cancel reasonableness 尚存合理性的脱轨论辩修复 — 253
- 9.6 Two diverging proposals for dealing with perceived fallacies 公认谬误的两种处理方案 — 257
- 9.7 Re-railing repairable derailments of strategic maneuvering 可修复脱轨策略操控的校正 — 261

CHAPTER 10 第十章
Setting up an agenda for further research 后续研究计划设定 — 263

- 10.1 Recapitulating the basics of the extended pragma-dialectical theory 语用论辩学理论拓展中的重点回顾 — 263
- 10.2 Maintaining coherence and vitality in the research program 保持研究计划的连贯性和持续性 — 265
- 10.3 Reviewing dialectical and rhetorical perspectives philosophically 从哲学层面审视论辩与修辞视角 — 266
- 10.4 Defining types of strategic maneuvering and soundness conditions theoretically 从理论层面确定策略操控类型与合理性条件 — 267
- 10.5 Describing modes of strategic maneuvering and their effects empirically 从实证层面描述策略操控的模式与效果 — 269
- 10.6 Reconstructing strategic maneuvers and broader strategies analytically 从分析层面重构策略操控具体形式及其构成的策略 — 271
- 10.7 Characterizing communicative activity types praxeologically 从行为角度识别不同交际活动类型 — 273

References 参考文献 — 275
Index of names 人名索引 — 295
Index of terms 名词索引 — 299

Preface 前言

Strategic Maneuvering in Argumentative Discourse is dedicated to the memory of my former student, co-author, and friend, Peter Houtlosser, who died on February 14, 2008. It is the final result of a research project that we started together in 1996, and it is to a large part based on our joint work. After my long and close collaboration with Rob Grootendorst, who died of cancer in 2000, had ended, Peter accepted my invitation to extend the pragma-dialectical approach to argumentation that Rob and I had developed with a rhetorical dimension. This extension should enable us to increase the analytic and evaluative power of our theory. When cancer struck again, hitting Peter this time, I decided to complete the project in the way we had envisaged, writing in conclusion the monograph on strategic maneuvering in argumentative discourse we had in mind.

Peter Houtlosser (1956–2008) was a – youthful – man of great character who had a striking personality. As a student he amazed his teachers and fellow students by his typical combination of genuine enthusiasm, pig-headed stubbornness and cheerful playfulness. After he had defended his doctoral dissertation and became a fellow argumentation theorist his enthusiam turned into dedication, his stubbornness into perseverance, and his playfulness into spirituality. Always eager to be involved in everything, and accepting every task that needed to be done, Peter was a much-appreciated member of the Department of Speech Communication, Argumentation Theory, and Rhetoric of the University of Amsterdam. A great many of his colleagues and students were really fond of him. I am convinced that the great support I received when writing this monograph is largely due to the general affection for Peter. Personally I remember Peter as the most loyal friend one could wish to have, and I miss him dearly.

This research program "Strategic manoeuvring in argumentative confrontations: Norms and criteria, manifestations and effects," concluded by means of this monograph, was subsidized by the Netherlands Organisation for Scientific Research (NWO project no. 360-80-030). Peter and I developed this program to make it possible to involve more, in particular younger, students of argumentation in the research. Thanks to the NWO grant, we were able to work together with such talented young researchers as Dima Mohammed, Corina Andone, and Yvon Tonnard. All three of them devoted their doctoral dissertations to theoretical issues pertinent to the pragma-dialectical theory of strategic maneuvering in argumentative discourse. In their research, they were advised by Peter and me together, a task which Peter fulfilled until the very end with great energy and conviction. Jan Albert van Laar, who joined our team as a postdoctoral researcher, was also vital to the well-functioning of the team and the successful completion of its task.

From the beginning of my academic career I have worked together very closely with other members of the Department of Speech Communication, Argumentation Theory, and Rhetoric. Since the early 1980s this emphasis on collaboration has been an important element in the fertility of the research program Argumentation in Discourse carried out at the University of Amsterdam, currently under the auspices of the Amsterdam School for Cultural Analysis (ASCA). Accordingly, in writing the drafts of the various chapters of this monograph I relied on the other participants in this research program and its associates for criticisms and further feedback. I asked 13 colleagues (I am not superstitious) to read two chapters each and to send me all comments they might have. For their useful remarks and constructive suggestions I thank with great appreciation Corina Andone, Eveline Feteris, Ton van Haaften, Constanza Ihnen Jory, Henrike Jansen, Jan Albert van Laar, Bert Meuffels, Dima Mohammed, José Plug, Sara Rubinelli, Francisca Snoeck Henkemans, Jean Wagemans, and David Zarefsky.

I would also like to thank Renske Wierda, Jasmin Taraman and Nanon Labrie, students in the Research Master's program Argumentation, Rhetoric and Philosophy, for technical assistance in various forms. Finally, a special word of thanks goes to Bart Garssen, Erik C. W. Krabbe, and J. Anthony Blair for their invaluable support. All three of them played a vital role in making the final text become what it now is. By their friendship and advice, Bart and Erik have stimulated me to bring this project to completion. Both of them read all chapters and did not spare me their doubts and (often detailed) criticisms. Tony graciously offered to be my copy-editor. He performed this task meticulously and thoroughly, presenting me with a great number of corrections and helpful editorial remarks. I hasten to add that it goes without saying that all remaining errors and mistakes are mine. Whatever the demerits of this monograph may be, I hope that it will stimulate its readers to join me in critically reflecting on argumentative discourse and developing theoretical instruments for dealing with it.

Frans H. van Eemeren   Amsterdam, August 28, 2009

CHAPTER 1 第一章

论辩话语分析
Analyzing argumentative discourse

论辩话语中的合理性范畴
1.1 The scope of reason in argumentative discourse

It is a truism that argumentation always arises in response to, or in anticipation of, a difference of opinion, whether this difference of opinion is real or merely imaginary. When people argue their case, they are defending an opinion, or "standpoint," that they assume not to be shared by the addressee or by some third party the addressee might associate with – otherwise the argumentation would be pointless (van Eemeren & Grootendorst, 1984, pp. 39–46). The need for argumentation, the requirements of argumentation, and the structure of argumentation are all adapted to a context in which doubts, opposition, objections, and counterclaims arise.

Argumentation is basically aimed at resolving a difference of opinion about the acceptability of a standpoint by making an appeal to the other party's reasonableness (van Eemeren & Grootendorst, 2004, pp. 11–18). When people argue with each other without really wanting to convince each other but are in the first place out to win over an audience of onlookers ("the gallery"), as is the case when two political rivals are debating each other on television in election time, they still have to conduct their argumentative discourse with each other as if it is aimed at resolving a difference of opinion on the merits in order to maintain decorum and to appear reasonable to the viewers who are their intended audience. Even in the extreme case of the seemingly irresolvable controversies known as "deep disagreements" the parties usually go through the motions of trying to resolve a difference of opinion on the merits, if only to give the impression of being reasonable to a third party consisting of outsiders.[1]

The standpoints at issue in the difference of opinion can pertain to any kind of subject and they can be descriptive as well as evaluative or prescriptive.[2] An evaluative judgment of the ethical or esthetic quality of something ("The film *Infamous* is brilliant") or a prescriptive incitement to do something ("You should join me at that meeting") can just as well be at issue in argumentative discourse as a descriptive claim about

---

1. Cf. Memedi (2007).

2. Argumentation can be used for truth finding and truth preservation but also for getting certain judgments approved and making certain actions happen. As Tindale (2004, p. 174) puts it, "Those most eager to enlist a truth requirement among their criteria of argument evaluation are those who see truth as the principal aim of argumentation." In this connection, it is worthwhile to emphasize the important distinction between argumentation and demonstrative proof. See also Perelman and Olbrechts-Tyteca (1958/1969, pp. 13–14).

a factual state of affairs ("Amsterdam is much bigger than Rotterdam"). Standpoints of any of these types, and the argumentation to defend them, can be encountered in all areas of life, from the family circle and the classroom to the legal and political arenas.[3]

Some philosophers have a *parti pris* that normative statements expressing evaluative and prescriptive (often referred to as "practical"[4]) standpoints can never be subjected to a reasonable discussion. They assign a higher status to descriptive claims, because these are deemed to fulfill a special role in the epistemic process of truth finding and truth preservation.[5] The ultimate consequence of excluding evaluative and prescriptive standpoints from the realm of reasonableness is that value judgments and choices for action can only be viewed as based on subjective preferences and personal interests. Contrary to such philosophers with an "exclusionist" outlook, Mill – who showed a keen interest in discussing ethical, political and religious standpoints – and likeminded "inclusionist" philosophers believe that all subjects can be the objects of a reasonable discussion (Finocchiaro, 2005a, 2005b; Hansen, 2006).[6] I emphatically agree with them and see no justification for *a priori* pronouncing positions implying a value hierarchy or an action principle unsuitable for a reasonable discussion. This inclusionist outlook fits in with a long-standing analytic tradition that distinguishes, besides the reasonableness scientists adhere to when dealing with physical reality, reasonableness bearing on value judgments and reasonableness relating to the desirability of actions.

It is in my view not only unnecessary but also highly undesirable to limit the scope of the notion of reasonableness to descriptive standpoints, because in certain domains of discourse such a limitation would give free rein to those who are not at all interested in maintaining reasonableness. In politics, for instance, it would provide politicians with an alibi for abstaining from making out a case for their actions and would offer them a chance to "immunize" their standpoints against criticism by proclaiming them beyond discussion. Let me elaborate on the discussion of standpoints in politics, in

---

3. As is explained in van Eemeren (1987b), standpoints can be conveyed by speech acts of all the types distinguished in Searle's (1979) taxonomy, but they can always be reconstructed as being aimed at gaining acceptance from the addressee(s). See also Houtlosser (1995).

4. The traditional term *practical* is nowadays often replaced by terms such as *inciting* and *prescriptive*. When I use the term *prescriptive* I intend to cover the content of all these terms.

5. Biro and Siegel promote viewing argumentation as "*a fundamentally epistemic affair* whose purpose is to bring reasoners from recognized truths or justified beliefs to previously unrecognized truths or not otherwise justified beliefs" (1992, p. 99, italics added, FHvE). However, they do not rule out that evaluative and prescriptive standpoints can have truth values as well. From an entirely different angle argumentation scholars who favor a rhetorical approach to argumentation sometimes take a position that fosters the exclusion of descriptive and evaluative standpoints by claiming that rhetoric is only about action claims (Kock, 2007).

6. Hansen sees "a great deal of similarity" between Mill's view and the pragma-dialectical view I defend (2006, p. 103).

particular where democracies are concerned, because this area is of vital interest to all of us and should clearly not be excluded from argumentative reasonableness.

Ideally, participation in democracy amounts first and foremost to an engagement of the members of the community, or society at large, in a continual and public discourse about common interests, policies to be developed, and decisions to be taken. Acknowledging that preferences may change as a result of communication, Schumpeter, one of the most influential modern theoreticians of democracy, calls the will of the people "the product, not the motive power of the political process" (1950, p. 263). In representative democracies, however, the outcomes of the political process tend to be predominantly the product of negotiations between political leaders rather than the result of a universal and mutual process of deliberative disputation. More often than not, allegedly political discussions are in fact no more than a one-way traffic of leaders talking down to their voters, and only when elections are close do politicians adjust their campaigns, sometimes in a blatantly opportunistic way, to the opinions of their voters. This adjustment, however, is by no means the result of an intensive and elaborate discussion of potential issues (van Eemeren, 2002).

At this juncture, it is expedient to make a distinction between "discussion" as a serious attempt to have a regulated critical dialogue aimed at resolving a difference of opinion on the merits, and "quasi-discussion" that is in fact a monologue calculated only to win the audience's consent to one's own views. Only in the first case, when a critical discussion is aimed for, can one speak of a dialectical discussion; in the latter case, the discourse is rhetorical in a very narrow sense of the term. The discourse may only be called a genuine (i.e. dialectical) discussion if it involves a serious attempt to have an intellectual exchange and does not simply boil down to a unidirectional feeding of the audience. In a discussion that aims at complying as much as possible with the normative ideal of resolving a difference of opinion on the merits (van Eemeren & Grootendorst, 1984), the protagonist of a standpoint and the antagonist of that standpoint try to establish together through an orderly exchange of argumentative moves whether the protagonist's standpoint is capable of withstanding the antagonist's criticism. At its best, democracy should always have promoting such a critical discussion of standpoints as a central aim. Only if this is the case can stimulating participation in political discourse enhance the quality of democracy.

If one views argumentation as occurring within a discourse that is supposedly aiming at having a critical discussion, the argumentative moves that are made in the discourse are approached from a dialectical perspective. Argumentation is then considered to be part of a regimented procedure for testing the standpoint at issue in relation to critical reactions. The dialectical discussion procedure can be thought of as representing a "code of conduct" for rational discussants who aim to achieve their argumentative goals in a reasonable way (van Eemeren & Grootendorst, 2004, pp. 187–196). In the domain of politics, such a code of conduct indicates how in argumentative discourse justice can be done to the fact that democracy is quintessentially a system for dealing institutionally with uncertainty, and provides a solution to the problem of how in this domain uncertainty can be managed in a reasonable way. In my opinion, the dialectical rules for argumentative discourse that make up a code of conduct for political discourse are therefore of crucial importance to giving substance to the ideal of participatory democracy.

In real-life contexts, it has to be taken into account that human interaction is not always automatically "naturally" and fully oriented toward the ideal of dialectical reasonableness. In the political domain, for instance, those who are involved in a disagreement generally enter a discussion without being prepared to subject their thinking to critical scrutiny, and more often than not they have a vested interest in a particular outcome. The circumstances in which they argue typically involve an inequality in power and resources. In addition, the discussants may well have different levels of critical skill. On top of that, the circumstances giving rise to argument may create at the same time a practical demand for an immediate settlement, thereby placing constraints on the possibilities for truly resolving the disagreement – like when you have to decide instantaneously which film you are going to see when all movies that are shown are about to start when you and your friend enter a cinema.

In view of the predicament I have just sketched one might ask whether maintaining the dialectical ideal of critical discussion in political and other real-life contexts is not utopian. In my view, it might seem like that on first thought, but on second thought the argumentative state of affairs is different. The ideal of a critical discussion is by definition not a description of any kind of reality but sets a theoretical standard that can be used for heuristic, analytic and evaluative purposes. The model of critical discussion gives substance to what it means to be critical in dealing with argumentative discourse. It is an instrument for doing justice to the vital intellectual, social and cultural interests that can be at stake in argumentative practice. Argumentative discussion of standpoints plays, or should virtually always play, a crucial part in joint decision-making, not only in politics, law, science, education and other domains of the public and technical sphere, but also in the personal or private sphere. If this decision-making is taken seriously, the quality of the discussion is to be protected in all argumentative exchanges systematically and critically, even if the argumentative discourse falls short of the dialectical ideal.

作为一种理论视角的规约语用学
1.2 Normative pragmatics as a theoretical perspective

Scholars of argumentation are often drawn to studying argumentation by their practical interest in improving the quality of argumentative discourse where this is called for. In order to be able to realize this ambition, they have to combine an empirical orientation with a critical orientation toward argumentative discourse. In order to give substance to this challenging combination, a comprehensive research program must be carried out that ensures that argumentative discourse is not only examined empirically as a specimen of verbal communication and interaction but also measured critically against normative standards of reasonableness. If "pragmatics" is taken to be the study of communicative and interactive language use, as is customary among discourse analysts, the need for uniting the descriptive empirical angle of research and the normative critical angle of research can be honored by construing the study of argumentation as a branch of "normative pragmatics" (van Eemeren, 1986, and, more in particular, 1990).

In normative pragmatics, as I envisage it, argumentation scholars make it their business to clarify how the gap between the normative dimension and the descriptive dimension of argumentation can be bridged to integrate critical and empirical insights systematically. The complex problems that are at stake in this endeavor can only be solved with the help of a comprehensive research program consisting of five interrelated components (van Eemeren & Grootendorst, 2004, pp. 9–41). On the one hand, the program has a philosophical component in which a philosophy of reasonableness is developed, and a theoretical component in which, starting from this ideal of reasonableness, a model for acceptable argumentation is devised. On the other hand, the program has an empirical component in which argumentative reality as it can be encountered in argumentative exchanges is investigated qualitatively and quantitatively. Next, in the analytical component the normative and the descriptive dimensions of studying argumentative discourse are systematically linked together. Finally, in the practical component the problems are identified that occur in the various more or less institutionalized argumentative practices, and methods and designs are developed to tackle these problems systematically.

As it happens, the conceptions of reasonableness argumentation scholars have developed in what I regard as the philosophical component of their research programs diverge from the outset, so that in the theoretical component different outlooks emerge on what is considered to be acceptable argumentation. When developing the "pragma-dialectical" approach to argumentation, which can be characterized as a *discourse dialectic*, Rob Grootendorst and I were strongly influenced by Barth and Krabbe's (1982) "formal dialectic" and started also from a critical conception of reasonableness that replaces self-defeating "justificationism" with a critical testing procedure (van Eemeren & Grootendorst, 1984, pp. 15–18).[7] This critical conception of reasonableness is associated with the (Popperian) "critical rationalist" philosophy of reasonableness, which claims that, ultimately, nothing is a certainty, and takes as its guiding principle the idea of critically testing all claims that are made to acceptability (van Eemeren & Grootendorst, 1994). As Albert (1975) has emphasized, the critical rationalist conception of reasonableness is all embracing: it pertains – as it should – to *any* issue that can be subjected to a regulated discussion and covers the discussion of descriptive as well as evaluative and prescriptive standpoints.[8]

---

7. Although justificationism goes against irrationalism and authoritarianism by requiring argument and evidence for accepting claims, by relying on intellectualism (intuition) or empiricism (observation) *to achieve a final justification involving a definitive legitimization*, instead of bringing about a critical testing of one's conjectures, it depends on arbitrary standards or is open to infinite regress. See Popper (1962) and Bartley (1984).

8. In combining pragmatic and dialectic insight, pragma-dialecticians rely on four meta-theoretical principles, which serve as their methodological starting points. "Functionalization" is achieved by making use of the fact that argumentative discourse occurs through – and in

By implementing the critical rationalist view in the theoretical component of the research program one pursues the development of a model of critical discussion that gives substance to the idea of resolving differences of opinion on the merits by means of dialectically regulated critical exchanges in which the acceptability of the standpoints at issue is put to the test (van Eemeren and Grootendorst, 1994, pp. 19–20). The outcome of the discussion between the protagonist and the antagonist of a standpoint depends fully on the adequacy of the protagonist's responses to the antagonist's critical questions. The systematic interaction that takes place between the speech acts performed by the protagonist to defend the standpoint and those performed by the antagonist to respond critically to the standpoint and the protagonist's defense of it is characteristic of a pragma-dialectical resolution procedure. This systematic interaction can only lead to a reasonable resolution of the difference of opinion at issue if the discussion is in accordance with a proper regulation. The rules for critical discussion must specify, for the various discussion stages, in which cases the performance of certain speech acts contributes to or hinders a resolution of the difference of opinion on the merits.[9]

---

response to – speech act performances. Identifying the complex speech act of argumentation and the other speech acts involved in resolving a difference of opinion on the merits makes it possible to specify the relevant "identity conditions" and "correctness conditions" of these speech acts (van Eemeren & Grootendorst, 1992a). In this way, for instance, a specification can be given of what is "at stake" in advancing a certain standpoint that makes clear how the argumentative discourse is organized around this context of disagreement. "Socialization" is achieved by identifying the discussion roles of protagonist and antagonist in the collaborative context of argumentative discourse. By extending the speech act perspective to the level of interaction, it can be shown in which ways positions and argumentation in support of positions are interrelated. "Externalization" is achieved by identifying the specific commitments created by the speech acts performed in a context of argumentative interaction. Rather than being treated as internal states of mind, notions such as "disagreement" and "acceptance" can be defined pragmatically in terms of discursive activities. "Acceptance," for instance, can be externalized as giving a preferred response to an arguable act that commits the respondent who accepts to not attacking this act anymore. Finally, "dialectification" is achieved by regimenting the exchange of speech acts aimed at resolving a difference of opinion on the merits in an ideal model of critical discussion.

9.   Van Eemeren and Grootendorst opted for developing a model of critical discussion that is a theoretical model based on "etic" *analytic* considerations. Although their model is not a reproduction of the perspective of an ordinary arguer, where this is appropriate it nevertheless makes use of – or is "informed by" – "interpretive" insights stemming from their "emic" perspective as arguers. Cutting across the distinction between an "interpretive" and an "analytic" model is the distinction between an *a priori* model and an *a posteriori* model. The model of critical discussion is *a priori* in the sense that it provides a description of what argumentative discourse would be like if it were ideally tailored to the task of resolving a difference of opinion. At the same time, the model could not have been developed without a certain understanding, based on experience, of the organization and proceeding of argumentative discourse. In *Reconstructing Argumentative Discourse* (van Eemeren et al., 1993) the authors argue for a model that is not only analytic and *a priori*, but also *rational*, because such a model is the most suitable model for

The model of a critical discussion Grootendorst and I devised in the 1970s provides an overview of the argumentative moves that are pertinent to a constructive development of each of the discussion stages to be distinguished in a critical discussion, i.e. pertinent to a proceeding that furthers the process of resolving a difference of opinion on the merits in each particular stage. In this model, the critical norms of reasonableness authorizing the performance of speech acts in the various stages of a critical discussion are reflected in a set of dialectical rules (van Eemeren & Grootendorst, 1984; 2004). The rules for critical discussion state norms that are all pertinent to resolving a difference of opinion on the merits and cover the argumentative discourse in its entirety. In a critical discussion, the protagonist and the antagonist of the standpoints at issue must therefore observe in every stage all these rules, which are instrumental in resolving a difference of opinion.

Each of the rules constitutes a distinct standard or norm for critical discussion. Although the practical impact of violating the rules may vary from case to case, every rule violation, in whatever discussion stage it has been committed and by whatever party, is a discussion move that obstructs or hinders the resolution of the difference of opinion on the merits and must therefore be regarded as fallacious (in this particular sense). Thus, in pragma-dialectics the use of the term *fallacy* is systematically connected with the rules for critical discussion. Fallacies may range from preventing the other party from expressing a position he wishes to assume in the confrontation stage, which violates the so-called Freedom Rule (rule 1), to unduly generalizing the result of the discussion in the concluding stage, which violates the so-called Concluding Rule (rule 9) (van Eemeren & Grootendorst, 1992a, pp. 107–115 and 184–194, respectively). Another of the ten rules that constitute together a code of conduct for conducting a critical discussion is, for instance, the Standpoint Rule (rule 3), which says that attacks on standpoints may not bear on a standpoint that has not actually been put forward by the other party.[10] If a fictitious standpoint

---

covering argumentative discourse and is able to subsume and explain much of what is expected from a conventional model or a sequential model. In this view, an integration of "conventional" Searlean insight (Searle, 1969; 1979) into the communicative aspects of argumentative discourse and "rational" Gricean insight (Grice, 1989) into its interactional aspects provides the most adequate basis for developing a model for dealing with argumentation, because it brings together in a pragmatic framework the rules and regularities of actual discourse and the normative principles of goal-directed discourse.

10. The pragma-dialectical code of conduct for critical discussion consists of the following rules (van Eemeren & Grootendorst, 2004, pp. 190–196): (1) Discussants may not prevent each other from advancing standpoints or from calling standpoints into question (Freedom Rule); (2) Discussants who advance a standpoint may not refuse to defend this standpoint when requested to do so (Obligation-to-Defend Rule); (3) Attacks on standpoints may not bear on a standpoint that has not actually been put forward by the other party (Standpoint Rule); (4) Standpoints may not be defended by non-argumentation or argumentation that is not relevant to the standpoint (Relevance Rule); (5) Discussants may not falsely attribute unexpressed premises to the other party, nor disown responsibility for their own unexpressed premises (Unexpressed Premise Rule); (6) Discussants may not falsely present something as an accepted starting point or falsely deny that something is an accepted starting point (Starting Point Rule);

is attributed to the other party, this results in committing the fallacy of the "straw man." A different variant of the straw man fallacy comes about when the other party's standpoint is misrepresented by taking his utterances out of context or oversimplifying or exaggerating what he has said (van Eemeren & Grootendorst, 1992a, pp. 124–131).

重构意见分歧的消除过程
1.3 Reconstructing the process of resolving a difference of opinion

The pivotal constituent of the pragma-dialectical research program is the analytical component, because this component integrates the normative and the descriptive dimensions of the study of argumentative discourse by linking the philosophical and theoretical components systematically with the empirical and practical components (van Eemeren & Grootendorst, 2004, pp. 40–41). When concentrating on the analytical component of the study of argumentative discourse, a terminological issue that needs to be clarified first concerns the difference between "analysis" and "interpretation." Although in ordinary usage these words may often seem to be used interchangeably, it is clear that even in everyday language there is a difference between the two. Letting your interlocutor know how you have "analyzed" her words has a different meaning from telling her in what way you have "interpreted" what she said.[11] I will build on this distinction when stipulating the meaning of "analysis" as a technical term in contradistinction to "interpretation."

Giving an interpretation refers, in my use of this term, to any assignment of meaning to a certain piece of discourse (or other cultural artifact). A first difference between an analysis and an interpretation I propose to make is that an analysis is more focused. It concentrates on certain aspects of the discourse while abstracting from others. A second difference is that an analysis is conducted within a certain theoretical perspective and is put in terms of the conceptual framework defining this perspective. A third difference ensuing from the second is that an analysis is always of a well-delineated type: it is a linguistic analysis, a historical analysis, a psychological analysis, a sociological analysis, or, for that matter, an argumentative analysis. A fourth and last difference to be mentioned is that an analysis must be accounted for more thoroughly and precisely than a mere interpretation. Every analysis should be justified in terms of the conceptual framework

---

(7) Reasoning that in an argumentation is presented in an explicit and complete way may not be invalid in a logical sense (Validity Rule); (8) Standpoints may not be regarded as conclusively defended if the defense does not take place by means of appropriate argument schemes that are applied correctly (Argument Scheme Rule); (9) Inconclusive defenses of standpoints may not lead to maintaining these standpoints and conclusive defenses of standpoints may not lead to maintaining expressions of doubt concerning these standpoints (Concluding Rule); (10) Discussants may not use any formulations that are insufficiently clear or confusingly ambiguous, and they may not deliberately misinterpret the other party's formulations (Language Use Rule).

11. Some people use their language in a rather pompous way and call their interpretation an analysis, but most speakers and writers will not use these words interchangeably.

defining the theoretical perspective that determines the angle of analysis and is to be supported empirically by means of pertinent communicative and interactional data.

The analysis I am interested in here can be described as a theoretically motivated and empirically justified pragma-dialectical reconstruction of what is going on in the discourse. Depending on the theoretical perspective determining what kind of analysis is carried out and the matching conceptual framework used in the analysis, an analysis will always amount to a specific kind of reconstruction that highlights particular elements and aspects of the discourse. What is considered relevant in the discourse from one perspective may be regarded as not so relevant, or even irrelevant, from another perspective. Where a psychoanalyst finds his client's constant boasting about his achievements and successes pertinent to diagnosing his "inferiority complex" and comes up with a reconstruction that reflects this interest, a pragma-dialectical analyst of argumentative discourse will rather be interested in reconstructing the process of resolving a difference of opinion taking place in the discourse and consider those moves to be relevant that have a potential role in resolving the difference on the merits. Just as in the case of psychoanalysis the Freudian (or some other) model is the theoretical starting point, in the case of the pragma-dialectical analysis the model of a critical discussion will be the theoretical starting point. In both cases the model that is the theoretical starting point serves as a guide for what is worth noting in the discourse, and in both cases the reconstructive analysis that is given must also be based on empirical evidence from the discourse. Just as the psychoanalyst upon having met his client cannot simply conclude their first encounter by stating "I see, inferiority complex," but needs to establish his diagnosis through a thorough investigation, the argumentation analyst has to carefully examine the discourse in full before he can come to any definitive analysis.

Analyzing argumentative discourse pragma-dialectically amounts to interpreting the various moves that are made in the discourse systematically from the theoretical perspective of a critical discussion, exploiting in the process the conceptual instruments needed to implement this perspective and making use of the terminological conventions that go with them. Such an analysis is pragmatic in the sense that the discourse is viewed as essentially a contextualized exchange of speech acts and dialectical in the sense that this exchange is viewed as a methodical attempt to resolve a difference of opinion on the merits by having a regulated critical exchange. The model of a critical discussion constitutes a valuable tool for analyzing argumentative discourse because it has a heuristic function in indicating which speech acts need to be taken into consideration in the analysis. The model points out by means of which speech acts the argumentative moves are prototypically conveyed that are "analytically relevant" (van Eemeren & Grootendorst, 2004, p. 73), because they are pertinent to the resolution process, acknowledging that these speech acts may also be performed implicitly or indirectly in the discourse.[12]

---

12. For analytic relevance, and the distinction between interpretative, analytic and evaluative relevance, see van Eemeren and Grootendorst (2004, pp. 71, 73, 88) and, more in particular, van Eemeren and Grootendorst (1992b).

The four stages that are distinguished analytically in the model of a critical discussion correspond to the different phases any argumentative discourse must pass through, albeit not necessarily explicitly, in order to resolve a difference of opinion on the merits. First, without a confrontation of views, there is no occasion for having a critical discussion. In actual argumentative discourse, the "confrontation stage" manifests itself in those parts of the discourse where it becomes clear that there is a standpoint that meets with – real or projected – doubt or contradiction, so that a potential disagreement arises. Second, the "opening stage" is manifest in those parts of the discourse where the people engaged in the difference of opinion commit themselves to act as a protagonist or antagonist and explore whether there is sufficient common ground to have a critical discussion. Without having an opening for an exchange of views, conducting a critical discussion does not make sense. Third, the parties go through the "argumentation stage" in those parts of the discourse in which the one party advances argumentation to overcome the other party's doubts, and in which the other party continues to be critical until he has been convinced. Without the advancement of argumentation in response to criticism, no critical discussion takes place and the difference of opinion remains unresolved. Finally, without a "concluding stage" in which the parties draw a conclusion about the result of their attempts to resolve the difference of opinion, no true completion of a critical discussion will be reached.[13] As stands to reason, however, such a completion of a critical discussion does not preclude the same parties from embarking upon another discussion.[14]

In Figure 1.1, I have indicated which speech acts in argumentative discourse are analytically relevant and should be included in an "analytic overview" of the discourse because they convey argumentative moves that are potentially constructive in the various stages of the resolution process reconstructed with the help of the model of a critical discussion. It should be borne in mind, however, that in actual argumentative discourse – like in other types of actual discourse – a great many speech acts are performed implicitly or indirectly, so that other types of speech acts may occur that, after they have been reconstructed, also prove to fulfill a constructive role in a critical discussion.

---

13. Following Goffman, Vuchinich (1990, pp. 136–137) points out that real-life argumentative discourse does not always lead to one "winner" and one "loser." There may even be no consensus on whether there is a winner or a loser, or on who is the winner. Unlike in game theory, the parties do not automatically agree on the interpretation of outcomes. This is why pragma-dialecticians consider it vital that in analyzing argumentative discourse the normative model of a critical discussion is systematically brought together with careful empirical description.

14. If another discussion begins, it must go through the same stages again – from confrontation stage to concluding stage.

15. This categorization starts from a typology of speech acts largely based on Searle (1979, pp. 1–29).

16. This category of speech acts has been introduced in van Eemeren and Grootendorst (1984, pp. 109–110).

Chapter 1. Analyzing argumentative discoruse

Components analytic overview	Stages & Moves		Prototypical types of speech acts[15]
	Protagonist	Antagonist	
Difference of opinion	I Confrontation stage		
	Advancing standpoint		Assertive
		Accepting or non-accepting standpoint; Upholding non-acceptance of standpoint	Commissives
	[Requesting usage declarative]	[Requesting usage declarative]	[Directive]
	[Definition/ Specification/Amplification/ Etc.]	[Definition/ Specification/Amplification/ Etc.]	[Usage declarative[16]]
Procedural and material starting points	II Opening stage		
		Challenging to defend standpoint	Directive
	Accepting challenge to defend standpoint		Commissive
	Agreeing on premises and rules of discussion; Deciding to start discussion		Commissives
	[Requesting usage declarative]	[Requesting usage declarative]	[Directive]
	[Definition/Specification/ Amplification/Etc.]	[Definition/Specification/ Amplification/Etc.]	[Usage declarative]
Arguments (explicit, implicit or unexpressed); argument schemes; argumentation structure	III Argumentation stage		
		Requesting argumentation	Directive
	Advancing argumentation		Assertive
		Accepting or non-accepting argumentation	Commissive
	[Requesting usage declarative]	[Requesting usage declarative]	[Directive]
	[Definition/ Specification/Amplification/ Etc.]	[Definition/ Specification/Amplification/ Etc.]	[Usage declarative]
Outcome of discussion	IV Concluding stage		
		Accepting or non-accepting standpoint	Commissive
	Upholding or retracting standpoint		Assertive
	[Requesting usage declarative]	[Requesting usage declarative]	[Directive]
	[Definition/ Specification/ Amplification/Etc.]	[Definition/ Specification/Amplification/ Etc.]	[Usage declarative]

Figure 1.1. Table of the distribution of speech acts playing an immediate constructive role in resolving a difference of opinion on the merits

构建论辩话语的分析概览
1.4 Constructing an analytic overview of argumentative discourse

The analytic overview aimed for in the reconstruction of argumentative discourse with the help of the model of a critical discussion consists of the following components: it indicates the difference of opinion at issue in the confrontation stage; it identifies the procedural and material premises agreed upon in the opening stage that serve as the point of departure of the discussion; it surveys the arguments and criticisms that are – explicitly or implicitly – advanced in the argumentation stage, together with the types of argument that are used, and the clusters of arguments that have developed; it determines the outcome of the discussion that is reached in the concluding stage. All theoretical concepts employed in constructing the analytic overview are defined from the pragma-dialectical perspective of a critical discussion, which also provides the theoretical terms used to refer to these concepts: "type of difference of opinion," "unexpressed premise," "argument scheme," "argumentation structure," etc.[17] In identifying the unexpressed premises, for instance, first a differentiation is made between the "logical minimum" or "associated conditional" covering the reasoning involved in the argument concerned, and the "pragmatic optimum" involving a contextualized specification or generalization of the premise representing the logical minimum that is justified by pragmatic considerations (van Eemeren & Grootendorst, 1992a, pp. 60–72). In analyzing the argument schemes that are used, it is determined whether in view of the kind of critical questions the arguer anticipates he establishes a causal relation, a symptomatic relation, or a comparison relation between a reason he advances and the standpoint he defends (van Eemeren & Grootendorst, 1992a, pp. 94–102). In analyzing the argumentation structure, depending on how the arguments support the standpoint in relation to each other, "multiple," "coordinative," and "subordinative" structures are distinguished (van Eemeren & Grootendorst, 1992a, pp. 73–89).

The components of an analytic overview are all pertinent to judging the soundness of an argumentative discourse. If it is not clear exactly what difference of opinion underlies the discourse, there will be no way of telling whether the difference has been resolved by the discourse. If it is not clear precisely which positions the parties have adopted in the difference of opinion, it will be impossible to tell in whose favor the discussion has ended. If implicit or indirect premises are not taken into account, crucial arguments may be overlooked, so that the evaluation is inadequate. If the argument schemes employed in supporting standpoints and sub-standpoints are not recognized, it cannot be determined whether the links between the individual reasons and the standpoints are resistant to the kinds of criticism their specific make-up is bound to elicit. If the structure of the argumentation advanced in favor of a standpoint is not laid bare, it cannot be judged whether the argumentation put forward in

---

17. These concepts are explained in van Eemeren, Grootendorst, and Snoeck Henkemans (2002). See also van Eemeren and Grootendorst (1992a) and van Eemeren (Ed., 2001).

defense of the standpoint constitutes a coherent whole that provides sufficient support for the standpoint.

Due to a variety of factors, argumentative reality seldom resembles the ideal of a critical discussion – as is to be expected when comparing reality with an ideal. According to the model of a critical discussion, for example, in the confrontation stage antagonists of standpoints must state their doubts clearly and unambiguously, but in practice the disputants usually have to operate circumspectly, for one thing because being straightforward can be "face-threatening" to both parties.[18] As in other types of discourse, in argumentative discourse much remains unsaid. Not only is there seldom any mention of discussion rules and remain the material starting points often unstated, but other vital aspects of the resolution process, including even the perceived outcome, are often not clearly indicated either (van Eemeren, Houtlosser, & Snoeck Henkemans, 2007). In argumentative practice, elements that are indispensable to the resolution process are regularly left unexpressed, either because they are considered evident or because they are not considered worth mentioning (but also for less honorable reasons). Such unexpressed elements may include the exact make-up of the disagreement, the division of the discussion roles and other starting points, the relation between the arguments put forward in defense of a standpoint, the way in which premises are supposed to support the standpoint, and even some of the premises employed. These elements are left implicit in the discourse or concealed in the argumentative context because they are taken to be clear or easy to detect, and they need to be recovered in a reconstructive analysis.[19]

In order to be able to give a fair evaluation of the discourse, a reconstructive analysis is needed of all and only those argumentative moves that are analytically relevant because they play a potential part in resolving a difference of opinion on the merits. A pragma-dialectical analysis should result in an analytic overview that provides an outline of how these moves are to be analyzed in conceptual units that are pertinent to judging the quality of the resolution process – identifying a difference of opinion, for instance, as a "mixed difference of opinion" ("I do not agree at all; in my opinion, it is just the opposite") or an argument that has been advanced as a "symptomatic argument" ("North Americans are competitive; therefore, Paula will do her utmost"). In an analytic overview all ingredients of the discourse that are relevant to resolving a difference of opinion on the merits are identified and represented in well-defined theoretical

---

18. Expressing doubt may also go against the "preference for agreement" that governs ordinary conversation. See Heritage (1984, pp. 265–280), Levinson (1983, pp. 332–336), and van Eemeren et al. (1993, Chapter 3).

19. The obvious fact that in ordinary argumentative discourse the various stages of a critical discussion are often implicit, unclear, distorted and accompanied by diversions, should neither give rise to the premature conclusion that the discourse is deficient nor to the superficial conclusion that the ideal model of critical discussion is not realistic. The former is contradicted by pragmatic insight concerning the conduct of ordinary discourse, the latter by dialectical insight concerning the requirements for resolving differences of opinion. See van Eemeren and Grootendorst (1984, Chapter 4; 1992a, Chapter 5); and van Eemeren et al. (1993, Chapter 3).

terms, so that the overview offers a suitable point of departure for a systematic evaluation of the discourse.

The analytic overview is conditional upon the discourse or the part of the discourse that is to be analyzed being argumentative. The most decisive criterion for calling a discourse argumentative is, of course, whether there is argumentation advanced in the discourse (whether expressed directly or indirectly), and whether this argumentation is put forward in a serious attempt to defend a standpoint. If this is indeed the case, the discourse is automatically, partially if not *in toto*, argumentative. In practice, however, it is not always fully clear whether a discourse is aimed at overcoming some other party's – real or projected – doubt regarding a standpoint in a way that can be considered argumentative going by the prevailing definition (van Eemeren et al., 1996, p. 5). For this reason, and for similar reasons having to do with the uncertainties involved in reconstructing natural argumentative discourse, an analytic overview is always tentative in the sense that it remains open to improvement. The analytic overview provides never more than the best result that could be achieved based on the outcome of the reconstruction process.

A reconstructive analysis of argumentative discourse aimed at creating the basis for constructing an optimal analytic overview of the discourse comprises a number of specific analytic operations. These operations consist in carrying out transformations that are instrumental in identifying the elements in the discourse that play a constructive (albeit not necessarily impeccable) part in resolving a difference of opinion on the merits. Each of these transformations is instrumental in reconstructing certain parts of the discourse in terms of a critical discussion by externalizing the commitments of the participants that are to be taken into account in determining the merits and demerits of the discourse (van Eemeren, Grootendorst, Jackson, & Jacobs, 1993, Chapter 4). Due to the transformations, the reconstruction may differ in several respects from the argumentative discourse as it has been recorded (or transcribed) in the case of oral argumentation, or has appeared in the original text in the case of written argumentation. Because in argumentative discourse a great many speech acts are performed implicitly or indirectly, a constructive role in conducting a critical discussion can be fulfilled by a great many speech acts that going by the way in which they are literally presented do not belong to the categories of speech acts included in the model of a critical discussion.

The reconstruction taking place in the analysis amounts to leaving out of consideration all speech acts that do not play a part in the resolution process ("deletion" transformations of irrelevant digressions, etc.), rearranging in an insightful way speech acts whose order does not reflect their function in the resolution process ("permutation" transformations of separated parts that belong together, etc.), making explicit such speech acts as remain implicit in the actual discourse but are pertinent to the resolution process ("addition" transformations of elliptical and implicit premises, etc.), and reformulating in an unequivocal way those speech acts whose function would otherwise be opaque ("substitution" transformations of confusingly ambiguous expressions, etc.) (van Eemeren and Grootendorst, 2004, Chapter 5).

In the analysis of argumentative discourse the reconstruction transformations are carried out in a cyclic process, returning in a later round, whenever such is appropriate, to parts of the discourse that were already dealt with and carrying out new transformations in as many rounds as necessary to achieve an optimal analytic overview.[20] In analytic practice it is a rule of thumb that the reconstruction in each round starts with deletion, so that the discursive situation becomes easier to survey, then goes on to permutation, so that it becomes clearer to what extent the successive stages of the resolution process are represented in the discourse, continues with addition, so that a more complete picture is offered of the elements vital to the resolution process, and ends with substitution, so that the various steps made in the resolution process are made more easily recognizable. It goes without saying, however, that any other way of going through the reconstruction procedure will do equally well if for some reason or other this suits the analyst better.

In analyzing argumentative discourse it often happens that various reconstruction transformations have to be carried out together. In reconstructing a non-assertive speech act that serves as an indirect standpoint, for instance, both the transformation of substitution and the transformation of addition need to be carried out. A directive, for instance, that serves as a standpoint must first be reconstructed as an assertive by means of a substitution transformation, and then this assertive must be explicitly designated as having the communicative function of a standpoint by means of an addition transformation (see the example provided by van Eemeren & Grootendorst, 2004, p. 116). Of the three types of standpoints distinguished in Section 1.1, only descriptive standpoints, which have an epistemic flavor but often lay claim to acceptability rather than truth,[21] are characteristically expressed by means of assertives ("Dutch women are the tallest in the world"), even though they can also be conveyed indirectly by

---

20. There is a need to return to a certain part of the discourse and to continue the reconstruction process if the analysis of that part of the discourse still remains unsatisfactory because it contains elements that seem superfluous, or lacks necessary elements, or puts elements in an order that does not make sense, or includes elements whose function is not clear. When a particular reconstructive transformation has been made it always needs to be established in the next round whether the incongruency that made the earlier representation of the discourse unsatisfactory has been resolved. Otherwise the reconstruction process should go on.

21. According to Johnson (2000, p. 336–337), "The truth criterion concerns the relationship between the premise and the state of affairs in the world. The acceptability criterion concerns the relationship between the premise and the audience." I think, however, that the difference is somewhat more complex, because truth too has to be recognized, i.e. accepted, as such, which means that in both cases the audience plays a part. In neither case, however, is the audience entirely free to accept whatever it wants to accept; it rather has to comply with certain standards of reasonableness. In the case of claims to truth, these standards will be different in some respects, and presumably also stricter, than in the case of (other) claims to acceptability. I share Tindale's (2004, p. 26) view that "acceptability not only avoids the problems associated with truth, but better meets the requirements of argument evaluation and communication" (see van Eemeren & Grootendorst, 1984, pp. 95–97).

other types of speech acts (van Eemeren, 1987b). Normative views as expressed in evaluative standpoints are perhaps most characteristically conveyed indirectly by expressives ("What a marvelous view"), but can also be expressed directly by means of assertives ("This is a bad copy") or indirectly by commissives ("You may take it from me that Slovenian wine is delicious") or even declaratives ("I call this bad behavior"). Prescriptive standpoints, having a practical character, are characteristically expressed by means of directives ("Go home now"), although – again – by no means exclusively ("It is time to go home"). To do justice to the fact that all these speech acts function in a particular communicative and interactional context as standpoints, whether directly or indirectly, all of them are in a pragma-dialectical analysis reconstructed as assertives, so that the claim to acceptability involved in advancing a standpoint, of whatever type this standpoint may be, is explicitly recognized in the analysis and can be duly taken into account in the evaluation.[22]

解释论辩话语的分析概览
1.5 Accounting for an analytic overview

In *Reconstructing Argumentative Discourse* (van Eemeren et al., 1993) Grootendorst, Jackson, Jacobs and I emphasized that it is crucial that the reconstructions proposed in a pragma-dialectical analysis are indeed justified. The transformations carried out that go beyond a naïve reading of the discourse should be faithful to the commitments that may be ascribed on good grounds to the speaker or writer concerned. Only when this is the case, can the reconstruction result in an analytic overview that constitutes a sound basis for carrying out an evaluation that will bring out in a fair way which fallacies, if any, have been committed in the discourse.

The theoretical tools of pragma-dialectics for reconstructing argumentative discourse and accounting for the reconstruction consist primarily in the model of a critical discussion, with the four stages of the resolution process, the accompanying specification of the various argumentative moves instrumental in each of the stages, the specification of the types of (elementary and complex) speech acts by which these moves are made, and the commitments ensuing – according to the identity and correctness conditions – from performing these speech acts.[23] In addition, there are the pragma-dialectical "communication rules" that combine Searlean and Gricean insight in verbal communication and interaction, the associations and connections at a higher

---

22. Since the presentational form of standpoints can influence the kind of responses that are expected and the kind of arguments that can be put forward to support these standpoints, the choice of presentational form may have strategic significance. I will return to this point in Chapter 4.

23. For the distinction between elementary and complex speech acts and the commitments ensuing from performing these speech acts, see van Eemeren and Grootendorst (1984, pp. 19–46). For the distinction between identity and correctness conditions, see van Eemeren and Grootendorst (1992a, pp. 30–33).

level of the discourse between certain types of speech acts in terms of "adjacency pairs" and "repairs," and the philosophy of critical reasonableness behind the critical discussion model that indicates what it means to act reasonably in argumentative exchanges (van Eemeren & Grootendorst, 1992a).

The requirements that an analytic overview based on a reconstructive analysis needs to satisfy as much as possible are, first, economy, efficacy, and coherence. The requirement of economy means that the analytic overview should represent in a succinct way only those elements in the discourse vital to resolving a difference of opinion on the merits. The requirement of efficacy means that the analytic overview should provide a functional categorization of all elements of the discourse pertinent to a fair evaluation. The requirement of coherence means that the analytic overview should offer an optimally consistent view of the discourse. Second, the analytic overview needs to satisfy to the greatest possible extent the requirements of realism and well-foundedness. The requirement of realism means here that the analytic overview should offer a representation of the discourse that is as plausible and credible as possible, which means that the representation involved should make sense with respect to the argumentative reality in which the discourse takes place and should be intersubjectively acceptable as a likely representation of this discourse. The requirement of well-foundedness means that the analytic overview should be backed up by pragmatically informed empirical observations concerning the discourse which offer a justificatory account of the analysis that is provided.

In accounting for the reconstruction of a discourse given in an analytic overview the analyst can refer to various sources. First, there is the *text of the discourse* (and the visual accompaniments of the discourse, if any). The text of the discourse is always the first and the ultimate source for justifying a reconstruction. In his justification the analyst has to refer to passages in the discourse that immediately support his analysis, if possible by pointing in addition to certain structural and functional properties of the discourse that support the analysis.

Second, there is the *context* in which the passage of the discourse that is being reconstructed appears. As far as the context is concerned, the analyst's source of justifying information can be the *micro-context*[24] that consists of the parts of the text immediately preceding or following the fragment of the discourse that is to be reconstructed. The micro-context is often referred to as the "linguistic" context. The analyst's source of justifying information can also be the context in a wider sense. Then he refers to specific properties of the setting and situation – the "constituation" – in which the passage that is reconstructed occurs (*meso-context*),[25] or to the text genre or speech

---

24. It goes without saying, however, that in particular in oral argumentative discourse the so-called paralinguistic phenomena need to be taken into account too.

25. The "meso"-context is also referred to as the "extra-linguistic" context, but the extra-linguistic context includes also what I call the "macro"-context and the "interdiscursive" context, and in these contexts linguistic phenomena play a part too.

event of which this passage is a part (*macro-context*), or to other texts or speech events with which the discourse passage or the text or speech event as a whole is somehow connected (*interdiscursive* or *intertextual context*).[26] The context may, for instance, be a decisive source when justifying the construction of the "pragmatic optimum" in making an unexpressed premise explicit.[27]

Third, there are inferences the analyst can make by carrying out certain discursive operations that can be a source for justifying a particular way of understanding what is going on in the discourse. Apart from the analyst's references to discursive operations that involve an externalizing reconstruction of a *logical reasoning process* in which he points to certain presuppositions or implications of what is said in the discourse, his references to discursive operations can also involve reconstructions of *pragmatic inferences* supported by the use of common sense, such as when he points to pragmatic inconsistencies in the discourse or to Gricean implicatures.

Fourth, there is *background information* the analyst can use as a source for justifying his analysis. Among the *general background information* he can refer to in justifying his reconstruction of a certain passage in the discourse may be knowledge of general rules and regulations in a certain society that are pertinent to coming to an understanding of that passage. Such general background knowledge that members of a society share may, for instance, play a part in justifying the reconstruction of the argumentation advanced in "Bart cannot be in the swimming pool because his swimming trunks are on the line," where the analyst – just like the addressee – can refer to the rule that in public swimming pools men are obliged to wear swimming trunks and to the generally known fact that they normally own only one pair of them (which may in some circumstances not be general but rather special background information). In many cases, the analyst may also be able to refer to *specific background information* as a source of justification for his reconstruction. Such specific background information can be of several kinds. It can consist of *inside information*, such as that Bart has just bought new swimming trunks, which is only available to those who are familiar with the issue at hand – friends, relatives, colleagues, or other people who are in the know about something. Specific background information can also consist of

---

26. The analysis of William of Orange's *Apologie*, for instance, in which Orange defends the Dutch revolt against King Filip of Spain, can only be accounted for if it is taken into account that the *Apologie* is a response to Filip's *Ban Edict* (van Eemeren & Houtlosser, 1999b, 2000b). Wodak distinguishes "interdiscursivity" from "intertextuality" (2009, pp. 39–40). In her usage, intertextuality refers to "the linkage of all texts to other texts, both in the past and in the present" (p. 39), whereas interdiscursivity indicates "that topic-oriented discourses are linked to each other in various ways" (p. 40).

27. Context is sometimes wrongly taken to be something permanent and fixed, but in practice the context changes continually during an argumentative exchange, because the participants in the exchange reshape the micro-context by every argumentative move they make, and the meso-context changes accordingly. See Chapter 6.4 on "dialectical profiles" and Chapter 6.6 on the "argumentative situation."

expert information that some people have due to their special training with regard to the topic or field at issue in the discourse. Special forms of expert information are *ethnographic information*, which may be of help to an analyst when cultural peculiarities play a role in understanding the discourse, and *expert information about argumentative discourse*, which is utilized when argumentation theorists refer to their knowledge of the conventional patterns and structures occurring in argumentative discourse to support their understanding of certain aspects of the discourse. The analyst may, for example, make use of his expertise as an argumentation theorist when referring to a prolonged pause before a standpoint is responded to as an indicator of non-agreement and to the use of the expression "apart from this" as an indicator of a multiple argumentation structure.

All these sources can, in my view, be used as resources for giving a justified account of a reconstruction of argumentative discourse with the help of pragma-dialectical analytical instruments. In most cases, the analyst may exploit these resources in the way he thinks most pertinent, without one source being necessarily superior to the other, provided that ultimately the analysis is in agreement with a possible interpretation of the discourse that is plausible and credible (van Eemeren *et al.*, 1993, pp. 44). In many cases, however, and most certainly in problematic ones, the analyst has to refer to a combination of sources. If this happens, he must make sure that the various sources referred to do indeed reinforce each other and do not instigate inconsistent results.[28]

论辩现实的更佳把握
1.6 Getting a better grip on argumentative reality

The theory of argumentation as explained in the preceding sections may be called the "standard theory" of pragma-dialectics. This theory aims at enabling the analyst of argumentative discourse to make a reconstruction of the discourse that results in an analytic overview of all elements that are pertinent to a critical evaluation. The theoretical tools that have been developed for this purpose need to be such that they provide the analyst with all the means that are necessary to construct an analytic overview of the discourse and to account for this overview by utilizing the available resources. In order to show in what respects the standard theory of pragma-dialectics as a method for analyzing argumentative discourse is not yet as adequate as one might wish, I shall present a reconstruction of a discourse that demonstrates that in certain cases there is more at stake in argumentative reality than the "standard" pragma-dialectical method developed so far is capable to cover.

Because argumentative discourse centering on normative standpoints — which is of particular significance for my endeavor — is often neglected in the study of argumentation, I will take such a discourse as my object of analysis. I will give a (partial)

---

28. If two or more sources instigate inconsistent results, the analyst must explicitly acknowledge that this is the case.

reconstruction of a discourse in which a prescriptive standpoint is at issue that recommends a certain course of action, in this case urging the addressees to refrain from taking up a certain habit.

The case stems from an "advertorial" that appeared in many American magazines in the mid-1980s at the time when in the United States public attitudes toward smoking had started to shift dramatically. In the context of a call for Congressional hearings to consider further restrictions on the advertising of cigarettes, the argument was put forward that tobacco companies were advertising to children in order to replace the growing number of adult smokers who were quitting or dying. Among the responses issued by R.J. Reynolds Tobacco Company was the following:

Some surprising advice to young people from R.J. Reynolds Tobacco.

> Don't smoke.
> For one thing, smoking has always been an adult custom. And even for adults, smoking has become very controversial.
> So even though we're a tobacco company, we don't think it's a good idea for young people to smoke.
> Now, we know that giving this kind of advice to young people can sometimes backfire.
> But if you take up smoking just to prove you're an adult, you're really proving just the opposite.
> Because deciding to smoke or not to smoke is something you should do when you don't have anything to prove.
> Think it over.
> After all, you may not be old enough to smoke. But you're old enough to think.

Analysis. After the announcement preceding the text has created the "surprising" perspective desired by Reynolds, the text begins with the pronouncement "Don't smoke." This pronouncement initiates the confrontation stage by expressing – by way of an advice – the normative standpoint that young people should not smoke, which, viewed dialectically, the protagonist Reynolds is expected to defend against the antagonist consisting, in this case, of the young people the advertorial is addressed to. After having tried to establish as common starting points in the opening stage that smoking has always been an adult custom and has become very controversial, these starting points are then used as arguments to support the standpoint presented by Reynolds. This means that the argumentation stage develops in a way that from a dialectical point of view could have been expected after Reynolds advanced its confrontational standpoint. A reconstruction of the structure of the argumentation put forward by Reynolds in defense of its standpoint shows that this argumentation is coordinatively compound because the arguments that are advanced are interdependent:

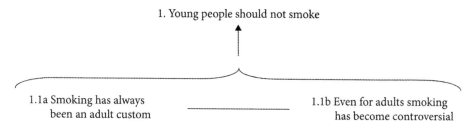

Although there is more to say about the arguments that are used, the argument schemes they employ, and several other aspects of the discourse, I leave the analysis at this, because this partial reconstruction should be enough to make clear in what respect a reconstructive analysis on the basis of the standard theory of pragma-dialectics is still found wanting.

In the Reynolds advertorial more is at stake that is pertinent to an evaluation of this piece of argumentative discourse than my analysis provides. Although Reynolds is – as they explicitly acknowledge – fully aware that young people are usually not inclined to accept the kind of paternalistic advice Reynolds is giving, the company puts its advice bluntly and in the strongest possible terms, thus taking the considerable risk that exactly because of its presentation their advice will be resisted. It is also fully clear that there is something odd about the arguments put forward by Reynolds. They leave conspicuously unmentioned the readily available arguments that smoking can become an addiction and causes cancer, which are much more obvious and much stronger arguments than the ones they put forward. In addition, the wording of the arguments has been chosen in an awkward way. That smoking is "controversial," as Reynolds asserts, implies that there are valid reasons for *not* smoking, but also that there are valid reasons to smoke – in other words, that the opinions on this matter are (literally) divided. Paradoxically, it is already clear from the start that the arguments that are put forward by Reynolds will not appeal to young people. It is more than doubtful – to say the least – that considerations of age and convention will be decisive reasons for young people to decide not to smoke. It is much more likely that highlighting the conventional presupposition that smoking is the privilege of "adults" will give the average young person a motive to participate in that privilege. And that smoking has become "controversial" will make it only more interesting to the young.

Because Reynolds must have known that it was likely that the way they designed their advertorial would have the negative effect I just described, it seems plausible that in this advertorial they in fact aimed at rendering their official argumentation counterproductive. Although a final evaluation of the discourse is, of course, possible only after a full analysis has been given, I nevertheless dare to claim that the observations I have made in commenting on the way the discourse would be analyzed according to standard pragma-dialectics already enable us to come to the conclusion that something pertinent is absent from such an analysis because in a case like this it misses the point in a crucial sense. According to my observations, the cause of this oversight is that the intended interactional ("perlocutionary") effect of the moves made in argumentative discourse is not taken into account.[29] It seems therefore worthwhile to make an effort to extend the scope of pragma-dialectical analysis in such a way that, next to the dimension of reasonableness of argumentative discourse, the dimension of its effectiveness is methodically taken into account in the analysis and the evaluation of argumentative discourse – a challenge taken up in this monograph.

语用论辩学的理论拓展
1.7 An extended pragma-dialectical theory

Strategic Maneuvering in Argumentative Discourse is a study aimed at extending the standard pragma-dialectical theory of argumentation (van Eemeren & Grootendorst, 1984; 1992a; 2004; van Eemeren et al., 1993; van Eemeren et al., 2007) by integrating insight concerning the intended effectiveness of argumentative discourse into the theoretical framework of analysis and evaluation. The extended theory should offer a theoretical perspective on argumentative discourse that enables a systematic reconstruction of such discourse which takes into account not only the ways in which dialectical reasonableness is, or is not, maintained in the discourse, as the pragma-dialectical standard theory does, but also the ways in which attempts at being effective are made in the discourse (van Eemeren & Houtlosser, 2000a; 2002a).

In order to expound such a theoretical perspective, in Chapter 2, I will first discuss the concepts of reasonableness and effectiveness, and the way in which they relate to each other. Starting from this background I introduce the notion of "strategic maneuvering" that will make it possible to integrate insight concerning intended effectiveness systematically into the pragma-dialectical framework of analysis and evaluation. In Chapter 3, I explore theoretical perspectives on reasonableness developed in classical and modern dialectical approaches and on effectiveness developed in classical and modern rhetorical approaches, followed by an investigation of the relationship between dialectic and rhetoric.

Having established in this way a theoretical basis for an extended theory of pragma-dialectics, I will introduce in the next chapters a series of theoretical concepts that are instrumental in developing the necessary analytical tools for refining the reconstruction of argumentative discourse, strengthening the justificatory account of the analysis, and attuning the evaluation of the discourse more systematically to the functional variety of argumentative practices that characterizes argumentative reality. In Chapter 4, I distinguish analytically between three inseparable aspects of strategic maneuvering and discuss some relevant theoretical contributions made by other authors to the analysis of each of these aspects. In Chapter 5, the contextualization of strategic maneuvering in various kinds of conventionalized communicative practices

---

29. For a conceptual clarification of the notion of perlocutionary effect, see van Eemeren and Grootendorst (1984, pp. 69–74).

is at issue. I distinguish between communicative activity types instrumental in different more or less institutionalized communicative domains. Next I make clear in which ways in argumentative discourse communicative activity types impose certain institutional preconditions on the strategic maneuvering. Chapter 6 is devoted to the problem of determining the strategic function of argumentative moves made in argumentative discourse, offering pragma-dialectical theoretical tools for dealing with some of the most crucial parameters.

In Chapter 7, fallacies committed in argumentative discourse are characterized as derailments of strategic maneuvering. I explain how this characterization relates to the pragma-dialectical view of fallacies as violations of a critical discussion (developed in response to the challenge involved in Hamblin's critique of the so-called logical Standard Treatment of the fallacies), and how it provides more insight in the deceptiveness of the fallacies, an issue that had earlier largely been ignored. In connecting the treatment of the fallacies with the conventional preconditions for strategic maneuvering prevailing in particular communicative activity types, I make a distinction between context-independent criteria ensuing directly from the norms involved in the rules for critical discussion, and context-dependent criteria for judging fallaciousness serving the particular institutional needs of specific communicative activity types. Chapter 8 is devoted to a discussion of strategic maneuvering with the burden of proof from the perspective developed in this study. Chapter 9 concentrates on strategic maneuvering that occurs in response to presumed inconsistency and presumed fallaciousness. Special attention is paid to the problem of re-railing derailments of strategic maneuvering. In conclusion, in Chapter 10, setting up an agenda for further research regarding strategic maneuvering is considered for each component of the pragma-dialectical research program.

CHAPTER 2 第二章
有效性和合理性之间的策略操控
Strategic maneuvering between effectiveness and reasonableness

论辩的理论界定
2.1 Defining argumentation theoretically

Rather than being merely stipulative, a theoretical definition of argumentation should, in my view, connect as much as possible with commonly recognized characteristics of argumentation. Therefore due account must be taken of the lexical meaning of the word "argumentation" in ordinary usage. In this endeavor it is important to realize from the outset that there are striking differences between the meaning of the pivotal word "argumentation" in English and the meaning of its counterparts in other European languages, such as Dutch ("argumentatie"), French ("argumentation"), German ("Argumentation"), Italian ("argomentazione"), Spanish ("argumentación"), Portuguese ("argumentação") and Swedish ("argumentation"). The differences cannot be simply dismissed as just funny peculiarities, because they involve vital characteristics of argumentation that may have significant consequences for the way in which argumentation is viewed.[1] It is noteworthy that the word "argumentatie" in my own language, Dutch, and the equivalents in other languages, are much more commonly used than the word "argumentation" in English.[2] More importantly, these expressions lack some of the properties the word "argumentation" has in English that complicate a theoretical definition of argumentation starting from the perspective of ordinary language use. Put positively, the counterparts of the English word "argumentation" already display certain characteristics that are crucial to a theoretical definition of argumentation.[3]

A first noteworthy difference between the English word "argumentation" and its counterparts in several other languages is that the meanings of the latter include naturally both the meaning of argumentation as a process and the meaning of

---

1. Without falling back on a Sapir-Whorf hypothesis concerning the relationship between language and thinking I conclude from personal experience that certain linguistic idiosyncrasies can have a distinct impact on people's conceptualizations.

2. Because I am a native speaker of Dutch in comparing with English usage I rely in the first place on that language, but my observations apply equally well to the other languages I mentioned.

3. This explains that, apart from the technical jargon, the theoretical definition of argumentation provided in *Fundamentals of Argumentation Theory*, presently the most comprehensive handbook of argumentation studies (van Eemeren *et al.*, 1996, p. 5), is virtually in agreement with ordinary usage in these languages.

argumentation as a product. Without having to stretch ordinary usage in any way, the Dutch word "argumentatie," for instance, can be used to refer both to the process of argumentation ("Don't interrupt me just now since I am in the middle of my argumentation [argumentatie]"), and to the product resulting from the argumentative process ("I have looked into your argumentation [argumentatie] but I don't find it very strong"). This means that the process-product combination that is characteristic of our object of study, and is to be preserved in the definition of the theoretical term *argumentation*, is in these languages already inherent in ordinary usage, whereas this is not the case in English (where the process side is predominant), or at any rate not so clearly. This double meaning is therefore more naturally preserved if one starts from non-English usage.

A second vital difference is that the non-English words for argumentation are immediately and exclusively connected with constructive efforts to resolve a difference of opinion on the merits by convincing the other party of the acceptability of one's standpoint. This means that they are immediately associated with reasonableness and acting reasonably – a crucial property of the pragma-dialectical conception of argumentation (van Eemeren & Grootendorst, 2004, pp. 11–18). The Dutch word "argumentatie," for instance, refers – just as the term *argumentation* used in argumentation theory – to a deliberate effort to resolve a (real or projected) difference of opinion by convincing the addressee(s) in a reasonable way of the acceptability of the standpoint(s) at issue. In this endeavor the audience is presumed to be a reasonable judge, irrespective of whether it consists of only one interlocutor or of all potential readers of an essay. Unlike the word "argumentation" in English, the non-English words for argumentation have nothing to do with quarrelling or other negatively charged verbal activities, such as skirmishing, squabbling, bickering, wrangling and haggling.[4] This lack of any negative connotations allows the non-English words for argumentation to be easily adopted as a technical term for theoretical purposes, without a need to first introduce artificial stipulations that rule out undesired aggressive meanings.

A third difference worth mentioning here is that, unlike the English word "argumentation," its counterparts refer only to the constellation of reasons put forward by a speaker or writer in defense of a standpoint while the standpoint itself is not included. According to Dutch usage, for instance, the argumentation ["argumentatie"] put forward in "You should not listen to Peter, because he is prejudiced" consists only of the explicit statement that he (Peter) is prejudiced and the implicit unexpressed premise that prejudiced people are not worth listening to, while the advisory statement that you should not listen to Peter is not part of the argumentation but constitutes the standpoint that is being defended by argumentation. This distinction connects very well with a theoretical definition of argumentation in which the argumentation put forward in defense of a standpoint and the standpoint that is

---

4. In *Negotiation: An A-Z guide*, Kennedy (2004, p. 22) describes the headword *argument* as follows: "Argument is a destructive form of debate. Some negotiations never get beyond argument."

defended by means of this argumentation are regarded as separate speech act complexes, so that the relationship between the two can be more easily analyzed and evaluated (van Eemeren & Grootendorst, 1984, p. 18). Although not too much should be made out of such largely coincidental language differences, it is clear that conceptually the lexical meaning of the non-English counterparts of the English word "argumentation" constitutes a better basis for a theoretical definition of the technical term *argumentation* than the meaning of the ordinary English word "argumentation" (if it is even an ordinary word).

There are some other conspicuous characteristics of argumentation as an ordinary phenomenon of generally shared everyday reality that are also vital to a theoretical definition but which are independent of any specific language. I consider them vital because in my view they must have methodological consequences for the way in which argumentation research is to be conducted. To start with, rather than being just a structural entity, argumentation is in the first place a *communicative act complex*, which is realized by making functional verbal (and sometimes non-verbal) communicative moves.[5] In the pragma-dialectical theorizing this characteristic leads to the adoption of the meta-theoretical principle of "functionalization," which serves as a methodological starting point for how to give a theoretical account. Second, rather than being just a one-way monologue, argumentation is an *interactional act complex* directed at eliciting certain responses from the people to whom it is addressed. This makes argumentation part of a dialogue, which may be explicit, as in the case of argumentation advanced in a discussion, or implicit, as in the case of argumentation delivered for an audience or readership that is not directly responding or is not even physically present. The associated meta-theoretical principle of pragma-dialectics is called "socialization." Third, rather than being just a free-flowing expressive act, argumentation involves putting forward propositions in a way that creates commitments for which one can be held *accountable*. The meta-theoretical principle that, in the pragma-dialectical approach, goes with this accountability is "externalization" – in this case, of commitments. Fourth, rather than merely speculating on instincts and emotional entanglements, argumentation involves by its constructive nature an *appeal to reasonableness* that derives its force from the idea of common critical standards. This critical characteristic of argumentation leads pragma-dialecticians to adopt the meta-theoretical principle of "dialectification," which is the fourth methodological starting point defining the pragma-dialectical theory of argumentation.

The four principles I have just introduced in association with four vital characteristics of argumentation are meta-theoretical in the sense that adopting them precedes the actual theorizing. After they have been adopted, the theoretical tools need to be found or developed to implement these principles systematically, and the endeavor of

---

5.   In the past I used to speak of "verbal" or "linguistic" moves (e.g. van Eemeren *et al.*, 1996, p. 2), but because these moves can also be non-verbal, or partly non-verbal, I think it is better to refer to them more generally as "communicative" moves.

creating means for implementing them poses its own problems. However this may be, the meta-theoretical principles of functionalization, socialization, externalization, and dialectification are part and parcel of the pragma-dialectical approach to argumentation. This does certainly not mean that these four principles are shared unreservedly by other argumentation theorists – establishing the extent to which they are shared is in fact one of the most telling ways of distinguishing between the various approaches.

Functionalization is in the pragma-dialectical approach to argumentation achieved by doing justice to the fact that argumentative discourse (as far as it is conducted linguistically) occurs through – and in response to – speech act performances. Giving a functional definition of the complex speech act of argumentation and the other speech acts performed in the discourse that are pertinent to resolving a difference of opinion on the merits makes it possible to specify the relevant "identity conditions" and "correctness conditions" of all argumentative moves (van Eemeren & Grootendorst, 1984, pp. 39–46; 1992a, pp. 30–33). In this way, for instance, a specification can be given of what is "at stake" in advancing a certain "standpoint," so that it becomes clear what the "disagreement space" is and how the argumentative discourse is organized around this context of disagreement (Jackson, 1992, p. 261). Socialization is achieved by identifying exactly which participants take on the discussion roles of protagonist and antagonist in the collaborative context of argumentative discourse. Through an extension of the speech act perspective from the communicative level of the *illocution* to the interactional level of the *perlocution* it can be shown in which ways standpoints and argumentation in support of standpoints are developed in response to the moves made by (or projected onto) the other party. Externalization is achieved by identifying on the basis of the relevant identity conditions and correctness conditions the specific commitments that are created by the speech acts performed in a particular context of argumentative interaction. Rather than being treated as internal states of mind, notions such as "disagreement" and "acceptance" are in such an externalized perspective defined in terms of discursive activities that create well-defined commitments. "Acceptance," for instance, is externalized as giving a preferred response to an arguable act committing the respondent to not attacking the act anymore. Finally, dialectification – regulating the critical exchange – is achieved by regimenting the performance of speech acts in argumentative discourse systematically in an ideal model of a critical discussion aimed at resolving a difference of opinion on the merits by putting the acceptability of the standpoints at issue to a critical test.[6]

Starting from the conceptualization of argumentation achieved by taking account of the vital characteristics of argumentation in ordinary language and doing justice to the principles of functionalization, socialization, externalization, and dialectification

---

6. In practice, this means that it is checked methodically by the parties involved whether or not the argumentative support given to the standpoints concerned justifies accepting them.

that serve as methodological starting points for studying argumentation, argumentation can be theoretically defined as follows:[7]

> Argumentation is a communicative and interactional (speech) act complex aimed at resolving a difference of opinion before a reasonable judge by advancing a constellation of reasons[8] the arguer can be held accountable for as justifying the acceptability of the standpoint(s) at issue.

保持论辩话语的合理性
2.2 Maintaining reasonableness in argumentative discourse

Since the pragma-dialectical definition of argumentation refers the assessment of argumentation to a "reasonable judge," I must clarify what I mean by *reasonable*. In ordinary language the word "reasonable" is often used indiscriminately and interchangeably with the word "rational." In my theoretical approach to argumentation, however, I would like to make a practical distinction in the meanings of these two expressions. Because I use *reasonable* as a technical term in my theorizing, I must make a distinction between the meanings of reasonable and rational, so that the scope of the two concepts referred to by the terms *reasonable* and *rational* will be clearly delineated. Following the dictionary descriptions, I assign a normative dimension to "reasonable" that is largely lacking in "rational:" I use "rational" for the activity of *using reason* and "reasonable" for using reason *in an appropriate* ("well-considered") *way*.[9] Taking also into account that in careful usage "reasonableness" is primarily reserved for indicating the quality of the use of reason in a situated context of communication and interaction, I relate the meaning of the term *reasonable* to a context of *interpersonal* reasoning[10] not automatically presupposed in the term *rational*.[11] My stipulative (but lexically based) definition delineating the meaning of the term *reasonable* is: *using reason in a way that is appropriate in view of the situation concerned*.

---

7. This is a stipulative-lexical definition as discussed by Naess (1966, p. 48, type b) without using the same terminology. See also Copi (1986, p. 142), who uses the term *precising definition*.

8. In Dutch, each of these reasons by itself is called an "argument," and the "argumentatie" (argumentation) consists of the whole complex of "argumenten" (reasons) put forward in support of a standpoint.

9. In ordinary usage the scope of the word "reasonable" is not limited to verbal behavior but covers also non-verbal behavior. Recently I read in an English newspaper that "Madonna divorced her film director husband citing 'unreasonable behavior' which she claimed was 'continuing' but not affecting her health." The scope of "reasonableness" seems to be wider than that of "rationality." One can, for example, speak quite well of "reasonable desires" but not so easily of "rational desires."

10. Interpersonal does not necessarily mean collectivist. See Popper (1971b, pp. 225-226).

11. "Rational" often refers to egoistical behavior calculated exclusively to maximize the desired payoff, as when this term is used in economic models.

To give further substance to the notion of reasonableness, it may seem sensible to turn to scientific procedures because they are often seen as the paragon of reasonableness. Philosophers of science and methodologists dealing with scientific procedures have indeed attempted to tackle the notion of reasonableness, specifying rules and criteria that are pertinent to conducting scientific discussions aimed at resolving scientific problems. They have formulated some rules and criteria of scientific discussion, but a clear-cut and infallible method for solving scientific problems they could not provide.[12] The rules and criteria of scientific discussion they formulate based on intersubjective understanding and the conventions of scientific tradition depend in the end on the agreement of what has been termed the *Science Forum* (de Groot, 1984).[13] If the rules and criteria are no longer satisfactory to the Science Forum, they will eventually have to be replaced by others, on the basis of arguments that the Forum considers cogent. According to de Groot, ultimately scientific methodology derives its reasonableness from the fact that consensus in the Science Forum is aimed for by means of a critical discussion *relying on the force of argumentation*.[14] In this approach, however, it is too readily assumed that the problem of establishing methodological rules and criteria can be easily transposed to that of establishing rules of discussion and criteria for sound argumentation.[15] Argumentation theory does not allow for such a solution,

---

12. The suggestion that a set of methodological rules can be compiled for maintaining reasonableness in an absolute sense is linked with a heavily contested ideology that suggests the existence of a final point in a scale of reasonableness.

13. The Science Forum, consisting of all experts in the field, is considered to have the final say and has to reach agreement on the matter concerned. A fundamental reason, however, why the reasonableness problem cannot be solved so easily by relying on philosophy of science is that there is not just one scientific methodology but a collection of competing methodologies, so that the Science Forum either has to make a choice or is not really in agreement – as seems in fact to be the case.

14. Because the Science Forum must establish which arguments are acceptable, this Forum functions as a monitor of reasonableness. A problem is that some philosophers think it necessary to distinguish various forums associated with different kinds of questions or question types. Combined with the fact that the Forum is a normative model that implies total openness, this poses not only a practical but also a theoretical problem. All the relevant experts should be able to participate in the scientific discussion and the quality of the Forum is supposed to be maintained by a process of self-selection. Only to an uncertain degree, however, can the company that constitutes the Forum be said to consist of a clearly identifiable group of people. It seems to me that the Science Forum could better be characterized the other way around, by first establishing which rules of discussion are taken into account and then identifying which scientists are committed to apply them.

15. While philosophers of science seem to place excessive trust in the problem-solving potential of argumentation theory, they seem on the other hand to undervalue the scope argumentation theory needs to have. The latter misconception is caused by the *parti pris* mentioned in Chapter 1 that a fundamental distinction should be made between factual judgments and value judgments, and that the value judgments cannot be the subject of a reasonable discussion because they can only be based on subjective preferences and conflicts of interests. It is precisely to

because among argumentation theorists there is presently an equally strong division as to when argumentation is to be considered reasonable.

As Grootendorst and I have argued elsewhere (van Eemeren & Grootendorst, 1994), prominent argumentation theories such as Toulmin's model (1958/2003) and Perelman and Olbrechts-Tyteca's new rhetoric (1958/1969) suffer from "justificationism." Justificationism manifests itself both in the "geometrical" and in the "anthropological" conception of reasonableness distinguished by Toulmin (1976) in *Knowing and Acting*. The geometrical (demonstration-oriented) conception of reasonableness eventually leads to a form of justificationism that Popper and Albert refer to as "intellectualism" or (Cartesian) "rationalism," the anthropological (consensus-oriented) conception of reasonableness to "empiristic" justificationism (British empiricism). According to Albert (1975, p. 13), justificationism, whatever its make, can never escape from the *Münchhausen trilemma*, i.e. justificationists are in the end always forced to choose between three unacceptable options: an infinite regress, a logical circle, or breaking the justification process off at one or more arbitrary points. When, as often happens, the last option is chosen, the process of *Begründung* is abandoned. Because no further foundation is deemed required, the justificatory claims made at the points where the justification process halts are given a more or less unassailable status. Their truth is regarded evident on the grounds of intuition or experience. In this way a starting point made immune to criticism serves as an *a priori* or as an *axiom* – or perhaps even as a dogma. In different forms, such justificatory starting points play a crucial part in both the geometrical and the anthropological conception of reasonableness.

I agree with Albert (1975, 15 ff), who warns in his *Traktat über kritische Vernunft* against any "revelation model" of the truth, and consider it necessary to distance the pragma-dialectical argumentation theory from the justificationism of the geometrical and anthropological conceptions of reasonableness. Instead, I opt for what Toulmin (1976) calls a "critical" conception of reasonableness, which focuses not on demonstration or consensus but on discussion. In contradistinction to protagonists of the geometrical approach, who are predominantly product-oriented logicians, and protagonists of the anthropological approach, who are predominantly process-oriented rhetoricians, protagonists of a critical approach are predominantly procedure-oriented dialecticians. They view argumentation as part of a dialectical procedure for solving problems regarding the acceptability of standpoints by means of a methodical discussion aimed at testing the tenability of these standpoints. In a dialectical discussion procedure, elements from both the product-oriented logical approach and the process-oriented rhetorical approach are duly taken into account.[16]

---

remedy this misunderstanding about the required scope of argumentation theory that the founding fathers of modern argumentation theory, Perelman and Toulmin, set out to develop their theories.

16. The purpose of the dialectical approach to argumentation is to establish how discussions must be carried out systematically in order to test standpoints critically. Wenzel, a supporter of

A dialectical discussion procedure derives its reasonableness from a dual criterion: *problem (solving) validity* and *intersubjective* (or *conventional*) *validity* (Barth & Krabbe, 1982, pp. 21–22).[17] This means that the various components that together constitute a pragma-dialectical discussion procedure are to be checked, on the one hand, for their capability "to do the job" they are designed to do,[18] namely for their adequacy for resolving differences of opinion, and, on the other hand, for their intersubjective acceptability to discussants – which can lend them conventional validity (acceptance by a company in Crawshay-Williams' (1957) sense[19]). For the pragma-dialectical approach to argumentation this means that evaluating the acceptability of argumentative moves for a reasonable judge will consist in checking whether or not these moves are in agreement with dialectical standards that (1) do the job of determining when an argumentative move contributes to resolving a difference of opinion on the merits and that (2) have been accepted intersubjectively as appropriate means for resolving a difference of opinion.

In *Speech Acts in Argumentative Discussions* (van Eemeren & Grootendorst, 1984), the authors introduced a pragma-dialectical procedure for conducting a critical discussion aimed at resolving a difference of opinion on the merits, which we amended slightly in *A Systematic Theory of Argumentation* (van Eemeren & Grootendorst, 2004). By adopting the viewpoint of a Popperian critical rationalist, we replaced the geometrical and the anthropological conceptions of reasonableness in this procedure by a critical conception. This means that we propose a discussion procedure based on a philosophy of reasonableness that takes the fallibility of human reason as its starting point and elevates systematic critical testing to the guiding principle of problem solving by means of argumentation in all areas of human communication and interaction. In the pragma-dialectical theory of argumentation this critical rationalist philosophy of reasonableness manifests itself by the promotion of dialectic in a Socratic sense. Having a regimented critical discussion is made the basic principle of reasonableness.[20] As Albert emphasizes, the dialectical method of systematic testing by critical discussion is of general scope, not subjected to any restrictions

---

this approach, believes that argumentation in the dialectical sense should be regarded as "a systematic management of discourse for the purpose of achieving critical decisions" (1979, p. 84).

17. This dual criterion was first proposed in Barth (1972).

18. If Perelman and Olbrechts-Tyteca's (1958/1969) "universal audience" represents an ideal that is connected with achieving problem-validity it may be expected to employ similar norms as those incorporated in the rules for critical discussion.

19. An external evaluator may be part of this company but may also be part of some other company accepting standards that are to some extent different from those of the discussants. Then there is in fact a difference of opinion about the problem-validity of the standards.

20. Eventually Perelman also seems to have come to terms with Socratic dialectics. In *Justice, Law and Argument* he describes argumentation as "the technique that we use in controversy when we are concerned with criticizing and justifying, objecting and refuting, of asking and giving reasons." He believes that aside from logic as a formal proof theory, an argumentation theory should be developed: "This enlargement would complete formal logic by the study of what, since Socrates, has been called *dialectics*" (1980, p. 108).

regarding the issues and types of standpoint or beliefs that are dealt with.[21] In such a critical discussion, whether it is a discussion about facts or about values, reasonableness is only limited by the boundaries drawn by the participants themselves (Albert, 1975).

In pragma-dialectics it is assumed that a difference of opinion comes into being when a party (the would-be protagonist) advances a standpoint on which doubt is cast (or assumed or projected to be cast) by another party (the would-be antagonist). After the parties have decided that there is enough common ground to conduct a discussion, the protagonist advances argumentation in defense of the standpoint, possibly followed by another critical response of the antagonist, and so on. The difference of opinion is resolved when the antagonist accepts the protagonist's viewpoint on the basis of the arguments advanced or when the protagonist abandons his viewpoint as a result of the critical responses of the antagonist. This view of the argumentative discussion process implies that a pragma-dialectical regulation of argumentative discourse in a procedure which furthers the resolution of differences of opinion on the merits cannot be limited to the inference relation between the premises (interpreted as "concessions" of the other party) and the conclusion of the reasoning involved, but must cover all speech acts performed in the discourse that are pertinent to the resolution process.

Since the pragma-dialectical theory is concerned with argumentative communication and interaction conducted in ordinary language, the concept of contradiction, which is vital to the dialectical testing process (Albert, 1975, p. 44),[22] should in that theory not be limited to the formal inconsistencies known as logical contradictions, but must also incorporate pragmatic inconsistencies leading to incompatible consequences in argumentative reality. The promise, for instance, "I shall pick you up in the car," may not logically contradict the statement "I don't know how to drive," but in ordinary communication making this promise and adding the statement are pragmatically inconsistent, which can be explained by referring to the correctness conditions of the speech act of promising and taking account of the commitments ensuing from performing this speech act. Among the procedures proposed in pragma-dialectics to evaluate argumentative discourse as a means for resolving a difference of opinion on the merits figure therefore, next to the "inference" procedure, several other intersubjective devices: an "identification" procedure, an "explicitization" procedure and a "testing" procedure (van Eemeren & Grootendorst, 2004, pp. 123–157).

---

21. Replacing Bartley's "comprehensive critical rationalism," Barth (1972, p. 17) speaks of "alles-omvattend rationalistisch criticisme" [all-embracing rational criticism].

22. Following Popper, critical rationalists equate dialectical testing with the detection of contradictions and emphasize that the consequence of the fact that an assertive and its negation cannot both be acceptable at the same time is that one of the speech acts concerned must be withdrawn. In *From Axiom to Dialogue*, Barth and Krabbe (1982) propose methods designed to establish whether a certain standpoint ("thesis") is tenable in relation to certain premises ("concessions") – in other words, whether criticizing the standpoint, given these premises, leads to (a kind of) contradiction (or, more precisely, to the contrary dialogue attitudes: admitting that p and attacking p).

In *Argumentation, Communication and Fallacies* (van Eemeren & Grootendorst, 1992a), the authors established the problem validity of the pragma-dialectical discussion procedure by showing that each of the norms incorporated in the rules for critical discussion has a distinctive function in keeping the discussion on track through the prevention of certain impediments to resolving a difference of opinion on the merits. The intersubjective acceptability we attribute to the procedure, which is eventually expected to lend conventional validity to the procedure,[23] is primarily based on its instrumentality in doing the job it is intended to do: resolving a difference of opinion. This means that, philosophically speaking, the rationale for accepting the pragma-dialectical procedure is *pragmatic* – more precisely, *utilitarian*.[24] A utilitarian discussion attitude involves striving for a resolution of the difference of opinion satisfactory to all concerned, irrespective of whether this means victory for the protagonist or the antagonist. Bearing Popper's plea on behalf of falsification in mind, a "negative" variant of the basic principle of utilitarianism seems to us more effective than "positive" utilitarianism. Rather than maximization of agreement, minimization of disagreement is to be aimed for,[25] because a procedure that encourages discussants to pronounce their doubts and to work out how far their differences can be resolved by critical testing is preferable to a procedure that seeks to ensure agreement.[26] This philosophical explanation illustrates how in the conception of reasonableness upheld in pragma-dialectics insights from critical-rationalist epistemology and utilitarian ethics conjoin.

---

23. Barth and Krabbe would probably call this *semi*-conventionality, since the company of discussants agrees only implicitly about the rules of discussion (1982, p. 22, 38ff.).

24. Pragmatists judge the acceptability of norms depending on the extent to which they appear successful in solving the problems they are designed to solve. In fact, to them a norm *is* a norm only if it performs a function in the achievement of objectives set by the pragmatist. Cf. William James' (1907) maxim "A difference which makes no difference is no difference." Those wanting to resolve differences of opinion and judge resolution procedures primarily on instrumental grounds, having as their main purpose to achieve an optimally satisfactory result for as many as possible of those involved (instead of, for example, as much personal gain or enjoyment as possible), can be characterized as *utilitarians*. This kind of utilitarianism goes back to Jeremy Bentham (1838–1843) and John Stuart Mill (1863), but is also connected with the eudaemonistic ethics rehabilitated in modern times by Kamlah (1973). Unlike the pure egoist or the hedonist, the utilitarian strives for optimal results for all concerned.

25. This alters the perspective by a U-turn. Broadly speaking, negative utilitarianism means that instead of the maximization of happiness, the minimization of suffering is sought. In this respect, the critical attitude pragma-dialecticians advocate corresponds with the negative utilitarian starting point. Cf. Popper in *The Open Society and Its Enemies* (1971a, Ch. 5, n. 6).

26. Although Habermas' ideal of consensus (1971) in a speech situation of communication unimpaired by power relations rests on philosophical starting points different from ours, his ideal is in some respects not dissimilar to ours, but in view of the pragma-dialectical conception of intellectual doubt and criticism as the driving forces of progress, it is eventually not consensus that we are after but rather a continual flux of ever more advanced opinions. In this perspective, aiming for agreement is just an intermediate step on the way to new, and more advanced, disagreements.

It is important to bear in mind that the pragma-dialectical procedure deals only with "first order" conditions for resolving differences of opinion on the merits by means of a critical discussion. These first order conditions provide general and vital guidance for their conduct to those people who are willing and ready to act as reasonable discussants and are in the circumstances to have a critical position. But in order for people to be willing and ready and to have the opportunity for concluding a critical discussion, certain further prerequisites need to be fulfilled. In principle, if they wish, all individuals can fulfill the prerequisites for a reasonable discussion attitude and become contributors to what Popper calls the Open Society. [27] In argumentative reality, however, their freedom to do so may be restricted by factors beyond their control, which can be referred to in a general way as *compulsion*. Following Barth and Krabbe (1982, p. 75), pragma-dialecticians consider the further prerequisites for a reasonable discussion attitude as second order conditions that must be fulfilled to be able to comply with the (first order) dialectical discussion procedure.[28] The theoretical clarification of the notion of reasonableness provided in pragma-dialectics can only be of practical significance if it is taken into consideration to what extent the higher (second, third, etc.) order conditions have been fulfilled that are prerequisites for critical reasonableness.[29]

In 1995, Bert Meuffels and I, soon joined by Bart Garssen, started Conceptions of Reasonableness, a comprehensive research project investigating the conventional validity of the pragma-dialectical discussion rules (van Eemeren *et al.*, 2009). The aim of this project was to examine empirically which norms ordinary arguers use, or claim to use, when evaluating argumentative discourse and how far these norms are in agreement with the critical norms proposed in the pragma-dialectical theory.[30] Our experimental design allowed us to abstract from the fulfillment or non-fulfillment of higher order conditions. It is interesting to note that this experimental empirical research has shown indisputably that the norms of reasonableness incorporated in the

---

[27]. Members of the Open Society are anti-dogmatic, anti-authoritarian, and anti-*Letztbegründung* – in other words, they are against monopolies of knowledge, pretensions of infallibility, and appeals to unfaltering principles.

[28]. The "internal" conditions for a reasonable discussion attitude ("free mind") are called *second order* conditions; the "external" conditions pertaining to the circumstances in which the discussion takes place ("free communicative situation") are called *third order* conditions. If the higher order conditions are fulfilled the argumentation takes place in circumstances that are similar to those in Habermas' (1971) "ideal speech situation."

[29]. It should be noted that the first order rules of the dialectical procedure corresponding to the first order conditions are not foolproof algorithmic rules, but informal rules of conduct that can only be used by people who reflect upon the argumentative reality in which the discussion takes place. This is another consideration as to why we cannot do without second and third (an perhaps even higher) order conditions.

[30]. The expression "ordinary arguers" refers in this case to people who are neither experts in the field of argumentation theory nor students who have received some specific training in argumentation analysis.

pragma-dialectical discussion procedure are to a large extent intersubjectively acceptable to ordinary arguers. They are congruent with norms these arguers already prove to have internalized (van Eemeren et al., 2009). One important proviso, however, is that this result was reached in experiments testing the subjects' judgments in "neutralized" circumstances that abstracted from non-fulfillment of "higher order" conditions that might influence their compliance with reasonableness in argumentative reality.

追求论辩话语的有效性
2.3 Aiming for effectiveness in argumentative discourse

In principle, language users performing speech acts do not do so with the sole intention of making the persons to whom they address themselves understand what speech act they are performing; by means of those speech acts they rather hope to elicit from their addressees a particular response (verbal or otherwise). They do not only wish their words to be understood, but they also want them to be *accepted* – and dealt with accordingly. To achieve this effect, the way they use their language must serve a communicative as well as an interactional purpose. Translated into the terminology of speech act theory, the communicative purpose is expressed in attempts to bring about the *illocutionary* ("communicative") effect of understanding and the interactional purpose in attempts to bring about the *perlocutionary* ("interactional") effect of accepting (van Eemeren & Grootendorst, 1984, pp. 23–29).

Some speech acts performed in ordinary discourse are specifically calculated to elicit a verbal or non-verbal response from listeners or readers in which they indicate acceptance in addition to understanding. This applies pre-eminently to the complex speech act of argumentation. Argumentation put forward in a discussion or debate is designed to achieve precisely defined verbally externalized illocutionary and perlocutionary effects immediately related to the complex speech act performed. In order to distinguish between the perlocutionary effect of *acceptance* and the broad range of further consequences argumentative and other speech acts may have in practice (varying from a furious look to starting a new life), Grootendorst and I introduced in *Speech Acts in Argumentative Discussions* a conceptual and terminological distinction between *inherent* perlocutionary effects and *consecutive* perlocutionary consequences (van Eemeren & Grootendorst, 1984, p. 24). Inherent perlocutionary effects consist of the acceptance of the speech act by the addressee and consecutive perlocutionary consequences comprise all other consequences of the speech act. To the extent that these effects and consequences are consciously aimed for in performing the speech act, inherent perlocutionary effects may also be termed *minimal* and the desired consecutive perlocutionary consequences *optimal*. If the communication and interaction go well, the illocutionary effect of understanding will be in principle a necessary condition for bringing about the inherent perlocutionary effect of acceptance and the consecutive perlocutionary consequences, but in neither case will it be a sufficient condition.

An illocutionary act – referred to as *communicative act* by pragma-dialecticians – is "happy" or "felicitous" if it achieves the effect that the listener or reader understands the communicative ("illocutionary") force and the propositional content of the utterance. A perlocutionary act – referred to as *interactional act* by pragma-dialecticians – is happy only if *another* (a further) desired effect on the addressee occurs. In order to make clear what this effect involves I have to make some distinctions.[31] First, I distinguish between effects of the speech act that are *intended* by the speaker or writer and consequences that are brought about accidentally. In agreement with a long-standing social science tradition, I reserve the term *act*, in contradistinction with "mere behavior," for conscious, purposive activities based on rational considerations for which the actor can be held accountable. As a result, bringing about completely unintended consequences cannot be regarded as acting, so in such cases there can be no question of the performance of perlocutionary *acts*.[32] Second, I draw a distinction between consequences of speech acts that are *not* brought about on the basis of an *understanding of an illocutionary act* on the part of the listener or reader and consequences where this *is* the case. I shall concern myself exclusively with *illocutionary perlocutions* realized on the basis of such an understanding. Third, I distinguish between consequences of speech acts whose occurrence may be regarded to be based on *rational considerations on the part of the addressee* and consequences that are divorced from reasonable decision-making, like being startled when someone shouts *boo*. In discussing perlocutionary acts, Searle and other speech act theorists do not make a distinction between "perlocutionary effects" the addressee can play an *active role* in bringing about, and effects where this is not the case. In their accounts, the addressee is always deemed to play a purely *passive role* and no account is taken of the *interactional aspect* of language use. In contradistinction, pragma-dialecticians concern themselves with interactional ("perlocutionary") acts whose success is, in principle, to some extent dependent on rational considerations on the part of the addressee. The alternatives I have just discussed are summarized in Figure 2.1.[33]

I am interested in a perlocution which is quintessential in connection with argumentation and conventionally associated with it: the perlocutionary act of convincing (van Eemeren & Grootendorst, 1984, pp. 63–68). By *convincing* I mean using argumentation to induce the addressee to accept a certain (positive or negative) standpoint on the basis of the argumentation that was advanced. Convincing is the "associated

---

31. Some more clarity must be created, because Austin uses the term *perlocutionary effect* to refer to a waste basket covering the most disparate and dissimilar consequences of language use (van Eemeren & Grootendorst, 1984, p. 26).

32. A rough-and-ready criterion for distinguishing between the performance of perlocutionary acts and the bringing about of unintended consequences is whether the speaker can reasonably be asked to *provide his/her reasons* for causing the consequence in question.

33. The "perlocution cube" presented in Figure 2.1 is a simplified version of the one introduced in van Eemeren and Grootendorst (1984, p. 29, Figure 2.3).

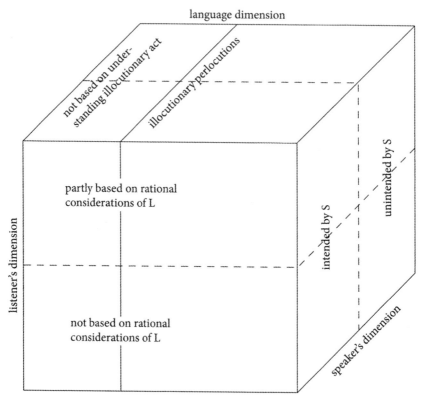

Figure 2.1. Perlocution cube of perlocutionary distinctions

perlocution" of arguing – an association Cohen (1973, p. 497) defines as a perlocution brought about by means of an illocution that "it belongs with." Grootendorst and I described such a perlocution as "something like the rationale" for performing the illocution; it is, as it were, in the nature of the illocution to bring about the perlocution (van Eemeren & Grootendorst, 1984, p. 53). In *Speech Acts in Argumentative Discussions* we explained that the relation between the illocution argumentation and the perlocution convincing can be characterized as "conventional" in Lewis' (1977) sense (van Eemeren & Grootendorst, 1984, ch. 3, esp. p. 63).

In a fully externalized argumentation process a discussion partner who takes his turn to perform the illocution of acceptance, following a successful performance by the other partner of the "illocutionary perlocution" argue/convince, *may be deemed to have the "conviction" presupposed in the standpoint* on the grounds of the *sincerity conditions* – more aptly called *responsibility conditions* – applying to this illocution (van Eemeren & Grootendorst, 1984, p. 21). By expressing a formula of acceptance the discussion partner performs an illocutionary act, viz. that of *accepting*, which in its turn entails certain interactional obligations regarding his further behavior (verbal or otherwise). In oral communication, acceptance of a standpoint may be expressed by non-verbal means (e.g. by nodding), but it may also be expressed verbally by performing the illocutionary act of accepting. The conventions that the performance of the illocutionary act of accepting is subject to are summarized in the identity (propositional content and essential) conditions and the correctness (preparatory and sincerity) conditions for carrying out this speech act. As I already implied when referring to the sincerity conditions, the propositional content condition is that the propositional content of the speech act of accepting must be the standpoint to which the argumentation pertains. The essential condition is, of course, that carrying out this speech act counts as an acceptance of the standpoint concerned.

作为理论分析工具的策略操控概念
2.4 The notion of strategic maneuvering as an analytic instrument

People engaged in argumentative discourse are characteristically oriented toward resolving a difference of opinion and may be regarded as committed to norms instrumental in achieving this purpose, maintaining certain critical standards of reasonableness and expecting others to comply with the same standards. At the same time, however, these people are also, and perhaps even primarily, interested in resolving the difference of opinion effectively in favor of their case, i.e. in agreement with their own standpoint or the position of those they represent. In examining actual cases of argumentative discourse, the conceptualization of argumentation as a communicative and interactional (speech) act complex aimed at resolving a difference of opinion for a reasonable judge by advancing a constellation of reasons the arguer can be held accountable for as justifying the acceptability of the standpoint(s) at issue therefore needs to be complemented by taking into account, besides the presumption of reasonableness involved in argumentation, also its quest for effectiveness. It should be noted that "effectiveness" is not completely synonymous with "persuasiveness," because aiming for effectiveness is not limited (as is the case with persuasiveness) to those parts of argumentative discourse (arguments) that can be reconstructed as belonging to the argumentation stage but applies also to the parts of the discourse that belong to the confrontation stage, the opening stage or the concluding stage, to which the term *persuasiveness* does not naturally pertain.[34]

---

34. One can speak of "persuasive arguments" in defense of prescriptive standpoints urging the addressee to do something or to refrain from doing something, but speaking of "persuasive arguments" in defense of descriptive standpoints is odd, just as speaking of "persuasive standpoints," "persuasive doubts," "persuasive starting points," "persuasive conclusions," etc. The term "convincingness" too applies only to parts of the discourse that can be reconstructed as arguments in the argumentation stage. Therefore, "reasonable plus effective equals convincing" cannot be used as a general characterization.

In all stages of argumentative discourse the aims of maintaining reasonableness and achieving effectiveness go together in every move that is made. It is the simultaneous pursuit of these two aims that characterizes the actual conduct of argumentative discourse. In order to do justice to the "argumentative predicament" of having to combine effectiveness with reasonableness, Peter Houtlosser and I introduced the concept of "strategic maneuvering" (van Eemeren & Houtlosser, 1997).[35] Strategic maneuvering refers to the continual efforts made in all moves that are carried out in argumentative discourse to keep the balance between reasonableness and effectiveness.[36] In principle, people engaged in argumentative discourse always have to reconcile their pursuit to maintain reasonableness and their pursuit to achieve effectiveness; because of this argumentative predicament they always have to maneuver strategically. Their strategic maneuvering does not manifest itself just in the complex speech act of argumentation, but also in all other speech acts performed in argumentative discourse that are pertinent to resolving a difference of opinion on the merits. Eventually the speech acts performed in argumentative discourse are all aimed at bringing about the perlocutionary effect of acceptance of the standpoint(s) at issue in a reasonable way that is in accordance with a procedure appropriate for resolving differences of opinion that is carried out correctly.[37]

Why have Houtlosser and I chosen the term *maneuvering* to refer to the efforts of dealing with the argumentative predicament? And why do we speak of *strategic* maneuvering? Maneuvering comes from the verb "maneuver," which has performing maneuvers as its first meaning. The noun "maneuver" can refer to a planned movement (in particular of armed forces) or a movement to win or do something. When boats are "maneuvering for position," they are *moving about to get to advantageous positions*. This moving about aimed at ending up in the best possible position in the situation at hand is exactly what we wanted our term *maneuvering* to mean – in this case, of course, referring to: moving toward the best position in view of the argumentative circumstances.

---

35. Krabbe (2002a, p. 35, note 13) thinks it necessary to distinguish between the goal of an activity and the aims of its participants once they are engaged in that activity: "Arguably, the primary goal of speeches, as a practice, is [...] to resolve disputes, whereas the aim of the rhetor is to persuade the audience." For certain purposes it may be useful to distinguish between these two objectives in this way when studying argumentative discourse in specific types of communicative activity, but for the purpose of illuminating the strategic maneuvering that takes place in every piece of argumentative discourse I find it more enlightening to assume that the arguer always has to combine pursuing at the same time the objectives of being reasonable and being effective.

36. It should be emphasized that the pursuit of effectiveness in reasonableness is not necessarily aimed at achieving effectiveness for the individuals who carry out the strategic maneuvering but may just as well be aimed at achieving effectiveness that is to the benefit of others whom they represent. As Jacobs (2002, p. 124) emphasizes, "at the level of institutional functioning" "arguments may fulfill public interests."

37. This view of strategic maneuvering is in the first place based on van Eemeren and Houtlosser (2002a).

The term *strategic* we have added to maneuvering because the goal aimed for in the maneuvering taking place at the operational level has to be reached by clever and skilful planning, doing optimal justice to both reasonableness and effectiveness.[38] In our terminology, *strategic maneuvering* in argumentative discourse refers to the efforts that are made in the discourse to move about between effectiveness and reasonableness in such a way that the balance – the equilibrium – between the two is maintained.[39]

In conducting argumentative discourse, strategic maneuvering is required at all times because the argumentative predicament of having to combine effectiveness with reasonableness leads to a potential tension between the simultaneous pursuit of the two goals that makes the balance that is to be kept in the maneuvering a delicate one. The conditions that need to be fulfilled in order to ensure effectiveness do not necessarily always agree with the conditions that have to be met to guarantee reasonableness. More often than not argumentative discourse that may be considered reasonable in a critical perspective will also be effective in an empirical perspective,[40] but there are also cases in which this is not so. The pursuit of effectiveness may in some cases get the better of the simultaneous pursuit of reasonableness. Then the combination of effectiveness and reasonableness is out of balance. Making use of a railway metaphor, it can be concluded that the strategic maneuvering *has derailed*. In case of a derailment of strategic maneuvering the pursuit of effectiveness has gained the upper hand at the expense of the pursuit of reasonableness, so that the process of resolving a difference of opinion on the merits gets distorted. It is because of the serious consequences for the resolution process that I consider imbalances of this type as more serious than a possible lack of effectiveness due to overemphasizing the need for reasonableness – if such a danger does indeed exist.

---

38. "Maneuvering" comes from the French "main" and "oeuvre," originally referring to manual work (medieval Latin *manu operari*). Later its meaning has changed into making a move to achieve the best possible position. "Strategic" is in all modern languages directly based on the Greek adjective *stratêgikos*, which is connected with the noun *stratêgos*, composed of the elements "strat-" = army and "-êgos" = leading. The main meaning of *stratêgos* is commander or general; *stratêgikos* means belonging to the prerogatives of the commander, which includes designing plans for the attack and defense. Only in later Greek (1st Century A.D.) did the noun *stratêgia* acquire the meaning of strategy. I am grateful to the classicist Albert Rijksbaron (University of Amsterdam) for explaining the etymological background of these words to me.

39. An alternative term to "strategic" might be "tactical," but the latter term highlights in the first place the local expediency of the maneuvering at the operational level and brings the terminology too close to the effectiveness pole while getting automatically too far removed from the reasonableness pole. I also think that in ordinary usage a "tactic" is in the first place a tool to reach a strategic goal, coming close to a ploy. In a more neutral fashion, I shall refer to tools used in maintaining the equilibrium between effectiveness and reasonableness as (argumentative) "techniques."

40. Within an empirical perspective "effectiveness" can be identified with the maximization of gain that represents one sense in which an actor is said to be "rational" (Goffman, 1970, p. 86).

Just as the pursuit of reasonableness in argumentative discourse can best be examined from a dialectical perspective, the pursuit of effectiveness can best be examined from a rhetorical perspective. Viewed from the perspective I have just sketched, there is always both a dialectical and a rhetorical dimension in argumentative discourse. The same argumentative discourse can be examined for its dialectical as well as for its rhetorical characteristics and this leads in each case to different kinds of observations. One could say that in argumentative discourse the need to balance a resolution-minded dialectical objective with the rhetorical objective of having one's positions accepted is what occasions strategic maneuvering by the parties in a difference of opinion. By means of their strategic maneuvering the parties attempt to reconcile the pursuit of their acceptance-oriented rhetorical aims with their resolution-minded dialectical obligations. In this endeavor, they attempt to exploit the opportunities which the argumentative situation provides to steer the discourse, within the dialectical boundaries, into the direction that serves their rhetorical interests best.[41]

Rhetorical insights can be used in combination with dialectical insights to get a clearer understanding of the strategic rationales behind the various moves that are made in the discourse. Because Houtlosser and I viewed strategic maneuvering taking place in argumentative discourse as a means for arguers to realize their rhetorical aims while complying at the same time with the requirements of resolving differences of opinion in a reasonable way, we put strategic maneuvering in our pragma-dialectical framework of analysis. In developing this conception of strategic maneuvering it is important to realize that the rhetorical pervasion of argumentative discourse in no way means that the parties involved in the discourse are only interested in having things their way. However hard they may be trying to have their points of view accepted, arguers also have to maintain the image of people who play the resolution game by the rules. This means that they may be held committed to what they have earlier said, assumed or implicated. If a move they have made proves to be fallacious, they can certainly not escape their dialectical responsibility by simply saying "Never mind, I was only being rhetorical." As a rule, the participants in argumentative discourse will be primarily interested – or will at least pretend to be primarily interested – in having the difference of opinion resolved on the merits.

Taking the pragma-dialectical perspective as point of departure, I think it can be shown that taking rhetorical considerations into account in the pragma-dialectical reconstruction of argumentative discourse will strengthen considerably not only the analysis and the evaluation of the discourse but also the way in which the analysis and the evaluation are justified. This approach implies that when in practice means other than conducting an argumentative discourse reconstructable as a critical discussion are used to gain acceptance for disputed standpoints – say appealing pathetically to the emotions of the audience – then from a pragma-dialectical perspective the means used

---

41. Cf. McHugh's (1968) discussion of the problems involved in defining the situation.

are no longer considered reasonable even if they may be rhetorically effective.[42] If effectiveness is aimed for by other means than argumentation, say by using flattery to influence the other party to accept standpoints that would otherwise not have been accepted, then, even though a rhetorician might still be appreciative, from a pragma-dialectical perspective one of the rules for critical discussion (the Relevance Rule) has been violated, and so the strategic maneuvering cannot be regarded as reasonable, but must be regarded as fallacious.

分歧消除过程中的阶段性策略操控
2.5 Strategic maneuvering in the various stages of the resolution process

An understanding of the role of strategic maneuvering in argumentative discourse can be gained by examining how the opportunities available to reach the objective of resolving of a difference of opinion in a dialectically reasonable way can be used by a certain party in the rhetorically most effective way. Each of the four stages in the resolution process is characterized by a specific dialectical aim and because the parties involved want to realize this aim rhetorically in the best possible way, they can be expected to make at every stage the dialectically allowed moves that serve their rhetorical interests with the greatest effectiveness. In this way, the dialectical objectives of the various discussion stages always have a rhetorical analogue and the presumed rhetorical objectives of the participants can be specified according to dialectical stage. It depends on the stage one is in what kind of results can be achieved by each of the parties. In all stages, both parties have to reconcile their own preferences for rhetorical effectiveness with the dialectical requirements of reasonableness inherent in the stage concerned.

In the confrontation stage, to begin with, the dialectical objective of the parties is to achieve clarity about the specific issues that are at stake in the difference of opinion and about the positions that each of the parties assumes in the difference of opinion. Viewed rhetorically, with a focus on the pursuit of effectiveness, each party will aim to direct the confrontation in the way that is the most beneficial from its own perspective. This means that each party will attempt to achieve a definition of the difference of opinion that favors the issues this party wants to discuss and the position this party likes to assume. For participants in the discourse who are going to act as protagonists this means that at every step they make in the confrontation stage they will try to get to an articulation of the standpoints that are to be discussed that agrees with the interests they represent. For participants who will be antagonists it means that at every step in the confrontation stage they will advance their critical doubts in the way they regard most appropriate.

---

42. It goes without saying that for other purposes, when a different perspective is chosen, reasonableness may be defined in other ways. This is not to say, however, that reasonableness is per se a relative concept.

The dialectical objective of the opening stage is to establish an unambiguous point of departure for the discussion. The point of departure consists of mutually accepted procedural starting points regarding the division of the burden of proof and other aspects of the conduct of the discussion and also material starting points regarding the premises of the discussion, which can be viewed as "concessions" that may be built upon in the discussion. The rhetorical counterpart for both parties is that they aim for effectiveness in the sense of arriving at the point of departure for the discussion that serves their interests best. Each party will try to establish the procedural starting points it considers most workable, including the most opportune division of the burden of proof, and the material starting points it regards as pertinent to having an effective exchange.

In the argumentation stage, the dialectical objective is to test the acceptability of the standpoints – descriptive, evaluative or prescriptive – that have shaped the difference of opinion, starting from the point of departure established in the opening stage. For participants who act as protagonists this means that they have to advance argumentation responding to the critical doubts expressed by (or ascribed to) the antagonists, until no further questions remain to be discussed. For participants who act as antagonists it means that they have to express their critical doubts about the standpoints and about each part of the argumentation that is advanced clearly and consistently. Viewed from the rhetorical perspective of effectiveness the protagonists try to make the strongest possible case by articulating in their argumentation those (combinations of) reasons that satisfy the antagonists and continue doing so until no critical doubts remain unanswered – using multiple, coordinative and subordinative argumentation depending on the antagonists' (anticipated) responses and exploiting the argument schemes they consider most effective in the situation at hand. The antagonists, for their part, will make a concentrated effort to launch the most effective attacks by expressing critical doubt wherever this seems appropriate from their perspective.

In the concluding stage, finally, the dialectical objective of the parties is to establish the result of the completion of the critical procedure and to determine whether the protagonist may maintain his standpoint in spite of the criticisms advanced by the antagonist or whether, alternatively, the antagonist may maintain his position of doubt in spite of the arguments advanced by the protagonist. Viewed rhetorically, each party will be out to claim that its own position has carried the day and its strategic maneuvering will be designed accordingly. This means that protagonists will do their best to make clear that the standpoint defended can be maintained whereas antagonists will try to establish that this standpoint cannot be maintained because the protagonist has not succeeded in removing all critical doubt. As in all other discussion stages, in these endeavors both parties have to make sure that the pursuit of their rhetorical aim of being effective can be reconciled with the dialectical requirements of reasonableness inherent in the concluding stage.

An overview of the rhetorical analogues of the dialectical aims of the various stages of the process of resolving a difference of opinion on the merits is given in Figure 2.2.

	Dialectical aims	Rhetorical aims
Confrontation stage	To achieve clarity concerning the specific issues at stake and the positions held by the parties in the difference of opinion	To establish the definition of the difference of opinion that is optimal for the party concerned
Opening stage	To achieve clarity concerning the point of departure for the discussion with regard to both the procedural and the material starting points	To establish the procedural and material starting points that are optimal for the party concerned
Argumentation stage	To achieve clarity concerning the protagonist's argumentation in defense of the standpoints at issue and the antagonist's doubts concerning these standpoints and the argumentation in their defense	To establish argumentation that constitute an optimal defense of the standpoints at issue (by the protagonist) or to establish critical doubts that constitutes an optimal attack on the standpoints and the argumentation (by the antagonist)
Concluding stage	To achieve clarity concerning the results of the critical procedure as to whether the protagonist may maintain his standpoints or the antagonist his doubts	To establish the results of the critical procedure in the way that is optimal for the party concerned as to maintaining standpoints or doubts

Figure 2.2. Overview of the dialectical and rhetorical aims of the various stages of resolving a difference of opinion on the merits

I have shown that the dialectical objectives characterizing the discussion stages that need to be passed through in order to resolve a difference of opinion on the merits always have their rhetorical analogues. This does not only go for all stages, but also for each separate move, made in a particular stage, that is instrumental in completing the stage concerned in a reasonable way. As a consequence, in argumentative discourse strategic maneuvering takes place in all the individual moves that are instrumental in achieving this purpose and in all discussion stages that have to be passed through in resolving a difference of opinion on the merits. This means that strategic maneuvering is not a theoretical concept at a level of abstraction far removed from actual argumentative discourse but a theoretical concept immediately connected with what is going on in argumentative practice.

协同性策略操控与讨论策略
2.6 Coordinated strategic maneuvering and discussion strategies

In determining the strategic function of particular modes of maneuvering my starting point is that each instance of strategic maneuvering belongs to a broader category, connected with one of the four different stages of a critical discussion. There is *confrontational* maneuvering that is to be reconstructed as part of the confrontation stage, *opening* maneuvering to be reconstructed as part of the opening stage, *argumentational* maneuvering to be reconstructed as part of the argumentation stage, and *concluding* maneuvering to be reconstructed as part of the concluding stage. Each of these four categories encompasses a variety of specific modes of strategic maneuvering whose make-up is instrumentally attuned to realizing the dialectical and rhetorical aims pertinent to the discussion stage the arguers are in.

If (and only if) the strategic maneuvers made in a particular discussion stage hang together in such a way that they can be regarded as being systematically coordinated, I say that a specific *discussion strategy* has been employed.[43] Apart from general discussion strategies applying to the argumentative discourse as a whole, there may be specific confrontational strategies, opening strategies, argumentational strategies, and concluding strategies. Among the confrontational strategies used in defining the difference of opinion there is, for instance, a strategy that Houtlosser and I dubbed "humptydumpty-ing" that pertains to making a self-serving choice from the issues comprising the "disagreement space" in determining what the difference of opinion is about (van Eemeren & Houtlosser, 1999a, p. 486). In employing this particular strategy a systematic effort is made to deviate from any preconceived idea of what the difference of opinion is about by determining the issues completely in one's own way (thus imposing, as Humpty Dumpty did with the meaning of words, one's own definition of the difference of opinion on the discussion). Examples of opening strategies are "broadening the zone of agreement" (e.g. by establishing a great number of starting points acceptable to all concerned), which allows for exploiting in the discussion a large array of starting points, and "creating a smokescreen," which amounts to distracting the attention away from one's "actual" starting points by strongly emphasizing starting points that are in fact irrelevant so that the other party is left in the dark about what one's point of departure effectively amounts to. An example of a well-known argumentational strategy consists in trying to convince the other party by resorting exclusively and completely to "instantaneous" pragmatic argumentation. In following this argumentational strategy the arguer limits himself deliberately to spelling out the immediate desirable – or, as the case may be, undesirable – consequences that accepting the standpoint at issue will have for the other

---

43. The general kind of strategies I have in mind resemble the strategies distinguished in political discourse by Martel (1983) and Schütz (1992, 1993), who also distinguish some techniques ("tactics") used in realizing these strategies. Even the "institutionally codified practice" of "strategic deception" in missile defense advocacy described by Mitchell (2000) provides examples, albeit that the term *strategy* is in these cases interpreted more loosely. Perelman and Olbrechts-Tyteca's (1958/1969) concepts of association and dissociation are sometimes referred to as argumentative strategies, but in my view they are general categories of *argumentation techniques* that can in the argumentation stage be applied in all kinds of strategic maneuvers and strategies. Anyway, these techniques may be applied locally in one or two particular moves and do not agree with my coordination requirement.

party, if not for all concerned. This strategy may work particularly well in the case of practical standpoints. A notorious concluding strategy is "making the audience bite the bullet," which means getting it through to the audience that the outcome is as it is, however undesirable it may be, and that they have to accept this outcome as unavoidable.

Discussion strategies as I envision them are combinations of moves – coordinated modes of strategic maneuvering – that are methodically designed to influence the result of a particular stage of the resolution process, or the discussion as a whole, in a way that is at the same time reasonable and effective. Such discussion strategies manifest themselves in a systematic, coordinated and simultaneous use of the available dialectical and rhetorical opportunities. Only if the strategic maneuvers carried out in a certain stage of the resolution process, or in the argumentative discourse as a whole, converge both "vertically" – by coordination of all aspects (see Chapter 4) of the strategic maneuvering realized in individual argumentative moves – and "horizontally" – by coordination of the successive argumentative moves – can it be said that a full-blown discussion strategy has been employed. Vertical convergence means that all aspects of a strategic maneuver made by the speaker or writer reinforce each other; horizontal convergence means that the separate maneuvers made in a certain stage, or in the discussion as a whole, reinforce each other when taken together. The various aspects of strategic maneuvering that are supposed to be part of the vertical convergence will be discussed in Chapter 4. Horizontal convergence can be described in the same terms that are used to describe the various argumentation structures, albeit that now the terminology pertains equally to the strategic maneuvering in all stages, instead of just to strategic maneuvering in the argumentation stage. In every stage, "multiple strategic maneuvers" that are part of the same argumentative strategy are independent of each other but serve the same strategic purpose, "coordinative strategic maneuvers" are interdependent components of a strategy, and "subordinative strategic maneuvers" are dependent on each other in the sense that the one maneuver supports the other.

In practice, multiple, coordinative and subordinative strategic maneuvers can be combined. The horizontal convergence of strategic maneuvering may exceed one particular discussion stage and stretch over various (if not all) stages, keeping the strategic moves that are made in line with each other. If this is the case, the strategic maneuvers are systematically coordinated at the level of the discussion as a whole. The strategy concerned is then no longer a discussion strategy belonging to one of the four categories of strategies but becomes in a more general sense a "discussion strategy."

在分析中阐释策略操控
2.7 Accounting for strategic maneuvering in the analysis

Let us now return to the analysis I presented in Chapter 1.6 of the Reynolds advertorial against smoking by young people. I had come to the point that the argumentation put forward by Reynolds in favor of its standpoint that (1) young people should not smoke is coordinative and consists of two parts: (1.1a) smoking has always been an adult custom and (1.1b) even for adults smoking has become controversial. What can observing Reynolds' strategic maneuvering in favor of their standpoint add to this analysis?

In Chapter 1 I already observed that it is clear from the start that the arguments advanced by Reynolds will not appeal to young people and that it is more likely that the conventional presupposition that smoking is the privilege of adults will for young people be a reason to go against that restriction, while smoking having become controversial will make it only more interesting to them. I also observed that Reynolds' reason for not mentioning the readily available and much stronger arguments that smoking easily becomes an addiction and causes cancer is that committing itself to them would leave the company with an inconsistency, because the health argument would strongly undermine the credibility of Reynolds' not-discussed standpoint that adults should be allowed to smoke.

Strategically, the arguments advanced for the standpoint that young people should not smoke seem selected for their *incapacity* to contribute to the defense of this official standpoint. By advancing arguments that so evidently do *not* support the disputed standpoint, Reynolds evokes the *topos* "If only bad reasons are advanced for not doing something, then there are no good reasons for not doing it," because one may expect an arguer to advance the strongest available arguments supporting his case. The reasoning induced in the young readers toward the conclusion desired by Reynolds can be reconstructed in the following way (unexpressed steps are put in parentheses[44]):

(1)   (There are no good reasons for young people not to smoke)
   ((1).1)   (There are only bad reasons advanced for young people not to smoke)
   ((1).1')   (If there are only bad reasons advanced for not doing something, then there are no good reasons for not doing it)
      (((1).1).1a)   (*Smoking has always been an adult custom* is a bad reason)
      (((1).1).1b)   (*Even for adults smoking has become controversial* is a bad reason)
      (((1).1).1a-b)   (These are the only reasons advanced for young people not to smoke)

It is evident that Reynolds tries to convey standpoint (1) – there are no good reasons for young people not to smoke – through implication, without committing the company to this standpoint. It can be left to the young readers to draw the desired conclusion themselves.

Having thus "argued" why young people should not smoke, viewed analytically, Reynolds returns to the opening stage of the discussion to acknowledge a concession: "We know that giving this kind of advice to young people can sometimes backfire." On the face of it, this acknowledgement is followed by a move aimed at preventing the dreaded effect from occurring: "But if you take up smoking just to prove you're an adult, you're really proving just the opposite." On closer inspection, however, a different effect must be aimed

---

44. An apostrophe indicates that the (often unexpressed) premise concerned serves as a connection ("major premise") between the other premise(s) and the standpoint defended by the premise(s).

for, because it is obvious that this warning will not be effective. Although Reynolds may suggest that young people who take up smoking only do so to prove that they are adults, strictly speaking, they say that those who take up smoking *just to prove that they are adults* prove exactly the opposite. In other words, there is no problem when you take up smoking *for some other reason*. In that case, you *do not* prove that you are not an adult. The addition of "just" even allows for taking up smoking to prove that you are an adult as long as you *also have other reasons* for smoking. In sum, you are almost always in the right.

In the concluding stage of this advertorial it would be normal – and pertinent in light of a critical discussion – to repeat the advice not to smoke ("So, once more, we emphatically urge you not to smoke"). Instead, Reynolds advises the young readers to "reconsider" the matter, while deliberately avoiding stating the conclusion that should be obvious. The advertorial ends in fact with a contradictory statement. Although the young readers are advised to think about it first, the phrasing "you may not be old enough to smoke, but you're old enough to think" suggests that it is already clear to them that they should not smoke. What is there left to think about if they have already accepted that they are too young to smoke?

I concentrated in this analysis on one striking aspect of Reynolds' strategic maneuvering: the choice of arguments. The analysis can be strengthened by taking other aspects into account. Take, for instance, the choice of the word "controversial" when Reynolds states that smoking is controversial even for adults. *Controversial* suggests that the matter is, in fact, *undecided* and that there is something to be said *both* for the positive and for the negative view of smoking. This means that smoking might well be acceptable in the end. In this and other ways, R.J. Reynolds Tobacco Company's text is pervaded with sly efforts to get young people to reject rather than accept Reynolds' case. I have made plausible that the strategy Reynolds followed in this advertorial is, in fact, aimed at rendering its official argumentation *counter-productive*, and a more elaborate analysis of the company's strategic maneuvering to this effect would add even more support to that analysis. Their strategic maneuvering is in fact aimed at achieving different dialectical and rhetorical aims than Reynolds' official standpoint calls for.

The analysis of the Reynolds Tobacco advertorial shows that at every stage of the implicit discussion with their readers Reynolds maneuvers strategically. On the one hand, they make an effort to comply publicly with their formal commitment to keep young people from smoking. On the other hand, they try to serve their business mission of protecting the commercial interests of the firm. Although Reynolds Tobacco does its utmost to maintain throughout its advertorial the image that their position is consistent, the analysis shows that indirectly the company's efforts are in the first place directed toward undermining its official standpoint that young people should not smoke.

My extended analysis of the Reynolds advertorial makes clear that a pragma-dialectical reconstruction and its justification become stronger and more pertinent when rhetorical insight is incorporated regarding the arguer's aiming for effectiveness. Of course, a final evaluation of this argumentative discourse is possible only after the analysis has been carried out completely. All the same, the analysis I have provided already enables us to observe that Reynolds, because the company advances arguments that are – as any independent observer will confirm – from the outset unlikely to convince, violates the Relevance Rule for critical discussion that standpoints may not be defended by non-argumentation or argumentation that is not relevant to the standpoint (van Eemeren & Grootendorst, 2004, p. 194). This makes Reynolds Tobacco company guilty of committing a relevance fallacy when defending their official standpoint that young people should not smoke – in this case a variant of *ignoratio elenchi* (van Eemeren & Grootendorst, 1992a, p. 205).

Thus, the extended method of analysis opens up new possibilities for a critical evaluation of argumentative discourse. In such a critical evaluation some specimens of the strategic maneuvering that takes place in the discourse may stand up as acceptable while other cases of strategic maneuvering involve a violation of one or more of the pragma-dialectical rules for critical discussion. The Reynolds example makes it clear that making smart argumentative moves toward effectiveness does not lead to acceptable strategic maneuvering if the moves that are made are not at the same time in agreement with the prevailing standards of reasonableness.

CHAPTER 3 第三章

论辩话语的论辩学与修辞学视角
Dialectical and rhetorical perspectives on argumentative discourse

论辩学与修辞学的不同原理论辩
3.1 Diverging meta-theoretical outlooks on dialectic and rhetoric

After having introduced the notion of strategic maneuvering between reasonableness and effectiveness in Chapter 2, I have connected reasonableness with a dialectical perspective on argumentative discourse and effectiveness with a rhetorical perspective.[1] To answer the question of how these perspectives can be put to good use in studying strategic maneuvering, it must first be clear what they involve. The dialectical perspective, and the meaning of dialectical reasonableness, has already been explained in expounding the pragma-dialectical approach to argumentative discourse in Chapter 1 – at least, for one particular outlook on dialectic. The rhetorical perspective, however, still needs to be elucidated, together with other outlooks on the dialectical perspective, so that it becomes clear what rhetorical effectiveness means and how the studies of dialectical reasonableness and rhetorical effectiveness can be fruitfully combined.

As may be expected of a handbook, in *Fundamentals of Argumentation Theory* (van Eemeren *et al.*, 1996) a standard account is given of both the classical dialectical and the classical rhetorical perspectives on argumentative discourse (cf. Tindale, 2004, p. 38). According to the standard version, dialectic is prototypically concerned with regulated critical exchanges between parties involved in a difference of opinion, and rhetoric is generally concerned with influencing people by means of communication – in the case of argumentative discourse, by argumentative means. As Foss and Griffin confirm in their proposal for a rhetoric that goes beyond persuasion, "as far back as the discipline of rhetoric has been explored, rhetoric has been defined as persuasion" (1995, p. 2).[2] When looking more precisely at the way in which rhetoric is viewed by

---

1. I agree with Foss, Foss and Trapp that speaking of "perspectives" is in this case to be preferred to speaking of "theories" because a perspective "can suggest both an organized and coherent body of knowledge and one that is less organized" (1985, p. 13). Because a perspective concerns a particular way of interpreting a phenomenon, a perspective becomes, as they say, "a set of conceptual lenses."

2. Cherwitz (1990, p. 1) observes that, although the various definitions of rhetoric he considers "are suggestive of the varied purposes, functions, processes, ends, and effects of communication, they all underscore the centrality of 'persuasion' to rhetoric." According to Bitzer, "rhetoric as a discipline is justified philosophically insofar as it provides principles, concepts, and procedures by which we effect valuable changes in reality. Thus rhetoric is distinguished from the

specific scholars of rhetoric, however, the complexities of the rhetorical perspective come into view. Because in contemporary education as a rule a standardized version of classical rhetorical theory is taught and explained, the diversity among rhetoricians regarding the definition of rhetoric remains most often hidden from view.

Reflecting upon the relationship between rhetoric and dialectic, Leff observes that "the historical record is one of almost constant change as the identity, function, structure, and mutual relationship [of the arts of dialectic and rhetoric, FHvE] become issues of argumentative contestation" (2002, p. 53). In *Contemporary Perspectives on Rhetoric*, Foss, Foss and Trapp sketch the diversity as follows: "One person might see rhetoric as telling a story, another as creating a particular reality, and a third as using persuasion and argumentation" (1985, p.13). In their "Introduction: Rhetorics and Roadmaps," which opens Part I of the recently published *The Sage Handbook of Rhetorical Studies*, Lunsford, Wilson, and Eberly (2009, p. xix) illustrate the variety of views on rhetoric in this way: "Rhetoric has been viewed as the 'counterpart' of dialectic (Aristotle), as the art of speaking well (Quintilian), as the purview of elocution and pronunciation alone (Ramus), as the study of misunderstandings (Richards), as the 'symbolic' means of inducing cooperation in beings that by nature respond to 'symbols' (Burke, 1945/1969a, p. 43), and as 'hot air' or deceptive practices (Plato, Chaucer, Locke, and a host of others)." "As a plastic art that molds itself to varying times, places, and situations," they conclude, "rhetoric is notoriously hard to pin down, and arguments about how to define rhetoric and what its scope should be characterize the long history of Western rhetoric" (2009, p. xix).

Swearingen and Schiappa state in the same *Handbook*, "We can no longer assume or impose any uniform definition of rhetoric. As a result, its very nature is being reconceived in ways that are troubling to some and exciting to others" (2009, p. 10). It can be observed that in the United States the study of rhetoric has survived more robustly during the 19th and 20th centuries than in Europe, both in the academic curriculum and in contributions to new rhetorical theories and methods. In the 20th century the American theories of rhetoric grew in scope "to the point that everything, or virtually everything, can be described as 'rhetorical'" (Swearingen & Schiappa, 2009, p. 2).[3] "Such accounts," Swearingen and Schiappa add, "can be called theories of 'Big Rhetoric' and are credited with popularizing or at least rationalizing what Simons (1990) calls

---

mere craft of persuasion which, although it is a legitimate object of scientific investigation, lacks philosophical warrant as a practical discipline" (1968, p. 14). Rhetoric is "always persuasive," however, in the sense that "the rhetor alters reality by bringing into existence a discourse of such a character that the audience, in thought and action, is so engaged that it becomes mediator of change" (p. 4).

3. Rhetoric in the European tradition is discussed by Conley (1990). See also Conley (2005), who also pays attention to the language-immanent topics of Anscombre and Ducrot.

the 'rhetorical turn' in a variety of disciplines" (p. 2).[4] "Whereas the Greco-Roman origins of the term *rhetoric* previously limited what scholars analyzed *as* rhetoric, Big Rhetoric made it possible for scholars to describe a far broader range of phenomena as rhetorical, as long as important and interesting insights could be gained through such descriptions" (Swearingen & Schiappa, 2009, p. 2). The 1960s are often viewed as a turning point: "broad definitions of rhetoric and the popularization of rhetorical studies is partly due to scholarly attention begun in the rhetorical practices of the 1960s, partly due to specific positions advanced by influential theorists and partly due to the understandable desires of members of a discipline to see what they are doing as important" (Swearingen & Schiappa, 2009, p. 3).

In spite of the fact that both "dialectic" and "rhetoric" are words that are also used on the "object level" of argumentative conduct ("a rhetorical argument"), I prefer to use these terms on the "meta-level" where they refer to theoretical perspectives on argumentation and the various kinds of theoretical outlooks on argumentative discourse that can be distinguished within each perspective. I agree with Tindale (2004, p. 4) that logic, dialectic, and rhetoric are "three distinct ways of conceiving argument," albeit that in the pragma-dialectical approach the logical perspective is incorporated in the dialectical perspective, as is usually the case in dialectical approaches.[5] The problem I am now confronted with is that within the dialectical and the rhetorical perspectives several views can be distinguished in the scholarly literature concerning what the choice of a dialectical or a rhetorical perspective on argumentative discourse involves. Since no dialectician or rhetorician has taken out a patent for the use of the terms *dialectic* and *rhetoric*, a free choice can be made and must be made in view of the incongruities between the various definitions that have been given or can be given.

Two general approaches by argumentation theorists to what a "dialectical" or a "rhetorical" perspective involves can be distinguished. First there is an approach that has primarily an empirical-historical basis. Those who follow this line of approach make the definition of dialectic and rhetoric – in a descriptive fashion – dependent on what a certain historical source claims dialectic or rhetoric to be. When it comes to rhetoric, the historical source taken as authoritative may, for instance, be Aristotle, Cicero or Quintilian – a recent tendency is to go back all the way to the Sophists and make them into the legitimizing force. When a certain authoritative source is selected the empirical-historical approach may sometimes acquire essentialist traits. In that case the definition of dialectic and rhetoric is not only made dependent on what the

---

4. In his introduction to *The Rhetorical Turn* Simons states that "most neutrally, perhaps, rhetoric is the study and practice of persuasion. But this broad conception permits varying emphases or narrowings: thus, rhetoric as invention, as argumentation, as figuration, as stylistics, as audience and situational adaptation, and as an art of composition or arrangement" (1990, p. 5).

5. By adding a "dialectical tier" to his informal logical approach to argumentation, Johnson (2000) makes clear that one can also view the dialectical perspective and the logical perspective as distinct perspectives. See also Section 3.3.

historical source has understood dialectic and rhetoric to be but this view is also declared unquestionable ("This is what rhetoric *is*"). A "technical" problem associated with the empirical-historical approach is that the conceptions of dialectic and rhetoric developed in antiquity are, in the way they are passed down through the ages, not always fully clear to the modern mind, so that a philological clarification or even an adaptation to modern argumentative reality is required. In any case, it is hard to make out on purely empirical-historical grounds which choice of paradigmatic dialectical or rhetorical approach among the various potential choices is the best one. This does not prevent some scholars from making explicit choices and promoting these choices emphatically, although in a great many other cases the choice remains implicit and its rationale is at best explained cautiously.[6]

Second there is an approach that is in the first place motivated by systematic theoretical considerations. Those who follow this line of approach make the definition of dialectic and rhetoric – in a stipulating fashion – primarily dependent on what conception fits best with the characteristics of the theoretical framework they are starting from and the nature of the problems their research aims to resolve. When it comes to defining dialectic and rhetoric, they will not necessarily follow any historical source they consider most authoritative, but try to develop, for instance, the view of rhetoric that is most helpful to their research and to make use of those rhetorical insights available in the rhetorical tradition that serve their theoretical purposes in a systematic way. Which dialectical and rhetorical insights will make sense to them depends, of course, also on the philosophical angle they have chosen in studying argumentative discourse – anthropological, geometrical or critical.[7]

The theory-based approach to dialectic and rhetoric favored by argumentation theorists such as myself is guided by theoretical considerations concerning what conception of dialectic and rhetoric is most helpful for realizing the analytic and evaluative objectives of their research program. Rather than being a philologist, I am an argumentation theorist who tries to make good use of (historically documented and philologically certified) insights stemming from the dialectical and rhetorical tradition to enrich the theoretical framework of pragma-dialectics.[8] Currently my

---

6. The latter is, for instance, the case in Battistelli (2009). By declaring that the conception of rhetoric that argumentation scholars such as Jacobs, Rescher, and Slob adhere to has as a drawback that it "is not consonant with the full range of rhetorical theory available," he implicitly shows himself to be a representative of the empirical-historical approach to rhetoric, as his reference to some authoritative historical sources confirms.

7. In choosing these names for referring to the various philosophies of reasonableness I stick to the terminology discussed in Toulmin (1976), see Chapter 2.2, but other views are possible.

8. As I have explained in Chapter 1, the pragma-dialectical theory of argumentation starts from a critical rationalist conception of reasonableness. In developing this theory Grootendorst and I paid tribute (like other critical rationalists did before us) to the sources of inspiration for pursuing the critical rationalist cause in argumentation theory found in classical dialectic as described by Aristotle and portrayed earlier in Plato's Socratic dialogues. Now that I am

Chapter 3. Dialectical and rhetorical perspectives on argumentative discourse

theoretical interest concentrates on the combination of aiming for reasonableness and effectiveness that characterizes strategic maneuvering in argumentative discourse described in Chapter 2. This means that I am out for insights from the classical and modern dialectical and rhetorical traditions that can be helpful for a systematic implementation of this combination.

合理论辩话语的古典论辩术路径
3.2 Reasonable argumentative discourse in classical dialectical approaches

In antiquity the term *dialectic* was used in different ways, referring to various kinds of theoretical models for dealing critically with argumentation and reasoning. Because Wagemans (2009) prepared the ground for me in his doctoral dissertation (in Dutch) by scrutinizing the classical dialectical approaches for distinctive features vital for making a systematic comparison with the pragma-dialectical theorizing, my brief discussion of these approaches relies in the first place on his exposé. In describing the various approaches, Wagemans concentrates in each case on the aims that are ascribed to the dialectical procedure, the structure of the dialectical procedure that is envisaged, and the norms that are regarded as applicable in implementing the dialectical procedure.

The aim of Zeno's model of "dialectical reasoning," the first dialectical approach developed in antiquity, is to refute a standpoint and to defend by way of this refutation the opposite standpoint. Zeno's dialectical reasoning takes the form of a monologue, although in certain specific cases it can be reconstructed as a dialogue between Zeno and another party, whose only contribution consists of volunteering the opposite standpoint. Zeno implicitly uses logical rules, but he does not refer explicitly to any norms for sound argumentation.

Plato viewed dialectic as a means of finding the truth.[9] In his dialogues three forms of dialectic manifest themselves. First, there is the "Socratic *elenchus*" aiming at testing the tenability of someone's standpoint in view of his other opinions. An *elenchus* that is part of a coherent series of *elenchi* aims also at increasing the plausibility of a standpoint by refuting an alternative standpoint regarding the same topic. Second, there is the "method of hypothesizing," which Wagemans reconstructed as consisting of three interdependent components having as their common aim to increase – in three different ways – the certainty of claims to knowledge. In the "critical" component the hypothesis is subjected to a critical test, in the "deductive" component it is derived from "higher" principles or hypotheses, and in the "concluding" component a conclusion is

---

concentrating on rhetorical effectiveness, I intend to do justice in a similar way to the classical and modern views closest to my current project.

9. In their rhetorics Plato and Aristotle require the speaker to convince the audience of standpoints that are true or good. As Wagemans (2009, Chapter 8.2) observes, in pragma-dialectics such "quasi-epistemic norms of reasonableness" regarding standpoints do not play a role.

derived from the hypothesis. Third, there is the "method of collection and division," which aims at defining a certain concept by first bringing it together with a number of kindred concepts under the umbrella of a generic concept ("collection") and next dividing the generic concept into *species* and *subspecies*.

The Socratic *elenchus* is structured as a dialogue between a questioner and an answerer. The answerer does not defend the standpoint by means of arguments but by preventing the questioner from deriving the opposite proposition (standpoint) from his concessions. The structure of the critical component of the method of hypothesizing is virtually the same, albeit that now both the questioner and the answerer are committed to testing the standpoint. In the deductive component the hypothesis is not critically tested but efforts are made to derive it from higher principles or hypotheses which can be viewed as arguments advanced in defense of the hypothesis. The only difference between the structure of the concluding and that of the deductive component is that in the former the hypothesis is not a standpoint but a starting point. The method of collection and division uses the structure of a dialogue in which each step in the reasoning of the questioner is confirmed by the answerer.

The various kinds of philosophical discussions in Plato's dialogues are governed by explicit as well as implicit norms. In the reconstruction provided by Wagemans the norms pertaining to the suitability of the discussants or the nature of the topic that is discussed are dubbed *conditions*, the norms pertaining to the soundness of the contributions to the discussion *rules*, and the norms pertaining to the attacking and defending by the parties in their various discussion roles *strategies*.[10]

Aristotle developed in the *Topics* a dialectical model of regulated dialogues for refuting a claim, starting from concessions of the other party.[11] In both the *Topics* (Aristotle, 1960, Trans.) and *Sophistical Refutations* (Aristotle, 1928c, Trans.)[12] the aim of the dialectical discussion is to find out whether a standpoint is acceptable in the light of generally accepted views or views accepted by the answerer. The answerer defends the standpoint and the questioner is out to refute it.[13] The structure of an Aristotelian dialectical discussion resembles closely the structure of the Socratic *elenchus*. Contributions to the discussion are made by two parties, the questioner and the answerer. The answerer does not defend his standpoint by means of arguments but by

---

10. An example of a strategy is that the questioner attempts, by asking his questions in an order that does not seem "logical," to hide as long as he can which concessions he is going to use to refute the answerer's standpoint.

11. Dialectic reasoning is defined as reasoning from premises (ἐνδόξα) (*Top.* I 1, 100a 29-30) that "commend themselves to all or to the majority, or to the wise – that is, to all of the wise or to the majority or to the most famous and distinguished of them" (*Top.* I 1, 100b 21-23).

12. In explaining Aristotle's views I also draw on his *Prior Analytics* and *Posterior Analytics* (Aristotle, 1928a, 1928b).

13. According to Leff (2002, p. 54), "Dialectic need consider only the *logos* of argument and can bracket matters of character (*ethos*) or emotion (*pathos*)."

choosing his concessions in such a way (staying within certain limits of reasonableness) that the questioner does not succeed in refuting the standpoint on the basis of these concessions or, if he succeeds, that this will not appear as a fault of the answerer. The Aristotelian dialectical discussion too is governed by "conditions" pertaining to the suitability of the participants and the nature of the standpoint at issue, "rules" pertaining to the soundness of the contributions to the discussion, and "strategies" pertaining to the way in which the questioner and the answerer fulfill their tasks. Unlike Plato, Aristotle discusses the norms explicitly (see Wagemans, 2009, pp. 146–152).

In explaining the dialectical character of the pragma-dialectical approach to argumentation, Grootendorst and I referred to Aristotle's conception of dialectic as the *technē* (τέχνη) of regulated debate (van Eemeren & Grootendorst, 2004, p. 42). Wagemans concludes from this reference, combined with the observation that the pragma-dialectical point of departure regarding the norms for argumentative discourse agrees well with the dialectical view in antiquity, that the pragma-dialectical view on norms is "inspired" by Aristotle's and – at least as far as the "rules" regarding the validity and reasonableness of argumentation are concerned – "implicitly related" with the views on norms held by Zeno and Plato (2009, p. 190).

There is indeed a connection between pragma-dialectics and Plato's dialogues in the sense that the aim of an argumentative discussion is in both cases viewed as determining the acceptability of a standpoint by subjecting the standpoint to a critical test (Socratic *elenchus*, critical component of the method of hypothesizing). Among the characteristics pragma-dialectics shares with Aristotle's dialectic are not only that argumentation is viewed as aimed at determining the acceptability of a standpoint, but also that the argumentative discussion consists of a systematic exchange between two parties and is governed by rules incorporating norms for validity and reasonableness (Wagemans, 2009, pp. 185–187).

A dialectical rule applying to the Socratic *elenchus* and the Aristotelian dialectical discussion that has a remarkable resemblance to the pragma-dialectical Language Use Rule is that in an *elenchus* and the Aristotelian dialectical discussion the answerer is allowed to ask for clarification when the questioner uses an ambiguous term. This rule prevents the questioner at a later stage of the discussion from taking advantage of this ambiguity by giving a term a different meaning than the meaning the answer's response was based on, thus refuting the standpoint in an unreasonable way – a discussion technique allegedly practiced by the Sophists. The Validity Rule and the Argument Scheme Rule also are similar to explicit and implicit dialectical rules from antiquity. Their antique counterparts regulate in the same way how acceptability may be transferred from the reasons that are put forward in defense of a standpoint to the standpoint itself. The pragma-dialectical Freedom Rule, on the other hand, goes against the antique dialectical norms reconstructed by Wagemans as "conditions." Whereas the Freedom Rule gives the discussants the right to advance or put into doubt any standpoint they like, those conditions contain all kinds of restrictions regarding the suitability of the discussants and the topics of discussion. Another difference is that the pragma-dialectical rules regarding defending and attacking standpoints do not correspond in all cases to the antique dialectical rules because the notions of "defense" and "attack" are defined differently. According to the pragma-dialectical Obligation-to-Defend Rule, someone who advances a standpoint is obliged to defend that standpoint by means of argumentation if challenged to do so, whereas the rules of the Socratic *elenchus* and the Aristotelian dialectical discussion require a different kind of defense of the standpoint (see below). In addition, the nature of the pragma-dialectical norms is different from the antique dialectical norms Wagemans reconstructs as strategies. The pragma-dialectical norms are to be viewed as rules on the basis of which the reasonableness of argumentation is to be judged whereas the antique strategies are, according to Wagemans, recommendations pertaining to the persuasive power of argumentation. Wagemans concludes that the antique backgrounds of the dialectical views of the extended pragma-dialectical theory is to be found in antique dialectic, and that of the rhetorical views is to be found in antique rhetoric (2009, p. 192).[14]

When the pragma-dialectical views concerning aim, structure and norms of the dialectical procedure are considered in their interrelationship, Wagemans feels impelled to add a qualification concerning the relation between the pragma-dialectical views about the rhetorical aim and the antique dialectical views about norms for argumentative discourse. The antique norms pertain not only to the reasonableness of argumentation ("rules"), but also to its persuasive power ("strategies"). Although, according to Wagemans (2009, pp. 192–193), strictly speaking, the antique views about strategies do not belong to the intellectual background of the pragma-dialectical view about norms for argumentative discourse, a conceptual analysis of the notion of strategic maneuvering and a reconstruction of the antique dialectical strategies show an important commonality. The point of departure in the pragma-dialectical view of strategic maneuvering is that the conduct of the discussants results from their efforts to resolve a difference of opinion both in a reasonable way and to the benefit of their own position. In antique dialectic the point of departure is that a dialectical discussion can be distinguished from an "eristic" discussion because the participants in the dialectical discussion do not aim at winning the discussion at the expense of the reasonableness of their contributions to the discussion. According to Wagemans, the antique dialectical strategies form, therefore, part of the background for the rhetorical views of extended pragma-dialectics.

As mentioned above, there are also some striking structural differences between pragma-dialectics and the antique approaches to dialectic. In a critical discussion the standpoint is defended by advancing argumentation, but in Zeno's dialectical reasoning the defense consists in refuting the opposite standpoint and in the Socratic *elenchus* and the Aristotelian dialectical discussion it consists in the answerer's effort to prevent

---

14. This view is not generally shared. According to Rubinelli (personal communication), the antique strategies are to be viewed as recommendations pertaining to the reasonableness of argumentation rather than its persuasive power.

Chapter 3. Dialectical and rhetorical perspectives on argumentative discourse

the questioner from acquiring the concessions that would enable him to refute the standpoint. Another difference is that in a critical discussion the standpoint is attacked by criticizing the argumentation advanced by the protagonist in defense of his standpoint whereas in Zeno's dialectical reasoning the standpoint is attacked by showing that it leads to contradictory consequences, and in the Socratic discussion and the Aristotelian dialectical discussion the standpoint is attacked by making an effort to refute the standpoint on the basis of the other party's concessions. In the critical component of the method of hypothesizing, the standpoint is not attacked, but it is examined whether the collection of standpoints for which the hypothesis serves as a common argument is consistent or not. In the deductive and the concluding component, the arguments advanced by the one party are not criticized by the other party but only "doubted" if this party does not understand (the reasons to accept) them. Another difference is that a critical discussion consists of a systematic exchange of arguments for and criticisms of a standpoint, whereas in none of the antique dialectics are arguments for and criticisms of a standpoint present simultaneously. In dialectic in which the defense of a standpoint takes place by means of argumentation for that standpoint the arguments that are advanced are not criticized by the other party and in dialectic in which the standpoint is attacked the other party does not advance any arguments for that standpoint.[15]

合理论辩话语的现代论辩学路径
3.3 Reasonable argumentative discourse in modern dialectical approaches

Modern argumentation theorists choosing a dialectical approach use the word "dialectic" in somewhat different ways, which are as a rule only in a very general sense related to classical dialectical approaches. As Krabbe (2002b) notes, whether they are formal dialecticians or pragma-dialecticians, what they have in common is not only that they are interested in dialogue as a context of argumentation, but that the position they assign to dialogue is more special. They look upon all argumentation "as occurring in an explicit or implicit discussion or dialogue with at least two parties" (2002b, p. 153). The distinctive element in this view is "the part about implicit discussions that are presumed to underlie ostensibly nondialogical argumentative texts or speeches with only one author or *rhetor* expressing his or her views." Consequently, Krabbe observes, "interest in dialogue structure is not restricted to explicit cases of dialectical exchange, but encompasses the implicit cases contained in such texts or speeches. Thus the

---

15. To close this brief discussion of classical dialectic it might be worthwhile to point to Sara Rubinelli's reminder (personal communication) that Plato and Aristotle often refer to dialectic in the sense of academic dialectical debates, which are gamelike competitions of debates with a very specific structure for training students, and that Aristotle mentions in the second chapter of book 1 of the *Topics* a use of dialectic in encounters (enteuxeis, ἐντεύξεις) that is considerably different from this.

analysis of argumentation in general depends upon the analysis of dialogues, i.e., the study of dialectic." Pragma-dialecticians characterize the dialectical perspective on argumentation more specifically as viewing argumentative discourse as an exchange between two parties in which an attempt is made to resolve a difference of opinion on the merits by means of a regulated discussion.[16]

Naess, one of the pioneers of modern dialectic in argumentation theory, has a view of dialectic that comes close to a classical view of dialectic. He, too, assumes that differences of opinion should be solved in a critical dialogue, and he also holds that discussions can follow a rational course only if the interlocutors are agreed on the procedures that are to be followed. According to Naess (and other dialecticians), discussions do not center on the absolute truth of statements, but on their tenability in the light of contra-arguments. Discussion, or debate, he regards as a "dialectic" amounting to a form of "systematic intersubjective verbal communication" (Naess, 1992, p. 138). This verbal communication must be conducted in accordance with certain discussion rules, procedural as well as material. The aim of a dialectic is in his view in the first place to clear up misunderstandings and in the second place to prepare individual standpoints for testing.[17] The dialectic envisaged by Naess is close to classical dialectic: "Understood in this way the *philosophical dialectic (dialektikè)* seems to me to be today a new edition [...] of the classical dialogue (*dialogos*) in so far as this was [...] a method for the joint labor of several philosophers" (p. 138).

In order to determine which of two conflicting standpoints is the more acceptable, Naess thinks it necessary to examine both the evidence for and the evidence against those standpoints. Here the link between his thinking and classical dialectic becomes even clearer. In this connection, Naess (1966, p. 101) refers to the Greek philosopher Carneades, who believed that there is always something to be said for and against an opinion. According to Naess, absolute certainty is not possible, and for assessing an argumentation it is not necessary. In Naess' practical method for evaluating individual standpoints the pieces of evidence both for and against a standpoint are weighed up. In order to acquire proficiency in examinations of this kind, Naess recommends doing exercises in compiling surveys of the available evidence. For this purpose, he differentiates between two sorts of survey: a "*pro-et-contra* survey" and a "*pro-aut-contra*

---

16. Thus the dialectical perspective means that argumentation is in the first place viewed as part of a procedure to test the acceptability of a standpoint in terms of its tenability in the light of critical reactions (van Eemeren et al., 1996, p. 278). For such a notion to be fruitful, it is unnecessary to determine whether or not Aristotle would have endorsed it, and immaterial if it happened that he did not.

17. According to Naess, "one will have to distinguish between eristics (rhetoric) and dialectics, between sophistics and philosophical investigation, roughly in the way Aristotle and Plato did. The debate or dialectic constitutes in my terminology [...] a systematic intersubjective verbal communication, whereby misunderstandings are eliminated and the various standpoints undergo the necessary precization (*Präzisierung*), so that recommendations for research programs may be subjected to testing" (1992, p. 138).

survey." A *pro-et-contra* survey contains the most important arguments which in a given discussion will most likely come to be adduced (a) in favor of a standpoint and (b) against that standpoint. A *pro-aut-contra* survey contains the most important arguments which, according to the surveyor or some particular party, may very likely be adduced for or against a standpoint. According to Naess, a *pro-aut-contra* survey "ends in a conclusion and implies that the arguments have all been weighed against one another" (1966, p. 102).[18]

Hamblin (1970, 1971), who inspired the modern formal dialectical approaches, coined the term *formal dialectic* to refer to strictly regimented – hence the indication "formal" – dialogue games. According to Hamblin (1970), the study of dialectical systems can be pursued *descriptively* or *formally*. In the first case, we look at the rules and conventions that operate in actual discussions. A formal approach, on the other hand, consists in "the setting up of simple systems of precise but not necessarily realistic rules, and the plotting of the properties of the dialogues that might be played out in accordance with them" (1970, p. 256). In Hamblin's view, however, "neither approach is of any importance on its own; for descriptions of actual cases must aim to bring out formalizable features, and formal systems must aim to throw light on actual, describable phenomena" (1970, p. 256). Krabbe (2002b, p. 153) calls this dichotomy between descriptive and formal "a bit surprising." As the opposite of descriptive, he would have rather expected "normative," and as the opposite of formal, "informal." He concludes that Hamblin is actually making a contrast along two dimensions: "Conceptually the two dimensions are independent: descriptive studies as well as normative studies may proceed either formally or informally" (Krabbe, 2002b, p. 154).

Another important factor in the development of formal dialectic is dialogue logic. In dialogue logic, as developed by Lorenzen and other members of the Erlangen School, one sets up dialogue games between a "proponent" and an "opponent" of a "thesis." The parties try to establish together whether the thesis can be defended successfully against critical attacks.[19] In his defense the proponent can make use of the propositions the opponent is prepared to be committed to. The proponent attempts to bring the opponent to a contradictory position by skillfully exploiting these concessions. If the proponent succeeds, the thesis has been successfully defended given the concessions (*ex concessis*). Building on the "semantic tableaux" method introduced by Beth (1955), Lorenzen proposed a method using "dialogical tableaux" to determine in what cases a critical discussion about a particular thesis can be won or lost. The development of

---

18. Naess assumes that the *pro-aut-contra* surveyor "considers the conclusion to be adequately derived from the arguments in its favor" (1966, p. 103).

19. The systems of formal dialectic developed by Hamblin differ from the Lorenzen approach (and the related Hintikka (1968) approach) in that they do not yield a concept of logical validity. Further development of the Hamblinian systems was undertaken by Mackenzie (1979a, 1979b, 1981, 1985, 1989, 1990).

Lorenzen's insights relating to the dialogical definition of logical constants signal the initiation of a pragmatic approach to logic (Lorenzen & Lorenz, 1978).

The first initiatives toward a modern dialectical theory of argumentation are worked out by Barth and Krabbe (1982), adopting Hamblin's term *formal dialectic* in this endeavor. Their formal dialectic, however, is not primarily based on Hamblin's proposals, but on Lorenzen's work. In *From Axiom to Dialogue* Barth and Krabbe (1982) describe a "formal-dialectical" procedure to determine whether a standpoint can be maintained in the light of certain starting points or "concessions." Formal dialectic comprises both rules for the use of logical constants in attack and defense, and general rules and norms for discussion.[20] Two roles are distinguished: the role of proponent and the role of opponent. The rules presented in formal dialectic lay down what moves are permissible in a discussion, in which circumstances a proponent has successfully defended a thesis, and in which circumstances an opponent has successfully attacked one. Like Kamlah and Lorenzen (1967), Barth and Krabbe distinguish three main alternatives for a system of regulations of dialogue: classical, constructive, and minimal dialectics. They discuss nonmaterial (purely formal) variants, using uninterpreted formulas, as well as material variants, using interpreted statements, of each of these.[21]

The rules of formal dialectic lay down the manner in which the opponent may attack the thesis, the manner in which the proponent may defend the thesis, the conditions under which one of the two parties wins, and who the winner is. Formal dialectic consists of five different sorts of rules, each of which serves a different purpose. These five sorts of rules are preceded by a number of "elementary" rules and are rounded off by rules establishing "winning and losing." The nonelementary rules of formal dialectic are grouped to correspond to the various requirements that the system is intended to meet, namely that the system be "systematic," "realistic," "thoroughgoing," "orderly," and "dynamic." Barth and Krabbe have shown the completeness of several of their dialectical systems (minimal, constructive, and classical) in terms of equivalence with extant systems of formal deduction or logical semantics, but they do not claim that

---

20. As Barth and Krabbe (1982, p. 75) explain, "The subject called 'Logic' corresponds to that part of the Theory of Argumentation that studies systems of language-invariant formal$_3$ dialectic rules and language-dependent formal$_2$ dialectic rules based on (formal$_2$) syntactical rules."

21. The initial situation in Barth and Krabbe's dialogues represents a stage in the resolution of a difference of opinion that does not arise until after the arguments in defense of the arguer's standpoint have been advanced, and the parties decide to examine together whether this standpoint is tenable on the assumption that the arguments are acceptable. This means that they set out to check whether the conclusion contained in the standpoint indeed *follows* from the premises contained in the argumentation. Van Eemeren and Grootendorst (1984) therefore included in their evaluation procedures a method, the "intersubjective reasoning procedure," corresponding to Barth and Krabbe's device for use in a later stage of the resolution process. For a different point of view, see Krabbe (1988), where the initial situation of formal dialectic is interpreted as a natural starting point.

Chapter 3. Dialectical and rhetorical perspectives on argumentative discourse

with their formal dialectic they have produced a "'complete,' ready-for-use theory of argumentation" (1982, p. 307).

As Krabbe (2002a, p. 39) observes, "Within dialogue theory, Walton & Krabbe (1995) have moved toward a more encompassing theory of dialectic, bringing in various types of dialogue besides the persuasion dialogue." A similarity between their approach, which aims at an integration of the Lorenzen and the Hamblin approach, and the pragma-dialectical approach is that both approaches aim to combine a pragmatic perspective on argumentative discourse with a dialectical orientation toward critical standards of reasonableness. The concept of types of contexts is in both approaches viewed as at the same time an indispensable tool for a description of what is happening in a given argumentative situation and a locus of application of certain standards of assessment (Walton & Krabbe, 1995; van Eemeren & Houtlosser, 2005a). All the same, the two approaches differ as to the solutions they propose and the form these solutions take.

Walton emphasizes Hamblin's fundamental assumption that "dialectic is the study of contexts in use in which arguments are put forward by one party in a rule-governed, orderly verbal exchange with another party" (1998b, p. 6). The roots of Walton's concept of dialogue types as "conversational contexts of argument" can be traced back to the "systems of dialogue rules" developed by formal dialecticians, which pertain to game-like and self-contained dialogues defined by the goal of the game and regulated by strict logical rules determining how this goal can be reached in an acceptable way. As Walton and Krabbe observe, the use of Lorenzen systems was highly specialized, as they had to provide solutions to problems of logic and mathematics; "each system of dialogue rules (or dialectical system) defines its own concept of logical consequence (its concept of validity, its 'logic')" (1995, p. 4).[22] As Walton and Krabbe note, Hamblin, who was unaware of Lorenzen's dialogue logic, took an important step from such abstract constructs to actual arguments, arguing "that such dialectical systems could be used to model contexts of dialogue in which argumentation takes place in everyday conversations of various kinds" (1995, p. 5). Despite this move toward argumentative reality, the goal of such modeling was decidedly normative – dialectical systems were to help the analysts to "justify critical judgments that an argument in a real case is fallacious or nonfallacious" (Walton & Krabbe, 1995, p. 5).

A different and influential angle of approach is Rescher's (1977).[23] In *Dialectics*, he revitalized the "disputation model" of argumentation from the scholastic tradition. His disputation model emphasizes "the communal and controversy-oriented aspects of rational argumentation and inquiry" (1977, p. xiii), and counters the Cartesian model, which supposes an isolated reasoner building chains of proofs constructed from undisputed truths. Rescher's modeling of dialectical argumentative exchanges makes

---

22. In other words, each system prescribes how one can win a particular game of dialogue in a valid way, and thus defines its own set of cases where the proponent has a winning strategy, so that the thesis "logically follows" from the concessions
23. See Blair and Johnson (1987).

room for cautious and provisoed initial assertions, alongside the standard categorical opening statements, in dialectical exchanges. That leads, in turn, to a richer inventory of dialectical countermoves. Rescher's burden of proof analysis implies that a proponent carries a variety of changing commitments during a dialectical exchange. Rescher makes a distinction between the probative "burden of initiation," which rests with the party who initiates by asserting, and the "evidential burden," which may shift from proponent to respondent during the exchange. Intimately connected with any account of the burden of proof will be a doctrine about presumption, namely about what may be taken as standing in the usual, normal, customary course of things. The need to identify how presumption works in different contexts leads Rescher to a discussion of plausibility, which he regards as the crucial determinant of presumption (see van Eemeren et al., 1996, pp. 172–173).

In *Manifest Rationality*, Johnson (2000) develops an informal logic approach based on a pragmatic and dialectical conception of argument. In his view, the basis of a normative theory of argument should be a proper understanding of the practice of argumentation. Johnson (following Govier, 1987) rejects both deductive theories that hold that all arguments are, or are reducible to, deductive arguments and "positivist" theories that hold that there are two kinds of argument, deductive and inductive. According to his conceptualization of argument the main purpose of argument is rational persuasion of "the Other," while taking the criticism of the Other into account. The premise-conclusion structure constituting the "illative core" of an argument derives from its function of rational persuasion. Because persuasion through argument takes place against a background of controversy, in addition a dialectical tier[24] is also required in which the arguer anticipates and tries to defuse the objections and criticisms of the Other.[25] In answer to the problem of specifying which objections and criticisms

---

24. According to van Rees (2001), Johnson's illative core "is nothing but the constellation of propositions making up premises and conclusion which as of old has been the main concern of informal logic." If an argument possesses in addition a dialectical tier in which the arguer discharges his dialectical obligations, producing reasons and discharging one's dialectical obligations are, according to van Rees, two different things. "But in actual fact," she continues, "if the notion of argument is indeed to be rooted in the dialectical practice of argumentation [as Johnson claims, FHvE], the two should coincide." In a truly dialectical account, argument *per se* would be defined as an attempt to meet the critical reactions of an antagonist, that is, to take away anticipated objections and doubt. Johnson's conception of argument, however, remains "*in the very core* [...] unchangedly logical in nature" (van Rees, 2001, p. 233). Even the dialectical tier itself, van Rees adds, is not rooted in argumentative practice, because the arguer is supposed to deal with "all standard objections." In a truly pragmatic conception of dialectic, "what the arguer needs to answer are nothing more (but also nothing less) than the actual or anticipated objections of the opponent that he tries to convince" (van Rees, 2001, p. 234).

25. A different way of incorporating dialectical insight in the theorizing about argumentation can be found in Freeman's (1991) *Dialectics and the Macrostructure of Arguments*. Freeman aims for a revision of the Toulmin model by adding a dialectical dimension to the model and rejecting the data-warrant-backing distinction as applicable to arguments as artifacts. He claims that

the arguer is required to deal with, Johnson opts for "the standard objections." The criteria for the illative core – to Johnson truth, acceptability, relevance and sufficiency – he regards as complete, but the criteria for the dialectical tier are an issue for future research, just as the questions of how the various criteria must be integrated and in what order they must be applied.[26]

Finocchiaro (2006) gives an overview of modern views of dialectic by discussing conceptions of "argument" that are to a varying degree dialectical. First, he mentions the view of argument as "just an attempt to support a conclusion with reasons," in which dialectic does not play a role (p. 52). In a "moderately dialectical" definition, the second view, an argument is seen as an attempt to justify a claim by supporting it with reasons *or* defending it against objections, so that "the dialectical tier as well as the illative tier are each a sufficient but not necessary condition to have an argument" (p. 53). Third, in a "strongly dialectical" definition of argument, as proposed by Johnson (2000), an argument is conceived as an attempt to justify a claim by supporting it with reasons *and* defending it from objection, so that "both tiers are necessary conditions for an argument, but neither is sufficient" (Finocchiaro, 2006, p 53). In the fourth view, the "hyper dialectical" definition of argument, "of which van Eemeren's pragma-dialectical definition is the best known," an argument is "an attempt to justify a claim by defending it from objections," so that the dialectical tier is both necessary and sufficient to have an argument, "whereas the illative tier is neither necessary nor sufficient" (2006, p. 53).[27] In pragma-dialectics, to be sure, the logical "illative tier" is – in a similar way as in Barth and Krabbe's formal dialectic – incorporated in the dialectical system, and it is allowed to concentrate on the (not separately distinguished) "dialectical tier" only if the argumentation does not convey a fully explicit logical argument (van Eemeren & Grootendorst, 2004, pp. 193–194).[28]

In *Galileo and the Art of Reasoning*, Finocchiaro (1980, p. 419) himself formulated and defended the hyper dialectical definition of argument as a defense of its conclusion against actual or potential objections. He endorses Johnstone's (1959, p. 82) point that apparently "constructive" arguments are really critical, i.e. justify their conclusion

---

this model captures the structures of the arguments that can be found in real life and is sufficiently complete and comprehensive to apply to any possible argument.

26. As Leff (2000) observes, Johnson's conception of a dialectical tier is essentially logical and abstract and makes the need felt for a dialectic "conceived in relationship to the controversies and disagreements that enter into our real world experience." According to van Rees (2001), the fact that Johnson's dialectical tier addresses imaginary objections gives rise to the pernicious infinite regress pointed out by Govier (1998).

27. Finocchiaro is right in thinking that the hyper dialectical definition is to be justified in due course by "holistic indirect arguments" in which the definition is combined with other theoretical claims (2006, p. 54).

28. It is also important to emphasize that van Eemeren and Grootendorst (1984, 1992a, 2004) are dealing with argumentation, not with argument.

by criticizing objections and counterarguments. In addition, Finocchiaro (2006, p. 58) claims, there is a "much longer, and very different" argument advanced in his own previous work that is "essentially [...] an inductive generalization." According to Finocchiaro (2006, p 58), in the sample of arguments provided in Galileo's *Dialogue on the two chief world systems, Ptolemaic and Copernican* "most arguments are critical, rather than constructive." Via this empirical support for the "Johnstonian thesis" one arrives then at the hyper dialectical definition of argument.

有效论辩话语的古典修辞术路径
3.4 Effective argumentative discourse in classical rhetorical approaches

In spite of the fact that Aristotle's *(On) Rhetoric* and the *Rhetoric for Alexander* (ascribed by some to Anaximenes of Lampsacus) are the only two theoretical studies from that period that survive, thinking about rhetoric in fourth-century B.C. Greece has shaped the study of rhetoric. Starting from these Greek sources, in particular Aristotle, rhetoric came to be seen as the study of discourse, especially argumentative discourse (Kennedy, 1991, Trans.).[29] From this perspective, rhetoric can be generally defined as the study of persuasion, albeit that persuasion is then to be taken broadly, involving not only the use of *logos* (λόγος), but also the use of *ethos* (ἦθος) and *pathos* (πάθος).[30] However, in order to avoid any misunderstanding arising from the use of the term *persuasion*, I shall speak of rhetoric as the study of *aiming for effectiveness* in discourse – in my case, argumentative discourse.[31] If phrased in this way, another misunderstanding can be prevented as well, i.e. that rhetoric is equivalent to the study of *successful* discourse, argumentative or otherwise.[32] The (empirical) study of successful (argumentative) discourse is more aptly called *persuasion research*.[33] Theoretically, the notion of "effectiveness" allows for various kinds of interpretation and various layers of depth. In this section I shall indicate in what way the effectiveness of rhetoric is perceived in the main rhetorical approaches that can be distinguished in antiquity.

As Kennedy explains, the word *rhetor* (ῥήτωρ) in Greek means a public speaker, but often, he adds, it had "the more dubious connotation of a 'politician'" (1994, p. 7).

---

29. The *Rhetoric for Alexander* had not much influence in antiquity, but in medieval times it was three times translated into Latin.

30. According to Krabbe, "*logos* constitutes the core-business of rhetoric (*Rhet.* I 1.3-4, 1354a11–18), but other means of persuasion are not neglected by Aristotle" (2002a, p. 33).

31. Aristotle does not define rhetoric in terms of persuasive effect, but as the faculty for observing in any given case the available means of persuasion.

32. Nicolaus of Damascus, who plays an important part in the reception of Aristotle, already points out that the goal of rhetoric is not to persuade, but to speak persuasively.

33. See O'Keefe (2002). As Leff (2002, p. 54) observes, "effective persuasion is measured by audience response. But this conclusion misrepresents the position of Aristotle and most other classical rhetoricians."

Chapter 3. Dialectical and rhetorical perspectives on argumentative discourse

Before the word "rhetoric" came into use in Greek, its closest equivalent was *peitho* (πειθώ), "persuasion," the power in *logos*. According to Kennedy (1994, pp. 12–13), "The first explicit identification of [the goddess] Peitho with rhetoric comes in Plato's *Gorgias* (453a2)." The "invention" of rhetoric as a theory is usually ascribed to Corax and Tisias, but according to Schiappa (1999), *rhētorikē* (ῥητορική) originates in Plato's works. Schiappa challenges the view that the Sophists used this term to refer to a systematic and deliberate set of practices and procedures.[34] As Tindale observes, "By identifying arguing with *logos* and opposing it to rhetoric, Schiappa challenges the popular distinction between success-seeking [Sophists and kindred spirits, FHvE] and truth-seeking [Platonists and Aristotelians, FHvE] (rhetoric vs. philosophy) that has influenced so many accounts" (2004, p. 31).

Tindale emphasizes that "the images of rhetoric as 'the art of persuasion' and the Sophist as 'the craftsman of persuasion' are both caricatures that have distorted our vision" (2004, p. 31). In his view, the Sophists' argument was aimed at much more than persuasion: "it sought to create insight and understanding, and to provide an invitation to modify one's views" (2004, p. 54). He refers to Poulakos (1997), who has a more positive engagement with the Sophists than argumentation scholars such as Hamblin (1970) who base themselves completely on Aristotle's account of the Sophists.[35] From his reading of the literature, Tindale concludes that the Sophists introduced "interesting and varied strategies and types of argument" which indicate that "Sophistic argument must have aims beyond the simple persuasion of an audience" (2004, p. 45; 2004, p. 46).[36]

In *The Art of Persuasion in Greece*, Kennedy explains that in the development of rhetoric in the early fourth century B.C. the tradition of the Sophists, "who taught mainly by example and imitation," and the "more pedestrian" handbook tradition, came together in the school of Isocrates (1963, p. 19). According to Murphy and Katula (1994, p. 46), Isocrates' school is largely responsible for making rhetoric the accepted basis of education in Greece and later in Rome. The Isocratean tradition – known in the first place for its concentration on style and literary aspects – emphasizes, Kennedy elucidates, "written rather than spoken discourse, epideictic rather than deliberative or judicial speech, style rather than argument, amplification and smoothness rather than forcefulness" (1963, p. 49). Bons (2002, p. 16) explains that, according to Isocrates' philosophy, "the ideal of absolute knowledge (ἐπιστήμη) of useful matters, i.e. those that pertain to making choices in one's personal life or as a member of a community," is unattainable. Therefore, the reasoning goes, it is better to have "the right opinions

---

34. According to Murphy and Katula, on the other hand, the Sophists "did not invent rhetoric as much as they codified its rules, applied those rules to public discourse, and exemplified the rhetorical arts in their speaking" (1994, p. 19).

35. Aristotle may have been particularly polemic with regard to the Sophists, but because he was chronologically and "socially" closer to them than we are, Sara Rubinelli thinks we have good reason to trust what he says about them (personal communication).

36. In Tindale's opinion, the Sophists are in need of rehabilitation (2004, p. 24).

(δόξα)" about these matters than "scientific knowledge of what is in this sense considered useless."[37] As the adverb "reasonably" (epieikôs, ἐπιεικῶς) qualifying the verb "to form an opinion" (doxazein, δοξάζειν) here indicates, Bons adds, "these opinions are based upon what is probable (eikos, εἰκός)."

In *Gorgias*, Socrates argues against the sophistic tradition because it has no subject matter of its own, deals with speech about appearances, and is neither good for the individual nor for society, since it often allows the evildoer to go unpunished and leads to persuasion instead of the truth. According to Socrates, rhetoric is "a sham art," "a form of flattery and a counterpart to cookery" (1961 edition, 463a-d). To Plato, speaking via Socrates, rhetoric was only defensible as a vehicle for conveying indisputable knowledge. In condemning the rhetorical practices of his time, he condemned in fact the essential point of rhetoric: that it lends cogency to views about matters on which more than one opinion is possible. Besides Plato there have always been critics of rhetoric, also in antiquity, particularly among philosophers. Their criticisms pertained as a rule in the same way to the fundamental objectives of rhetoric as Plato's, not to any specific developments within rhetoric. Nevertheless in antiquity no growing disrepute of rhetoric was discernable. On the contrary, rhetoric became increasingly important

In *Phaedrus*, Socrates' position is softened compared to that in *Gorgias*. Rhetoric is now portrayed as a neutral art. In a philosophically valid art of rhetoric, the goal of persuasion should be virtuous action, justice, and belief in the truth (Kennedy, 1994, pp. 42–43). These demands later become the basis for Aristotle's theory of rhetoric, "though Aristotle adapts them to a greater extent to practical realities than Plato seems to allow" (Kennedy, 1994, p. 43). Aristotle's *Rhetoric* can be seen as an expanded *Phaedrus* in which he assimilates the opposing views of Plato and the Sophists. According to Kennedy in *A New History of Classical Rhetoric*, Aristotle showed that "rhetoric, like dialectic, is a morally neutral art, which can argue both sides of an issue but which draws on knowledge from other disciplines in the interests of determining what is advantageous, just, or honorable and employs a distinct method of its own" (1994, p. 8).[38] The orator – in particular the political and juridical orator – should, in

---

37. Isocrates teaches *sophia*, wisdom in a practical sense, which is sometimes presented as coming close to what Aristotle termed *phronesis* and is often translated as "good sense" or "prudence," although "common sense," "practical wisdom," and "shrewdness" have also been proposed, which would involve a different view. I would not make the connection that easily because to Aristotle *phronesis* is practical wisdom (see Broadie & Rowe's edition of Aristotle's *Nicomachean ethics* (Aristotle, 2002)).

38. Among the more specific views on Aristotle's rhetoric is Lord's (1981). According to Lord, "the ultimate intention" of the *Rhetoric* is "to transform the theoretical and conceptual understanding of rhetoric by political men" (1981, p. 168). In Lord's view, Aristotle is concerned above all to show that rhetoric can become an instrument of political prudence or of a political science which educates in prudent behavior. "If Plato and Aristotle disagree in their view of the character of that science of politics to which rhetoric must be subordinated," he says, "they are in fundamental agreement on the need for such subordination" (1981, p. 168).

Chapter 3. Dialectical and rhetorical perspectives on argumentative discourse

Aristotle's view, prevent the truth from being kept hidden from the audience and ensure that truth and justice prevail. This view clearly confirms Kennedy's conclusion, which also applies to Aristotle, Cicero, and Quintilian, that the leading classical rhetorical theorists are certainly not "unscrupulous tricksters with words" (1994, p. 9).[39]

According to Kennedy (1991), Aristotle's rhetoric is an art, a *technē* (τέχνη), of "civic discourse."[40] It is "a body of knowledge, derived from observation and experience, about how to persuade an audience," and – as is true of other arts – it can be used both for good and for evil purposes (Kennedy, 1994, p. 57). By his "argumentative" definition of rhetoric as an ability or capacity (δύναμις) in each case to see the available means of persuasion,[41] Aristotle provided in the *Rhetoric* the *conceptual framework* for the study of rhetoric as it is predominantly practiced (*Rhet.* I 2.3–6, 1356a1–20). Kennedy (1994, p. 57) notes that it is the phrase "in each case" in Aristotle's definition that differentiates rhetoric from dialectic, since rhetoric deals with particular issues involving specific persons and actions, later called "hypotheses" and dialectic with "theses" (universal or general questions). In the rhetorical art of civic discourse Aristotle distinguishes, according to the circumstances, between the (juridical) *genus iudiciale*, the (political) *genus deliberativum*, and the (ceremonial) *genus demonstrativum*.[42] Of the means of persuasion "according to the art" mentioned by Aristotle *logos* is the argumentative means par excellence, *ethos* and *pathos* are not necessarily argumentative but can provide content in the construction of enthymemes.[43] The argumentative tools the speaker may call to his aid are the "enthymemes" (rhetorical deductive syllogisms, ἐνθύμηματα) and the "examples" (rhetorical inductive syllogisms, παραδείγματα).

---

39. On the contrary, "rhetoric was at times a greater liberalizing force in ancient intellectual life than was philosophy, which tended to become dogmatic" (Kennedy, 1994, p. 9).

40. Hill (1994) observes that *Rhetoric* is about reasoning rather than the unrestricted use of the emotions.

41. Havet (1846) observes from a different perspective, "Aristotle reduces rhetoric to argumentation." For Havet what Aristotle did is a reduction, for a great many other scholars it is progress in the development of rhetorical theory.

42. Aristotle's definition of rhetoric covers a wide range of speech activities that must all be related to persuasion. According to Krabbe (2002a, p. 33), "later on the range of rhetoric is narrowed down to three main types or genres [...]; there is an alleged proof that these are all the kinds there are (*Rhet.* I 3.1, 1358a36–b8)."

43. Relying on the speaker's trustworthiness is to Aristotle not necessarily emotional. For someone who has no other means of determining whether something is true, it is reasonable to be persuaded by *ethos*. Tindale envisions a more complex relationship between the means of persuasion: "The rational person, we might say, is subsumed by the aspect of *logos* [argumentation, FHvE]. The reasonable person supplements this with *pathos* and *ethos*, and the *logos* pursued becomes transformed through its alliance with these other components of the human reasoner" (2004, p. 134).

In all three genres, the audience for whom the discourse is intended is the most important factor to be taken into account, since the means of persuasion are characteristically chosen to suit the listeners.[44] A speaker who can assume that the audience will automatically accept certain premises as obvious or taken for granted can do without making these premises explicit. When setting up an enthymeme, it is first and foremost important that the speaker chooses the right, i.e. acceptable, premises. Aristotle distinguishes in this regard between sure signs, probabilities, and indications. The premises that are plausible, which often contain value judgments, are the most important to rhetoric.[45] Although premises that are certain are more likely material for demonstrative arguments, they can, if they are available, also be used for rhetorical arguments. In order for the *rhetor* to be effective, Aristotle suggests that he should undertake some kind of demographic analysis of the audience that is to be addressed.

The development of Hellenistic and Roman-Hellenistic rhetoric was connected with the earlier rhetoric of the Sophists and built only partly on Aristotle's work. The Aristotelian enthymeme was taken over in the extended form of an *epicheirema* (ἐπιχείρημα). For use in the *argumentatio* Hermagoras of Temnos developed the doctrine of *stasis* (Latin *status*), which replaced Aristotle's doctrine of the three means of persuasion.[46] Depending on the *status* chosen by the defender in a dispute, a certain issue will be central.[47] Hermagoras – whose work is only known to us via Cicero's (1949, Trans.; 2001, Trans.) *De inventione* – developed a four-part system for identifying the issue in dispute,[48] which is best suited to the forensic speech of accusation or defense. In Roman and Hellenistic rhetoric the doctrine of the *status* and the *loci* matching its issues enabled orators to determine their position and to find their arguments in preparing their speech.[49] The moves included among the *loci* became so specific that listing them would almost amount to giving an inventory of all possible

---

44. As an example of attuning the means of persuasion to the audience, Aristotle mentions that deductive reasoning can best be used in the presence of experts whereas inductive reasoning, because examples are being given, is better suited for a discourse addressed to an unlettered multitude.

45. In finding the plausible premises the speaker is assisted by the *topoi*. See Chapter 4.3.

46. *Stasis*, originally meaning "stance," is usually translated as (stock) "issue." According to Fahnestock and Secor (1983), the *staseis* (or *stases*) are basically a taxonomy, a system of classifying the kinds of questions that can be at issue in a controversy.

47. In the Roman *Rhetorica ad Herennium*, which is strongly influenced by the doctrine of status and is much less abstract than Aristotle's rhetoric, issues are suggested to a prosecutor who wants to make plausible that the accused is guilty of the deed he is accused of.

48. In Cicero's later works and in Quintilian's the fourth *stasis* is no longer included, to be restored (in a hierarchical order and for various genres) by Hermogenes of Tarsos.

49. According to Rigotti (2009, p. 159), contemporary argumentation theorists do not consider the heritage of "the dialectical-rhetorical tradition" adequately as far as the topics (or *loci*) are concerned.

premises. Again, the choice of elements an orator wishes to use must depend on the audience he is going to address.

Cicero tried in *De oratore* (1942, Trans.; 2001, Trans.) to fuse into a new synthesis several of the classical rhetorical approaches I have discussed – the Isocratean, the Aristotelian, and the Hellenistic traditions – to contribute to the education of the future Roman leaders and statesmen.[50] In his rhetorical system the three Aristotelian means of persuasion are as it were replaced by the three functions of the orator: to win over the audience's sympathy; to prove what is true; and to steer the emotions to the desired action.[51] Although, according to Wisse (1989), the classification of the "tasks" speakers must perform (*inventio, dispositio, elocutio, memoria, actio* or *pronunciatio*) when making a speech and the classification of the "components" of the speech (*exordium, narratio, propositio, argumentatio, peroratio*) were in the historical situations two systems that were used independently, they are nowadays often connected and presented together as "the classical rhetorical system," which is in fact largely Ciceronian.

Quintilian, the next leading Roman rhetorician, sees rhetoric very generally as the "science of speaking well" (*bene dicendi scientia*). He blends in his *Institutio oratoria* (Quintilian, 1996, Trans.), aimed at educating the perfect orator, the theoretical and educational aspects of rhetoric. In his view, resembling that of Cicero in *De oratore*, the perfect orator's essential characteristic is that he is a "good man" (*vir bonus*), who advances the cause of truth and good government. Quintilian emphasizes the value of rhetoric as a moral force in the community.[52]

Due to the Roman tendency to design more detailed classifications, rhetoric became in the course of time increasingly systematized. The next important (late) antiquity contributions containing new theoretical insights are Boethius' *De consolatione philosophiae libri quinque* (On the consolation of philosophy) and, particularly, his treatise *De differentiis topicis* (On topical "differentiae"), also known as *De topicis differentiis*. In the latter, Boethius demonstrates that rhetorical topics can be subsumed under the same headings as dialectical topics. Boethius' Ciceronian view of rhetoric, including stasis theory and the figures of speech, and his ideas about the relationship

---

50. As a result of this fusion, according to Ochs (Murphy & Katula, 1994, p. 129), Cicero "remains pre-eminent" of all the classical rhetoricians. In any case, until the 17th century western rhetorical theory was foremost Ciceronian.

51. Whereas Aristotle regards all emotions as *pathetic*, even those used solely to elicit the audience's sympathy for the speaker, Cicero (just like later Quintilian) considers these kinds of emotion as *ethical*, leaving only the "heavy" emotions under the rubric of pathos. Ethos is for Cicero an emotional means of persuasion. See Wisse (1989, p. 33).

52. Longinus re-emphasizes in *The Art of Rhetoric* that rhetoric is, or should be, a practical art of persuasion.

between rhetoric and dialectic were accepted as authoritative by rhetorical scholars in late antiquity and the middle ages.[53]

From examining these classical approaches to rhetoric it transpires that a common characteristic of the approaches – and one that is preserved in the notion of effectiveness employed in pragma-dialectics in defining the concept of strategic maneuvering – is that in a (classical) rhetorical perspective discourse in general, and argumentative discourse in particular, is in principle always viewed as being aimed at increasing the audience's acceptance of the viewpoints that are brought forward. However, as Wagemans (2009, p. 192) observes, the qualification that is required here is that the rhetorical insight used in examining the conduct of strategic maneuvering in pragma-dialectics is theoretically embedded in a dialectical framework of analysis and evaluation whereas in classical rhetoric this is generally not the case.

有效论辩话语的现代修辞学路径
3.5 Effective argumentative discourse in modern rhetorical approaches

A common characteristic of all modern rhetorical approaches is, in my view, their tendency to stick to a large extent with classical rhetorical insights and to continue using them in the analysis of argumentative and other types of discourse.[54] In modern times, starting already during the Enlightenment, a distinction can be made between primarily philosophically oriented rhetorical approaches inspired by Aristotle (and later by Whately), in which persuasion and effectiveness are central, and rhetorical approaches that are in the first place elocutionary and concentrate in an Isocratean way more on belletristic and decorative elements. Leff (2002) reminds us that effectiveness is not the only kind of normativity that enters into rhetoric. Already in the pre-modern traditions, he explains, there is a tendency toward a norm of "appropriateness," referring to the capacity to adapt one's discourse to changing local circumstances. It is "a norm of accommodation and flexibility, connected with *phronesis* (φρόνησις) or *prudentia*" (Leff, 2002, p. 56).[55]

---

53. Conley (1990) discusses not only classical approaches, but also rhetoric in the Latin Middle Ages, Renaissance Humanism, and the seventeenth, eighteenth, and nineteenth century. After its survival through medieval times, influenced by the Christian tradition started by Saint Augustine, rhetoric was brought into disrepute. According to Murphy (1994), the cause of the decline is not the Roman predilection for playing on the audience's emotions and the heavy emphasis on *elocutio*, as was the eighteenth-century view, but rather that in the Renaissance, the parts of rhetoric dealing with *inventio* and *dispositio* became part of dialectic, leaving rhetoric only with *elocutio*.

54. As Tindale observes, "Rhetorical argumentation draws features from the rhetorical tradition and mixes them with newer innovations" (2004, p. 20).

55. "The more stable context of dialectical argument," Leff (2002, p. 56) observes, "encourages a norm that more closely approximates abstract rationality."

In spite of the general inclination to hold on to classical rhetorical insights, in the twentieth century the scope of rhetoric has been broadened considerably, as Lunsford, Wilson, and Eberly (2009, p. xix) remark in their introduction to *The Sage Handbook of Rhetorical Studies*. Swearingen and Schiappa note in Part 1 of the *Handbook*, for instance, that the classical concept of audience has been widened "to include readerships, communities of discourse, and the formation of voluntary political and religious communities" (p. 2). Although in the introduction to their overview of contemporary rhetorical approaches Foss, Foss, and Trapp view "the use of the spoken word to persuade an audience" as the "paradigm case" of rhetoric (1985, p. 12), they define rhetoric much more broadly as "the uniquely human ability to use symbols to communicate with one another" (p. 11). The terms "rhetoric" and "communication," they add, are then "essentially synonymous" (p. 11).

Among the rhetorical scholars that Foss, Foss, and Trapp discuss in *Contemporary Perspectives on Rhetoric* are Richards, Weaver, and Grassi. Richards (1936) raises objections to the traditional view of rhetoric and he rejects both Aristotle's and Whately's views of rhetoric as the study of persuasion. Their study of rules for effectiveness is not what he envisages the study of rhetoric to be: a "philosophic inquiry into how words work in discourse." A second major objection he makes to their rhetoric is that its central theme is persuasion. In his view, which he shares with Campbell, rhetoric is "the art by which discourse is adapted to its end" (Foss, Foss & Trapp, 1985, p. 21).[56] Weaver (1970, 1985) believes that what he considers as the limitations of dialectic can be overcome (and its advantages maintained) through the use of rhetoric as a complement to dialectic. He defines rhetoric as "truth plus its artful presentation," which means that it takes a "dialectically secured position" and shows "its relationship to the world of prudential conduct" (Foss, Foss & Trapp, 1985, p. 56). In his view, rhetoric supplements the knowledge gained through dialectic with a consideration of the character and situation of the audience. A sound rhetoric presupposes dialectic, bringing action to understanding. Grassi (1980) aims to return to the definition of rhetoric espoused by the Italian Humanists to give rhetoric a new relevance for contemporary times, making use of the concept of *ingenium* – recognizing similarities – to grasp our ability to distinguish relationships and make connections. Returning to the ancient valuing of rhetoric as an art fundamental to human existence, Grassi identifies rhetoric with "the power of language and human speech to generate a basis for human thought." For Grassi the scope of rhetoric is much broader than argumentative discourse. It is the basic process by which we know the world.

Some scholars can be considered to have a rhetorical approach only if rhetoric is taken in a very broad sense. In this way, even Foucault is claimed to be rhetorical because some concepts he introduced can be used to provide a basis for a coherent

---

[56]. Richards is out to distinguish the different sorts of ends, or aims, for which language is used. He sees a task for rhetoric as "a study of misunderstanding and its remedies" (Foss, Foss & Trapp, 1985, p. 21).

perspective on rhetoric. His central concept of an "episteme" – in *The Archaeology of Knowledge* (Foucault, 1972) replaced by "discursive formation" – refers to "the total set of relations that unite, at a given period, the discursive practices that give rise to epistemological figures, sciences, and possibly formalized systems" (Foss, Foss & Trapp, 1985, p. 193). An episteme is the code of a culture that governs "its language, its schemas of perception, its exchanges, its techniques, its values, the hierarchy of its practices," and imposes on all branches of knowledge "the same norms and postulates, a general stage of reason, a certain structure of thought that the men of a particular period cannot escape" (Foss, Foss & Trapp, p. 193). The aim of "archeology" – later called "genealogy" – (Foucault's method of investigating epistemes or discursive formations) is to determine which rules govern the discourse and to describe the various relations among statements in a discursive formation. By making clear that a particular discursive formation produces particular kinds of knowledge, Foucault supports the idea that rhetoric is epistemic.[57] Another contribution to rhetoric is Foucault's power conception.

Habermas' theory too is sometimes reckoned to have a rhetorical basis. Habermas (1981) recognized the crucial role of symbolic exchanges in social life, which made critical theorists aware of the importance of analyzing communication, dialogue, and discourse. The meaning of speech acts expressing people's intentions cannot be determined unless it is known in which context these speech acts were performed. Entering the discourse presupposes for Habermas that the discourse will be conducted in accordance with principles of an ideal speech situation of symmetry between the partners in the interaction; principles which rule out any constraints.[58] In addition, unimpaired self-representation is presupposed, and all participants have equal rights to issue directives to others. When a problematic claim is discussed, the participants in the exchange suspend the usual assumptions about communication and move to the level of argumentation to examine and either accept or reject the claim.

As Gaonkar (1990) explains, in the United States there is also a rhetorical tradition that stems from Burke and expands the frontiers of rhetoric from "persuasion" to "identification" as an explanation of social cohesion. In *A Rhetoric of Motives* (1950/1969b), when dealing with the strategies people use for persuasion,[59] Burke discusses traditional principles of rhetoric and then suggests that a concept crucial for rhetoric is "identification." Burke's revisionism in considering aspects of persuasion

---

57. Departing from the traditional view of rhetoric as persuasion, Scott (1967) declared rhetoric "epistemic," a way of knowing. In Scott's view, knowledge can be the result of a process of interaction at a given moment. Rhetoric may be viewed not as giving effectiveness to truth but as creating truth. Scott, however, does not claim that all facets of "creating knowledge" are rhetorical ones. His work contributed to the belief that truth is relative to argument and to audience.

58. Like the pragma-dialectical ideal model of a critical discussion, Habermas' ideal speech situation should not be taken as anything but an ideal model.

59. Maneuvering has for Burke a very general meaning. In his view, rhetoric helps the *rhetor* maneuver through life.

does not make him drift apart from a persuasion-centered definition of rhetoric, although he widens its scope to cover more aspects.⁶⁰ Persuasion is, in his view, the result of identification: "You persuade a man only insofar as you can talk his language by speech, gesture, tonality, order, image, attitude, idea, *identifying* your ways with his" (1950/1969b).⁶¹ He thus expands the notion of rhetoric but does not mean to make *identification* the key term for rhetoric in place of the traditional term "persuasion."⁶²

Although he is not a rhetorician, Toulmin is another scholar whose work is relevant to rhetoricians – in fact not just to rhetoricians, but to argumentation theorists in general. This goes in the first place for the model of argumentation he developed in *The Uses of Argument* (Toulmin, 1958/2003) as an alternative to the logical treatment, but it also applies to the philosophical views he expressed in *Return to Reason* concerning the banishment of rhetoric from the scientific scene since the seventeenth century (Toulmin, 2001). Toulmin's central thesis is that rationality can, in principle, be claimed for every sort of argumentation. He rejects the view that there are universal norms for the evaluation of argumentation and that these norms are supplied by formal logic. The scope and function of contemporary formal logic is, according to Toulmin, too restricted to serve this purpose. Formal validity in the logical sense, says Toulmin, is neither a necessary nor a sufficient condition for soundness of argumentation. In his view, a requirement of formal validity *in quite another sense* is required for making a rational judgment. Ultimately, the evaluation criteria depend on the nature of the problem or the kind of problems at issue. Sound argumentation, that is, argumentation containing arguments that may be called valid in a broader sense, is to Toulmin argumentation conducted in accordance with a formally valid procedure and in conformance with the specific soundness conditions of the field or subject concerned.⁶³ According to Brockriede and Ehninger, the model of the layout of argumentation that Toulmin provided to replace formal logic in the analysis of argumentation is "an appropriate structural model by means of which rhetorical arguments may be laid out for analysis and criticism."⁶⁴

The New Rhetoric developed in *La nouvelle rhétorique: Traité de l'argumentation* (Perelman & Olbrechts-Tyteca, 1958/1969) constitutes a major modern rhetorical

---

60. Burke's expansion of the aspects of persuasion includes, for instance, unconscious intent, and nonverbal elements that have meaning for an audience.

61. Burke (1950/1969b) summarizes his view as follows: "Wherever there is persuasion, there is rhetoric. And wherever there is 'meaning', there is 'persuasion.'"

62. Since in Burke's view rhetoric is directed at contending symbolic actions, and dialectic at transcending this contest by discovering a more general term that covers and reconciles the opposing positions, Burke unites rhetoric with dialectic.

63. Willard (1995) focuses on fields as "organizations," thus emphasizing relationships among games.

64. For an elaborate exposition of Toulmin's views, see van Eemeren *et al.* (1996, pp. 129–160). For a collection of essays on the argumentative aspects of his work, see Hitchcock and Verheij (Eds., 2006).

approach to argumentation that leans heavily on classical rhetoric. The New Rhetoric aims to provide the theoretical tools for capturing sorts of argumentation that can be successful in practice.[65] Instead of being a normative theory that establishes norms to which argumentation ought to adhere, the New Rhetoric is a phenomenological theory. According to Perelman, it constitutes a reaction to "positivistic empiricism" and "rationalistic idealism" in which important areas of rational thinking, such as legal reasoning, are simply passed by. In his view, argumentation aimed at justification is a rational activity which stands alongside formal argument – it is complementary to it. There is an urgent need of a theory of argumentation that describes the manner in which argumentation takes place – as a complement to formal logic. This theory of argumentation should deal with disputes in which values play a part, which can be resolved neither by empirical verification or formal proof, nor by a combination of the two. Perelman and Olbrechts-Tyteca's New Rhetoric is an attempt to create an argumentation theory that shows how choices and decisions, once made, can be justified on rational grounds. In the New Rhetoric it is postulated, just as in classical rhetoric, that argumentation is always designed to achieve a particular effect on *"the ensemble of those whom the speaker wishes to influence by his argumentation"* (1958/1969, p. 19). In both rhetorics the audience therefore plays a crucial part. The soundness of argumentation depends on its success with the audience for whom it is intended, whether this is a particular audience or the "universal audience."[66] If argumentation is to have the desired effect, it is very important that the audience should be approached in an effective manner. The techniques used in argumentation must be attuned to the audience's frame of reference. In *La nouvelle rhétorique* Perelman and Olbrechts-Tyteca give an overview of the starting points and the argument schemes (*schèmes argumentatifs*) that can play a constructive role in this persuasive endeavor.[67]

Against the background of these classical and "neo-classical" modern approaches to rhetoric a great many other modern approaches to rhetoric have developed,[68] particularly in the United States.[69] When it comes to studying argumentation, generally speaking, one can say that a rhetorical perspective is taken when the discourse is in the first place viewed as aimed at achieving communion by having an audience agree with the acceptability of a standpoint, because rhetoric is strongly associated with the aim

---

65. A new approach to rhetoric was called for since rhetoric concentrated too much on style at the expense of reasonableness.

66. The *universal* audience is composed of all reasonable and competent people; a *particular* audience is just any group of people.

67. For an elaborate exposition of Perelman and Olbrechts-Tyteca's views, see van Eemeren *et al.* (1996, pp. 93–128). For a collection of essays on the New Rhetoric, see Kopperschmidt (2006).

68. See, for instance, Bizzell (2006).

69. Among the subjects chosen as a topic for rhetorical study in Europe, where rhetoric experiences a modest revival, is practical argument (Kock, 2007). See also Ilie (2009).

Chapter 3. Dialectical and rhetorical perspectives on argumentative discourse

of creating consensus.[70] As I already mentioned, Leff points out that effectiveness in the sense of creating consensus is not necessarily the rhetorical standard and certainly not the only one.[71] He explains that the rhetorical standard may vary from author to author: "For Quintilian, the standard for speaking well is ethical; for renaissance humanists, often it is to achieve eloquence in expression; for speech act theorists (see Kauffeld, 1999), it might be to fulfill the obligations imposed by a certain kind of discursive situation; and for other contemporary rhetoricians (see Wenzel, 1998), it might be to demonstrate an enlarged and embodied sense of rationality" (Leff, 2002, p. 55). He thinks that rhetoricians are "far more likely to divide argument into different fields or genres and to consider how subject-matter, institutions, and traditions condition the conduct of argument" (Leff, 2002, p. 54). This may explain the considerable proliferation and diversification of modern rhetoric.[72]

According to Schiappa, in the United States rhetoric may mean a lot of things since the "rhetorical perspective" includes a "variety of methodological and theoretical approaches" (2002, p. 67).[73] He explains that for some of them "rhetorical studies" has even become a label coterminous with "cultural studies" (Schiappa, 2002, p. 7). "There would seem to be little in common among a narrative analysis of George Bush's discourse about the Persian Gulf War, a psychoanalytic reading of the movie *Aliens*, and an analysis of visual iconography in the advertisement of 'Heroin Chic', but few American scholars would object to categorizing them all under the rubric 'rhetorical perspective on argumentative discourse'" (p. 67). Generally speaking, scholarship that enacts a rhetorical approach to argumentative discourse often shares the following characteristics: a focus on texts of written or spoken words but also considering non-verbal forms, and guidance by "the belief that our communicative interactions are epistemic and inform most of what we come to know about the world" (Schiappa, 2002, p. 67). As a result, Schiappa concludes, "rhetoric/argument is important because it is both the *how* and *what* of socially-constructed reality. Rhetorical/argumentation analysis is thus also ideological analysis, since all understandings of the world serve particular interests" (p. 67). With regard to the American situation, he claims that the vast majority of argumentation studies in the United States is informed by a rhetorical perspective, that "rhetorical analysis of argumentative discourse" in the United States

---

70. An interesting connection between rhetoric and Critical Rationalism is made by Orr (1990).

71. Pertinent here is also Farrell's reminder that "rhetoric cannot operate effectively [...] unless we let it" (1993, p. 251).

72. Brummett, to give just one example, aims in *A Rhetoric of Style* to "place style at the center of popular culture today in late-capitalist societies globally" (2008, p. xii), thus addressing what he diagnoses as a crucial failing of contemporary rhetorical theory.

73. In an effort to bring system into the diversity, Foss and Griffin (1995) distinguish between four types of rhetoric: "Conquest," "Conversion," "Advising," and "Invitational." The first three types all involve an attempt by the *rhetor* to change the views or behavior of others, the invitational type is characterized by openness.

is best understood as a loosely-related set of social practices rather than a unified specialty guided by a strong consensus concerning methods and purposes of argumentation research; and that the closest to a common thread in such research is the belief that persuasive discourse is epistemic and thus has cultural-political significance (Schiappa, 2002, p. 65).

A distinct and fruitful branch of present-day American rhetoric consists of "rhetorical criticism" directed at answering the question why certain speech performances succeed or fail from a rhetorical perspective (Foss, 2004). The case-based analyses that are provided concern, for instance, campaign speeches made by politicians and other public speeches that have played a prominent role in society. Exemplary cases are Zarefsky's rhetorical analysis of President Johnson's "War on Poverty" (1986/2005) and Leff's analysis of Martin Luther King's letter from Birmingham jail (2003).[74] Such analyses are, as a rule, rather explanatory than critical (normative). Although they usually do not contribute in an immediate sense to theory-building they are pertinent to the strategic maneuvering project I am pursuing, because they point in a detailed and precise way to the kind of phenomena that are to be accounted for in a pragma-dialectical analysis of the strategic maneuvering that takes place in argumentative discourse.

In his State of the Union message of January 8, 1964 President Johnson declared "unconditional war" on poverty.[75] According to Zarefsky (1986/2005, p. 19), the War on Poverty offers a fitting case to examine the role of rhetoric in public policy because there rhetoric is seen to play a central role in the construction of social reality. Johnson's decision to call the effort a "war" had significant symbolic implications, because such a choice creates a perspective. Zarefsky explains that rhetoric as the study of public persuasion encompasses "a concern for the terms in which issues are defined, since a definition will highlight some aspects of an issue while diminishing others, and the choice of what is highlighted will make the issue more or less persuasive" (1986/2005, p. 5).

Goodwin (2002), who is interested in well-considered rhetorical theory-building, observes that dialectic tends to treat issues as "given," whereas issues "are not found but made." After consulting the dictionary she learns that an issue is "a point or matter in contention between two parties" (p. 85). Her provisional conclusion is that "an issue is a more or less determinate object of contention that is, under the circumstances, worth arguing about" (p. 86). Although she acknowledges that the rhetorical tradition has maintained a general interest in how issues are designed, she agrees with McEvoy (1999, p. 51) that the crucial matter of issue construction is "a point which the theory

---

74. See also Zarefsky (2006).

75. Referring to the agenda-setting power of the presidency Ceaser, Thurow, Tulis, and Bessette (1981) speak in this connection of the "rhetorical presidency." According to Zarefsky, the trend toward the rhetorical presidency has been intensified by the prominence of the electronic mass media (1986/2005, p. 8). The symbol of war "was picked up by influential audiences and [...] gave rise to the related symbols of soldiers, ammunition, a battle plan, and an enemy" (Zarefsky, 1986/2005, p. 15).

Chapter 3. Dialectical and rhetorical perspectives on argumentative discourse

of argumentation [...] has tended to set aside." "What we need are accounts of what an arguer designing issues must do – normatively and pragmatically plausible accounts" (2002, p. 88). To make an issue of something, the arguer will have to (a) render it as determinate as required for the particular situation, and (b) show that, under the circumstances, it is worth arguing. "The stasis system has proved surprisingly robust," Goodwin observes, but what the stasis system misses is "specifically an account of the normative pragmatics of issue design: an account of why going through this process leads to just the effects it has. Luckily we can turn to the work of Fred Kauffeld for help" (Goodwin, 2002, p. 89).[76]

According to Kauffeld (2002, p. 97), for rhetoricians the question is whether there are specifically rhetorical norms of adequacy. In his opinion, classical theories of *stasis* cast relatively little light on the norms, standards, duties, etc. proper to persuasive argumentation (p. 100). He is out to find a normative basis for *stasis*.[77] After analyzing "an example of issue management in which stasis was established between initially disparate positions," Kauffeld concludes that the strategy which produced this result had two principal components: (a) a "communicative based allocation of probative obligations" and (b) "an interpretation of the issues which rendered contending positions commensurable" (p. 113). There is, however, another respect in which the "probative obligations and strategies for issue management" fit the traditional orientation of rhetoric (p. 115). As Leff observes, "attention to [these] situational features of argumentation characterizes a rhetorical perspective" (2000, pp. 234–244). Kauffeld concludes that "rhetoricians should give more attention to the normative dimensions of persuasive argumentation, especially to situation-specific probative obligations and concomitant strategies for issue management" (2002, p. 116).

Kauffeld thus opts for a rhetorical approach but admits that rhetoricians do not pay enough attention to the normative dimensions of issue design. In his view, such a normative basis can be provided by making use of the philosophy of language, which has taught us that "in trying to communicate with one another, speakers commonly incur sets of obligations related to what they say" (2002). An elaboration of this view induces Kauffeld to relate certain types of issues to certain types of speech acts: the classical juridical stases of conjecture, definition, quality, and jurisdiction (or translation) to the speech act of accusing, the "stock issues" of deliberative argumentation to the speech act of proposing. As far as its aims and its theoretical orientation are concerned, Kauffeld's rhetorical enterprise is immediately related to the strategic maneuvering research I have in view for pragma-dialectics.

---

76. Kauffeld (1986, 1995, 1998) put forward accounts for two distinct design strategies common in deliberative settings: proposing and advising. Goodwin offers "the preliminaries of a case study of yet one more" (2002, p. 91).

77. According to Kauffeld (2002 p. 115), "rhetoricians ought to dedicate clearer, more explicit attention to the normative dimensions of persuasive argumentation."

Battistelli and Jacobs point to rhetorical insights that can be relevant to argumentation theory in what I would call a preliminary way.[78] Battistelli suggests that rhetoric offers useful insights for making clear how certain verbal or non-verbal moves may be helpful in establishing or restoring the fulfillment of what pragma-dialecticians would call "higher order" conditions for conducting a critical discussion (van Eemeren & Grootendorst, 2004, pp. 189–190). According to Battistelli, "once argumentation has derailed, rhetoric can provide the means for opening up solidified attitudes through appeal to the ambiguity and plurality of opinion existing in a given rhetorical setting" (2009).[79] Battistelli's observations show that rhetoric can have an important role to play in indicating how to promote the reasonableness that is presupposed in argumentative reality in a critical discussion.[80] His views resemble those of Jacobs (2002), who goes much further in bringing rhetoric and dialectic together. In his opinion, the "emerging understanding of fallacies in dialectical theories could profit from taking into account some rhetorical considerations;" in this perspective, Jacobs calls it "somewhat ironic that rhetorical theorists have largely ignored the problem of fallacies" (2002, p. 123). The "traditional rhetorical emphasis on adaptation to audience" and "to the constraints, demands, and opportunities of the situation," Jacobs says, "should be more clearly acknowledged" in the study of the fallacies (p. 123). Apart from acting "so as to adjust the conditions of deliberation for the better," effective rhetoric, Jacobs claims – in what one might call a pragma-rhetorical fashion or by rhetorizing dialectic – consists also in making "do with the limitations of deliberation so as to make the most of a bad situation" (p. 125).

---

78. There are also large parts of rhetorical scholarship that can be enlightening with regard to other matters but are not taken into account here because they do not pertain to the effectiveness of argumentative discourse in strategic maneuvering.

79. "The rhetorical mindset is always inhabiting an unspoken dialogue," Battistelli (2009) contends. I agree with his preference for a "multilateral" rhetoric, if only because this fits in nicely with my conception of strategic maneuvering. The more parallel the rhetorical and the dialectical perspective (are made to) run the easier it will be to utilize the insights their combination provides in analyzing and evaluating strategic maneuvering. Because both parties may influence the progress of the argumentation process at every point in a critical discussion, pragma-dialectics presupposes an active audience. Pragma-dialecticians do by no means view the rhetorical dimension of strategic maneuvering (running parallel with the dialectical dimension) in terms of a *static* set of expectations concerning the audience.

80. In pragma-dialectics, reasonableness viewed as a characteristic of a testing procedure for determining the acceptability of standpoints (and, as a consequence, as a characteristic of argumentative discussions and texts that are in accordance with the rules that constitute the testing procedure). The "reasonableness" Battistelli refers to corresponds with what pragma-dialecticians would call: fulfillment of second order conditions.

对论辩学与修辞学之间关系的不同看法
3.6 Different views on the relationship between dialectic and rhetoric

After having made a rough inventory of both prominent classical and modern dialectical approaches and prominent classical and modern rhetorical approaches that are pertinent to explaining the dialectical and the rhetorical perspectives, I need to explore the relationship between dialectic and rhetoric in order to work out how they can be employed together in analyzing strategic maneuvering in argumentative discourse.[81] In so doing I first examine in what way this relationship is perceived by some modern argumentation scholars and then work out my own position on the matter. Because most argumentation theorists define their positions in close connection with the relationship between dialectic and rhetoric envisioned, or thought to be envisioned, by Plato, Aristotle and other classical scholars, I start my exploration there.[82]

For Plato's Socrates, the basis for practicing rhetoric is dialectic. Without dialectic, it would not be possible to find the appropriate content for one's speeches. Where Plato opposes dialectic to rhetoric, Aristotle chooses a different tack. His *Rhetoric* starts by bluntly stating that rhetoric is the "mirror image" or "counterpart" (αντίστροφος) of dialectic.[83] Aristotle seems to express in this way that he considers both perspectives on arguing, which share the same inferential tools, as branches of the study of reasoning, and that he wants to lend the status of "art" to each of them. Dialectic and rhetoric

---

81. The issue of the relationship between dialectic and rhetoric is an old one and the discussion about this issue can easily be prolonged to become an eternal one. In order to be able to take strategic maneuvering into account in the analysis of argumentative discourse I need nevertheless to define my position on the matter.

82. Wagemans' (2009) doctoral research concerning the commonalities and differences between present-day pragma-dialectics and classical dialectic and rhetoric to which I referred earlier serves a different purpose and has a different scope. Wagemans aims to situate the pragma-dialectical theory against the historical background of the various approaches to dialectic and rhetoric developed in Greek antiquity and concentrates on those aspects pertinent to pragma-dialectics.

83. As Reboul observes (1991, 46), for *antistrophos* the translators "donnent [...] tantôt 'analogue,' tantôt 'contrepartie.'" He adds: "Antistrophos: il est gênant qu'un livre commence avec un terme aussi obscur!" Green (1990) examines the various interpretations of *antistrophos* and the history of their development in detail. He concludes that the issue reached an "impasse" by the end of the Renaissance, "and the arguments have not advanced significantly in four hundred years" (1990, p. 6). According to Rainolds, one of the commentators he quotes, "there are as many interpretations of this little word as there are interpreters" (Green, 1990, p. 7). Strikingly, Green observes that the word *antistrophos* is used a great deal more frequently in the *Analytics* and the *Topics* than in the *Rhetoric*, in every instance indicating "a transformation which is reciprocal and reversible, and in which one part of a two-part relationship necessarily implies the second part by virtue of such reciprocity and reversibility" (1990, p. 9). Green concludes (just as Zarefsky, 2006, suggests) that dialectic and rhetoric "always imply one another, and can be transformed into one another, without actually being one another" (p. 9). His own view is "that Aristotle meant just what he said by choosing the word αντίστροφος – a reciprocal and rule-governed transformation" (1990, p. 27).

employ parallel forms of reasoning that can only be distinguished because they deal with different types of propositions and are explicit to a different degree. However, since enthymematic arguments (the rhetorical demonstrations, 1355 16–7) are in the first place the province of dialectic and dialectic provides the justificatory principles for enthymematic arguments that rhetoric needs, one might conclude that Aristotle sees rhetoric as a part of dialectic and that rhetoric is theoretically subordinated to dialectic. A little later on in the *Rhetoric* Aristotle seems to confirm the view that dialectic and rhetoric are at the same time on an equal footing and hierarchically related when he characterizes rhetoric also as an "offshoot" (paraphues, παραφυές) of dialectic (1356a 25–26), but shortly after that he characterizes rhetoric as a sort of division or likeness of dialectic (1356l 31) which seems to imply that dialectic would be the more encompassing unit and would include rhetoric. If this reading is correct, rhetoric is both a part of dialectic and to some extent independent of it.[84]

In *De oratore*, Cicero makes Crassus strongly attack dialectic. In line with the Isocratean tradition, he portrays dialectic as liable to degenerate into empty formalism. Boethius, on his part, argues against this position and presents dialectic as the crucial art because it provides the methods of inference. Only by means of the dialectical rules of inference can rhetorical inferences be made. In Boethius' view, rhetoric is therefore subordinated to dialectic.

Since the main classical sources differ considerably as regards their perception of the relationship between dialectic and rhetoric it will not come as a surprise that the views of modern argumentation theorists relying on these sources differ to a similar extent. It is no problem that most modern argumentation theorists base their positions on classical sources, but it becomes a problem if they appeal to these sources to *legitimize* these positions. From my brief summary of prominent classical views on the relationship between dialectic and rhetoric it can be concluded that the sources contradict each other and that none of the sources can straightforwardly be considered as authoritative. Moreover, of course, the preliminary question remains why a vision from ancient times should be accepted today as legitimating a particular view on the relationship between two disciplines that are to resolve certain problems of analysis and evaluation occurring in the framework of a contemporary argumentation theory.

Modern argumentation theorists disagree as to whether it is desirable and, if so, possible, to combine dialectic and rhetoric, or insights taken from dialectic and rhetoric, in one and the same theoretical approach to argumentation. Depending on their own disciplinary background, theoretical orientation, and cultural preferences, they have different positions on the matter. These positions vary from the "zero" position,

---

84. My reading of Aristotle here comes close to Reboul's (1991). According to Reboul, Aristotle wrote "que la rhétorique est le 'rejeton' de la dialectique, c'est à dire son application, un peu comme la médecine est une application de la biologie. Mais ensuite, il la qualifie comme une 'partie' de la dialectique" [that rhetoric is the "offshoot" of dialectic, that means its application, more or less as if medicine is an application of biology. But after that he qualifies rhetoric as a "part" of dialectic] (p. 46).

Chapter 3. Dialectical and rhetorical perspectives on argumentative discourse

in which no explicit stance is taken, to one of the variants of the "combination" position according to which dialectic and rhetoric can, or must, in some way or other be combined together in the analysis and evaluation of argumentative discourse. When examining which positions regarding the relationship between dialectic and rhetoric have been taken up by modern argumentation theorists having an articulated stance on the matter, I decided to make a selection from their various contributions to the ongoing discussion. I have selected in each case a representative of a particular position who explicitly discusses the relationship, indicates what it is or ought to be, and argues his or her case.[85]

Argumentation scholars taking the zero position are all those who have not made any statements about the relationship issue. They are just pursuing their own research approach in their own preferred way, whether this approach is dialectical, rhetorical or – in exceptional cases – not linked to either of these perspectives. They may be entirely satisfied with the approach they have chosen – I am not in the position to know – and may remain so in the future. In any case, a great many rhetoricians and dialecticians seem simply to continue their rhetorical or dialectical projects without being bothered by the question that concerns me here.[86] In practice, most contemporary dialecticians do not incorporate a great deal of rhetorical insight in their research, and neither do most contemporary rhetoricians include a great deal of dialectical insight – at least not in so many words. If, exceptionally, they report their views about the alternative perspective, this is usually only done to demarcate their own position as a dialectician or a rhetorician (as Ramus did in favor of dialectic in the sixteenth century and Cicero did much earlier in favor of rhetoric).[87]

Several modern argumentation scholars consider combining dialectical and rhetorical insights in some way or other.[88] Among those who are in favor of a combination is – somewhat reluctantly – Hohmann, but he would like to restrict the combination to the practical level of applying such insights in analyzing argumentative discourse. Hohmann's position concerning the desired relationship between dialectic and rhetoric of favoring a limited combination is based on an analysis of some important

---

85. In this endeavor the essays collected in *Dialectic and Rhetoric* (van Eemeren & Houtlosser, 2002) were a useful source because several of them tackled the issue in this way.

86. From the fact that certain authors do not express themselves about the relationship between dialectic and rhetoric it cannot be automatically concluded that they think that dialectic and rhetoric are both mature and independent disciplines which happen to only share a common subject-matter but have no further relationship with each other.

87. See Ong (1983).

88. Some authors have clearly chosen for a certain perspective but claim to have included insights from the other perspective without this being really noticeable in their theorizing. This goes, for instance, for Perelman and Olbrechts-Tyteca, who rightly call their approach rhetorical but claim that they could also have called it the New Dialectic (1958/1969, p. 5) whereas distinctive dialectical characteristics are *de facto* lacking in the New Rhetoric (see van Eemeren et al., 1996, p. 96).

historical developments in the interaction between the two disciplines which shows that every effort to demarcate the two disciplines strictly and to establish a hierarchical relationship between the two is doomed to fail (2002, p. 50). Hohmann is suspicious that combining the two disciplines in a more structural way may have negative consequences. He criticizes an existing tendency perceived by him to emphasize "somewhat one-sidedly the negative potentials of rhetoric and the positive aspects of dialectic" (p. 41). "And even when it is conceded that rhetoric at least *can be* theoretically sound and used for good, it is often assigned an auxiliary role as a kind of handmaiden of dialectic," he adds, referring to the views advanced by van Eemeren and Houtlosser and putting the blame for the one-sidedness one-sidedly on the dialecticians.

Hohmann emphasizes that "Aristotle's characterization of rhetoric as an *antistrophos* to dialectic is notoriously difficult to interpret" (2002, p. 43). On the whole, however, Aristotle "appears to envision a coordinate relationship here, emphasizing the parallels between the two fields" (p. 43). Nevertheless, Hohmann claims that "the *mutual dependence* of dialectic and rhetoric on each other is shown nowhere more clearly than in Aristotle's pioneering analysis of the rhetorical foundation of dialectical reasoning in the audience acceptance of its premises, and of the dialectical justification of rhetoric by the corrective interplay of opposing viewpoints" (p. 50, italics FHvE). In his opinion, legal argumentation highlights "perhaps more clearly than any other forms of reasoning [...] the need to link dialectical soundness and rhetorical acceptability in the analysis and design of good arguments" (p. 50). Hohmann recognizes that Aristotle sees rhetoric as a part of dialectic, "and thus as theoretically subordinated to dialectic," insofar as it deals with enthymematic arguments, but because dialectic relies, according to the *Topics*, on premises that are "accepted opinions" (*endoxa*, ἔνδοξα), he concludes – practicing what he criticizes in others[89] – that dialectic is also a special case of rhetoric, "since rhetoric deals generally with arguments based on premises acceptable to whatever audience is at hand, while dialectic relies particularly on premises acceptable to a special limited kind of audience" (p. 43).

After reminding us that Boethius "does reverse Cicero's preferential hierarchy very decisively, and unequivocally claims theoretical primacy for dialectic over rhetoric" (p. 45), Hohmann refers to Stump (1978, p. 79ff.) in stating that Boethius "claims this primacy by pointing out that 'the rhetorician always proceeds from dialectical topics, but the dialectician can be content with this own topics'" (p. 45). He brings Hegendorff's *Dialectica legalis* (1534) and *Rhetorica legalis* (ca. 1541) to bear to claim that rhetoric adds a concern for pragmatic effectiveness to dialectic but is not limited to that concern. "The difference between the two fields here appears to be rather one of different audiences," because "rhetoric deals with discourses addressed to a broader

---

89. According to Hohmann (2002, p. 42), van Eemeren and Houtlosser "link rhetoric, as a method of strategic maneuvering, with the objective of having one's own position accepted, aiming at successful persuasion." Even worse, in Hohmann's view, "they also propose to subtly subordinate rhetoric to dialectic in their model." Cf. Section 3.7.

public, while dialectic focuses on the more limited sphere of expert discussions" (p. 47). Hohmann's conclusion is that "territorial claims could be eliminated even more decisively by treating dialectical and rhetorical aspects of argumentation analysis as complementary, rather than asserting primacy of one over the other" (p. 49). "Such complementarity," he says, "appears to me to be borne out by the failure of efforts to establish either clear boundaries or unequivocal conceptual or moral hierarchical relationships between rhetoric and dialectic" (p. 49). Although I sympathize with Hohmann's anti-imperialistic sentiments, I think that a failure to establish clear boundaries and an unequivocal relationship between dialectic and rhetoric calls for clarification and definition rather than keeping the confusion hidden behind the vague banner of complementarity.

One of the argumentation scholars who are in favor of a combination of dialectic and rhetoric on the theoretical level is Leff (2002), who thinks that such a combination can have a corrective function. Emphasizing that a simple contrast between a normative dialectic and a merely empirical rhetoric does not exist,[90] Leff (2002, pp. 54–55) points out that both disciplines have their own character, dialectic dealing with abstract issues and rhetoric with circumstantial issues, dialectic following norms of logical rationality and rhetoric norms referring to appropriateness, dialectic proceeding through questioning and answering and rhetoric through uninterrupted discourse, dialectic employing technical language and rhetoric embellished persuasive language (p. 57). "Dialectic," says Leff, "tends to generate procedures that work autonomously within the practice of the art," whereas "rhetoric tends to adjust argumentation to public situations" (p. 57). In his view, the disciplines can best be positioned "at opposite ends of [the] space [of argumentation]" (2002, p. 62). Neither their independence nor their differences, however, prevent combining the two disciplines in any way. Leff envisages a "conversation" between dialectic and rhetoric in which they correct each other's "vices" (p. 62).[91]

According to Leff, the advantage of combining dialectic and rhetoric overrules the disadvantage that the disciplines may risk their autonomy (p. 61). In response to Johnson's (1996) proposal to add a "dialectical tier" to the logical approach to argumentation, Govier (1998) signals that this proposal leads to a problem of infinite regress arising from his requirement that every argument at the level of the illative core must receive support at the dialectical level. Leff points out that Aristotle already discovered that this process cannot continue all the way down. "Somewhere there must be a stopping point, a concession that emerges from agreements not secured through the inferential sequence." Then Leff ascribes Rescher the view that "this is precisely the point at which rhetoric comes into play" (Leff, 2002, p. 60). "'Effective persuasion,'" Leff

---

90. Campbell (1963) proposed in the eighteenth century a theory of rhetoric in which both truth and strategic effectiveness are founded empirically.

91. A similar suggestion with regard to the corrective function of dialectic with regard to rhetoric is made by Zarefsky (2006, p. 400, 415).

concludes, "must be disciplined by dialectical rationality" (p. 62). In this way "rhetorical evocation" turns "dialectic away from regressive abstraction, and the disciplined voice of dialectic" turns "rhetoric away from vicious relativism" (p. 62). Leff thus explains Aristotle's insight that rhetoric is the *antistrophos* of dialectic by claiming that dialectic "must depend upon rhetoric to close and define the situations in which it can operate" (p. 61). According to Leff, this is precisely the point at which rhetoric comes into play to provide "a provisional, local closure" (p. 61). On the other hand, Leff says, "once [rhetoric] sets the wheels of reason into motion, its effort to achieve 'effective persuasion' must be disciplined by dialectical rationality" (pp. 61–62).

There is at least one modern argumentation theorist who is in favor of a combination of dialectic and rhetoric that involves a "full integration" of the two: Krabbe (2002a). According to Krabbe, at the theoretical level (and to some extent also at the practical level) dialectic and rhetoric are already "intertwined" (p. 39). "This closeness," he says, "accords with Aristotle's characterization of rhetoric as a 'counterpart of Dialectic'" (p. 29). It was Plato's negative appreciation of rhetoric that gave rise to a tradition of mutual antagonism between the two fields, the "common reproaches" being that rhetoric produces "feigned and untruthful speeches, addressed to man's lower instincts, rather than to reason, and possessed of unnecessary bombast and flowery use of language," while dialectic "will be described as useless logic chopping, full of sophistry and leading to no practical gains" (p. 30). According to Krabbe, this is not Aristotle's view. Although Aristotle's dialectic is not primarily a dialectic of persuasion, "both rhetoric and the dialectic of persuasion (the persuasion dialogue) share the primary goal of arriving at a shared opinion, or, more precisely, of resolving a (supposed) dispute" (p. 33).[92]

Krabbe observes that the embedding of speeches in conversations, and of conversations in speeches, that can be witnessed in argumentative practice calls for an integration of the dialectical and rhetorical theories. In his view, this integration has been achieved to some extent by pragma-dialectics, where the analysis of dialogues is fundamental and speeches are analyzed in terms of the dialogues implicit in them: "In this respect the theory of persuasive speech has already been integrated in that of the persuasion dialogue" (2002a, p. 39).[93] "A further integration of rhetorical points of view with pragma-dialectical analysis," Krabbe adds, "is undertaken [...] by van Eemeren and Houtlosser [...]: They show how by [...] strategic maneuvering the discussants may achieve rhetorical aims without (necessarily) abandoning dialectic norms" (p. 39).[94]

---

92. Krabbe (2002a, p. 33) observes that there is "a black rhetoric besides a white rhetoric that Aristotle recommends," and that in dialectic the situation is not different, "but here the black side is known by a special name: sophistry (cf. *Rhet.* I 1.14, 1355b18-21)" (p. 33).

93. The reference made to van Eemeren and Grootendorst (1992a) makes clear that Krabbe is talking here about the standard pragma-dialectical theory that I described in Chapter 1.

94. Note that Krabbe argues elsewhere that "much of what Van Eemeren & Houtlosser present as rhetorical behavior is more adequately designated as dialectical behavior. This does not detract from the importance of their analyses" (2002a, p. 39 note). See also Krabbe (2004).

Chapter 3. Dialectical and rhetorical perspectives on argumentative discourse

Without explaining in more detail what he means, Krabbe's final statement on the matter is that "[a] fully integrated theory of speech and conversation [...] will also deal with the various degrees of rhetoricity in persuasion dialogues and of dialecticity in persuasive speeches and with the shifts between these various types of speech event as well as with their mutual embeddings" (p. 39).

架构论辩学与修辞学桥梁的策略操控概念
3.7 Strategic maneuvering as a concept bridging dialectic and rhetoric

As my discussion of the classical roots of contemporary views on the relationship between dialectic and rhetoric has made clear, from antiquity onward there always have been scholars who saw a certain connection between rhetoric and dialectic.[95] Aristotle considered rhetoric to be the mirror image or counterpart of dialectic as well as its offspring.[96] In late antiquity, Boethius subsumed rhetoric under dialectic.[97] According to Mack, the development of humanism "provoked a reconsideration of the object of dialectic and a reform of the relationship between rhetoric and dialectic" (1993, p. 15). In *De inventione dialectica libri tres* (1479/1967), Agricola incorporated dialectic and rhetoric into one theory, which is dialectic in name but contains a great deal of rhetorical insight hidden behind new terms.[98] In fact, by concentrating on developing a method for resolving problems of uncertainty in disputation, Agricola made a major contribution to the development of a humanist argumentation theory.[99] As Meerhoff (1988, p. 273) points out, "pour Agricola, [...] loin de réduire la dialectique à la seule recherche de la vérité rationelle, il entend parler de celle-ci en termes de *communication*" [far from reducing dialectic solely to the search for rational truth, Agricola wants to speak about it in terms of communication].

In medieval times, dialectic had achieved a new importance at the expense of rhetoric, which was reduced to a doctrine of *elocutio* and *actio* (delivery) after the study of *inventio* and *dispositio* had been moved from rhetoric to dialectic. With Ramus this development culminated in a strict separation between dialectic and rhetoric, rhetoric being devoted exclusively to style, and dialectic being incorporated in logic

---

95. The short historical expose I am about to give is partly based on van Eemeren and Houtlosser (1998).

96. According to Murphy and Katula (1994, Ch. 2), Aristotle assimilates in the *Rhetoric* the opposing views of Plato and the Sophists.

97. According to Mack, dialectic is for Boethius the more important because it provides rhetoric with "its basis" (1993, p. 8, note 19).

98. Mack explains that Agricola's work is unlike any previous rhetoric or dialectic: "He has selected materials from the traditional contents of both subjects" (1993, p. 122).

99. Agricola changed dialectic from a theory about securing logical validity in argument into a method for dealing with uncertainty in argumentative discourse.

(Meerhoff, 1988). Although there were already these precursory symptoms of a widening gap between rhetoric and dialectic, according to Toulmin (2001), the division did not become "ideologized" until after the Scientific Revolution.[100] The division (which is still very much alive in present-day argumentation theory) then resulted in two separate and mutually isolated paradigms, each conforming to different conceptions of argumentation, which were considered incompatible. Within the humanities rhetoric has become a field for scholars of communication, language and literature while dialectic, which was incorporated in logic and the sciences, almost disappeared from sight with the further formalization of logic in the late nineteenth century.

In the second half of the twentieth century the dialectical approach to argumentation has been taken up again, and the rhetorical approach has experienced a remarkable revival thanks, in the first place, to Perelman and Olbrechts-Tyteca's New Rhetoric and Toulmin's argumentation model. In spite of some recent overtures, made by the very same scholars whose views on the relationship between dialectic and rhetoric I discussed in Section 3.6, in contemporary argumentation theory there is still a yawning gap in conceptualization as well as understanding between theorists opting for a dialectical approach to argumentation and the protagonists of a rhetorical approach.[101] Aiming for the inclusion of rhetorical insight into a dialectical approach to argumentation, as I emphatically do in the examination of strategic maneuvering, means making an effort to bridge the gap and to create a basis for fruitful collaboration. This effort is backed by the intellectual support of all argumentation theorists, classical as well as modern, who share my purpose and work into the same direction, varying from Agricola to Reboul.[102]

---

100. Although I do not think, as Toulmin (2001) suggests, that such a precise date can be put on the turning point as 1648, when the Peace of Westphalia was concluded, I agree with his more general view that the division became ideological and had most negative consequences. For the Scientific Revolution see Shapin (1994, 1996).

101. The division is reflected in separate infrastructures of scholarly organizations and associations, journals, book series and conferences. In North America most rhetoricians are organized in the National Communication Association (NCA) and its many branches, such as the American Forensic Association, whereas dialecticians tend to be part of the Association for Informal Logic and Critical Thinking (AILACT). The International Society for the Study of Argumentation (ISSA) aims to stimulate a rapprochement.

102. For Reboul (1991) dialectic is the intellectual instrument of rhetoric. He is one of the theoreticians who recognize that rhetorically strong argumentation should comply with dialectical criteria: "On doit tout faire pour gagner, mais non par n'importe quels moyens: il faut jouer [le jeu] respectant les règles" (1991, p. 42). See also Wenzel (1990). Among the more far-reaching proposals, in which rhetoric is subordinated to dialectic, is Natanson (1955). See also Weaver (1953/1985), who thinks – like later Leff – that separating dialectic and rhetoric is dangerous because "rhetoric alone does not have knowledge of the truth, and an isolated dialectic does not engage the issues of the empirical world" (Foss, Foss, & Trapp, 2002, p. 166).

Chapter 3. Dialectical and rhetorical perspectives on argumentative discourse

To overcome the sharp and infertile division between dialectic and rhetoric, dialectic is in pragma-dialectics – more or less in line with Agricola – viewed as a theory of critical argumentative exchanges in natural discourse (van Eemeren *et al.*, 1997, p. 214). The question now is how rhetorical insight can best be fitted into this approach.[103] By conceiving dialectic pragmatically as discourse dialectic, a conception of dialectic is promoted that brings dialectic closer to the argumentative reality of ordinary communicative practices than the conceptions of dialectic sponsored in Aristotelian dialectic and formal dialectic. If rhetoric is viewed in the general sense of the theoretical study of aiming for communicative and interactional effectiveness in discourse – which is with regard to argumentative discourse the best thing to do – there is no reason to assume that this interpretation of the rhetorical norm of artful persuasion is necessarily in disagreement with the ideal of critical reasonableness that lies at the heart of pragma-dialectics.[104] Why would it not be possible to comply with critical standards for argumentative discourse when one attempts to shape one's case in the most effective way? In fact, it is more likely than not that argumentative moves that are in accordance with the dialectical norms applying to the discussion stage concerned will be considered rhetorically strong by a critical audience and, the other way around, that argumentative moves that a critical audience considers to be rhetorically strong will be in accordance with the dialectical norms applying to the discussion stage concerned – although it goes without saying that this is certain in neither case.[105] At any rate, no immediate impediment to combining the two perspectives, and overcoming the ideological division between dialectic and rhetoric, arises from this preliminary consideration.

When Houtlosser and I introduced the notion of strategic maneuvering in order to do justice to the joint pursuit of reasonableness and effectiveness taking place in argumentative discourse, and proposed to take the strategic design of the discourse into account in the analysis and evaluation of discourse, we realized from the outset that this extension of pragma-dialectics would mean involving the discipline of rhetoric explicitly in our dialectical approach because vital insights concerning the effectiveness of argumentative discourse can be derived from rhetoric – to begin with, of course, from classical rhetoric. Having started from the division of labor between

---

103. As Fahnestock encouragingly says, with Melanchthon as a resource, the [Amsterdam] project of bringing rhetoric and dialectic together, "after their long divorce and current desuetude, does not have to build quite from scratch" (2009, p. 192).

104. When argumentation is in the first place viewed as aimed at resolving an difference of opinion on the merits, a perspective is taken that is primarily dialectical, and when argumentation is in the first place viewed as aimed at achieving agreement by having the acceptability of the standpoint at issue agreed upon by the audience, a perspective is taken that is primarily rhetorical. In this way dialectic is firstly associated with evaluating opinions by trying to resolve differences of opinion on the merits and rhetoric with creating consensus by trying to resolve differences of opinion in agreement with the parties concerned.

105. All kinds of violations of the rules for critical discussion are still possible, so that fallacies may occur.

dialectic and rhetoric suggested by Aristotle, we soon enough realized that to exploit insights from rhetoric systematically in our dialectical analysis and evaluation of argumentative discourse a merely parallel way of proceeding within both approaches would not do, and that an *integrated* dialectical and rhetorical approach was needed instead.[106] A "full" integration (whatever that may mean exactly) of dialectic and rhetoric, however, seemed to us neither necessary nor feasible. In order to achieve a productive integration, we decided, the integration should be *functional* – functional in the sense of incorporating all those and only those rhetorical insights in the pragma-dialectical theorizing that can play a constructive role as one wants to take the intended effectiveness of the strategic maneuvers made in argumentative discourse methodically into consideration, both in analysis and in evaluation.[107]

Because I am out to incorporate rhetorical insights concerning the pursuit of effectiveness of argumentative discourse methodically within the dialectical framework of analysis and evaluation of the pragma-dialectical theory of argumentation, my position concerning the relationship between dialectic and rhetoric cannot be characterized as favoring a limited practical combination of dialectic and rhetoric as Hohmann does. And since I am neither aiming at the mutually beneficial theoretical efforts Leff has in mind nor at the full combination of dialectic and rhetoric Krabbe considers desirable, my position concerning the relationship between dialectic and rhetoric cannot be characterized as favoring a corrective combination or a full combination of dialectic and rhetoric either. My position differs from Leff's because I intend to achieve a systematic integration of rhetorical insights in a dialectical theoretical framework, and it differs from Krabbe's because the integration I intend to achieve is not "complete" but focuses on a selective integration of rhetorical insights in the pragma-dialectical method of analysis and evaluation.[108] The nature of the differences between the other approaches I have discussed and my approach are methodological in the sense that

---

106. As far as dialectic is concerned, the pragma-dialectical theory is, as Wagemans (2009) has shown, related to various classical approaches; as far as rhetoric is concerned, it is related both to the general classical approach to rhetoric and to certain insights concerning strategies developed in classical dialectic.

107. In this way, we are "engaging the issues of the empirical world more closely," as Houtlosser and I had in mind when we started to include insights from rhetoric into dialectic (van Eemeren & Houtlosser, 2002a, pp. 137–138).

108. According to Krabbe (2004, pp. 6–7), strategic behavior aimed at winning the discussion that remains within the bounds of dialectical reasonableness "is most properly regarded as dialectical. To call such behavior rhetorical seems off the mark." However, I would call the behavior neither "dialectical" nor "rhetorical" because strategic maneuvering by definition always has both a dialectical and a rhetorical dimension and in my usage the terms *dialectical* and *rhetorical* do not pertain to a particular kind of behavior but to theoretical perspectives on what is going on in argumentative discourse.

Chapter 3. Dialectical and rhetorical perspectives on argumentative discourse

they stem from the fact that the various approaches are designed to serve different goals within different theoretical frameworks.[109]

It is worthwhile to note that both dialectic and rhetoric leave room for connecting the two disciplines in other ways or for involving the one discipline, wholly or partly, in the other discipline in another way, so that still other positions are possible than I have discussed. Tindale (2004), for one, favors a position in which rhetoric instead of dialectic is the primary theoretical source.[110] Like I do, he considers dialectic and rhetoric as different perspectives on, or conceptions of, arguments (just as logic, which dialectical approaches generally include). He emphasizes that focusing on the rhetorical perspective does not mean that the dialectical perspective (or the logical perspective) can be dismissed (p. 7). "Rhetoric aims at effectiveness rather than truth and completeness," Tindale confirms, although not at effectiveness alone; it has no "dialectical tier," but cannot ignore the dialectical dimension of argumentation (p. 13). So far I fully agree, just as I agree with Tindale's observation that if effectiveness is understood "in traditional terms" it is an easy "leap" to the judgment that, since effective persuasion is the goal, "any means can be employed to achieve it (Johnson, 2000, 163)" (p. 181).[111] I do not agree with him, however, that this explains "the opposition between effectiveness and reasonableness or rationality" (Tindale, p. 181).[112] As I have indicated earlier, there is not necessarily any opposition between effectiveness and reasonableness, but this does not mean, of course, that they should be identified.[113]

---

109. In this scholarly context, hierarchical relationships in a sociological or political sense do not play a part, let alone in an ideological sense. Just as mathematics is not the "handmaiden" of the natural sciences or medicine when its attainments are put to good use there, dialectic and rhetoric are not each other's handmaiden when in some combination or other they are put to good use in the analysis and evaluation of argumentative discourse.

110. Although I tend to agree with Tindale that "those who limit the rhetorical to matters of style have [...] failed to see how [the rhetorical] conditions and determines the organization of the logical choices and dialectical procedures," I certainly do not agree with his conclusion that arguments drawn from figures "demonstrate why the rhetorical is the primary most influential layer in any model of argument that seeks to integrate the logical, dialectical, and rhetorical" (p. 86). Tindale's later argumentation to defend his position even amounts to begging the question: "The 'addressivity' that permeates and characterizes the argumentative situation is the most compelling 'evidence' for why we should recognize rhetorical argumentation as preceding, ground, and conditioning the logical and the dialectical. Ultimately, these last two emerge from and respond to the rhetorical situations, which is already argumentative" (p. 179).

111. In response to Johnson (2000), who "subordinates" the rhetorical to the logical, Tindale states that "the rhetorical is the vehicle for the development and expression of the logical, for the logical is a product of audience and can be nothing more, nor less" (2004, p. 143).

112. Tindale (2004, p. 15) disagrees with van Eemeren and Houtlosser's statement that "effective persuasion must be disciplined by dialectical rationality" (2002, p. 16).

113. In my view, the rhetorical pursuit of effectiveness in argumentative discourse can only be understood as an effort to maintain reasonableness if it is viewed as being disciplined by

Effectiveness and reasonableness are basically different categories that need to be distinguished and treated in the ways that are most enlightening in each case, making use of the theoretical perspectives that are most illuminating — which are, in my view, the rhetorical perspective in the case of effectiveness and the dialectical perspective in the case of reasonableness. For dealing with strategic maneuvering in argumentative discourse, and being able to deal in a satisfactory way with the fallacies, however, making a functionally combined use of both the dialectical perspective and the rhetorical perspective is even a prerequisite.[114]

---

dialectical considerations, i.e. analyzed by putting the implementation of rhetorical means in a dialectical perspective.

114. In spite of the fact that Tindale observes disapprovingly that "success in terms that they [van Eemeren and Houtlosser] have now set out may mean no more than being able to match one's own rhetorical interests [or the interests of those one is speaking for, FHvE] with one's dialectical obligations" (p. 17), I cannot see that anything is wrong in matching one's rhetorical interests with one's dialectical obligations (although *success* is not the appropriate term to use here).

CHAPTER 4　第四章

策略操控的三个有机组成部分
Three inseparable aspects of strategic maneuvering

策略操控"三角"
4.1 The strategic maneuvering triangle

In order to permit a more sophisticated analysis and evaluation of argumentative discourse it is useful when examining strategic maneuvering to take a differentiated view of the maneuvering rather than viewing it as a monolithic whole. Although strategic maneuvering always manifests itself in argumentative practice in the performance of speech acts embodying indivisible argumentative moves, analytically several aspects can be distinguished in the strategic maneuvering that are helpful to provide a more precise characterization of the strategic function that the argumentative moves fulfill in the resolution process. In order to emphasize that the qualities which are then distinguished are in fact inseparable, I prefer to call them "aspects" rather than "elements" or "components" of strategic maneuvering. These aspects could also be referred to as "dimensions" of strategic maneuvering but I would like to reserve the word "dimension" for referring to more generic theoretical perspectives on argumentative discourse, such as the dialectical dimension and the rhetorical dimension of the study of argumentative discourse.

Distinguishing between different aspects of strategic maneuvering makes it easier to make sure that the analysis and evaluation of argumentative discourse do not concentrate on just one particular aspect of strategic maneuvering but take methodically – each individual aspect in turn – all aspects into account that are worth considering. This prevents an analysis and evaluation that would focus only on the aspect of the maneuvering that is in a particular case most conspicuous while ignoring aspects whose potential impact is – intentionally or unintentionally – hidden from view. Carrying out such a complete check systematically is, of course, especially worthwhile when in argumentative practice aspects that can be distinguished analytically do not stand out clearly by having a distinct appearance.

Houtlosser and I have distinguished three aspects of strategic maneuvering (van Eemeren & Houtlosser, 2002a). All three aspects are associated with distinct types of choices that are made in the maneuvering. However closely the choices that are made regarding each aspect may be related to each other, they pertain to different qualities of the maneuvering. First, there is the choice made from the available "topical potential," the (not always clearly delineated) repertoire of options for making an argumentative move that are at the arguer's disposal in a certain case and at a particular point in the discourse. In the part of the discourse that can be reconstructed as the argumentation stage, for instance, there are usually a great number of possible arguments the arguer can choose from for defending his standpoint, i.e. to select the line of defense that suits him best. Put in pragma-dialectical terms, in each particular case the arguer can make a choice from a variety of subtypes and variants of "causal" argumentation, "symptomatic" argumentation and "comparison" argumentation to select exactly the causal, symptomatic, or comparison argument he finds fitting.[1]

Second, there is the choice of how to adapt the argumentative moves made in the strategic maneuvering to meet "audience demand," the requirements pertinent to the audience that is to be reached. Among the starting points, for instance, that can be chosen as the point of departure in the part of the discourse that is to be reconstructed as the opening stage, arguers who maneuver strategically may be expected to try to make a selection that pleases the audience or places the case in a perspective that suits the audience. Put in pragma-dialectical terms, arguers who select the starting points in view of audience demand try to create a division of commitments regarding the procedural and material starting points of the discussion that constitutes a point of departure that is in agreement with what the audience is willing to accept and helpful to resolving the difference of opinion at issue.

Third, there is the exploitation of "presentational devices," which involves a choice as to how the argumentative moves are to be presented in the way that is strategically best. In the parts of the discourse that are to be reconstructed as the confrontation stage, for instance, arguers who maneuver strategically try to present their standpoints in a manner that makes them appear most acceptable. When choosing a presentational device for their standpoints arguers who maneuver strategically will in their presentation go for the communicative means they reckon to have the most beneficial effect. Put in pragma-dialectical terms, if they would like to keep the difference of opinion single and non-mixed they formulate their standpoints as reasonably and effectively as they can without provoking counter-standpoints. If for strategic reasons they are aiming for a single mixed or multiple mixed difference of opinion or want to achieve some other result in the confrontation stage, they will try to adjust their presentational devices accordingly.

It is important to emphasize that in argumentative practice making an opportune selection from the available topical potential, responding appropriately to perceived audience demand, and exploiting presentational devices as well as one can always go together and are represented in every argumentative move. No strategic maneuvering can occur without making simultaneous choices regarding how to use the topical potential, how to meet audience demand and how to employ presentational devices. When analyzing and evaluating argumentative discourse it is therefore necessary to try to identify for each argumentative move and for every series of moves the three

---

1. According to the pragma-dialectical theory, the causal, symptomatic and comparison schemes are the three generic argument schemes, of which all others are species or variants.

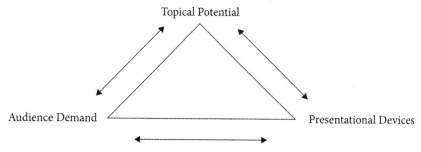

Figure 4.1. The strategic maneuvering triangle

aspects of the strategic maneuvering that takes place and to find out in what way exactly the three aspects are given shape in the maneuvering. Figure 4.1 summarizes the three aspects and the mutual relationship between them in the strategic maneuvering triangle (the arrows indicate interdependency).

It is no coincidence that in classical rhetoric developed in antiquity ancient argumentation theorists were already interested in all three aspects of strategic maneuvering I have distinguished and paid systematic attention to each of them. The three aspects represented in the strategic maneuvering triangle run in fact parallel to three prominent areas of interest of classical rhetoricians as well as modern rhetoricians: (1) the study of the systems of "topics" – traditionally referred to as *topoi* (from the Greek τόποι) or *loci* (from Latin) – which constitute the basis for selecting appropriate argumentative moves; (2) the study of audience orientation and the appeals to *endoxa* in persuading an audience; (3) the study of presentational means that can be used as stylistic devices in the pursuit of reasonableness and effectiveness. It may even not be too far-fetched to claim that the different views of rhetoric entertained by the various rhetoricians can be divided according to their primary interest, expressed in their scholarly works in one of these three areas.[2] In their theorizing some rhetoricians put the topical systems at the center of their attention; for other rhetoricians, audience orientation is the focal point; still other rhetoricians concentrate in the first place on stylistics and the use of presentational devices.[3]

Leaving the preferences following from the specific interests of the rhetoricians aside, it is clear that we need to examine which rhetorical insights can be gained from topical systems for developing analytic tools for dealing with choices from the topical

---

2. Meyer (2008) makes a similar division in the primary objects of rhetorical interest by distinguishing between rhetoricians concentrating on audience, style, and the arguer ("l'orateur").

3. Conspicuous examples among modern rhetorical scholars interested in the study of argumentation are: for topical systems Rubinelli (2009), for audience orientation Tindale (2004), and for presentational devices Braet (2007a, pp. 87–89; 2007b, 87) and Fahnestock (2009), but each of them is very much aware of the need not to separate one of the three areas of rhetorical study from the other two areas.

potential ("rhetoric as topics"), which rhetorical insights concerning audience management can be helpful to develop tools for dealing with adaptation to audience demand ("rhetoric as audience orientation"), and which rhetorical insights concerning presentational means can be exploited for developing tools for dealing with the use of presentational devices ("rhetoric as stylistics").[4] In each particular case, however, it is better not to limit the efforts to exploring the prospects that classical and modern rhetoric offer for realizing our theoretical and analytic purposes, but to include also an examination of the prospects offered by insights developed under other disciplinary headings, such as dialogue study, speech act theory and discourse analysis. To prepare the ground, I shall return, starting from the overview provided in Figure 4.2, to each of the three aspects I have just distinguished to explain in more detail what I have in mind.

策略操控中的话题选择
4.2 Topical selection in strategic maneuvering

The first aspect of strategic maneuvering I distinguished – the choice made from the available topical potential – has to do with the viewpoint, angle or perspective from which the arguer selects the argumentative move or moves he makes in strategic maneuvering, or at least in the piece of strategic maneuvering we are interested in. The expression "topical potential" refers to the range of topical options available at a certain point in the discourse that have a role similar to that of the *topoi* or *loci* in the classical rhetorical doctrine of *inventio*, the first of the five tasks (*officia oratoris*) an orator has to fulfill. Just as *topoi* can be seen as pointers to certain means the orator can use to solve a problem of choice he is confronted with at a specific point in an argumentative speech when fulfilling his oratorical task, the topical potential I am talking about represents the aggregate of options for maneuvering strategically that are generally available at a specific point in the discourse aimed at resolving a difference of opinion by means of a critical discussion. Just as in the case of an orator who makes a choice from the available *topoi* in the classical analogue, the topical choice the arguer makes in maneuvering strategically reflects a certain perspective, angle or viewpoint regarding the basic assumptions prevailing in the part of the discourse concerned.

The *topoi* of the classical *ars rhetorica* are connected within the rhetorical aims of the successive parts of a speech: *exordium, narratio, propositio, argumentatio* (subdivided in *refutatio* and *confirmatio*), *peroratio* (*epilogos*), with a *digressio* if desired. Although the pragma-dialectical model of a critical discussion with its confrontation,

---

4. In Fahnestock's view, the first two aspects of strategic maneuvering, topical selection and adaptation to audience demand, link to *logos* and *pathos*; the second aspect "could be expanded to include how rhetors construct themselves as well as their audiences in their language choices, thereby projecting an *ethos* appropriate to the occasion and their goals" (2009, p. 211). "In short, the complete rhetorical canon may be useful in the pragma-dialectical pursuit of how meeting rhetorical goals can still satisfy dialectical demands."

	Dialectical dimension	Rhetorical dimension	Aspect of topical choice	Aspect of audience demand	Aspect of presentational choice
	Reasonableness	Effectiveness	Reasonable and effective topical selection	Reasonable and effective handling of audience demand	Reasonable and effective use of presentational devices
Confrontation stage	Reasonable definition of difference of opinion	Effective definition of difference of opinion	Reasonable and effective choice of issues and critical responses	Reasonable and effective adjustment of issues and critical responses to audience	Reasonable and effective presentational design of issues and critical responses
Opening stage	Reasonable establishment of point of departure	Effective establishment of point of departure	Reasonable and effective choice of procedural and material starting points	Reasonable and effective adjustment of procedural and material starting points to audience	Reasonable and effective presentational design of procedural and material starting points
Argumentation stage	Reasonable development of lines of attack and defense	Effective development of lines of attack and defense	Reasonable and effective choice of arguments and criticisms	Reasonable and effective adjustment of arguments and criticisms to audience	Reasonable and effective presentational design of arguments and criticisms
Concluding stage	Reasonable statement of results	Effective statement of results	Reasonable and effective choice of conclusion regarding the results	Reasonable and effective adjustment of conclusion regarding the results to audience	Reasonable and effective design of presentation conclusion regarding the results

Figure 4.2. Three aspects of strategic maneuvering with two dimensions in four discussion stages

opening, argumentation and concluding stage is a far more abstract theoretical construct than the rhetorical model of the *partes orationis*, the topical choices that, viewed from the perspective of a critical discussion, are to be made in argumentative discourse are in a similar fashion connected with the stages of the resolution process and their dialectical and rhetorical aims (see Figure 4.2). Just as in the case of an *oratio* there are not only *topoi* for the *argumentatio* but also *topoi* pertaining specifically to the *exordium* (e.g. to underline the importance of the subject of the speech), the *narratio* (e.g. to establish a certain perception of the course of events), and the *peroratio* (e.g. to incite pity with the accused in the jury of a law case), so too in argumentative discourse there are specific topical options to choose from for every single stage of the process of resolving a difference of opinion on the merits.[5] A major difference, however, between the classical systems of *topoi* and our aggregates of topical potential is that so far no ready-made system to choose from exists for our topical options, and so choices generally have to be made from relatively open and fluid categories of possibilities.

In order to be able to specify the moves that can be instrumental in realizing the specific tasks the discussants have to perform in the various stages or sub-stages of the resolution process Houtlosser and I have developed a heuristic method consisting in the application of "dialectical profiles." Our dialectical profiles were inspired by the idea of "profiles of dialogue" developed by Walton and Krabbe (Walton, 1989; Krabbe, 1992, 1999, 2002b). Walton and Krabbe describe a profile of dialogue as "a connected sequence of moves and countermoves in a conversational exchange of a type that is goal-directed and can be represented in a normative model of dialogue" (Walton, 1999b, p. 53; quoted by Krabbe, 1999, p. 2). Unlike Walton's and Krabbe's profiles of dialogue, our concept of a *dialectical* profile is based on the concept of critical discussion and purely normative from the outset.[6] A dialectical profile is defined as a sequential pattern of the moves the participants in a critical discussion are entitled to make – and in one way or another have to make – to realize a particular dialectical aim at a particular stage or sub-stage of the resolution process (van Eemeren, Houtlosser & Snoeck Henkemans, 2007). The dialectical profile thus provides an overview of the analytically relevant moves in the part of an argumentative discourse covered by the profile.[7]

I will explain further what is meant by dialectical profiles by showing in what sense these profiles are designs that capture the moves instrumental to resolving a difference of opinion on the merits at a particular stage or sub-stage of a critical discussion.

---

5. Fahnestock emphasizes that the canonical rhetorical division "translates too easily into a chronological sequence so that it is assumed to represent steps in the process of composition. One thinks up material, arranges it to suit the occasion, and then finds a suitable means of expressing it" (1999, p. 31). This observation applies even more strongly, I would like to add, to the more abstract stages of the pragma-dialectical ideal model of a critical discussion, as well as to the analytic distinction between three aspects of strategic maneuvering I am discussing in this chapter.

6. Walton and Krabbe claim that their profiles are normative but in actual fact they seem to have in the first place a descriptive basis. See van Eemeren, Houtlosser, Ihnen and Lewinski (forthcoming).

7. In this way, Tindale's (2004, p. 135) requirement that "we should look to determine what is reasonable in that situation" can be responded to in a specific and concrete way.

To start with an example of a dialectical profile, I focus on the way in which agreement is reached in the opening stage of a critical discussion as to who will assume the burden of proof. In the simplest case, i.e. that of a single non-mixed difference of opinion with only one standpoint that meets with doubt, agreement about who will assume the burden of proof may consist either in a confirmation or in a disconfirmation of the conditional obligation to defend this standpoint that lies with the party who advanced it. In order to determine which of these two results is aimed for by a party in a particular case, it is helpful to have an understanding of the kind of deliberation that can lead to either of these results and the moves that are made to achieve them.[8] A dialectical profile of such deliberation is a means of achieving such an understanding.

In designing the dialectical profile of invoking the burden of proof, the first issues we have to deal with are which party is to start the deliberation and what kind of move this party must make. According to the pragma-dialectical procedure for conducting a critical discussion the party that has advanced a standpoint in the confrontation stage of the discussion, protagonist P, may in the opening stage be challenged by the other party, antagonist A, to defend this standpoint (van Eemeren & Grootendorst, 2004). Once A's challenging move has been made, it is up to P to respond. This response can consist of one of the following alternatives: P may accept the challenge or refuse to accept it. If P accepts the challenge, this particular deliberation is over, because it is agreed that P will defend his standpoint in the argumentation stage of the discussion. If P refuses to accept the challenge, A may react to this refusal in two ways. A's first option is to claim his right to maintain his doubts. Then, again, the deliberation is in fact over. A's second option is to ask P why he does not want to defend his standpoint. Then P must either retract his standpoint or initiate a procedural discussion in which he explains his reasons for not defending his standpoint here and now. In the latter case the deliberation may still go on with a discussion of P's reason-giving. As a reason for not wanting to defend his standpoint here and now, P can, for instance, say that A is such a skilled arguer that it would be good if he played the devil's advocate and made an attempt to defend P's standpoint. A, in turn, should react to this proposal, etc. For now, I leave it at the following dialectical "starting profile."

In representing the argumentative moves in this way, the design of the dialectical profile provides the analyst with a systematic sequential representation of the argumentative moves that are pertinent ("analytically relevant") to the process of coming to an agreement about whether or not to accept in the opening stage of the discussion the burden of proof for the standpoint at issue.

---

8. We use the non-technical word "deliberation" to refer to the parties' (sub-)discussion about the point of departure for the discussion. Some authors prefer to label such deliberations *meta-dialogues* (see Krabbe, 2003; Finocchiaro, 2005; Mackenzie, 1981), but we refer to "meta"-discussions only if they are about *procedural* starting points.

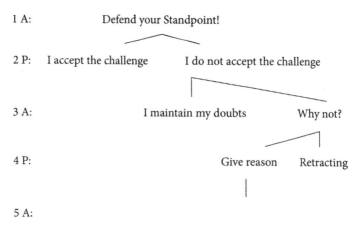

Figure 4.3. Dialectical profile of confrontational challenging

As Houtlosser, Snoeck Henkemans, and I have shown in *Argumentative Indicators in Discourse*, with the help of dialectical profiles the various kinds of dialectical developments that may occur in argumentative discourse can be portrayed, so that the indicators of argumentative moves used in argumentative practice can be identified and described (van Eemeren, Houtlosser & Snoeck Henkemans, 2007). At this juncture I will not go into the details of specific dialectical profiles. For the purposes of the current study, it is necessary first to give a general explanation of the aim of the management of the available topical potential in the strategic maneuvering taking place at the various discussion stages.

As regards choosing from the topical potential at the confrontation stage, a party's strategic maneuvering is aimed at making the most effective choice from among the potential issues for discussion (the "virtual" standpoints[9]) – thus utilizing the "disagreement space" available in the dialectical situation in such a way that the confrontation is defined in accordance with that party's preferences. In the opening stage, each party's strategic maneuvering is directed at creating a "zone of agreement" that offers the most advantageous procedural and material starting points; this aim can, for instance, be pursued by eliciting or calling to mind helpful "concessions" from the other party. In the argumentation stage, each party that acts as a protagonist chooses, starting from the *status topoi* associated with the type of standpoint at issue, a strategic "line of defense" involving a selection from the available potential of arguments that suits that party best in the dialectical situation at hand. On his part, each party that acts as an antagonist chooses the strategic "line of attack" that seems most effective in light of the dialectical situation. In the concluding stage, each party will direct all his efforts toward achieving through a strategic portrayal of the "scope of conclusiveness" the results of the discourse that come closest to the outcome desired by that party. He may

---

9. For the notion of virtual standpoints, see van Eemeren *et al.* (1993, pp. 95–102).

do so, for instance, by highlighting from his own perspective (positive or negative) implications of certain outcomes he wants drawn.

话题选择分析的理论资源
4.3 Theoretical contributions to the analysis of topical selection

As I have indicated, each of the three aspects of strategic maneuvering discussed in this chapter has also been studied, albeit usually from a somewhat different angle, by other authors. I would like to draw attention to approaches in the literature that share some common ground with what I have in mind, because I believe that insights can be gained from them that may be helpful to the analysis of strategic maneuvering. In this section I concentrate on approaches that are relevant to the selection from the topical potential – "topical selection" for short. By referring to one of the choices the arguer makes in strategic maneuvering as *topical selection*, I have already explicitly acknowledged that the study of this particular subject is not new. Already in antiquity the "topical" selection of argumentative moves, and the sources used to draw from in this endeavor, were the subject of substantial and systematic theoretical treatments, both from a dialectical and from a rhetorical perspective. Classical scholars, however, were not in agreement about what *topoi* are. This becomes apparent as soon as one considers the different translations of the term *topos* into English, which include "line of argument," "standard procedure," "point of view," "place," and "strategy."[10]

The classical *topoi*, which had been treated authoritatively by Aristotle both from a dialectical and from a rhetorical perspective, have often been supposed to fill the gap between the rigor of formal logic and the persuasive power of oratory.[11] As Levene (2009, p. xviii) observes, they consist of "a set of flexible schemata [informally valid argument schemes] which can be used in a wide variety of practical contexts." Aristotle's dialectical treatment in the *Topics* (1960, Trans.), which is the fullest and most systematic account of the *topoi* given in antiquity, is characterized by the central place given to critical argumentative exchanges (Topics I.1, 100a). On this conception, which is probably inspired by Socrates' cross-examinations, the *topoi* are strategies for conducting a critical debate of a type usually referred to as "dialectical." Aristotle's treatment of the *topoi* as argument schemes in the *Rhetoric*, however, which is more in line with that of his predecessors and at the same time more general and more specific and

---

10. Topos literally means "place." According to Kennedy (1994, p. 28), a "topic" may originally have been the place in a handbook or other written work "from which the idea, argument, or form of expression could be borrowed."

11. Bird (1962, pp. 322–323) argues that attempts such as Toulmin's to analyze inferences that seem outside the scope of formal logic amount to a rediscovery of the *topoi*. In my opinion, this applies more clearly to textbook applications of the Toulmin model, such as Ehninger and Brockriede's (1963), where existing textbook types of argument are fitted into the Toulmin model and are thus connected with the classical *topoi*. See van Eemeren *et al.* (1996, pp. 150–151).

context-oriented than his dialectical treatment,[12] has been more influential among "neo-classical" argumentation theorists such as Perelman and Olbrechts-Tyteca (1958/1969) (van Eemeren, 2006).[13] After Aristotle – and perhaps also before, but there is no convincing evidence for this – there were also argumentation scholars – Cicero, for one – who viewed the *topoi* in a rather different way by identifying them without much further ado with "ready-made arguments."[14] According to Levene, their impact had as a consequence that in contemporary literary scholarship the term *topos* has come to be used almost exclusively to refer to these ready-made arguments "or, by extension, to any theme or idea that has become a commonplace through repeated use" (2009, p. xix).[15]

In *Ars topica*, Rubinelli (2009) reviews the views of the *topoi* of the most prominent classical theorists, Aristotle and Cicero, and the relationship between these views, "with a particular focus on the interplay between the separate aims of rhetorical effectiveness (persuasiveness) and [...] maintaining dialectical standards (critical reasonableness)" (p. viii). Although Aristotle discussed the *topoi* extensively, he never defined the notion of *topos*.[16] According to Rubinelli (2009, p. 145), in the *Topics* the

---

12. Although Aristotle's rhetorical topical system is much more specific and content-oriented than his dialectical topical system, which had to apply to virtually any subject, his rhetorical topical system remains much more dialectical and much more argumentation-oriented than the topical systems of the Romans. The *idia*, special *topoi*, which are immediately related to the three *genera* of the *oratio*, are left out of consideration here. For the division between general *topoi* and special *topoi*, see Huseman (1965).

13. Aristotle's treatment of the *topoi* is often connected with the doctrine of *stasis*, a method – best known in Cicero's version of the doctrine of Hermagoras of Temnos – to defend oneself against accusations, described especially for criminal cases. It involves a combination of recommendations that serve both the reasonableness and the effectiveness of the arguments for which they were designed. After the accused has made a choice from the available lines of defense, the main claim is made out and then arguments in defense of the claim are searched for. In this endeavor the topical lists of standard arguments (*topoi, loci*) established for each *status* can serve as tools to find an optimal way of defense and a clue for searching systematically for arguments. The American doctrine of "stock issues" for policy issues in the domain of politics is developed on the basis of the doctrine of *stasis*.

14. Comparing Aristotle's approach to that of the Sophists, Stump (1978, p. 20) remarks that the Sophists enable their students to argue well by having them memorize *prepared arguments* on major issues whereas Aristotle does so by teaching them a method for *discovering arguments*.

15. According to Levene, the equation of *topoi* with ready-made arguments led "to a tendency to underestimate the role of rational argument in ancient rhetoric, in which the Aristotelian *topos* and its development, above all through Cicero, plays so large a part" (2009, p. xix).

16. According to Kennedy (1994), Aristotle views the *topoi* as "ethical or political premises on which an argument can be built or logical strategies such as arguing from cause to effect." Grimaldi (1972) distinguished between two categories of *topoi*: special material *topoi* of a pragmatic, ethical and pathetic nature that provide material ("information"), and general formal *topoi* that provide inferences. Ochs (1969), however, does not agree with this division.

topoi are viewed "as argument schemes of universal applicability" and have the appearance of strategic advice. According to Stump, for Aristotle a dialectical *topos* "seems to be originally or primarily a strategy of argumentation with which one can construct a number of particular arguments; secondarily, it is a basic principle that can serve to support a variety of arguments" (1978, p. 16). Rubinelli (2009, pp. 12–21) emphasizes that in Aristotle's treatment of the *topoi* a law and an instruction are to be distinguished,[17] the law being the principle that guarantees the reliability of the operations suggested by the instruction.[18]

The Aristotelian *topoi koinoi* as they are often called – Aristotle himself never used this expression but spoke of *topoi*[19] – are rather abstract argument schemes.[20] The name of a *topos*, which is always given in the "from" form, indicates "the main concept" on which the argument scheme plays.[21] Such *topoi* can only be used in argumentation if they are applied to premises that have a propositional content (*protaseis*). Although Aristotle originally systematized the *topoi* for their use in dialectical debates, he claimed that they are also useful for other purposes, even in casual conversations.[22] Rubinelli demonstrates that Aristotle introduced the dialectical *topoi* in the *Rhetoric* – emphasizing the link between the *Topics* and the *Rhetoric* – as part of an attempt to elevate the status of rhetoric to that of a proper technique. She points out that in the *Rhetoric* Aristotle uses the term *topos*, confusingly, not only to refer to argument schemes but sometimes also, for instance, to refer to propositions. This usage can be explained by the fact that in pre-Aristotelian rhetoric the term *topos* was already in use with the meaning of "subject-matter indicator" (referring to the subject-matter arguers might take into consideration in pleading their case) – a usage that, as Rubinelli notes,

---

17. According to de Pater (1965), "real" *topoi* consist (unlike the "*topoi* "in Aristotle's *Topics*) of three parts: (1) a reference to the thesis the questioner attempts to refute, (2) an instruction for the questioner, (3) a reference to a logical law justifying this instruction. In his view, the instruction part and the law part reflect the two functions of *topoi*: selecting (of a useful specimen from the possible data) and guaranteeing (the transition from this specimen to the intended conclusion). Rubinelli (2009) is in agreement with this three-part partition of the components of a *topos*.

18. In Aristotle's work the technique of finding arguments depends on the notion of "predicables:" genus, species, definition, differentia, property, and accident.

19. See Rubinelli (2009, pp. 61–62), who questions that the adjective *koinoi* should be used to name a specific type of Aristotelian *topos*.

20. As a matter of fact, there seem to be some considerable differences between the classical topics and modern argument schemes. The Aristotelian topics are much more abstract and do not always seem to characterize a specific relationship between an argument and a standpoint.

21. Rubinelli emphasizes that the expression *specific topoi* (Greek: ’ίδιοι τόποι) is not Aristotelian (2009, p. 63).

22. In Rubinelli's treatment of the *topoi* the emphasis lies on their use for the construction of arguments. I treat them also as analytic instruments for carrying out a reconstruction of argumentative discourse, not only with regard to argumentation, but also with regard to other types of argumentative moves.

became later very popular in the Roman context. Rubinelli observes that Aristotle uses the term *topos* in *Rhetoric* II.23 in a more general sense than in the *Topics* and in the earlier sections of the *Rhetoric*, which supports the case for claiming the possibility that the *Rhetoric* II.23 "was originally written independently from the previous sections of the *Rhetoric*" (2009, p. 147).

It is the interplay of dialectical and rhetorical elements in Aristotle's and Cicero's topical systems that makes these systems particularly interesting to me as a student of strategic maneuvering. This interplay is most clearly the case in the *Rhetoric*, where Aristotle points out that there is a topical relationship, such as a causal relation or a relation of comparison, between a standpoint and the argument that is explicitly put forward in defense of this standpoint. In Aristotle's approach, the *topoi* are thus considered to be at the center of the argument scheme – according to Rubinelli (2009), they are in fact argument schemes. The problems of interpretation that Aristotle's concept of *topos* poses to later scholars are, Braet (2007a, pp.156–171) claims, to be resolved in a different way depending on whether the point of departure is logic or argumentation theory.[23]

Since de Pater (1965, 1968), so Braet (2007a) observes, there has been a general agreement about the "selection" function and "guarantee" function of the *topoi koinoi* which Aristotle introduced in Chapter 23 of book 2 of the *Rhetoric*. According to de Pater, the guarantee function is based on the "logical" nature of this kind of *topoi*, but whether the *topoi* have indeed a logical character is subject to doubt. Another question is whether a *topos* is part of the enthymeme as a premise, or structures the enthymeme as an external principle, in a way analogous to the argument form *modus ponens* in logic. Braet (2007a) proposes the following solution to these problems. First, the *topoi koinoi* suggest that the orator view the standpoint that is to be defended in a certain way (selection function). The *topos* of causality ("When there is a cause, then there is also an effect"), for instance, suggests that the speaker present his standpoint as the effect of a certain cause. This *topos* will also lead him to look for a cause that has this effect. If he finds one, he has an argument that serves the purpose ("He will survive being poisoned because he took this antidote within the required time limit"). Second, the guarantee function has it that there is a plausible causal relation between the standpoint thus formulated and the argument that is advanced, the *topos* guarantees that for the public the acceptability of the argument is transferred to the standpoint. The *topoi konoi* can have the two functions Braet distinguishes because, although they can be very abstract principles, they always contain also content terms and usually express an empirical or normative

---

23. In a study published in Dutch, based on a careful analysis of the Rhetorica ad Alexandrum, the *Rhetoric* of Aristotle, and the rhetoric of Hermagoras of Temnos, Braet (2007a) makes a convincing case for his view of classical rhetoric as an early contribution to the formulation of rules for reasonable discussions instead of a collection of opportunistic advices for how to win an argument at all costs.

endoxon. Assuming that Aristotle requires an enthymeme to have at least two premises in order to be complete, the *topoi konoi* do not seem to be "external" principles like *modus ponens*. According to Braet, the Aristotelian *topoi koinoi* are relatively abstract principles that are hidden behind often implicit major premises, and this makes it possible to view the *topos* as the generalized if-then proposition in a modern argument scheme.[24]

Cicero built on Aristotle when developing his own topical system, which became in its turn the starting point on which Boethius later built a topical system that dominated the discussions of the *topoi* in medieval times and later.[25] According to Rubinelli, Cicero's work on the *topoi* "can only be grasped in juxtaposition with that of Aristotle" (2009, p. vii). Cicero's treatment of the *loci* in *De inventione* (in which the dialectical context is almost completely lost), however, resembles the pre-Aristotelian approach to rhetoric rather than Aristotle's treatment of the *topoi*.[26] Although Cicero uses the term *locus* with various different, more or less technical meanings, varying from "theme" and "subject-indicator" to "argument scheme" and "*locus communis*," he concentrates in *De inventione* in the first place on the *locus* as subject-indicator.[27] It is only in *De oratore* and the *Topica* that he discusses *loci* which he attributes to Aristotle. In this endeavor he refers in *De oratore* to the *Rhetoric* while he suggests in the *Topica* that his treatment is based on the *Topics*. Among the *loci* he discusses Cicero makes a distinction between *loci* inherent in the nature of the subject under discussion and *loci* brought in from without. From examining Cicero's list Rubinelli concludes that "important aspects suggest" that it "comes from a selection from Aristotle's *Rhetoric* II.23" (2009, p. 148). Rubinelli's daring claim is that Cicero's *loci* derive from "a selection and some further rearrangement of only those argument schemes listed in *Rhetoric* II.23 that are of universal applicability" (2009, p. 148). She observes that Cicero preserves in this way the characteristic property of the *topoi* that these residing places of

---

24. According to some, in Aristotle the *topoi* are more than premises in the sense that they include the instruction for how to reach a conclusion from a given set of premises of a certain type.

25. Stump (1978, p. 24) observes that Boethius was for a long time the direct, perhaps sole, source for the study of dialectic and that his work "remained an important indirect source even when it was superseded by later treatments of the subject, such as that of Peter of Spain's *Tractatus*," which has a chapter on the topics that is organized in the same way as *De differentiis topicis*.

26. Unlike Aristotle's *topoi*, Cicero's *topoi* are not always specifically argumentative but can be used in a more general sense to find the content of certain parts of an oration so that these parts can have their proper role in the speech. In Aristotle's case they also have a specific argumentative role in other parts of the oration.

27. In *De inventione* the doctrine of the *staseis*, which corresponds with subjects, is presented as a system for organizing the *topoi*. Fahnestock and Secor (1983) – who want to restore *stasis* theory to its "rightful place" as the first organizing principle of invention – explain that, once identified, the *stasis* leads the orator to the appropriate *topoi* for making a convincing argument. Invention based on the doctrine of the *staseis* can also be of help when agreement instead of victory is aimed for.

argumentative moves are "*sedes et quasi domicilia omnium argumentorum*" [the seats and, as it were, the dwelling places of all arguments], which is not only underlined in his *De oratore* 2.162, but also emphasized in Aristotle's *Topics* as well as his *Rhetoric* I.2, 1358a ff.

In her philosophical study of Boethius' *De differentiis topicis*, Stump (1978) explains Boethius' views and explores their relationship to the earlier views of Aristotle expressed in the *Topics* and to the later views of Peter of Spain expressed in the *Tractatus*.[28] Although, because he thinks primarily of dialogues, "the last of the Romans" gives in *De topicis differentiis* most attention to the method of finding arguments as used in dialectic, he also discusses the method as used in rhetoric and starts in his concern with the discovery of argument from a concept of *locus* that seems much closer to Cicero's than to Aristotle's *topos*.[29] The *locus* is the main instrument in Boethius' method of finding arguments. As Stump (1978, p. 16) explains, for Boethius a *locus* is (as its literal meaning indicates) a "place" which in the art of memorizing is pictured in the memorizer's mind so that he can recall ("retrieve") from there what he wants to remember after it has been "stored" in that place. The *locus* is thus used as an aide-mémoir in the large edifice representing the domain he is talking about.[30] In an analogous way, Boethius claims, the *topoi* can be used as an aid to find arguments.

Boethius distinguishes between two types of *loci*: maximal propositions and their *differentiae*. Maximal propositions are principles that are general premises containing self-evident truths or truths known per se which function as guarantors of the validity or soundness of argumentation. Although maximal propositions are indispensable for dialectical arguments, according to Stump (1978, p. 193), the *differentiae* are the real instruments of Boethius' art of discovering arguments. They do not provide particular arguments but "a reasoned path to finding them" (Stump, 1978, p. 199). As Stump explains, "To find an argument, we need to find an intermediate between the two terms in the question, something that can be joined to each of the two terms and connects them in the way wanted," and the *differentia* suggests what *sort of* intermediate term this can be (1978, p. 196).[31] According to Stump, *differentiae* are in two senses *loci* or places for arguments. First, they are *loci* for maximal propositions, "because they contain maximal propositions as their genera, and hence maximal propositions can be found with their help" (p. 204). Second, "as genera of intermediate terms, they contain

---

28. Of particular interest in this connection are also Peter of Spain's *De locus* in his *Summulae logicales* and Abelard's *Dialectica*.

29. In fact, further studies are required to answer the question whether this is indeed the case because Stump analyzed Boethius and Cicero without having analyzed Aristotle first.

30. Cooper (1932, p. xxiv) speaks with regard to a *topos* of "a pigeon-hole in the mind of the speaker."

31. According to Stump, a *differentia* differs from an Aristotelian *topos* "not only by being abbreviated, but also by being stripped of its association with a particular predicable" (1978, p. 203).

the intermediate terms from which arguments arise for all dialectical questions, and hence they provide arguments" (p. 204).

In my brief discussion of classical topical systems for making strategic choices in argumentative discourse I have concentrated on the way in which the *topoi* are conceived by the most prominent classical authors, without considering the exact divisions they have made within the various topical systems between different kinds of *topoi* and different categories of *topoi* (though that might be the next step). I also refrained from discussing examples of *topoi* and the application of the topical systems, since doing so would exceed the scope of my present study. In the topical systems discussed the emphasis was on arguments, because they are central in the classical treatments of the *topoi*. The scope of the rhetorical topical systems, however, is by no means limited to the *argumentatio* but covers also other parts of the *oratio* that have different aims, such as the *exordium* and (especially) the *peroratio*.[32] The *narratio* got its topical treatment only after Cicero.

The classical topical systems I have discussed have been an important source of inspiration and a starting point for modern argumentation theorists interested in the development and exploration of systematic sources for finding material for arguments and other argumentative moves, making appropriate selections from the available material, and valuing the selections that are made by comparing the consequences of the choice involved with those of their alternatives. The most prominent among them are no doubt Perelman and Olbrechts-Tyteca (1958/1969), who absorbed a great many classical topical insights in their New Rhetoric. In particular their treatment of associative "argumentation schemes" – with the quasi-logical arguments, the arguments based on the structure of reality, and the arguments creating a structure of reality as main categories – is strongly influenced by the classical topical tradition. In the New Rhetoric, however, the categorization of argumentation schemes is presented in the first place as a classification that serves as an analytic tool rather than as a system for invention. Another striking difference is that in the classical tradition the rationale of the categorization that is proposed is not so much that the argumentation schemes that are distinguished relate in different ways to the audience, which is the guiding principle in the New Rhetoric, but that their effectiveness in convincing or persuading an audience is judged to be based on different inference principles. Neither of these two conspicuous differences, however, stands in the way of making use of insights from the New Rhetoric when developing theoretical instruments for analyzing topical selection in strategic maneuvering.[33]

Among the other modern argumentation theorists who have an interest in the *topoi* and build on insights provided by Aristotle, Cicero, Boethius and their

---

32. In the Roman system the *inventio* was to be applied to each of the parts of the speech. Cicero's *De inventione*, for instance, suggests *loci* for each of these parts.

33. For a further characterization of the New Rhetoric and a general assessment of its merits and demerits, see van Eemeren et al. (1996, pp. 93–128).

contemporaries to develop their own (more or less encompassing) approaches are Ducrot (1988), Kauffeld (2002), and Rigotti (2007, 2009).[34] In spite of considerable differences of theoretical orientation between them, all of them aim in fact – just as I do – to combine certain classical insights about the *topoi* with certain modern insights concerning speech act conditions, conversational maxims, commitment sets and other theoretical concepts that have been more recently developed.[35] The conclusions of their explorations, which are still going on, are to benefit the further development of theoretical instruments for the analysis of topical selection in strategic maneuvering.[36]

策略操控中的受众需求调适
4.4 Adaptation to audience demand in strategic maneuvering

The second aspect of strategic maneuvering we have distinguished, adaptation to the audience, has to do with tuning the argumentative moves that are made to audience demand. The expression "audience demand" refers to the requirements that must be fulfilled in the strategic maneuvering to secure communion, at the point in the exchange, with the people the argumentative discourse is aimed at. In order to be not only reasonable but also effective, the strategic moves a party makes must at each stage of the resolution process connect well with the views and preferences of the people they are directed at, so that they agree with these people's frame of reference and will be optimally acceptable. This requirement makes it necessary to go into the question of how to take the views and preferences of the intended audience into account. In dealing with this question I shall first concentrate on the problem of identifying the audience that is supposed to be reached and next on the problem of cataloguing their relevant views and preferences.

As recognized in the meta-theoretical principle of socialization, argumentative discourse is always aimed at achieving certain communicative and interactional effects on other people. The person or persons the arguer intends to reach can be his immediate addressee, but he may also intend his argumentation to have additionally – or even

---

34. Starting from the legal domain, Hoppmann (2008) proposes in his doctoral dissertation, published in German, a modern doctrine of *status* based on an analysis of classical models (*ad Herennium*, Hermagoras of Temnos, Hermogenes of Tarsos).

35. There is, however, not only a danger of eclecticism involved in this enterprise, but also one of a too superficial approach that leads to finding subjectively in the classical sources exactly what one is out to find.

36. Rigotti (2009) describes a model of topics developed in a project called *Argumentum* that supports in the argumentation stage the choice of arguments from the topical potential (and argument evaluation in terms of logical validity and communicative effectiveness). The designers of the model "want to construct a new building, adopting, with respect and gratefulness, all the useful contributions inherited from the [Aristotelian] tradition" (Rigotti, 2009, p. 160). The model that is proposed links the topical potential aspect with the audience demand aspect by incorporating a component of *endoxon* in the model.

primarily – an effect on one or more others (or the argumentation may have such an effect unintentionally).[37] These others can be people who constitute a regular audience or bystanders who happen to be listening in, television viewers watching the broadcast of a speech delivered to a different public elsewhere or watching a television debate between politicians, readers of a polemic between newspaper columnists, researchers examining a scholarly discussion conducted in the correspondence between two eighteenth century scientists, etc.[38] In all these cases there are in fact two (and sometimes even more) antagonists, both of which may in principle consist of an audience that comprises more than one person. In such a "triadic argument" there is the "official" antagonist, who is addressed directly, and there is some other antagonist, a "third party," reached indirectly by the protagonist (intentionally or unintentionally) that also judges the acceptability of the argumentative moves that are made and whose verdict may in certain cases even be the more important one.[39] In cases where it is clear which audience the arguer considers the more important to reach, we call these people the *primary* audience and the person or persons instrumental in reaching them the *secondary* audience.[40] In a television debate between two politicians during election time, for instance, it may be clear from the outset that there is a dual audience and that the politicians consider the great mass of viewers their primary audience and each other only their secondary audience, even to the extent that in effect they aim not to convince each other but, based on the argumentation advanced to each other, the (largest possible part of the) viewers.

Another complication in identifying the audience and determining its views and commitments is that audiences – whether primary or secondary – are not always homogenous.[41]

---

37. Ede and Lunsford (1984) make a distinction between "audience addressed," in case the audience is physically present when a speech is delivered, and "audience invoked," in case the audience is intended. See also van Eemeren and Grootendorst (2004, p. 99).

38. A special case of an audience addressed by the parties in a dispute is the judge in a legal case. See Feteris (1987, 1993).

39. Govier (1999) and Bonevac (2003) also deal with third party audiences; Govier concentrates on a non-interactive audience. Van Rees (2003) responds to Bonevac's claim that the pragma-dialectical approach is ill-suited for dealing with a third party audience.

40. A special case of a "primary" audience can be distinguished when the audience is parasitic on a secondary audience that may in fact have been the speaker's or writer's primary audience. This happens, for instance, when the audience we concentrate on consist of persons who happen to listen in or to read the argumentation later (like a 21st century reader reading Newton's defenses of his views) to analyze and evaluate it.

41. In a public political debate, for instance, the official antagonists (being in this case the secondary audience), having rather different political views and preferences than those a protagonist represents, may consist of the leaders of the other political parties taking part in the debate, whereas the people attending the public debate are the primary audience consisting of listeners coming from different backgrounds whom the protagonist regards as his potential voters. If the audience is homogenous, it can be regarded as a "collective" antagonist (just as a homogenous group of advocates of a standpoint can be regarded as a "collective" protagonist).

The audience listening to a political speech, for instance, may consist of people who not only differ because they have diverse backgrounds (e.g. by being well-educated or not) and dress in different ways (e.g. by wearing a headscarf or not) but also because they vary in respects more immediately relevant to their appreciation of the argumentative moves that are made. They may, for instance, have different professional backgrounds which make certain issues and considerations more vital to them than others. This diversity may lead a politician who wants to convince at the same time the farmers and the educators among his audience to take refuge in multiple argumentation, so that the one argument serves the farmers, the other the educators and a third argument all of them. If an audience is heterogeneous with respect to the points at issue in the argumentative discourse or the starting points pertinent to the discourse, I call it a *composite* audience.[42] In fact, I think that it is advisable to make a terminological distinction within a composite audience between a "multiple" audience consisting of individuals or subgroups having different positions in the difference of opinion and a "mixed" audience consisting of individuals or subgroups having different starting points. A problem is that even an individual listener or reader may have "mixed feelings" regarding certain points at issue or starting points. As a father, for instance, someone may be inclined to agree with a starting point chosen by a politician, but as a businessman the same person may be inclined to think that this starting point involves financial consequences that make it in his opinion too costly to maintain. Although acknowledging this phenomenon, in such a case I do not speak of a "mixed audience."[43]

Whatever its make-up, if the whole audience is aimed at by the strategic maneuvering, all views and preferences of the audience that are pertinent to determining the starting point of the argumentative discourse must be taken in account. This means that a serious effort must always be made to identify the views and preferences of the audience which can be regarded as being part of the point of departure established in the opening stage of the resolution process. If they have been identified correctly, these starting points are *commitments* the audience can be held to in the argumentation stage and the concluding stage of the exchange. Some of these commitments are "descriptive" commitments relating to starting points concerning what Perelman and Olbrechts-Tyteca (1958/1969) call "the real;" some of them are "normative" commitments relating to starting points concerning what they call "the preferable." Descriptive commitments, as I call them, may in their opinion include facts, truths and presumptions, and among the normative commitments they include values, value hierarchies and *loci*. Whereas descriptive commitments relating to starting point concerning the real are, according to Perelman and Olbrechts-Tyteca, supposedly shared

---

42. Benoit and d'Agostine (1994) also use the term *multiple audience*. Perelman and Olbrechts-Tyteca (1958/1969, p. 21) and Myers (1999) use the term *composite audience* to refer to the phenomenon of trying to reach simultaneously different groups. Others just speak of a *heterogeneous audience* (e.g. Ede & Lunsford, 1984).

43. Doing otherwise would be confusing and would go against the presumed indivisibility of personhood.

universally, normative commitments are in principle connected with a particular audience or, if the audience's composition is more complex, with a specific part of a particular audience.

In argumentative practice, the discussants will rely in their strategic maneuvering on their (primary and secondary) audience's commitments – both the descriptive and the normative ones – wherever this is possible and serves their strategic purposes. This means that they try to exploit not only the specific "concessions" that are made by the other party in the opening stage, but also the "contextual commitments," which can also be called *pragmatic commitments*, pertaining to the argumentative situation they are in and the generally accepted commitments having to do with the "normal" (which Perelman and Olbrechts-Tyteca call the real) that have been known since Aristotle as "endoxa."[44] Together these commitments define the audience's frame of reference. In every specific case such a frame of reference will be less universal than the connection of *endoxa* with the normal or the real suggests. Not only are the commitments ensuing from specific concessions always connected with a particular audience, but also are the contextual commitments and the "generally accepted" commitments not always automatically shared by each particular audience. Different particular audiences, for instance, may well recognize different kinds of *endoxa*. This is even more clearly the case if, as I would like to endorse, the possibility of normative commitments entering the domain of *endoxa* is recognized (as seems to be the case in *Topica* III, where, starting from *endoxa*, the discussion concentrates on what is preferable).[45]

The commitments the parties have undertaken in the argumentative discourse itself by making the argumentative moves they have made can be traced by externalizing the commitments ensuing from the speech acts they have performed in making these moves; to the extent that their commitments can be externalized this also goes for audiences that do not play an active part in the discourse (in some cases the saying "silence is consent" applies). These commitments are connected with the identity conditions and the correctness conditions applying to the (direct or indirect) speech acts by means

---

44. *Endoxa* are the views generally accepted in a specific culture or subculture. Going back to Aristotle, Irwin (1988) refers to *endoxa* as commonly held beliefs (p. 8) and "beliefs of the many or the wise or both" (p. 37). He states that "common beliefs should be apparent [...] but apparent not to just anyone, but to people of a certain sort; for it is an indefinitely long task to examine the things that make something apparent to just anyone" (*Topica*, 170b6–8; cited by Irwin p. 38). Concluding from this, Irwin claims that "The relevant beliefs, then, are those held by fairly reflective people after some reflexion" (p. 38).

45. If *endoxa* also include normative commitments, the differences regarding *endoxa* between certain groups of people point to their representing different subcultures (or even cultures).

of which the argumentative moves that have been made are realized.[46] This connection makes it possible for an analyst to identify the *set of commitments* each of the parties involved in the discourse has accumulated at a certain point in the discourse, thus making clear in what way the "dialectical situation" at that point is defined. In order to get a full picture of what exactly the "argumentative situation" is, this inventory of the mutual commitments should be completed by the addition of relevant contextual information concerning the rhetorical commitments that can be ascribed to the parties at that point in the exchange in view of (1) the institutional conventions of the communicative activity type in which the argumentative discourse the parties are engaged in takes part and (2) the possibilities left to the parties for aiming for effectiveness at the point they have reached. I shall come back to these parameters in the Chapter 5 and Chapter 6.

In argumentative practice, adaptation to audience demand amounts to adjusting one's argumentative moves in such a way to the audience's views and preferences that there is as much agreement as possible between the arguer and the audience. On the one hand, in such an audience-directed adjustment the perspective is adopted that the audience, going by its recognized commitments, may be expected to have.[47] On the other hand, the audience-directed adjustment also articulates the perspective the arguer in pursuing his strategic aims invites his audience to adopt. In choosing his arguments in an audience-directed way, for instance, the arguer may take into account that certain arguments among the candidates available for topical selection connect well with the starting points the audience is committed to and that choosing these particular arguments rather than other candidates creates strategically the kind of perspective on what really matters in the case concerned that he intends his audience to have. In Section 4.6, I shall discuss how framing this perspective can be strengthened by the use of presentational devices such as the stylistic figures and the choice of words.[48]

Adaptation to the audience takes place – in combination with handling the other aspects of strategic maneuvering – in all stages of an argumentative discourse. In the confrontation stage, adaptation to the audience may manifest itself, for example, in the avoidance of the articulation of unsolvable contradictions between the position of the party whose maneuvering is the focus of attention and the position of the other party, so that the disagreement between the two parties is limited to a non-mixed difference of opinion instead of a mixed one. In this connection, Perelman and Olbrechts-Tyteca (1958/1969) point out that one way of avoiding unsolvable contradictions is to

---

46. In examining audience adaptation in the various discussion stages systematically, the best policy is to start from the preparatory conditions for performing the types of speech acts by which the various argumentative moves are made that play a constructive part in resolving a difference of opinion on the merits. These conditions indicate, among other things, which requirements regarding the addressee must be satisfied for a correct performance of these speech acts, so that audience adaptation can be realized by ensuring and emphasizing their fulfillment.

47. Cf. Bell's (1984, 2001) "audience design" and the "accomodation theory" of Giles *et al.* (1991).

48. The concept of "framing" as it is used here is inspired by Goffman (1974/1986). See Section 4.7.

communicate a disagreement with respect to values as a difference of opinion over facts, because differences over facts are generally easier to accommodate. In the opening stage, adjustment to audience demand may consist in mentioning only material starting points the audience will have no problems with and which are at the same time helpful in putting the discussion of the standpoint at issue in a perspective that is favorable to the arguer. In the argumentation stage, choosing only those arguments that agree with the audience's sphere of interest may serve the same purpose. In the concluding stage, finally, adapting to the audience may involve sketching the result of the discussion in a way that avoids exasperating the audience by rubbing in those parts or consequences of the outcome that are not to its liking.

迎合受众需求分析的理论资源
4.5 Theoretical contributions to the analysis of adjusting to audience demand

Most authors examining what exactly is involved in adjusting to audience demand, the second aspect of strategic maneuvering I have distinguished, start from a rhetorical angle. Although my approach certainly shares some common ground with theirs, and the study of strategic maneuvering can benefit from studying their views more closely, there are also clear differences. I will first point out some commonalities and then mention some differences. Although insights from classical rhetoric can, again, be brought to bear, I concentrate in the first place on modern rhetorical or rhetorically-minded theoretical approaches relevant to the analysis of adjusting to audience demand. Dialectical insights I shall bring in by comparing, where this is due, the various classical and modern dialectical perspectives on argumentation with the pragma-dialectical approach. There seems to be general agreement among argumentation theorists from all persuasions[49] that paying attention to audience demand and to the ways in which argumentative discourse is adjusted to audience demand in order to bring the arguer's and the audience's perspectives into alignment is of vital importance to the study of argumentation. If one is interested, as pragma-dialecticians are, in how argumentative discourse is used to bring about conviction rather than mere persuasion,[50] the audience needs in this endeavor to be viewed as consisting in principle of reasonable people who are out to establish in a reasonable way whether the standpoints at issue are acceptable.

In their New Rhetoric, Perelman and Olbrechts-Tyteca (1958/1969) give the audience a central place because a speech must be heard, as a book must be read.[51]

---

49. Except, perhaps, for some of those argumentation theorists who are in the first place epistemologists and view argumentation purely from a specific epistemological perspective, such as Lumer (2007).

50. For the distinction between conviction and persuasion, see van Eemeren and Grootendorst (1984, pp. 48–49).

51. Among the numerous other authors who take it as their starting point that discourses are always addressed to an audience are Burke (1950/1969b), Bitzer (1968), and Bakhtin (1986).

According to Perelman and Olbrechts-Tyteca, the aim of argumentation is "to create or increase the adherence of minds to the theses presented for their assent" (p. 45).[52] This means that they start from the idea that argumentation is always addressed to an audience and that the quality of argumentation depends on its acceptability to the audience. According to Crosswhite (1996, p. 139), an ardent supporter of the New Rhetoric,[53] we are always "in audience," because "audience is a mode of being, one of the ways human beings *are*," "something that happens in time, as an event in people's lives, in their talking and writing and communicating in general." Tindale (2004), who connects with Crosswhite and also views argumentation as communication (p. 2),[54] takes a similar view as Perelman and Olbrechts-Tyteca. He recognizes that knowing the intended audience is of the utmost importance to providing a well-justified analysis of argumentative discourse. Replacing "mutual knowledge" or "shared information" by "shared cognitive environment," he observes that "where our cognitive environments overlap, they will give rise to a shared cognitive environment" (p. 22).

Though pragma-dialecticians may use other kinds of theoretical instruments in analyzing what adjusting to audience demand amounts to, they agree on this fundamental level with the authors just mentioned that argumentation is communication and that addressing the audience is a central feature of argumentation, if not – as Bakhtin (1986) would have it – its most telling feature.[55] Although Bakhtin, in my opinion, pushes his point too far when making the general claim that an argument is as it were "co-authored" by the arguer and the addressee,[56] as a dialectician I cannot but agree with him (and Tindale and other authors) when he ascribes an *active* role to the audience. In pragma-dialectics the audience is certainly not "a passive consumer of arguments," as Tindale (2004, p. 21) puts it, but engages actively in the argumentative discourse. This is already clear in the model of a critical discussion as far as the

---

52. As a rule, Perelman and Olbrechts-Tyteca observe, each party's efforts are directed at "assigning [...] the status enjoying the widest agreement to the elements on which he is basing his argument" (1958/1969, p. 179). This explains, for instance, why in the opening stage the status of a widely shared value judgment may be conferred on personal feelings and impressions, and the status of a fact on subjective values. In the argumentation stage, strategic adaptation to audience demand may be achieved by quoting arguments the other party is known to agree with or by referring to argumentative principles that party may be expected to adhere to.

53. See also Crosswhite (1993, 2000).

54. Pragma-dialecticians too view argumentation as communication, but their theoretical framework for studying argumentation as communication (van Eemeren & Grootendorst, 1992a) is pragmatic and considerably different from Crosswhite's and Tindale's.

55. According to Bakhtin (1986), only in dialogue utterances acquire their meaning. In his view, not sentences but utterances, which can only exist if there are both an author and an addressee, are the basic linguistic acts, which creates unclarity as to the theoretical status of his observations.

56. Tindale (2004, p. 103) summarizes Bakhtin's view succinctly by saying that the argument, "while having the arguer as its principal author," can be said to be "co-authored by the addressee."

interlocutor is concerned, but even more so if one considers the role of a "silent" audience (or readership) taking into account how argumentative texts that seem at first sight monological – Bakhtin speaks of "hidden dialogicality" – are reconstructed dialogically in a pragma-dialectical analysis. In addition, in an analysis of strategic maneuvering that takes place in argumentative discourse, in order to do justice to the aspect of audience demand, the changing commitment sets of both the arguer and his outspoken or silent antagonists are specified as they are at each point in the discourse the analysis focuses on (see Chapter 6).

Involving the audience as an active discussion partner in the reconstruction of argumentative discourse makes the analysis dialogical, and taking the commitment sets into account that have developed at a certain point in the resolution process makes it dynamic. In these respects the approach developed in pragma-dialectics, however different its theoretical orientation may be, is in line with Tindale's ambition "to capture and express the dynamics of argumentation as a communicative process" (2004, p. xi).[57] Tindale appeals to a Bakhtinian model of argumentation – which is to be constructed from observations Bakhtin makes scattered over his work – a model he considers dialogical "in the surest sense" (p. 25). Bakhtin's approach connects well with Tindale's own interest in "how audiences collaborate with arguers in an argumentative situation so as to invite reflection and self-persuasion rather than impose a view on passive minds" (p. xii). Since, according to Tindale (p. 103), for Bakhtin there seems no distinction "between the audience and the 'counter-opinions' that a discourse must answer," one might think that in this respect too Bakhtin and Tindale remain close to pragma-dialectics, but this is too optimistic a view.

Tindale observes, fully in line with pragma-dialectics, that "each contribution changes the context relevant for the judgment" (p. 49). In addition, however, he considers "the rhetorical audience," to be a "complex and fluid" idea, because "audiences change, even in the course of argumentation" (p. 21). Granting that in a psychological sense an audience may subtly change during the exchange, I prefer to speak only of a change of audience if the audience's nature and composition have changed in respects that are relevant to the analysis of argumentative discourse and strategic maneuvering. This is, in my view, the case if some or all of the active members of the audience (including new active members that have joined the audience during the exchange) are no longer committed to the same definition of the difference of opinion at issue (confrontation stage) or to the same starting points of the discussion (opening stage) as previously agreed upon. If during the argumentative exchange in the discussion (argumentation stage) active members of the audience have acquired more and other

---

57. According to Tindale, although it is often not recognized, "Rhetorical argumentation is dialogical. That is, there is a dynamic sense of dialogue alive in the context" (2004, p. 89). For pragma-dialecticians such a dialogical rhetoric, of course, just makes it easier to establish connections with their own (dialogical) theoretical framework than would be the case if it were monological.

commitments than were part of their commitment set earlier on I take it that it is not the audience that has changed, but the argumentative situation.[58]

Another difficult issue seems to be the "ontological status" of the audiences we are concentrating on. In the New Rhetoric, Perelman and Olbrechts-Tyteca distinguish between a "particular" audience, which consists of a specific collection of one or more people, and the "universal" audience, which is supposed to represent reasonableness (see the more detailed discussion in van Eemeren *et al.* 1996, pp. 93–128).[59] Although many scholars take the particular audience to have the ontological status of a concrete group of persons, however small or big this group in particular cases may be, Bakhtin (1986) and Tindale (2004, p. 118) seem to understand this audience as "constructed" by the speaker. In that sense, it would be on a par with the universal audience, which is generally understood to be a construction. Although Tindale follows Gross and Dearin (2002) in observing that the construction of an audience is "an operation of the imagination," he claims that it is "an imaginative operation *on* a real audience that exists" (2004, p. 148). He rejects the criticism that the universal audience is "no more than a product of the arguer" by observing that "given that both universal audiences and particular audiences are constructed on this reading, the difference lies in the focus of the discourse – on the real or the preferable" (p. 138).[60] Because Perelman and Olbrechts-Tyteca connect the universal audience emphatically with facts, truths, and presumptions and the particular audience with values,[61] value hierarchies and *loci*, I find the identification of a constructed universal audience with "the real" and a constructed particular audience with "the preferable" hard to accept: suggests an unjustified subjectivization of not only the universal audience and – *bien étonnés de se trouver ensemble* – values, value hierarchies and *loci*, but also of particular audiences and facts, truths and presumptions.[62]

Nevertheless Tindale comes up with a view of the relationship between the particular audience and the universal audience that is worth considering for those

---

58. An important advantage of concentrating in the first place on the commitment sets ensuing from the performance of the speech acts by means of which argumentative moves are made is in my view that the analysis is more precise and its results are more concrete.

59. Perelman and Olbrechts-Tyteca claim to expand Kant's notions of conviction and persuasion by associating persuasion with a particular audience and conviction with a universal audience (1958/1969, pp. 28–29).

60. From the fact that Crosswhite notes that "the universalizing interest of reason is essentially an ethical one" (1996, p. 154), Tindale concludes that "universal audiences embody the evaluative rather than the factual." (2004, p. 142).

61. To answer the question of what is acceptable to a universal audience, Perelman and Olbrechts-Tyteca refer to the concept of "presumptions," which are connected with what is normal and likely, because they are so well-accepted that they can be used as a starting point. Gaskins (1992, p. 34), however, criticizes presumptions for being "localized biases or prejudices, characteristic of discrete groups but certainly not binding on the community as a whole."

62. In my perception, this is an example of a tendency noticeable among some of Perelman and Olbrechts-Tyteca's adepts, to read more and other things into their text than they actually say.

interested in the critical dimension of a universal audience, by making a distinction between "the particular audience being addressed and the universal audience somehow lying within, or framed by, or participating in, that particular audience" (2004, p. 128). In Tindale's view, the universal audience "is not an abstraction but a populated community." Far from being "a transcendental concept born out of rationalism (Ray, 1978)," the universal audience is "a concrete audience that changes with time and the speaker's conception of it derives from its conceiver, conditioned by her or his milieu" (Tindale, 2004, p. 128). If a universal audience "is anchored by a real, particular audience," then "there are recognized means of accessing and evaluating the standard" (p. 154).[63] As a principle of "universalization," a universal audience provides shared standards of agreement by which to measure argumentation.[64] According to Tindale, it provides the details of "what is 'reasonable' in any particular case" (p. 133).

Tindale observes a parallel between the universal audience and Bakhtin's (1986) *superaddressee*, "who bridges the internal dialogism of a situation and what lies outside of it" (2004, pp. 116–117). Just like Perelman and Olbrechts-Tyteca, Bakhtin makes a distinction between a more concrete personalized and a more abstract audience: "Each dialogue takes place as if against the background of the responsive understanding of an invisibly present third party who stands above all the participants in the dialogue" and whose responsive understanding is presumed (1986, p. 126). Like Perelman and Olbrechts-Tyteca (van Eemeren et al., 1996, pp. 99–100), Bakhtin stresses that universality does not mean that there is any *outside* position involved, the superaddressee is "presupposed" by the author and "controlled by the author." The claim that the

---

63. Somewhat confusingly, Tindale also observes that "the universal audience might make judgments – by appealing to principles of logic that, if not timeless, certainly endure over time and transcend particular audiences" (2004, p. 139). He refers to Crosswhite in preparing his solution: "In each case, one begins with a particular audience on which imaginative operations are performed. Thus we might set aside the local features of an audience and consider its universal features. Or we might exclude from the particular audience all members who are prejudiced, or irrational, or incompetent. Or we might combine particular audiences so as to cancel out their particularity (eventually reaching all humanity)" (2004, p. 139). If argumentation addresses us simply as reasonable people, without recourse to the values of the group or religion, or other involvement, then we are addressed as a universal audience (Crosswhite, 1996, p. 141). From the point of view of evaluation, Tindale observes (pp. 140–141), "argumentation may address us through our particular involvements. [...] Here it speaks to a specific audience to which we belong. Thus Crosswhite recognizes the inextricable link between the universal and particular audiences and, combined with his previous insight, we can realize these as two aspects of our way of being as audience – particularly or universally."

64. According to Tindale, "it is not a matter of each arguer deciding the universal audience in some arbitrary way, such that there could be as many universal audiences as there are arguers. It is a matter of the argumentative context dictating to the arguer how the universal audience can be conceived, and the respondent or particular audience playing a co-authorizing role in that decision. The argumentative context imposes clear constraints on the freedom of the arguer" (2004, p. 129).

superaddressee is not another voice, but represents an "extension of the author" poses in my view serious problems to any claim concerning the identification of the superaddressee with reasonableness (cf. van Eemeren *et al.*, 1996, pp. 119–120).[65]

Speaking about the kind of problems involved, Pareto (1935) skeptically puts forward that "the universal consensus invoked is often merely the unwarranted generalization of an individual intuition" (Perelman & Olbrechts-Tyteca, 1958/1969, p. 33). Tindale is fully aware of such criticisms. He acknowledges that there are serious concerns with regard to the universal audience, both with regard to "the vagueness of the concept itself, the details of its nature and its relationship to the particular audience" and with regard to its applicability – "its usefulness for a range of matters that occupy those interested in argumentation" (2004, p. 136). In his opinion, however, the universal audience "meets the central demands we must make of any third-person objective standard: (1) there must be a real source standing behind the "abstract" standard, and (2) there must be "some recognized means of accessing and evaluating that standard." In his interpretation, the universal audience is "more than just a projection of the arguer," because it meets standard (1) "in that it lies in, and is derived from, the standard of reasonableness that is alive in a real particular audience,"[66] and standard (2) in that "a real particular audience can be accessed and its ideas evaluated" (pp. 129–130).[67] In reaching this conclusion, Tindale (p. 157) leans on Crosswhite (1996, p. 115), who conveniently assumes that what we mean by the judgments of a universal audience are the principles of reason as seen in logical principles and rules, so that it is logic in the end that gives us "real universalizability."

策略操控的呈现方式选择
4.6 Presentational choices in strategic maneuvering

The third aspect of strategic maneuvering we have distinguished, the exploitation of presentational devices, pertains to the communicative means that are used in presenting the argumentative moves constituting a piece of strategic maneuvering. When maneuvering strategically, speakers or writers are not just trying to make the argumentative moves that suit them well and agree with audience demand, but they also make an effort

---

65. Contrary to Tindale's claim (2004, p. 127), the superaddressee does not fulfill a function similar to Blair and Johnson's (1987, p. 50) "community of model interlocutors."

66. Tindale reads Bakhtin as dealing with "a model that is *found in* the argumentative context, a constituent of the essential utterance and not merely a reflection of the author or arguer" (2004, p. 127).

67. In indicating his standard, Tindale opines that the achievement of agreement of understanding "is, arguably, a better measure than the correctness of arguments gauged through the instruments of validity and soundness" (2004, pp. 112–113). In the emphasis on understanding Tindale follows Bakhtin (1986, 150), who contrasts the mutual understanding of dialogism and the monologic rhetoric with persuasion aimed at the "complete victory and destruction of the opponent."

to present their moves in a specific way. In all stages of the discourse their presentation of the moves may be assumed to be systematically attuned to achieving the strategic purposes they are aiming for.[68] This means that in analyzing strategic maneuvering it is worthwhile to take due account of the presentational choices that have been made.

Speaking of "presentational choices" presupposes that when presenting argumentative moves arguers have some kind of communicative (or, more specifically, linguistic) repertoire available to choose from. In a very general sense this is indeed the case, because in principle one can always express the things one chooses to communicate in various ways, linguistically or otherwise. However, recognizing the unbreakable connection between expression and content observed already in antiquity (*vide* Cicero's (1942, Trans. version) view of *verbum* and *res*), my starting point is that whenever something is at one time expressed differently than it was expressed at another time it is pragmatically no longer "the same thing," because – however subtle – there is automatically a difference in meaning, if only because different expressions have different connotations. In human communication – this too has been clear since antiquity – there is always room for making presentational choices and expressing whatever one wants to say in pragmatically different ways, even if their reference remains "the same." When speaking of making presentational choices in strategic maneuvering I am referring to utilizing the pragmatic room for presentational variation to steer the discourse toward the achievement of certain communicative and interactional effects.

Exploiting the possibilities of presentational variation in strategic maneuvering in agreement with one's topical choices and adjustments to audience demand boils down, in my view, to "framing" one's argumentative moves in a communicatively and interactionally functional way (Goffman, 1974/1986). As regards the stylistic dimension, Dascal and Gross (1999) observe that there is a possibility of variation at two levels.[69] There is room for making a choice from the available repertoire of language varieties or "registers" at the level at which "discourse is pitched" (such as Queen's English and Cockney English) and there is room for making a choice at the level of "semantic, syntactic, and prosodic variants within that register" (p. 122). I elaborate on Dascal and Gross' characterization by explicitly taking account of the pragmatic dimension of stylistic variation and describing stylistic choices in strategic maneuvering as functional selections from the available repertoire of presentational options, both at the level of registers-as-linguistic-varieties and at the level of variants within a register. Strategically, like all other strategic choices, each stylistic choice serves the purpose of framing the argumentative move that is made in such a way that it introduces a

---

68. I agree with Perelman and Olbrechts-Tyteca that all argumentative discourse presupposes "a choice consisting not only of the selection of elements to be used, but also of the technique for their presentation" (1958/1969, p. 119).

69. Dascal and Gross made this observation in an article pursuing their interest in "a union of pragmatics and rhetoric" (1999, p. 107).

particular perspective. In argumentative discourse such choices have to be made in every argumentative move.

Although in strategic maneuvering it may be more conspicuous which stylistic choice is made in one case than in another, cases that are stylistically "neutral" do not exist, so each choice always has an extra meaning (which is sometimes referred to as "symbolic"). If in a certain case the presentational choice made gives the appearance of being stylistically neutral, this impression is in fact just as much the result of a presentational choice – functioning to achieve a strategic purpose by giving the move concerned a particular appearance – as it is in the more conspicuous cases. It can therefore be maintained that presentational choices are always stylistically marked. This means that they have in all cases certain discernible (but not always obvious) features which associate them with the achievement of certain communicative and interactional effects that give the argumentative move concerned a strategic function.

A basic distinction I propose to make in analyzing the strategic function of presentational choices in general is that between *explicit* and *implicit* presentations of argumentative moves. When viewing the argumentative moves that are made in terms of speech act theory the explicit-implicit distinction applies both to the presentation of the communicative function and the presentation of the propositional content of the speech acts by means of which an argumentative move is conveyed. A concession, for instance, that is made in the opening stage of the exchange may be explicitly presented as a concession, but its communicative function can also be indicated only implicitly. The same applies to the propositional content of the concession, which can be fully explicit or partly implicit.

Another basic distinction I propose to make is that between *direct* and *indirect* presentations of argumentative moves. Except when triggering a Gricean implicature, explicit presentations are always direct, but implicit presentations of argumentative moves may be direct or indirect. Implicit presentations are indirect if, in the context in which the move concerned is made, the communicative function or the propositional content of the speech act conveying the move is only a secondary function or content of the speech act that is literally performed whereas the primary function or content of the speech act is a different one. This is, for instance, the case when a standpoint is presented as having the communicative function of an expressive ("What a beautiful movie!") but is later defended by means of argumentation, so that it becomes clear that it is a standpoint after all, or if it is clear from the context that (the propositional content of) an apparent reason put forward in the argumentation is not to be taken literally because the utterance is ironic ("I should join the demonstration, since I really love to be in a crowd").

In making presentational choices that manifest themselves in the discourse in a marked fashion, the Gricean Maxim of Manner (Grice 1989, pp. 33–37) is exploited in a specific way, often in combination with other Maxims, to achieve certain communicative and interactional effects that serve a strategic function. Expressing oneself in a specific way is identified by Anscombre and Ducrot with giving orientation (1983, p. i) – or, as Anscombre (1994, p. 30) puts it, guiding the discourse into a certain direction ["diriger le discourse dans une certaine direction"]. Leading the discourse into a certain direction is something that can be achieved by "formal" presentational means whose effect is due to their appearance ("form"), but also by "informal" presentational means, whose effect depends on the content, or by a combination of both types of presentational means. Evident examples of formal ("syntactic") devices for a marked presentation are repetition, subordination, and paratactic, and hypotactic constructions. Among the clearest examples of informal ("semantic") devices are the "tropes," the various kinds of metaphor and metonymy characterized by a change of meaning involving a substitution of concepts. Easily recognizable examples of context-dependent combined formal-informal ("pragmatic") devices are, for instance, rhetorical questions, which have the grammatical form of a question but cannot be merely a question in the context concerned.

The stylistic means that can be exploited as presentational devices in strategic maneuvering in argumentative discourse include in the first place the various "figures" of speech and thought that are distinguished in classical and modern dialectic and rhetoric.[70] Perelman and Olbrechts-Tyteca regard such figures as argumentative if they bring about a "change of perspective" (1958/1969, p. 169), which is fully in line with the approach I am taking here. Depending on the stage the argumentative exchange has reached, a great many figures can be put to such argumentatively profitable use. As various authors have shown, this applies, for instance, to *praeteritio, conciliatio, metalepsis*, and rhetorical questions[71] (see Reboul, 1989; Rocci, 2009; Snoeck Henkemans, 2009). The study of presentational choices made in argumentative discourse by the use of figures (Fahnestock, 1999, 2005, 2009) can therefore be a helpful tool in analyzing the strategic maneuvering that takes place.[72]

Presentational choices that can be made in strategic maneuvering in the confrontation stage of an argumentative exchange may, for the listener addressed by the protagonist of a standpoint, include not making explicit his position with regard to the standpoint that has been advanced, so that the difference of opinion does not become unnecessarily or prematurely mixed. In the opening stage the protagonist can, for instance, maneuver strategically by presenting his starting points by using a metaphor that is likely to appeal to the audience. This is, in fact, what Senator Edward Kennedy did in his Chappaquiddick speech when he said that he had wanted to make it clear to the now deceased Mary Joe

---

70. There is a drift in the definition of some figures, as Poster (2000) observes, that hinders the authorization of any one historical characterization of the figures as the correct one.

71. In an interesting note, after mentioning the rhetorical question (*erotema*) Fahnestock (1999, p. 196, note 5) points to "its forgotten siblings, such as asking *and* answering a question (*hypophora*) or answering a question different from the question asked: 'Did you strike the victim?' 'He hit me first.'" See also Fahnestock (2009, pp. 198–199).

72. For a useful overview of ancient and contemporary treatments of figures of speech (also called "rhetorical figures" and "figures of rhetoric"), including both tropes and figures of speech in the narrow sense, see Kienpointner (1999).

Kopechne and the other secretaries that they "still had a home with the Kennedy family." By doing so and by describing the party he and Kopechne had attended by means of another presentational choice as a "cook-out" organized for secretaries who had worked for his deceased brother Robert and were devoted to him, he suggested by presentational means that the (extented) "family" party had offered only clean American outdoor pleasure, with hamburgers from the grill and similar attractions, thus excluding any association with the kind of parties where sexual misconduct could flourish. Among the presentational choices that can be appropriate in the argumentation stage are, for instance, presenting all the arguments advanced in defense of one's standpoint explicitly and numbered, so that the rigor and quantity of the reasons that speak in favor of the standpoint may seem overwhelming. In the concluding stage, a strategic presentational choice the party who claims to have won the discussion could make is to present his claim matter of factly, in a restrained manner, so that the outcome of the discussion is not rubbed in.

呈现方式分析的理论资源
4.7 Theoretical contributions to the analysis of presentational choices

A great many authors have examined the presentational choices that can be made in discourse, including argumentative discourse. In most cases they start from a rhetorical, literary or linguistic perspective. Invariably, the origins of their studies can be traced back to classical rhetoric. Only in some cases is classical dialectic also mentioned. In spite of the common origins, there is some variation in the way they approach presentational devices. In a great many cases the authors just provide a list of figures, explain their meaning and give some examples of how they are used taken from the kind of communicative practice they are particularly interested in, which is often literary or oratory.[73] In some cases, however, they make an effort to develop a coherent theoretical view on presentational devices or provide an explanation of how presentational devices can be viewed from a specific angle. Since Fahnestock combines in her work all these aims and ambitions while concentrating on the use of presentational devices for argumentative purposes, I think her insights deserve special attention. Because of my preoccupation with the analysis of presentational choices in strategic maneuvering, I am particularly interested in her concern with the "technique" of rhetoric, especially with regard to the expression of certain "well-used lines of argument" in "certain linguistic constructions called *figures of speech*" (1999, p. 8).[74]

---

73. A Dutch example is van Alphen *et al.* (1996), but similar examples can be found in a great many other languages.

74. According to Fahnestock, definitions of the figures as departures from acceptable usage or from statistically normal usage or even from "simple" usage all carry with them the underlying concept that the figure is "a substitution for another linguistic choice." "Thus, one consistent corollary of these definitions has been," she observes, "an implicit division of language into two domains, the literal and the figurative" (1999, p. 17).

Among Fahnestock's (2009, pp. 193–197) sources are not only manuals written by scholars representing the classical rhetorical tradition and classical and early modern grammars of Greek and Latin,[75] but also manuals of literary stylistics, ad hoc studies of significant word choices in a specific area, and – above all – "offshoots" of modern linguistics such as pragmatics, (critical) discourse analysis, and sociolinguistics that draw, much like the pragma-dialecticians do, on insights derived from ordinary language philosophy. Among her modern predecessors more specifically interested in the use of presentational devices for argumentative purposes are Perelman and Olbrechts-Tyteca (1958/1969), Burke (1945/1969a), and Reboul (1989).

In the New Rhetoric the emphasis is on the effects of the figures. The figures are considered argumentative only if they have a recognized structure that is codified, and bring about "a change of perspective" while "its use seems normal in relation to this new situation" (Perelman & Olbrechts-Tyteca, 1958/1969, p. 169). If the figure "does not bring about the adherence of the hearer to this argumentative form, the figure will be considered an embellishment, a figure of style" (p. 169). Perelman and Olbrechts-Tyteca add that "it is apparent, then, that it is impossible to decide in advance if a given structure is or is not to be regarded as a figure, or if it will be an argumentative or a stylistic figure" (1958/1969, pp. 169–170). Therefore, I am inclined to conclude that in the New Rhetoric a figure is considered "argumentative" only if it has proven to be rhetorically effective with regard to an audience; otherwise it is just an embellishment and called a "figure of style." However, because in the New Rhetoric effectiveness does not necessarily mean persuasiveness, Fahnestock (1999, p. 198, note 12) issues a warning by quoting Perelman and Olbrechts-Tyteca: "a figure may be seen as argumentative without its necessarily bringing about adherence to the conclusions of the discourse; all that is required is that the argument should be seen in its full value" (1958/1969, p. 170). She concludes, rightly, that "The New Rhetoric's redefinition of the figures [...] is highly problematic to the extent that it links the figures to an untraceable psychological experience" (p. 36).[76]

Reboul (1989) considers a figure "rhetorical" only to the extent that it contributes to persuading, which is in his view the goal of argumentation (p. 61). He wonders in what ways figures facilitate argumentation, and raises the fundamental questions whether the figure itself can constitute an argument and whether argument is not itself a figure "more or less" (1989, p. 170). A metaphor, for instance, is viewed as an argument, he observes, insofar as it is a condensed analogy (p. 176). A figure is an argument, Reboul concludes, "as soon as it is impossible to translate, paraphrase or

---

75. Advantages Fahnestock sees in recovering the older rhetorical stylistics are that "the language devices it identifies are already linked suggestively to argument strategies," and that the treatment of such devices, "particularly in the early modern manuals," is "both voluminous and precise" (2009, p. 195).

76. As Fahnestock (2009, p. 204) explains, "it is really better to operate with two great catalogs, one of argumentative moves and one of linguistic devices."

otherwise express it without weakening it" (1989, p. 181). In fact, his position comes close to Burke's (1950/1969b) in *A Rhetoric of Motives*. Fahnestock indicates that she, in turn, follows Burke in considering figures "to be able to express a particular line of argument and simultaneously to induce an audience to participate in that argument simply by virtue of their form" (1999, p. 34).

In the classical system of figures three broad categories are distinguished: (1) the figures of speech (including devices of word arrangement and patterning), (2) the tropes involving a transference of meaning, and (3) the figures of thought (representing interaction gestures and either the speaker's "illocutionary" [communicative] intent or the desired "perlocutionary" [interactional] effect or both) (Fahnestock, 1999, pp. 10–11).[77] Fahnestock rightly observes that some definitions of figures of speech given in the rhetorical manuals hinge primarily on formal features, others on the presumed effects of these devices (1999, p. ix). Although the grouping of figures shifts from manual to manual, the actual devices listed remain "surprisingly consistent" (p. 14). According to Fahnestock, however, the compilers of the figures are codifying two different things: verbal forms and discourse functions or speech acts, whereas, ideally, the placing of a figure requires both (p. 14). She refers to Melanchthon as a rhetorical (and dialectical) scholar who is grouping according to both principles, one formal, based on the semantic or syntactic change involved, and one functional, based on what the devices should communicate or achieve for the speaker (p. 12).[78]

In *Rhetorical Figures in Science*, Fahnestock (1999) sets out to "help to establish the centrality of the figures of speech in rhetorical theory." She motivates this ambition by stating that "these widely used devices epitomize fundamental mental operations" (p. xi).[79] After acknowledging that "this point has certainly been made for metaphor," she explains that it "needs to be extended to other figures so that they are no longer seen as decoration on the plain cloth of language but as the fabric itself" (p. xi). As she puts it succinctly, "a style argues" (p. xii). According to Fahnestock, "the figures epitomize lines of argument that have great applicability and durability" (p. xi-xii). Understanding the figures as epitomes of certain lines of argument requires also "reinstating these durable, completely general lines" (p. 24). Just as metaphor can be viewed as an epitome of analogical reasoning, so are certain other figures linked to corresponding modes of reasoning.

---

77. As Fahnestock points out, this division of the figures of speech as syntactic, the tropes as semantic, and the figures of thought as pragmatic "holds only roughly" (1999, p. 11).

78. According to Fahnestock (2009, p. 192), Melanchthon's vision of the "deep interdependence between dialectic and rhetoric may have come from his Biblical hermeneutics." Melanchthon "understood that language manipulation was at the center of all three arts. So he included sections in his rhetoric on the tie-in with dialectic and specifically linked figures of speech to different topoi."

79. Fahnestock (1999, p. 24) explains that the Greek verb *epitome* means "to cut short or cut upon." The figure, then, is "a verbal summary that epitomizes a line of reasoning."

Fahnestock claims that a small group of figures can be identified with certain forms of argument or reasoning, and scrutinizes several of them in her study. She discusses, for instance, examples of argumentative strategies epitomized by the figures *incrementum* and *gradiatio* that can, she claims, be found "in virtually any argument field" (p. 98). According to Fahnestock, "these lines of argument are truly common topics, based ultimately in the dialectical tradition of arguing from the more or the less" (p. 98). The *antimetabole*, to mention just one more figure discussed by her, "epitomizes arguments concerning reciprocal causality, a causal influence that goes in opposition directions, or a reversible process:" A causes B, B causes A (p. 141). The figure enables a slippage from definition to causal argument or from causal argument to definition. Fahnestock shows how Pasteur's use of *antimetabole* ("Life is the germ and the germ is life") allowed him "a certain useful ambiguity in the implications of his argument" (p. 140).[80]

Fahnestock's study of the figures makes clear that certain figures are associated with general lines of argument known as "topics" in the rhetorical tradition. Since the understanding of the figures as epitomes of lines of argument has been recovered, a whole repertoire of lines of argument comes in view that is part of rhetoric as well as dialectic, "its sister art of practical reasoning" (p. 24). Fahnestock (1999, p. 24) acknowledges that twentieth-century historians of rhetoric, such as Murphy (1990), have been aware of the intimate connection between the figures and the topics or lines of argument. Kibédi Varga (1983, p. 86) draws a practical consequence of this awareness: "Every *figure* should be defined as part of elocution, but at the same time it should be mentioned in relation to the topic within which it usually appears and functions, in the chapter on invention."

Because they promote acceptance, figures always have in principle a rhetorical function, not per se a dialectical one; but in certain cases they have a dialectical function as well. Just as Burke (1945/1969a) viewed the rhetorical devices as unifying speaker and audience, Fahnestock unites the presentational aspect through her study of the rhetorical figures that also have a dialectical function with the other two aspects of the conduct of argumentative discourse I have distinguished in the strategic maneuvering triangle, topical choice and adaptation to audience demand. The close intertwinement she recognizes corresponds to the interrelationship between the three aspects the triangle indicates. Although it is structured and intended differently, a similar intertwinement of the three aspects, starting from the presentational aspect, can be

---

80. Fahnestock also discusses *antithesis*, *ploch*, and *polyptoton*. According to Tindale (2004, p. 59), "we can go further than Fahnestock and show that figures do not just facilitate arguments; in some cases they *are* arguments." In his opinion, "many rhetorical figures are particularly suited to serve as arguments in rhetorical argumentation" because of the ways in which they are "constructed to engage the audience through their experiential nature and collaborative invitation" (p. 85). Rhetorical arguments "drawn from figures" can be effective, Tindale claims, not just in persuading an audience, but in "engaging them at a quite deep, often emotional level, before reason moves in as an organizing force" (p. 86).

found in the modern concept of "framing" that is widely used in the social sciences and in discourse analysis.

Framing uses presentational devices to call attention to particular facets of the matter at issue and simultaneously to direct attention away from other facets (cf. Kahneman & Tversky, 2000). Framing always involves an interpretation of reality that puts the facts or events referred to in a certain perspective. Viewed rhetorically, it amounts to creating a context by verbal means in which what is put forward makes sense to the audience in a way that is in agreement with the speaker's or writer's intentions. As a rule, framing is linked to a specific issue. Menashe and Siegel (1998) for instance, examined the framing of the smoking issue. They compared the framing of this issue by the tobacco industry and by the health campaigners of the tobacco control movement in research that examined 300 newspaper articles. Framing can be identified via "framing devices," which are the presentational means that are used to create an effective text; for example, the device of portraying the relationship between a boss and his employees as a family relationship between an uncle and his cousins. In a text, the devices manifest themselves not only in the choice of words and the rhetorical figures that are used, but also between the lines, and they can be identified through accurate observation. Pan and Kosicki (1993) have distinguished in news discourse framing devices having to do with syntactical structure, script structure, thematic structure, and rhetorical structure.

If it is successful, framing creates social facts. This happened, for instance, when President Bush framed the response to the September 11 attacks as waging a "war on terror," so that (at least for some time) the events of September 11 and their aftermath came to be viewed from the military perspective of a collaborative and necessary joint fight against a well-defined army of dangerous enemies that should lead to the downfall and surrender of the enemies. Greco Morasso rightly observes that "the linguistic characterization of reality is never neutral, because the definition that one gives of an issue is always deeply connected with the interpretation of that issue and, thus, with the value attributed to it" (2009, p. 76). Frame analysis, she says, has the merit of highlighting this. Goffman (1974/1986), the first theoretician of framing, viewed frames as cognitive resources through which people interpret and organize reality which are linked to the culture in which they are used and co-determine social reality in that culture. Since different cultures use different frames, the identification of frames is culture-bound – or in any case, I would say, bound to a particular domain of communicative activity. In studying mediation, Drake and Donohue define a frame in that macro-context as "the particular quality assigned [to] an issue" by linguistic choices made by the mediator (1996, p. 301).[81] Greco Morasso refers to the parties' implicit agreement upon using the same frames for referring to the dispute issues in mediation

---

81. Zarefsky (1986/2005), dealing with persuasion in a political context, seems to assign the power of framing in the first place to (rhetorical) definitions: "the power to persuade is, in a large measure, the power to define" (p. 1).

as "frame convergence" (2009, p. 78). Sometimes "reframing tactics" are used to put already given information in "a more durable form" (Donohue, Allen & Burell, 1988). In their efforts to put an end to the disagreement between the parties, mediators, for instance, often reframe issues for the parties by introducing "a different way to make sense of the same circumstances" (Gray, 2006, p. 195).

CHAPTER 5 第五章

惯例化交际实践中的策略操控
Strategic maneuvering in conventionalized communicative practices

不同交际活动领域中的论辩话题
5.1 Argumentative discourse in different domains of communicative activity

In the study of argumentation the term *argumentation* is not merely used to refer to a theoretical concept given shape in analytical models such as the ideal model of a critical discussion, but also, and even in the first place, to refer to an empirical phenomenon that can be observed in a multitude of communicative practices which are recognized as such by the arguers. Because these communicative practices are generally connected with specific kinds of institutional contexts in which they serve certain purposes that are pertinent to the *raison d'être* of the institution – i.e. purposes relevant to realizing the "institutional point" or rationale of the communicative practices concerned – they have become conventionalized in accordance with different kinds of requirements.[1] Due to this context-dependency of communicative practices, the possibilities for strategic maneuvering in argumentative discourse in such practices are in some respects determined by the institutional *preconditions* prevailing in the communicative practice concerned. This makes it necessary to situate the analysis and evaluation of strategic maneuvering in the macro-context of the "communicative activity type" in which it takes place.[2]

In this chapter, I will explain how, in my view, the relationship between strategic maneuvering and the macro-context of a communicative activity type can be captured. For

---

1. I use the terms *institution*, *institutional* and *institutionalized* in a very broad sense, so that they do not only refer to the formally established organizations of the law, administration, and schools, let alone just to those of prisons, mental clinics and the army, but to all socially and culturally established macro-contexts, irrespective of whether they are part of the personal, the technical or the public sphere, in which certain (formally or informally) conventionalized communicative practices have developed, including, for instance, the macro-contexts of commerce, public entertainment, and interpersonal relations. Like Searle (1995), I envision institutions as systems for dealing with rights and duties characterized by socially constructed rules and their associated sanctions.

2. This notion of activity types was introduced in van Eemeren and Houtlosser (2005b), which inspired this chapter. Earlier, Levinson used the term *activity type* in the related meaning of a "fuzzy category whose focal members are goal-defined, socially constituted, bounded, events with constraints on participants, setting, and so on, but above all on the kinds of allowable contributions" (1992, p. 69).

this purpose I first discuss a kindred theoretical approach to argumentation in context that was proposed by Walton in collaboration with Krabbe. In sketching next my own approach to the macro-contexts for strategic maneuvering I shall make clear how communicative activity types can be characterized argumentatively by relating them, where this is appropriate, systematically with the pragma-dialectical model of a critical discussion. This characterization provides the point of departure for tracing methodically the institutional preconditions pertaining to strategic maneuvering in the various communicative activity types because it points out the ways a certain communicative activity type is conventionalized in a manner pertinent to the conduct of argumentative discourse. As an illustration of the impact institutional preconditions can have on the strategic maneuvering in a specific communicative activity type I discuss in Section 5.7 an example of confrontational strategic maneuvering in a communicative activity type from the political domain.

In accordance with the institutional requirements that need to be satisfied, different kinds of conventionalized communicative practices have developed in the various communicative domains.[3] In principle, the institutionally determined conventions are always instrumentally related to the exigencies that caused the communicative practices concerned to come into being. These exigencies constitute in a sense the rationales of the communicative practices. Without aiming in any way for completeness, or even mutual exclusiveness, I mention by way of example some communicative domains in which certain generally recognized conventionalized communicative practices have become established: the domain of legal communication, which fosters some highly formalized conventionalized communicative practices; the domain of political communication, which has a number of communicative practices that are to a lesser degree formally conventionalized; the domain of interpersonal communication, which has communicative practices that may give on first sight the impression of lacking any conventionalization but are on second sight to some extent informally conventionalized.[4] Other communicative domains with conventionalized practices are, for example, the scholarly, the medical, the commercial, the problem-solving, and the diplomatic domain.

In aiming for a description of the way in which communicative practices are conventionalized, my starting point is that every communicative practice that can be recognized as such may be assumed to be characterized by a certain degree of conventionalization that is dependent on the institutional rationale – the institutional point – of the communicative practice concerned.[5] In other words, I believe that when

---

3. Instead of talking about communicative domains, Goodnight (1982) and other scholars inspired by Habermas (for an overview, see Gronbeck, 1989) distinguish between three communicative *spheres* (personal, technical, public), each of which includes a number of communicative domains. Rigotti and Rocci (2006) refer to *interaction fields* instead of domains of communication.

4. The terms *convention*, *conventionalized* and *conventionalization* are in this study used in accordance with the concept of convention introduced in van Eemeren and Grootendorst (1984, p. 59).

5. I believe my approach connects with "rational choice institutionalism" as practiced in political science, economics, anthropology and sociology within New Institutionalism. In dealing

tracking down the specific conventionalization of communicative practices it is useful to take as one's point of departure that the communicative practices that can be distinguished in each of the various communicative domains are conventionalized in a way that is dependent on precisely which function the practice has to fulfill in realizing its institutional point. Thus the conventionalization of court proceedings or a summons in the domain of legal communication is instrumental in realizing the institutional point of maintaining justice; the conventionalization of a presidential debate or a political interview in the domain of political communication is similarly instrumental in realizing the institutional point of preserving a democratic culture; etc.

When analyzing particular specimens of communicative activity it is necessary, in order to be able to take the different ways of conventionalization in the various communicative practices into account, to connect each token of communicative activity with the communicative activity type it is a specimen of. The defense pleading for O.J. Simpson delivered during the latter's famous murder trial, for instance, is to be viewed as part of a specimen of American court proceedings in a criminal case,[6] and the 1960 television debate between Richard Nixon and John Kennedy as a specimen of a presidential debate. These examples can be easily expanded with specimens of communicative activity types from the scholarly, the medical, the interpersonal, the commercial, the problem-solving, the diplomatic domain, etc.

语境中论辩理论分析
5.2 The theoretical treatment of argumentation in context

The problem of how to conceptualize the macro-contextual dimension of argumentation has led Walton and Krabbe (1995) to propose a theoretical treatment of

---

with the question of how to construe the relationship between institutions and behavior, New Institutionalism emphasizes the relative autonomy of political institutions and the importance of symbolic action (March & Olsen, 1984, p. 734). According to Hall and Taylor, rational choice institutionalism draws our attention to "the role that strategic interaction between actors plays in the determination of political outcomes" (1996, p. 951). Generally this approach is "functionalist" in the sense of explaining the origins of an institution largely in terms of the effects that follow from its existence, but also "intentionalist" in the sense of assuming that the process of institutional creation is a purposive one, whereas its analyses are "voluntarist" in the sense that they tend to view institutional creation as a quasi-contractual process marked by voluntary agreement among relatively equal and independent actors (Hall & Taylor, 1996, p. 952).

6. The fact that Simpson was not convicted of murder in the criminal court case but was later, based on virtually the same evidence, considered guilty of murder in a civil court case is a good illustration that even within the same genre of communicative activity the preconditions for argumentative discourse may vary from communicative activity type to communicative activity type. I thank Davida Charney for drawing my attention to this striking example of a different appreciation of evidence in different macro-contexts when I discussed the O. J. Simpson case in a lecture on strategic maneuvering at Bar-Ilan University, Israel, on March 24, 2009.

argumentation in context that has some ground in common with the theoretical approach of the macro-contextual dimension of argumentation I have developed with Houtlosser.[7] Therefore it may be enlightening to have the exposition of our account preceded by a brief discussion of Walton and Krabbe's approach of the contextuality of argumentation,[8] which centers on the concept of "dialogue types" as "conversational contexts of argument."[9]

The roots of Walton and Krabbe's approach can be traced back to Lorenzen's "systems of dialogue rules" pertaining to game-like and self-contained dialogues defined by the goal of the game and regulated by strict logical rules determining how this goal can be reached in an acceptable way.[10] As Walton and Krabbe observe, such systems had to provide solutions to problems of logic and mathematics: "Each system of dialogue (or dialectical system) defines its own concept of logical consequence (its concept of validity, its 'logic')" (1995, p. 4). An important step from such abstract constructs to actual arguments had already been made by Hamblin, who was not aware of Lorenzen's dialogue logic, but introduced the related concept of a *dialectical system* and argued "that such dialectical systems could be used to model contexts of dialogue in which argumentation takes place in everyday conversation of various kinds" (Walton & Krabbe, 1995, p. 5). Despite this move toward argumentative reality, however, the goal of such modeling was decidedly normative – dialectical systems were to help the analysts to "justify critical judgments that an argument in a real case is fallacious or nonfallacious" (Walton & Krabbe, 1995, p. 5).

This theoretical backdrop enables us to get a clearer picture of how Walton (this time without Krabbe) seeks to use their types of dialogue to extend the formal approach to the rich context of ordinary argumentation:

> The key here is that the concept of dialogue has to be seen as a context or enveloping framework into which arguments are fitted so they can be judged as appropriate or not in that context. So the concept of dialogue needs to be normative: it needs to prescribe how an argument ought to be used in order to fit in as

---

7. For an approach to argumentation in context closely associated with pragma-dialectics in which the specific conditions imposed on argumentative discourse in a specific argumentative context are described in terms of design, see Jacobs and Aakhus (2002), Aakhus (2003), and Jackson and Jacobs (2006). Unlike in the case of Walton and Krabbe's approach, there are no major differences that need to be spelled out here.

8. This section is to a large extent based on van Eemeren *et al.* (forthcoming).

9. Walton argues that the concept of dialogue types revives in fact – as so often happens in the study of argumentation – a classical Aristotelian idea, viz., that the soundness or fallaciousness of argumentation depends not just on form, but on the context of dialogue (1992, p. 143). One may add that Aristotle developed a rhetorically-minded conceptualization of the contexts of argumentation in his division of the deliberative, the forensic and the epideictic genre.

10. According to Walton and Krabbe, "a good argument is one that contributes to a goal of the type of dialogue in which that argument was put forward" (1995, p. 2).

appropriate, and to be used rightly or correctly (as well as incorrectly, in some cases). But the concept of dialogue also needs to fit the typical conversational settings in which such arguments are conventionally used to make a point in everyday argumentative verbal exchanges (Walton, 1998b, p. 29).

Thus Walton provides a characterization that attributes both "normative" and "conventionalized" qualities to dialogue types. This is how he summarizes his concept of dialogue:[11]

> The concept of a dialogue [...] is that of a conventionalized, purposive joint activity between two parties (in the simplest case), where the parties act as speech partners. It is meant by this that the two parties exchange verbal messages or so-called speech acts that take the form of moves in a game-like sequence of exchanges (1998b, p. 29).

Such a characterization gives this theoretical concept a double function. Not only should dialogues prescribe which argumentative behavior is correct, or reasonable, within the bounds of a well-delineated language game, but they also have to mirror in their structure "the typical conversational settings" or – as Hymes (1972) calls them – "speech events" that are characteristic of a given communicative reality. As used by Walton, the notion of context is limited to dialogue types understood as rule-governed and generic conversational entities.[12]

Walton and Krabbe organize the plurality of dialogues types they observe in a typology of six "general types" (1995, p. 66): *persuasion dialogue* (or – as they confusingly add[13] – *critical discussion*), *negotiation, inquiry, deliberation, information-seeking dialogue*, and *eristics*. These types of dialogues are primarily distinguished through their main goals: "resolution of [...] conflicts by verbal means" (critical discussion), "making a deal" (negotiation), "reaching a (provisional) accommodation in a relationship" (eristics), etc. Next, the six basic types differ as regards the initial situation, the participants' aims (not to be confused with the goal of a dialogue as such), and the side benefits of each.

---

11. According to Walton, each dialogue type constitutes a separate normative model of argumentation, with its own specific rules prescribing what good and fallacious argumentation is. Thus Walton proposes a "postmodern and relativistic standard of rationality" (1998b, p. 30). Cf. Lewiński (2010).

12. Recently, Walton and Macagno introduced a notion of "dialogue context" referring to "a broader notion of dialogue," which includes, among other things, "common ground," "interpersonal relationship," and "social constraints" between arguers (2007, p. 110). This approach extends the contextual considerations pertinent to argumentation analysis and evaluation beyond the goal-directed and rule-governed structure of the dialogue types, bringing Walton's theoretical framework closer to being a rhetorical perspective.

13. Confusingly, because in pragma-dialectics the term *critical discussion* has been in use for many years to refer to a theoretical construct rather than a communicative activity type or dialogue type, and in using the term *critical discussion* Walton and Krabbe refer to the pragma-dialectical concept but change its content. See van Eemeren and Houtlosser (2007a, p. 64).

According to Walton and Krabbe, the usefulness of the concept of dialogue types to argumentation theory lies in its capacity to account systematically for the difficulties related to the contextuality of fallacies. As is clear from the discussion above, their dialogue types are in the first place supposed to fulfill a normative function. In the simplest formulation this context-dependent normativity amounts to a claim that "a good argument is one that contributes to a goal of the type of dialogue in which that argument was put forward" (Walton & Krabbe, 1995, p. 2). In sum, their solution to the problem of the contextuality of the quality of argumentation is that each dialogue type (after sufficient specification, pp. 66–67) yields a separate normative model of argumentation, with its own specific rules prescribing what good argumentation is.[14]

For such a theoretical framework to be useful in the analysis and evaluation of actual argumentation, two interrelated issues need to be dealt with: (1) the relation of the six normative (general) dialogue types to the plethora of types of communicative contexts actually perceived by ordinary language users needs to be determined, and (2) the exact ways in which fallacies occur in the different types of dialogue need to be described. Walton and Krabbe make an effort to deal with the first issue through the introduction of the concept of "mixed dialogues." Because they are well aware that their six basic types of dialogue cannot cover all ordinary speech events, they assume (without claiming completeness) that many speech events are composites of two or more of the six dialogue types (Walton & Krabbe, 1995, p. 82). They take it, in other words, that there is a synchronic multiplicity of various types of dialogue constituting together a particular speech event. A political debate, for instance, as we know it in Western democracies, escapes any easy one-speech-event-to-one-dialogue-type classification. Walton (1998b, p. 223) regards Question Period, a kind of political debate, as a type of context for argumentation that involves a mixture of no less than four (out of six) main types of dialogue (two subtypes of persuasion dialogue being involved). It is partly an information-seeking dialogue, partly eristic dialogue, partly negotiation, and partly persuasion dialogue. In such a complex case some obvious problems arise concerning the evaluation, how it should take place, and what useful role the distinction between the six dialogue types still has to play. By which standards associated with the six basic types of dialogue should, for instance, the arguer's performance in the "mixed" speech event of political debate be judged? Walton's easy solution is that "it is conditionally permissible to evaluate a political debate [...] from the point of view of a critical discussion" (1998b, p. 224).

The second issue, concerning the fallacies, is dealt with by viewing the problem as a problem of a diachronic multiplicity of dialogues. The conceptual tool to solve this problem is the notion of "dialectical shifts." Walton's central observation is that discussions that emerge and develop are liable to take turns that – in his theoretical framework – can be perceived as shifts from one type of dialogue to another. The central

---

14. Basically the types are empirical entities and only if the rules and goals are precisely laid down by a theorist one gets a normative model (see Walton & Krabbe, 1995, pp. 66–67).

distinction between such shifts is the normative division between *licit* shifts and *illicit* shifts. Licit shifts are overt and mutually agreed upon moves away from the dialogue the participants were originally supposed to carry out to another type of dialogue that still serves, or at least does not block, reaching the goals of the original dialogue (Walton, 1992, pp. 138–139). Illicit shifts are, by contrast, covert and unilateral attempts to change the type of dialogue that is going on into one that is wrongly presented as being in line with the exchange in the original dialogue. It is the illicit type of a shift that is often "associated," as Walton puts it, with the informal fallacies. The problem, however, seems to me that for an analyst it is hard to determine when exactly a "dialectical shift" has taken place and whether or not it is illicit.

In my view, any theory of argumentative contexts derives its practical value from its functionality in *analyzing and evaluating real-life argumentative discourse*. Having a better understanding of how arguers typically behave in a given type of context, and what norms they are expected, or even required, to follow, must allow for a more differentiated appraisal of everyday argumentation than would result from a straightforward application of context-independent normative standards. When adopting such a pragmatic touchstone in assessing the value of Walton and Krabbe's theory we encounter some problems that their account presents to an analyst of actual argumentative discourse.

To start with, it is not precisely clear what the theoretical status is of the concept of a dialogue type. The notion lays claim to both a normative and a descriptive status, because dialogue types are at the same time defined as "normative ideal models" and as "conventionalized activities." Here a problem arises. On the one hand, normative concerns are given priority, which is made explicit when Walton and Krabbe emphasize that "structures or systems of dialogue are normative models that represent ideals of how one ought to participate in a certain type of conversation if one is being reasonable and cooperative" and warn that they should not be confused with "an account of how participants in argumentation really behave in instances of real dialogue that take place [...] in a speech event" (1995, p. 67). On the other hand, however, their concept of dialogue types has unmistakably a strong empirical flavor, as is evident in Walton's characterization of the various types of dialogue. When, for instance, he makes his case for the context-dependent fallaciousness of *ad baculum* arguments, he supports his position by observing that "during a negotiation type of dialogue, threats and appeals to force or sanctions are quite typical and characteristic" (1992, p. 141). In this case, and in many more cases adduced by Walton, the observation of an empirical regularity – describable in quantitative terms such as "often," or quantifiable terms such as "typically" and "characteristically" – creates in his approach the normative basis for giving a fallacy judgment.[15]

---

15. One of the reasons why it does not become clear that Walton and Krabbe's types of dialogue are – contrary to their normative claims – empirical categories is that the norms pertaining to the various dialogue types are not unequivocally related to the goals of the activity types concerned.

This conflation of normative and descriptive perspectives gives the impression that Walton's account ignores a pertinent philosophical, but also methodological, distinction regarding the concept of rule-governed behavior. When it comes to the study of language use, it is important to distinguish clearly between: (1) observable behavioral regularities or patterns of language use; (2) the norms underlying some of these regularities, which language users may have understood and internalized during their socialization; (3) external norms for judging language use that are analytically stipulated by the theorist because they are relevant from an external theoretical perspective. The corresponding research traditions concentrate on describing regularities, tracing internal norms, and developing external norms, respectively.

Traditionally, the study of behavioral regularities in argumentative discourse has been the domain of discourse analysts and other pragma-linguists, who have aimed to describe – with careful attention to detail – the sequential and other patterns of dialogical arguments, deliberately avoiding any normative theorizing. Even in such a purely empirical perspective, argumentation can be viewed as a rule-governed verbal activity aimed at managing disagreement and "organized by conventions of language use in which two cooperative speakers jointly produce the conventional structure" (Jackson & Jacobs, 1980, p. 251). The important dilemma facing the analyst in such empirical research is, as Jackson observes with regard to the order of turn taking in natural conversations, "whether these patterns represent [normative, FHvE] rules or [descriptive, FHvE] regularities" (1986, p. 142).

A problem normatively oriented scholars are confronted with in relation to this dilemma is how to distinguish between a pattern that is infrequent but correct and a pattern that is both infrequent and incorrect.[16] When it comes to language use, in order to be able to solve this problem, they need to have some further insight in the norms of correctness prevailing in a certain context in a given communicative community. In principle, these norms of language use can – *pace* the methodological difficulty just referred to – be abstracted ("deducted") from the behavior of the language users, be formulated by the language users themselves, or even be explicitly institutionalized in a written code, such as the rules of *netiquette* for Internet communication.[17] A systematic description of such existing norms yields descriptive models of actual "empirical" normativity. Using Pike's (1967) "emic"-"etic" distinction, in the case of such descriptive models we can speak "emically" about reconstructing the "internal" normativity that is regarded as sound in practice. Doing so is fundamentally different from speaking in the study of argumentation "etically" about an "external" normativity

---

16. Most interesting (and most worrisome) are, of course, the cases of frequent and incorrect patterns of language use. The notion of "an often committed fallacy" belongs to this category. Such cases clearly point to the need for distinguishing between descriptive and normative considerations in the study of language use and, more in particular, argumentation.

17. For a study of conventionalized (political) argumentative discourse in Internet communication, see Lewinski (2010).

based on analytic considerations concerning the goals the discourse has to serve in view of a critical ideal defined by the theorist and the procedures the discourse has to comply with to achieve these goals. It is the stipulation by an argumentation theorist of a set of norms for achieving a certain critical goal that leads to the construction of an ideal model of external normativity. Both the formal dialecticians and the pragma-dialecticians have taken this kind of approach – as logicians and lawyers do in other areas. Despite their theoretical differences, these dialecticians have similar general aims, i.e. to develop ideal models of argumentative dialogues that point out what optimally reasonable argumentative behavior amounts to, and to characterize argumentative behavior that falls short of this ideal as the commitment of some kind of fallacy.

Bearing in mind the distinctions I have just discussed, I cannot answer the question to which of the three traditions of studying language use I mentioned (describing regularities, tracing internal norms, developing external norms) Walton's research on dialogue types belongs. Even Walton and Krabbe's explicit treatment of the main point is not of much help:

> It would be nice if the answer were clear-cut and if each logic system had a tag on it, saying whether it is to be taken descriptively or normatively. But that is not the way things have worked out. All serious logic systems seem to have descriptive and normative uses, but to different extents. The point is that descriptive accuracy and normative content are both important and, moreover, interdependent. Purely descriptive systems cannot be used as instruments of evaluative criticism. A purely normative system that is too far removed from what actually goes on cannot be applied to what actually goes on (1995, p. 175).

Granting that "conventional validity" based on intersubjective agreement is indeed a prerequisite for reaching a conclusive judgment concerning the acceptability of argumentative moves, I would like to emphasize that, because of its overriding importance, determining their "problem-solving validity" should come first. Although I recognize the interdependence of problem-solving validity and conventional validity, and consequently of normative and empirical models of argumentation, if such models are to have any significance for the analysis and evaluation of actual argumentative discourse, I do not agree with keeping this interdependence vague, and even doing so deliberately, regardless whether the primary source for coming to a judgment concerning the reasonableness of argumentation is an external or an internal normative source.

Related to the problem of the source of Walton and Krabbe's normativity – and thus of the rules of particular types of dialogue – is a question that concerns the goals of the various types. Are they formulated based on empirical analyses or are they stipulated based on theoretical considerations? In other words, are these goals necessarily familiar, or at least reflectively recognizable, to the discussants or are they formulated by some theorist, in this case Walton and Krabbe themselves? The enormous diversity of the goals Walton and Krabbe assign to the various dialogue types raises the additional question of which of these dialogue types are really argumentative. Can, for example, "reaching a (provisional) accommodation in a relationship" be seen as an argumentative goal? And can the goal of the "mixed" dialogue type of political debate, presented by Walton and Krabbe as a "tool to make society possible" (1995, p. 83) be taken to be argumentative? If such goals – and, consequently, the types of dialogue concerned – are not inherently argumentative but may simply have an argumentative component, many more types of dialogue can be distinguished, whether "main types" or "mixed types," that are similarly argumentative – which presents a serious problem to a theoretical framework meant to provide context-based argumentative standards of normativity. If, on the other hand, all these types of dialogue are fundamentally argumentative, one would like to know what definition of "being argumentative" is applied in determining this quality. In particular the information-seeking dialogue, which Walton and Krabbe (1995, pp. 73–74) call *deliberation*, and the inquiry are then problematic, because these are basic types of dialogue that – according to Walton and Krabbe's descriptions – do not necessarily involve any conflict or confrontation as is commonly required for a discourse to be argumentative.[18] Whichever interpretation Walton and Krabbe may have intended to enforce, it seems to me that the point has to be made that there must be a theoretical rationale for considering discourses or verbal moves to be argumentative that is independent of the specific empirical environment – or type of dialogue – in which they occur.

Because the status of the goals of dialogue types has an immediate bearing on the typology of dialogues, and the extent to which these dialogues are argumentative is problematic, two interrelated questions are pertinent regarding the Walton and Krabbe typology. First, what exactly is the function of the typology? In other words, what is the purpose of dividing contexts of argumentation? Second, what is the principle of classifying types of dialogue in precisely this way? This second question enquires about the kind of underlying theoretical framework that justifies this classification. Or is the classification just based on categories recognized by ordinary language users? What kind of norms are at stake anyway? And how are the normative models to be given shape? Against the background of these largely unanswered questions I shall sketch my own theoretical approach of argumentation in context.

不同交际活动的类型区分
5.3 Distinguishing between communicative activity types

The different kinds of communicative practices that have developed within the various domains of communicative activity depending on the institutional needs that have to be satisfied will manifest themselves in the normal course of events time and time again in a continual succession of speech events. In some cases we may be particularly interested in the specifics of an individual speech event, such as when we are carrying

---

18. Interestingly, Walton and Krabbe themselves point out that an "argumentative" type of dialogue is "conflict-centered" (1995, p. 105).

out a case study concerning a particular argumentative text that has a special historical meaning – as Houtlosser and I did when we analyzed William the Silent's Apologia pamphlet published in 1580 that responded to the Ban Edict issued earlier by King Philip II of Spain (van Eemeren & Houtlosser, 1999b, 2000b). Generally, however, when examining conventionalized argumentative practices we are not interested in individual speech events as such but in speech events as instantiations of some general communicative practice. If so, we are examining these speech events as tokens or representations of a particular communicative activity type. When viewed from this perspective, all individual pleadings by the defense at a court case about a juridical dispute, for instance, are seen as representations of the communicative activity type of legal proceedings (or of one of its particular parts or subtypes), all individual television debates between American presidential candidates as representations of the communicative activity type of a presidential debate, etc.

Communicative activity types are conventionalized practices whose conventionalization serves, through the implementation of certain "genres"[19] of communicative activity the institutional needs prevailing in a certain domain of communicative activity.[20] The genres of communicative activity that may be implemented (alone or combined) in the various communicative activity types vary from adjudication and deliberation to mediation, negotiation, consultation, disputation, promotion, communion, and others.[21] The institutional mission that a communicative activity type is meant to fulfill in a certain communicative domain is accomplished by realizing the relevant institutional point through the use of the appropriate genre(s) of communicative

---

19. Following Fairclough (1995, p. 14), a genre of communicative activity can be characterized as "a socially ratified way of using language in connection with a particular type of social activity." Cf. Bakhtin, "Each separate utterance is individual, of course, but each sphere in which language is used develops its own *relatively stable types* of these utterances. These we may call *speech genres*" (1986, p. 60).

20. Rigotti and Rocci's (2006) notion of "interaction schemes" seems to have a similar function as the pragma-dialectical "genres" of communicative activity. They define them as "culturally shaped 'recipes' for interaction congruent with more or less broad classes of joint goals and involving scheme-roles presupposing generic requirements. Deliberation, negotiation, advising, problem-solving, adjudication, mediation, teaching are fairly broad interaction schemes; while more specific interaction schemes may correspond to proper 'jobs'" (p. 173). As is the case with genres of communicative activity, the same interaction scheme can be found in different interaction fields (in pragma-dialectical terminology *communicative domains*). In practice, the term *interaction scheme* seems to refer both to genres of communicative activity and communicative activity types. According to Greco Morasso (2009, note 169), "The notion of activity type corresponds to an interaction scheme applied to a precise interaction field."

21. Such genres can also be viewed as "families" or "conglomerates" of communicative activity serving certain clusters of communicative activity types. Communicative activity types whose mission is to be reached by implementing the same genre of communicative activity belong to the same family or conglomerate. Cf. Swales (1990, 2004) and Bhatia (1993, 2004).

activity.²² The names I have given to the genres are chosen in such a way that they indicate what kind of institutional point they are out to realize. In some cases the conventions of the communicative activity types implementing a certain genre of communicative activity will be expressed in fully explicit constitutive or regulative rules; in other cases they are found in largely implicit rules of some kind, established practices or simply common usage.²³

The communicative activity types that have come into being in the legal communicative domain implementing prototypically the genre of adjudication include, among many others, court proceedings, arbitration, and summoning. Some communicative activity types in this domain make use of less prototypical genres. There are also communicative activity types in the legal communicative domain that standardly combine making use of adjudication with the use of other genres, such as mediation, which are prototypical of communicative practices in other communicative domains. Similar observations can be made regarding communicative activity types in the political communicative domain implementing prototypically the genre of deliberation, such as a presidential debate, a plenary parliamentary debate, and Prime Minister's question time.²⁴ A political interview is an example of a communicative activity type in the political domain in which prototypical deliberation is combined with making use of information-seeking, a genre prototypical of communicative practices in the communicative domain of journalism.

Communicative activity types which belong to the same communicative domain making use of the same genre of communicative activity share a common institutional point. The general institutional point, for instance, that a great deal of the communicative activity types in the political domain have in common is arguably preserving a democratic political culture by means of deliberation.²⁵ On a more concrete level,

---

22. In my view, the appropriateness of a certain genre to serve a certain institutional mission is its vitality in realizing the "institutional point" of a communicative activity type, i.e. in satisfying the need that made the communicative activity type come into being. I think that the more formally institutionalized communicative activity types are, the more likely it is that their institutional goals and further characteristics will be explicitly specified.

23. Following the ethnographer Dell Hymes, communicative activity types can also be called *speech events*, but I prefer to use the term *speech event* for specific instantiations of a communicative activity type. My communicative activity types and speech events seem to relate to each other in a similar way as Hymes' "genres" and "speech events": "Genres often coincide with speech events, but they must be treated as analytically different of them. They may occur in (or as) different events" (1972, p. 61).

24. I use the term *deliberation* in its broad colloquial meaning, which is also the way in which it is used by Habermas and a great many political scientists in connection with political argumentative discourse. It goes without saying, by the way, that these terminological choices are not of any vital theoretical importance.

25. Under the influence of protagonists of the concept of "deliberative democracy" such as Habermas, political theorists have replaced the traditional view of political communication as

individual communicative activity types usually have their own specific goals which are instrumental in contributing in a certain way to realizing the institutional point the communicative activity type is associated with.[26] In the case of a "general" plenary parliamentary debate in the Netherlands, for example, the specific institutional goal is to confront the government with the views of the people's elected representatives about their policy plans and their financing in accordance with the institutional conventions for the conduct of a general debate constituting parliamentary tradition and the format laid down in parliamentary procedure. The institutional goal of Prime Minister's Question time in Great Britain, to take another example, is to hold the Prime Minister to account for his government's policies in accordance with the institutional conventions of Question Time and the format of the exchange of questions and answers determined by practice and by existing regulations: the House of Commons Rulings from the Chair, the so-called Standing Orders, and the parliamentary rules of order. The institutional goal of a political interview is to make the politician clarify and justify his or her position in accordance with the institutional conventions determined by the regulations pertaining to the medium and the professional requirements of the trade, which also determine the format. The institutional goal of an American presidential debate is to make clear to the voters by means of a television debate what their choice between the candidates is about; the institutional conventions of this public debate have developed for the most part in the American tradition; the format of the debate is spelled out and agreed upon in advance. In some not formally institutionalized communicative activity types, such as a friendly chat in the communicative domain of interpersonal communication, there are no specific instrumental goals apart

---

an activity conducted in formal institutions, such as parliaments, by a much broader view. Habermas considers informal and unregulated daily communication among citizens as equally important to rational democratic politics as legally institutionalized procedures of democratic deliberation and decision-making. As a source of "informal public opinion-formation" it may in his view even be considered fundamental to democracy (1994, p. 8; 1996, pp. 307–308). Although it may be a consequence of this view that political argumentation has more venues and can also take part in communicative activity types such as a chat, this does not mean that an informal type of political deliberation does not take place within a conventionalized institutional framework, albeit a much less formalized one. According to Mansbridge (1999), the lack of a formal institutional goal in everyday conversation does not mean that this is just talking for the sake of talking which does not produce any results. Instead, the exchange of arguments on matters of public concern among ordinary citizens may lead to a more informed, critical opinion-formation among those actively or passively involved. Mansbridge concludes that "everyday talk [...] differs from classic deliberation in an assembly not in kind but only in degree" and should be assessed according to the same standards (1999, pp. 227–22).

26. Although Aristotle emphasizes that political discourse is about future actions, so that it requires a prospective account, political theorists recognize that the argumentation put forward in political discourse is also often about past performance and requires a retrospective account. Cf. Schedler's "prospective ex ante accountability" and "retrospective or post accountability" respectively (1999, p. 27).

from realizing the institutional point of keeping the interpersonal relationship going by means of communion, but there will nevertheless be certain institutional conventions regulating the communicative practice to some extent and an informal format that must be observed.[27]

As an illustration of the relationships that generally exist between communicative domains, genres of communicative activity, communicative activity types and actual speech events in the macro-contextual dimension of argumentative discourse I list in Figure 5.1 some examples.

---

[27]. In communicative activity types that are not formally institutionalized, such as a chat in a pub, it is usually easier for the participants to refrain from accepting the rational consequences of the way in which an argumentative exchange turns out. This is why an informal discussion may end in a stand-off even if it is in fact clear who has won. Thus, the loser can maintain that he has not given in (cf. Vuchinich, 1990, pp. 133–135).

[28]. It goes without saying that, depending on one's purposes, communicative domains and communicative activity types can also be classified in other ways. Some authors, for instance, starting from Patton's (2005, p. 279) wide definition of negotiation in the Harvard Program on Negotiation as "back-and-forth communication designed to reach an agreement between two or more parties with some interests that are shared and others that may conflict or simply be different," consider facilitation (or mediation) as a subtype of negotiation (Uzqueda & Frediani, 2002), instead of a separate genre of communicative activity types, while other authors agree with my classification (e.g. Goldberg, Sander, Rogers, & Cole, 2007). Such differences, however, are not pertinent to my purpose of making clear that the possibilities for strategic maneuvering are dependent on constraints posed by the macro-context of a communicative activity type that are instrumental to reaching the institutional point of a certain genre of communicative activity occurring in a particular communicative domain.

[29]. For the purpose of illustration for one communicative activity type a concrete speech event is mentioned in italics each time that is an instantiation of this (italicized) activity type.

[30]. My conception of the genre of deliberation, which is different from Walton and Krabbe's (1995) and Walton's (1998b) conception, includes Auer's (1962, p. 146) *debate*, defined as: "(1) a confrontation, (2) in equal and adequate time (3) of matched contestants, (4) on a stated proposition, (5) to gain an audience decision," but it also allows for the possibility of communicative activity types such as television debates which do not always start from a stated proposition and an explicitly decisive audience (Martel, 1983, p. 3). Cf. Perlof (1998, pp. 380–381).

[31]. In contradistinction with legal dispute resolution by adjudication, problem-solving by mediation is also known as *Alternative Dispute Resolution* (ADR), but I avoid using this terminology because negotiation and certain types of adjudication, such as arbitration, are also reckoned to belong to ADR, in spite of vital differences between them and mediation. My division of domains of communicative activity is certainly not mutually exclusive and there may be combined or overlapping communicative activity types, such as "arb-med" (Ross & Conlon, 2000).

[32]. As an illustration of the problems of classification it might be mentioned that the peace talks leading to the Camp David Accords in 1978 are sometimes treated as a case of mediation, but this goes against some major characteristics of these talks as they are described by the

domains of communicative activity	genres of communicative activity	communicative activity types	concrete speech events
legal communication	adjudication	– court proceedings[29] – arbitration – summoning	defense pleading at O.J. Simpson's murder trial
political communication	deliberation[30]	– presidential debate – general debate in parliament – Prime Minister's Question Time	1960 Nixon-Kennedy television debate
problem-solving communication[31]	mediation	– custody mediation – counseling – informal intervention	mediated talks between Richard and Tammy about custody Vanessa
diplomatic communication	negotiation	– peace talks – trade treaty – diplomatic memorandum	Israeli-Palestinian exchanges at Camp David[32]
medical communication	consultation	– doctor's consult – prescription – health rubric	Bart's February 13 visit to his doctor
scholarly communication	disputation	– book review – scientific paper – conference presentation	Dr. Apt's critique of the *Controversy and Confrontation* volume
commercial communication	promotion	– advertorial – sales talk – classified ad	Shell's newspaper message about its role in Nigeria[33]
interpersonal communication	communion	– chat – love letter – apology	Dima's talk with Corina about how they spent the weekend

Figure 5.1. Examples of speech events representing communicative activity types implementing genres of communicative activity instrumental in certain communicative domains

participants and it requires the mediator to have a completely different set of qualifications than the usual ones in mediation: those of being neutral and disinterested.

33. For a detailed analysis of this advertorial, see Chapter 6.

交际活动类型与批判性讨论模型
5.4 Communicative activity types and the model of a critical discussion

The communicative activity types mentioned in Figure 5.1 represent different types of conventionalized communicative practices belonging to more general clusters of conventionalized communicative practices in which a specific genre of communicative activity is prototypically activated. The list I have provided is meant for illustration and is, of course, not exhaustive. Not only could it be extended by mentioning more communicative activity types, but also by mentioning communicative activity types making use of still other genres of communicative activity. In addition, it should be taken into account that next to the genre that is considered prototypical for a particular activity type other genres might also play a part in that activity type. Certain communicative activity types may even prototypically involve the activation of more genres of conventionalized communicative practices. In fact, in order to get a realistic picture of the various types of conventionalized communicative practices in which strategic maneuvering takes place, typical combinations, mixtures and overlaps between different communicative activity types should certainly be added as well.[34]

Communicative activity types can usually be distinguished from each other, and defined more precisely, by describing the specific goals they are supposed to serve in order to fulfill their mission in realizing the institutional point of the communicative activity, together with the distinctive conventions pertaining to the communication involved, and the characteristic design of their format. How far one should go in branching out communicative activity types depends in the first place on the aim for which the classification is made. Even if such an enterprise were possible, there would be no need to aim for an ontology of communicative practices that is complete in an absolute sense. In distinguishing and defining communicative activity types for the purpose of analyzing strategic maneuvering in argumentative discourse, the proliferation can end at the point where no longer any distinctions are made that are pertinent to the analysis. In Section 5.5, when dealing with characterizing communicative activity types argumentatively, I shall explain what the point of reference is in this endeavor, and why this is the benchmark.

The communicative activity types brought to bear in the communicative practices enveloped in a certain domain of communication are known to those actively engaged in that domain, due to their primary socialization as members of a communicative community, as in the case of chatting, or to their secondary socialization as members of a professional community, as in the case of a diplomatic memorandum. Because communicative activity types are more or less conventionalized communicative practices that manifest themselves as such in communicative reality, they can in principle, albeit often with some difficulty, be recognized by outsiders as well. Essentially, all communicative activity types can be distinguished and defined by entering the relevant domain of communicative activity and examining empirically through participation and observation what their

---

34. *Mutatis mutandis*, in these respects communicative activity types resemble Walton and Krabbe's dialogue types.

distinctive features are and what their conventionalization involves. In a great many cases, however, making such an effort is not necessary because the communicative activity types concerned are generally acknowledged cultural artifacts familiar to everyone. They can sometimes even be elucidated by consulting textbooks or other reference books.

Because of their empirical status, communicative activity types are not on a par with theoretical constructs such as the ideal model of critical discussion – or, for that matter, the calculus of first order propositional and predicate logic.[35] While theoretical constructs are analytic idealizations, the various communicative activity types are empirical conceptualizations of conventionalized communicative practices.[36] The model of critical discussion, for instance, is constructed on the basis of analytic considerations concerning the optimal way of resolving differences of opinion on the merits.[37] Unlike such theoretical constructs as a critical discussion, which are designed by concentrating on the necessary constituents of a problem-valid procedure for achieving a particular kind of analytic objective, the various communicative activity types refer to communicative practices that manifest themselves in concrete speech events and have come into being and have been conventionalized in the pursuit of realizing the institutional point of the communicative activity concerned.[38]

In studying the argumentative dimension of conventionalized communicative practices the argumentative properties of communicative activity types are focused on. Communicative activity types may be inherently or "essentially" argumentative, as is the case in parliamentary debates, predominantly argumentative, as is the case in political interviews, coincidentally argumentative, as is the case in prayers in which a claim made is supported by arguments, or not argumentative at all, as is generally the case in news bulletins broadcast on the radio. In the case of a communicative activity type that is inherently or essentially argumentative we can speak without reservation of an *argumentative* activity type.[39] As soon as a communicative activity type is inherently

---

35. Whereas the theoretical construct of critical discussion is based on analytic considerations of a dialectical kind, the theoretical construct of demonstration or proof is based on analytic considerations of a formal logical kind.

36. Theoretical constructs such as the ideal model of a critical discussion are sometimes referred to as *scenarios* (exemplified in dialectical profiles) and the conventionalized practices of the communicative activity types as *scripts*, but I fear that the conceptual difference between these two terms is not clear enough to make this terminological distinction helpful.

37. Dascal (2001, p. 316) distinguishes between a "problem-solving" model, a "contest" model, and a "deliberative" model, but his models are empirically based conceptualizations that seem related to communicative activity types (van Eemeren & Garssen, 2008, p. 6).

38. By distinguishing in this way between an analytic ideal model and conventional activity types, and making a fundamental distinction between the two categories, we deviate from approaches to argumentative discourse types such as Walton's (1998b) and Walton and Krabbe's (1995).

39. In argumentation theory, the term *argumentative activity type* is more generally used to refer to all communicative activity types that are examined for their argumentative dimension (van Eemeren & Houtlosser, 2005b).

or essentially argumentative or predominantly argumentative or when argumentation incidentally plays an important part in it, it is worthwhile to study the strategic maneuvering involved. Starting from the way in which the communicative activity type is to be defined, the communicative activity type concerned has to be characterized from the perspective of argumentation theory in order to be able to identify the constraints the communicative activity type imposes on the strategic maneuvering. The theoretical model of a critical discussion can be instrumental in this endeavor because in the various argumentative activity types the argumentative dimension can be substantiated in different ways, depending on the specific institutional requirements ensuing from the arguers' mission to realize the institutional point of the communicative activity type by concentrating on the empirical counterparts of the four stages of a critical discussion: the *initial situation*, the *starting points*, the *argumentative means*, and the *outcome of argumentative discourse*.[40]

Taking the four stages of a critical discussion as the point of departure, four focal points can be identified in the resolution process that need to be taken into account in an argumentative characterization of a communicative activity type. These focal points, corresponding to the four stages to be distinguished in a critical discussion, reflect the constitutive elements in the process of resolving a difference of opinion on the merits. In an argumentative characterization of a communicative activity type it needs to be determined exactly how these constitutive elements are represented in the argumentative discourse conducted in the communicative activity type concerned. A specification of the argumentative characteristics of the institutionally shaped counterparts of the four stages of a critical discussion can be achieved by a systematic comparison between the argumentative conditions prevailing in the empirically constituted communicative activity type at issue and the argumentative conditions stipulated in the ideal model of a critical discussion.

不同交际活动类型的论辩特征描述
5.5 Characterizing the argumentative features of communicative activity types

Communicative activity types can be completely non-argumentative, but more often than not, whether directly or indirectly, argumentation comes in inherently or incidentally, so that the communicative activity type concerned is wholly or partly argumentative. As a matter of course, only when argumentation is used will it be possible to characterize a communicative activity type argumentatively. For the purpose of showing that strategic maneuvering can be affected by the communicative activity type in which it takes place I concentrate on communicative activity types belonging

---

40. Using the ideal model of a critical discussion as an analytical instrument in all cases, whatever the complexities of the communicative activity may be, not only ensures unity in their comparison, but also a coherent and consistent appreciation of the argumentative dimension. In this way diversity is not the (relativistic) point of departure but could in some cases be shown to exist as a result of a systematic comparison. Cf. Walton and Krabbe's approach discussed in Section 5.2.

Chapter 5. Strategic maneuvering in conventionalized communicative practices 147

to the first four clusters of activity types mentioned in Figure 5.1: adjudication, deliberation, mediation, and negotiation. The communicative activity types mentioned there (in the third column) are institutionalized to a degree that their institutional goals, conventions and formats are sufficiently transparent and that the speech events associated with them are easily recognizable. With the help of the model of a critical discussion the argumentative features of communicative activity types prototypically implementing these four – and other – genres of communicative activity can be characterized in terms of the four categories representing the counterparts in real-life argumentative discourse of the four stages of a critical discussion.

Communicative activity types, such as court proceedings and summoning (as a distinct part of a legal procedure), that make use of the genre of communicative activity referred to as *adjudication*, aim for the settlement of a dispute by an authorized third party rather than by the parties themselves. Although, in practice, the scope of the communicative activities belonging to the cluster of adjudication is broader, communicative activity types making use of this genre are commonly understood as taking a difference of opinion that has become a well-defined "dispute" to a public court, where a judge makes a reasoned decision in favor of one of the parties after having heard both sides (and a jury, if that is part of the legal procedure). The judge determines in favor of one of the parties according to a set of rules. On closer analysis, most of the procedural rules are tantamount to specifications of rules for critical discussion aimed at guaranteeing that the difference of opinion is terminated in a fair and practical fashion. Usually there are special rules concerning the division of the burden of proof, the data that can be part of the common starting points, and the kinds of proof that count as acceptable. It is characteristic of adjudication that the parties adjust their discussion roles from trying to convince each other to trying to convince the adjudicator.

Adjudication is a genre of predominantly argumentative communicative activity that is strongly institutionalized in formal ways. It is applied in types of communicative activity that are explicitly scripted and have a precisely defined format, such as a civil law case, an administrative law case, and a criminal trial. Compared with weakly institutionalized communicative activity types, the initial situation from which adjudication starts is much more formalized, with an official definition of the dispute and with the jurisdiction to decide the case given from the outset to a fixed third party. The procedural and material starting points in adjudication consist of largely explicit codified rules (laws) and explicitly established concessions (evidence). The argumentative means that are used amount to an argumentative interpretation of the concessions in terms of established facts and legal evidence, and established material rules of law. The only outcome that is allowed, and is invariably reached, is a decision by the third party that is in control; a return to the initial situation of the dispute is not possible.

The term *deliberation* refers to a multi-varied genre of emphatically argumentative communicative activity types, varying from a plenary debate in parliament to an informal political Internet forum discussion, that start from a projected mixed disagreement between the parties about issues on which their views and those of a listening, reading or television-watching audience diverge.[41] Although some communicative activity types making use of the genre of deliberation may have a more clearly-defined format than others, these communicative activity types are usually not fully conventionalized. In deliberation taking the form of a public debate the disputants generally have clear starting points that differ for each disputant in crucial respects from those of other disputants. At all times the contestants take the listening, reading or watching audience into account up to the point that this third-party audience is in fact their primary addressee – or even their only "real" addressee. More often than not their argumentation will be aimed at convincing the third-party audience rather than their debate partners. This third-party audience determines then the outcome of the deliberation – by voting or in a less conspicuous way.

Communicative activity types relying on deliberation are particularly interesting to protagonists of democratic institutions because their institutional point generally is to preserve a democratic political culture. They are designed to enable an argumentative exchange that is optimal from both a dialectical and a rhetorical perspective, so that strategic maneuvering is of crucial importance at every point in the exchange. Often deliberation starts from largely implicit intersubjective rules and from both explicit and implicit concessions on both sides, an exception being the communicative activity type of an American presidential debate, in which the rules are largely explicit. Another important characteristic of that kind of communicative activity type is that the parties are first of all out to put forward argumentation defending their standpoints in critical exchanges with their contestants. The decision concerning the resolution of the differences of opinion at issue in their contributions to the deliberation is up to the individual listener, reader, or viewer.

The genre of *mediation* covers a cluster of communicative activity types that are to a large part argumentative, which include, for instance, custody mediation and counseling. These communicative activity types start from a difference of opinion that has grown into a conflict that the parties concerned cannot resolve by themselves, so that they have to take refuge in a third party who acts as a supposedly neutral mediator and guides the parties in their (more or less) cooperative discursive search for a reasonable and mutually acceptable solution. The mediator acts as a facilitator and is responsible for the process but not for its content. Unlike the adjudicator, he does not have the power to terminate the disagreement. Irrespective of whether the disagreement concerns custody of a divorced couple's child or the price to be paid for repairs to a car, the mediator aims to help the parties to have a reasonable discussion leading to an arrangement that is satisfactory to both of them.

Custody mediation is an excellent example of a communicate activity type using mediation. It is only weakly institutionalized and usually has a loosely defined informal

---

41. I am inclined to think that the presence of a third party audience is vital for the strategic maneuvering taking place in political deliberation, but there can also be political deliberation without a third party audience. In fact, without such an audience the conventional constraints on the strategic maneuvering will rather be those of disputation or some other genre of communicative activity.

format. The initial situation is such that the difference of opinion between the parties about a matter of vital interest to both has become a conflict that is hard to resolve. Although all concerned know that the mediating third party has no jurisdiction to decide and is only there to promote the adoption of a reasonable attitude by the contending parties, it is clear that the presence of a neutral outsider has a distinct influence on the contributions the parties will make. Due to the problematic nature of their disagreement, initially the parties will generally not be prepared to explicitly recognize any helpful concessions as a common starting point. In the process of deliberation, however, they will be inclined to accept, however reluctantly, the implicit procedural rules for their informally "scripted" speech event, cautiously forced upon them by the mediator. Instead of making their case in a businesslike manner, more often than not their arguments will be partially concealed in quasi-spontaneous but in fact calculating and sometimes emotional exchanges. Although in theory the conflicting parties may be just as free to draw their own conclusions as in ordinary conversations, in mediation they are expected to come to an arrangement because the disagreement they are having concerns an incongruity that needs to be overcome.[42]

The term *negotiation* refers to a cluster of communicative activity types that are sometimes wholly and at other times partially argumentative, varying from bargaining to more specific communicative activity types such as peace talks. These types start from an initial situation that is better described as a conflict of interests than as an ordinary difference of opinion.[43] Unlike adjudication and mediation, negotiation lets the parties be focused on each other rather than a third party. Negotiation typically aims for some kind of compromise,[44] usually consisting of the maximum amount of agreement the parties can reach on the basis of the concessions each of them is willing to make. A series of communicative activity types have been developed that are aimed

---

42. For a comprehensive study of the communicative activity type of mediation, see Greco Morasso (2009). See also van Eemeren et al. (1993), Moffitt and Bordone (2005), and Menkel-Meadow (2005).

43. According to Fisher, Ury and Patton, who promote concentrating on interests rather than positions in what they call "principled negotiation," negotiation, unlike positional bargaining, is to result in a "wise," and as far as possible, even "amicable" agreement (1991, p. 14). In their view, reconciling interests works better because "behind opposed positions lie many more interests than conflicting ones" (1991, p. 42).

44. In this connection, a fundamental distinction needs to be made between "integrative" negotiations, where the parties' interests are conflicting but not necessarily mutually exclusive, so that it is possible to have an outcome in which both parties gain something, and "distributive" negotiation, where the one party's loss is the other party's gain. In the longstanding tradition of viewing negotiations as games, distributive negotiation is treated as a "zero-sum game" in which the gains and losses of both parties necessarily add up to zero, and integrative negotiation as a "non-zero-sum game." Putnam and Poole (1987) observe that negotiation and bargaining are neither exclusively integrative nor exclusively distributive but involve both, depending on how the communication develops.

at reaching an outcome in which the interests of both sides are met to the maximum extent of what is mutually acceptable.

Negotiation is a genre of communicative activity that is generally moderately conventionalized, but its degree of conventionalization varies from the one type of negotiation to the other depending ultimately on the preferences of the parties involved. Negotiation plays a role in the domain of commercial ("business") communication but also very prominently in the domain of international relations, where peace talks offer an example of a communicative activity availing itself of negotiation. Usually, in communicative activity types making use of this genre of communicative activity the parties are initially free to define their own format but as soon as they have determined this format it becomes binding. The constitutive rules of a specimen of negotiation are fixed as soon as they have been accepted. The communicative activity types depending on negotiation may therefore be considered to be "semi-scripted." A distinctive feature of some communicative activity types belonging to this genre, such as bidding and bartering, is that the standpoints taken by the parties may change during the negotiation process, so that the confrontation that is at the heart of the discussion is variable (and the discussion must, in the analysis, be split into a series of interrelated discussions). Usually the concessions that each of the parties is prepared to make at the beginning of the negotiation or during the negotiation process are conditional and changeable. The final decision about the outcome of a negotiation is always up to the parties and each of them is free to return to the initial situation so that everything will stay the way it was.[45] Among the means the parties have at their disposal for reaching a decision in their own favor is argumentation, but often this argumentation will be incorporated in offers, counteroffers and other commissives, such as conditional promises ("If you allow X, we will do Y") and conditional threats ("No Y before you do X").[46]

Figure 5.2 presents an argumentative characterization, indicating the argumentatively relevant institutional conventions, of the four clusters of communicative activity types discussed in this section.

---

45. In another sense, of course, when a new process of negotiation starts after a failed negotiation, the initial situation will never be the same again, because the earlier failure will cast its spell. This earlier failure, however, is not part of the new definition of the difference of opinion. In some form or other it can be reflected in the new procedural and material starting points.

46. According to Tutzauer (1992, p. 67), "The nature, timing, and pattern of offers, and the concessions they elicit, constitute the very essence of bargaining and negotiation. Indeed, it can be argued that if there are no offers, there is no bargaining." Sawyer and Guetzkow (1965, p. 479) have a somewhat different emphasis: "The core of what is generally taken as the central process of negotiation [is] reciprocal argument and counter-argument, proposal and counter proposal in an attempt to agree upon actions and outcomes mutually perceived as beneficial." Axelrod (1977, p. 177) stresses the role of argumentation even more strongly: "After all, most of what happens in negotiation is the assertion of arguments by one side, and the response with other arguments by the other side."

critical discussion	confrontation stage	opening stage	argumentation stage	concluding stage
genres of communicative activity	initial situation	procedural and material starting points	argumentative means and criticism	possible outcome
adjudication	dispute; 3rd party with jurisdiction to decide	largely explicit codified rules; explicitly established concessions	argumentation from facts and concessions interpreted in terms of conditions for the application of a legal rule	settlement of the dispute by a motivated decision 3rd party (no return to initial situation)
deliberation	mixed disagreement; decision up to a non-interactive 3rd party audience	largely implicit intersubjective rules; explicit and implicit concessions on both sides	argumentation defending incompatible standpoints in critical exchanges	resolution difference of opinion for (part of) 3rd party audience (and/or deliberate return to initial situation)
mediation	conflict at deadlock; 3rd party intervening without jurisdiction to decide	implicitly enforced regulative rules; no explicitly recognized concessions	argumentation conveyed in would-be spontaneous conversational exchanges	mutually accepted conclusion by mediated arrangement between conflicting parties (or provisional return to initial situation)
negotiation	conflict of interests; decision up to the parties	semi-explicit constitutive rules; sets of conditional and changeable explicit concessions	argumentation incorporated in exchanges of offers, counter-offers and other commissives	conclusion by compromise parties as mutually accepted agreement (or return to initial situation)

Figure 5.2. Argumentative characterizations of some genres of communicative activity

策略操控的机构性先决条件
5.6 Institutional preconditions for strategic maneuvering

In each communicative activity type that is argumentative, whatever its make-up, the participants maneuver strategically to accomplish, in a reasonable and effective way, their mission of realizing the institutional point of the communicative activity in the specific macro-context in which the argumentative discourse takes place.[47] Due to the institutional requirements applying to a specific argumentative activity type, certain modes of strategic maneuvering may lend themselves particularly well or, as the case may be, not so well, or even not at all, to being used in that particular activity type. As a rule, the more explicitly the conventionalization of an argumentative activity type is articulated, the easier it is to recognize the institutional preconditions for strategic maneuvering prevailing in that activity type.[48]

As will be clear from the argumentative characterizations given in Figure 5.2, in some kinds of communicative activity types the definition of the initial situation may be more open than in others to being shaped by the preferences of an individual party. A similar variety may be observed regarding the choice of procedural and material starting points, the use of argumentative means and the advancement of criticism, and the possible outcomes of the argumentative exchange.[49] At every stage of an argumentative exchange all three aspects of strategic maneuvering can be affected by the institutional preconditions imposed on the argumentative discourse by the activity type in which the discourse takes place. There may be constraints on the topical choices that can be made, on the adaptation to audience demand, or on the use of presentational devices. In principle, these constraints are a limitation of the parties' possibilities for strategic maneuvering, but they can also create special opportunities for the strategic maneuvering of one or both of the parties. By means of some examples I will illustrate this preconditioning of strategic maneuvering by the macro-context of the argumentative activity type in which it takes place.

All argumentative activity types making use of *adjudication* aim for the termination of a well-defined dispute by the decision of an authorized third party. That decision is sustained by argumentation that is based on an understanding of relevant facts and

---

47. In some communicative activity types the parties have a different role in carrying out this mission. In Prime Minister's Question Time, for instance, the mission of holding the government to account for its policies and actions will generally involve that the opposition questions these policies and actions and that the Prime Minister defends them.

48. I dinstinguish between primary preconditions, which are as a rule official, usually formal, and often procedural, and secondary preconditions, which are as a rule unofficial, usually informal, and often substantial. Among the primary preconditions of the communicative activity type of a plenary debate in European parliament are, for instance, the rules of order guarded by the chair; among the secondary preconditions are, for instance, the "European predicament" that the parliamentarians need to combine serving the European interest with serving the interest of their home countries. See van Eemeren and Garssen (2009).

49. See, again, Vuchinich, 1990, pp. 133–135.

concessions, formulated in terms of conditions for the application of a legal or quasi-legal rule, and assessed by appealing to largely explicit codified rules.[50] For brevity's sake I confine myself to an example of strategic maneuvering in handling the topical potential for determining the issue in a legal case.[51] In dealing with this example I refer to the classical doctrine of *stasis* stemming from Hermagoras of Temnos – perhaps better known under its Latin name of "doctrine of *status*." The stasis doctrine provides distinct tools for answering the question of the choice of issue at the start of the argumentative process in a criminal court case in the legal domain (*genus iudiciale*).[52] According to the doctrine, in responding to an accusation of murder the defender can choose from four kinds of strategic options: (1) denying that the criminal act was committed (*status coniecturalis*), (2) redefining the act of killing as "manslaughter" (*status definitivus*), (3) appealing to extenuating circumstances such as the need for self-defense (*status qualitatis*), and (4) pointing to procedural flaws in the court case (*status translativus*). If the stasis doctrine is taken to be authoritative, the four options for managing the topical potential available in the confrontation stage serve as institutional preconditions of the possibilities for strategic maneuvering.[53] These preconditions constitute constraints that involve certain restrictions, but also open up opportunities.

In the prologue to Multatuli's *Max Havelaar*, a 19th century Dutch literary masterpiece about suffering injustice, Lothario, who is accused of having murdered a woman called Barbertje, defends himself in a criminal court case against this accusation by opting for the *stasis coniecturalis* and denying flatly that he committed this criminal act:[54]

> Your honor, I didn't kill Barbertje! I fed her and clothed her and looked after her. There are witnesses who will testify that I am a good man, and not a murderer.

---

50. In court cases, the judge usually fulfills the role of the third party. For reasons of legal certainty, he takes the prevailing legal codes and juridical rules as his starting point and checks whether the law indeed attaches the required legal consequence to the facts concerned and whether enough facts have been presented to make the legal ground of the claim acceptable. However strongly scripted such a speech event may be, there is always ample room left for strategic maneuvering. This room for maneuvering is, in fact, the basis of the legal profession.

51. Fahnestock (2009, pp. 208–209) observes that in third party adjudication, where one side must lose, there would be no point in maneuvering toward minimizing differences or in maneuvering toward overlapping positions. "In pragma-dialectical terms," she concludes, "the best 'rhetorical' strategy for arguers would be maximizing their difference to create a clear choice for third party deciders, while their 'dialectical' responsibilities, their desire to appear reasonable, would require their minimizing difference to reach resolution."

52. The doctrine, whose scope was probably much broader, was the basis for the distinction of "stock issues" in American "academic debate."

53. Braet (1984, pp. 173–192), who puts the classical doctrine of *stasis* in a modern perspective, claims that there is a strong resemblance between Hermagoras' doctrine and the way in which criminal justice is conducted in the Netherlands.

54. This example is taken from van Eemeren and Grootendorst (1992a, pp. 74–75).

This denial appears to be the strongest way of making a topical choice that Lothario could opt for. A moment later the denial is backed up by the appearance of Barbertje herself, so that it is a proven fact that she is still alive. Nevertheless, by some remarkable whim of fate, the effect of the strategic maneuvering is in this case spoiled, due to the additional remarks Lothario made about his good-heartedness. This is what the judge concludes:

> Man, you must hang! [...] It does not befit someone who has been accused of something to consider himself a good human being.

This fictional case shows in an ironic but not altogether unrealistic way that in practice strategic maneuvering does not always lead to the result that is aimed for and might even be counterproductive.

The second genre of communicative activity I discussed in Section 5.5 concerns the cluster of communicative activity types making use of *deliberation*. Deliberation as it is envisaged here usually starts from a mixed disagreement between two or more parties who are addressing each other but are in the first place out to gain the support of a listening, reading or watching audience in resolving one or more of the differences of opinion that might exist between them and (part of) these people, who are in fact their primary audience. In the critical exchanges all parties make use of each other's explicit and implicit concessions and act in accordance with explicit or implicit procedural rules. The listening, reading or watching audience is not interactive but its members determine nevertheless the outcome of the deliberation, because they decide at the end of the critical exchanges whether they (or some of them) have changed their minds so that (some of) their differences have been resolved or whether this is not the case, so that the initial situation will be maintained.

At all stages of the deliberation, there is room for strategic maneuvering. The conventional constraints imposed on the maneuvering are in the first place dictated by each party's mission to reach his primary audience of listeners, readers or watchers via a critical exchange with the secondary audience consisting of their actual interlocutors.[55] In order not to be perceived as non-cooperative, unresponsive, impolite or even rude by their primary audience, the participating parties cannot afford to ignore each others' questions, statements and other contributions to the exchange, and their strategic maneuvering has to be conducted accordingly. In addition, the format chosen for the deliberation may impose still other constraints on the parties. For instance, a chairman may have been installed who acts as an arbiter when it comes to assigning speaking turns, judges the relevance of contributions, and allows or does not allow interruptions. This is the case not only in parliamentary debate, but also in a great many other public debates. In all cases, the debaters have to conduct their strategic maneuvering in accordance with the prevailing institutional preconditions.

---

55. It might be useful to acknowledge that the terms *primary* and *secondary* audience introduced in Chapter 4.4 could also be assigned the other way around. In my choice of terms I have followed a tradition instigated by Searle (1979) in his treatment of indirect speech acts.

Chapter 5. Strategic maneuvering in conventionalized communicative practices

In the following example, taken from the 2008 general debate in Dutch parliament, the Prime Minister, Mr. Balkenende, maneuvers strategically in trying to avoid answering a question asked by a Member of Parliament (MP) by turning to another point. In this case, however, Balkenende does not get away with his evasive maneuver, because MPs have a right of information that entitles them to have all questions answered that they regard necessary to judge the government's performance. After the MP whose question is ignored has protested, the Chair of the Second Chamber of Parliament, Mrs. Verbeet, prevents Balkenende from completing this strategic maneuver successfully by using the Chair's right to intervene when a Member of Government denies an MP the information he requires.[56]

> *Prime Minister Balkenende:*
> "I will now start with the next part."
>
> *Mr. Rutte (Conservative Liberal Party):*
> "I thought you would also go into the refugee policy, but I did not get an answer to my question yet."
>
> *Chair, Mrs. Verbeet:*
> "Part of the refugee policy has been addressed in an earlier stage of the debate, but not your question. [...] You are right." (Parliamentary Proceedings, 18 September 2008)

This fragment illustrates how the institutional preconditions for strategic maneuvering may differ in some respects from type to type of communicative activity, depending on the impact that the need for realizing the institutional point of a communicative activity, and the goals and requirements of a particular type of communicative activity, have on the argumentative characteristics of the various stages of the argumentative process. The institutionalized macro-context of a general debate in Dutch parliament imposes certain conventional constraints on the strategic maneuvering considered acceptable in this argumentative activity type. Such constraints may obtain generally in a whole genre of communicative activity, but there can also be specific constraints applying to individual communicative activity types, due to their specific requirements, goals and formats.[57]

---

56. According to Tonnard (forthcoming), who examines in her doctoral dissertation the various ways in which standpoints (and doubt) can be excluded from further consideration in Dutch parliamentary debate, Mrs. Verbeet supports the Members of Parliament in their pursuit of clear and relevant answers (http://www.tweedekamer.nl). In a phone call with Tonnard on February 16, 2009, Verbeet explained that, although Parliament has a right for information, MPs can in fact only enforce this right by abandoning their trust in the Member of Government concerned.

57. In analyzing argumentative discourse one must ultimately specify the preconditions for strategic maneuvering pertaining to the specific communicative activity type concerned rather than to the cluster of communicative activity types this communicative activity type belongs to.

Mediation, representing the third genre of communicative activity I highlighted, aims to conclude a disagreement by a mediator-assisted arrangement of the parties, achieved with the help of argumentation conveyed in would-be spontaneous conversational exchanges that do not start from explicitly recognized concessions and are guided by implicitly enforced regulative rules. In principle, the mediator's only task is to facilitate the resolution process by structuring and otherwise improving the communication between the parties. In practice, however, he can exploit the room for strategic maneuvering that is left to him in order to contribute indirectly to the achievement of an arrangement. In the confrontation stage, for instance, the mediator can try to stimulate the parties to shift their attitudes toward the conflict to a more constructive level. In the opening stage he can encourage them to modify the perceived meaning of the implicit concessions in such a way that they can be used more easily to come to an agreement. In the argumentation stage he can help to give presence to the ideas of justice and fairness in order to make the conversational exchanges more effective. In the concluding stage he can prepare the ground for acceptance of an arrangement by the parties by allowing both parties to save face. In most cases he can try to achieve these strategic aims in an indirect way by using the appropriate kinds of presentational devices, such as questions and (re)formulations of the parties' positions and commitments.[58] Consider, by way of an example, the mediator's strategic maneuvering in the following exchange (rendered as recorded):[59]

Mediator:[60]
What about Bill's concern that this (could be a mutual decision).

Otherwise the problems of having to deal with all kinds of confusing mixtures, composites, and subordinative groupings of communicative activity that may occur in a cluster may be so overwhelming that they defeat proper treatment.

58. For strategic tools of the mediator see also Wall, Stark, and Standifer (2001).

59. This example and the explanation of it are taken from van Eemeren, Grootendorst, Jackson, and Jacobs (1993, pp. 126–127), where it is made clear how the mediator can be the architect of an argumentative discussion between the parties, in spite of the fact that he is not expected to express any standpoint or argument of his own to promote and support a specific resolution of the conflict between the parties. Greco Morasso (2009) explains that the mediator tries to achieve first a change in the parties' attitudes from disputants to "co-arguers," so that – in pragma-dialectical terms – a necessary "second order condition" has been fulfilled for resolving the difference of opinion by means of argumentation.

60. In this example an adaptation is used of Gail Jefferson's transcription notation (see Atkinson & Heritage, 1984). Single parentheses indicate material that was not clearly audible to the transcriber or not audible at all. Equal signs mark a continuous stream of talk between two speakers or by the same speaker. Double parentheses contain editorial descriptions. Repeated letters indicate stretched sounds. Punctuation marks usually indicate vocal intonation rather than grammatical form.

Wife:
I want Bill this is you know this is I I assume why we are here I want Bill to be close to them I want them to have time with them, with him, but I also want them to have a good stable (operating). And that's first and foremost in my mind. =

Mediator:
= Okay. How would you modify modify this ((PAUSE)) proposal then,

Wife:
What I would modify it to is every other weekend and maybe t an two evenings a week, I don't know
((Exasperated))
((Pause))

The mediator exploits here the presentational device of questioning to carry out some tasks of an advocate without having to advocate or challenge any particular standpoint or argument explicitly. Through lines of questioning he tries to get the respondent to commit to answers that could serve as common premises for arriving at a conclusion. The advantage of this strategic maneuvering is that the parties are the ones who make the assertions through their answers, so that the mediator has not publicly advocated any standpoint or made any personal commitment to any argument regarding the conflict. The mediator thus performs a balancing act to remain, at least in a formal sense, on the safe side of the boundaries of strategic maneuvering as they are drawn in mediation.

Negotiation, my last case, is a genre put to good use in a cluster of multi-varied activity types that are all aimed at ending a conflict of interests between parties by a compromise or a similar mutually acceptable result. In negotiation this outcome is brought about through rule-governed exchanges of offers, counter-offers and other commissives which convey argumentation or are interspersed with argumentation. These exchanges start from sets of explicit concessions that are conditional and may change during the negotiation process, depending on the way they are received and responded to by the other party. Establishing common endorsement of shared, complementary or non-conflicting diverging interests is vital to negotiation. As Putnam and Roloff (1992, p. 3) observe, "Negotiation differs from related types of communication by [...] employing strategies and tactics aimed at reaching a mutually acceptable agreement."

The fact that there is a conflict of interests does not mean that all interests the parties have are incompatible. Apart from the interests that are conflicting, each party always also has certain interests that are unrelated to the other party's interests. These other interests might be compatible, and the two parties may also have certain interests that they share. Since in a context of negotiation identifying and utilizing interests of the other party that are not part of the conflict can be a steppingstone to an agreement, adapting to the audience's perspective by taking their other interests into account is often a prominent element in strategic maneuvering in the communicative activity types making use of negotiation. This is not only so because a party can adjust to the other party's perspective by portraying its own interests as paralleling the other party's interest, or pose as an interlocutor who understands, and can help meeting, these latter interests,[61] but also because, by making creative use of the patterns of concessions constituted by the collection of recognized interests, more complex audience-oriented strategies can be brought to bear such as "package dealing."[62] A package deal is a compromise, based on the concessions that have been made, in which various interests of both parties that are unrelated but basically consistent are served optimally in a deal that is attractive to both parties and includes as it were automatically putting an end to the initial conflict. When taken together, the parties' avowed interests constitute as it were a pool from which various combinations of interests can be drawn in different strategic combinations.

In the following negotiation, which rather typically takes a series of exchanges, party 1 wants to borrow party 2's car for a few days. By offering quite a few unrelated concessions that are attractive to party 2, so that he adapts strategically to party 2's perspective, party 1 prepares the ground for making a package deal that includes him having the car:

> *Party 1:*
> You have been most generous in granting me this job. I shall finish it tomorrow, so that you will have a great bathroom again.
>
> *Party 2:*
> Fine.
>
> *Party 1:*
> Why don't you postpone paying me until next week, if that's easier for you? In any case I still wanted to paint the garden shed and to complete the other odd things that are still waiting to be done.
>
> *Party 2:*
> O.K.
>
> *Party 1:*
> I don't mind staying the night on Saturday, by the way, so that I can look after the kids and the two of you can go out.
>
> *Party 2:*
> Gee, thanks! But don't you have to eat then?

---

61. As Walton (1998b, p. 102) remarks: "Without empathy it is impossible for one party to understand what the other party really wants and what her priorities are within her list of wants."
62. According to Tutzauer (1992, p. 79), because the communication of offers is so central in this endeavor, having an understanding of negotiation requires an understanding of concessional patterns.

Party 1:
Some beer will be welcome, of course, and I would not mind a small bite, but I can take care of that myself. What do you say?

Party 2:
That's fine with me.

Party 1:
Oh, by the way, could I borrow your car for a few days?

Party 2:
Yes, I appreciate your doing all the extra work you are going to do and I don't need the car during the next couple of days, so you can have it. Except for Saturday night, of course, because otherwise we cannot go out. OK?

Party 1:
Sounds perfect to me!

政治领域的冲突策略操控个案分析
5.7 A case of confrontational strategic maneuvering in the political domain

In analyzing and evaluating argumentative discourse we need to take account not only of the dialectical and rhetorical aims intrinsic to strategic maneuvering but also of the institutional goals of the communicative activity types in which the argumentative discourse takes place, because activity types impose extrinsic constraints on strategic maneuvering. When we analyze and evaluate argumentative discourse, we start from a specific speech event. We examine its macro-context in order to determine its domain, the genre of communicative activity implemented, the institutional point thereof, and the specific communicative activity type which the speech event exemplifies. Next we examine the characteristics defining the argumentative dimension of this communicative activity type. My discussion in Section 5.6 of some preconditions for strategic maneuvering in argumentative activity types making use of some prominent genres of communicative activity shows how such preconditions discipline the strategic maneuvering. In order to give a more precise account of the contextually determined conventional constraints on strategic maneuvering, it is necessary to concentrate on specific communicative activity types because it is at the level of the individual activity types that the institutional preconditions for strategic maneuvering manifest themselves most specifically. As an illustration I turn to the communicative activity type of a political interview implementing deliberation.

In "Accusing someone of an inconsistency as a confrontational way of strategic manoeuvring," Andone (2009a) demonstrates that the argumentative activity type of a political interview creates, through a set of rules and conventions, certain contextual preconditions for the performance of confrontational moves.[63] In the pragma-dialectical fashion, she regards such moves as strategic maneuvers that arguers perform in an attempt to be effective while trying to remain reasonable at the same time. Andone concentrates on analyzing the strategic questions asked by the interviewer in a political interview and the strategic responses given by a politician who is confronted with an accusation of inconsistency. She shows how the institutional preconditions of the argumentative activity type of a political interview constrain the strategic choices made by the interviewer and the politician in a conventional way. Following other authors (Clayman & Heritage, 2002; Lauerbach, 2004), Andone acknowledges that the goals of a political interview can vary from informing the public about political acts and decisions to entertaining the public. She focuses on confrontational argumentative exchanges that serve the purpose of holding a politician to account.

Andone derives the preconditions for confrontational strategic maneuvering from her characterization of a political interview in terms of conventions for implementing the four stages of a critical discussion in this argumentative activity type. With the help of an example taken from a BBC interview she shows how knowledge of the institutional preconditions for strategic maneuvering can play a vital role in analyzing the strategic function of confrontational argumentative contributions. In her example, Jon Sopel interviews William Hague, a former leader of the Conservative Party, at this point the Conservative Shadow Foreign Secretary, in "Politics Show" of November 12, 2006:

Jon Sopel:

And Labor say the big thing that you could do to help would be to support identity cards. It's fair to say that this is an issue that your party has rather flip flopped on isn't it.

William Hague:

Well it's... I think it's become clearer over time where we stand on this, let's put it that way, because we've got the government adopting an identity card scheme, but one that is so bureaucratic and involves a vast data base and this is the government of serial catastrophes when it comes to data bases as we all know, costing now, according to the London School of Economics, up to twenty billion pounds and we said that if some of that money was spent instead on an effective border police and strengthened surveillance of terrorist

---

63. Besides Andone's (2009b) study of strategic maneuvering in political interviews, which I here briefly discuss, other pragma-dialectical studies of political communication making use of deliberation are Mohammed (2009a), who examines Prime Minister's Question Time in British parliament, Tonnard (2009), who concentrates on the general debate in Dutch parliament, Plug (2010), who investigates strategic maneuvering in parliamentary contexts and Lewinski (2010), who analyzes Internet Forum discussions. Ihnen (in preparation) focuses on law-making debates in British parliament. Pragma-dialectical studies regarding communicative activity types making use of other genres of communicative activity are carried out by Feteris (2009) for adjudication in the legal domain and Pilgram (in preparation) and van Poppel (in preparation) for consultation in the medical domain.

suspects, and strengthening special branch and things like that, we'd actually get a lot further.... (interjection)....having identity cards.
Jon Sopel:
Isn't that a detail of the legislation. I mean you supported identity cards back in December 2004, less than two years ago.
William Hague:
We supported, I and Michael Howard supported the principle of those. Subject to how the details were worked out. The details are not impressive and the grasp of detail and the ability to control the costs of the current government is so terrible, that it's not a scheme that we can support.

This question-answer exchange can be reconstructed in accordance with Andone's characterization of the argumentative activity type of a political interview as a mixed dispute over the introduction of biometric identity cards in Great Britain. In her analysis, Andone focuses on the way in which the participants realize the analytically relevant moves of expressing and maintaining a standpoint and expressing doubt. She explains the strategic function of the argumentative moves that are advanced on the basis of the argumentative characterization of a political interview and the institutional preconditions for confrontational moves. She justifies her analysis of the confrontational moves as strategic maneuvers by showing how for all three aspects of strategic maneuvering the preconditions influence the efforts the interviewer and Mr. Hague make to reach a satisfactory outcome.

The topical choice made by the interviewer in his first question is a realization of the analytically relevant move of expressing a standpoint (about the consistency of the politician and his party) through an accusation of inconsistency. In a political interview, the interviewer's strategic maneuvering regarding topical selection is limited to expressing his attitude with regard to stances or decisions for which the interviewee can be held to account in public. In this exchange, the interviewer makes an issue of a decision made by the politician concerning the introduction of biometric identity cards. This issue meets the institutional preconditions and is of real interest to the audience, as is required by the rules of a political interview. The strategic aim behind this choice of argumentative move is to make the politician accept the interviewer's standpoint according to which the decision of the politician is inconsistent. If the politician admits that he acted inconsistently, he thereby retracts any doubt he might have against the standpoint of the interviewer, which is, of course, the response favored by the interviewer, who can then maintain his standpoint without any further defense.

In reply to the interviewer's question, the politician makes the topical choice of responding with the analytically relevant move of expressing the opposite standpoint. This move is aimed at defending the position that no inconsistency was committed, thus giving a positive account of the politician's decision. Although defending the opposite standpoint is not easy, given the seriousness of the charge, it is in fact the only means available to the politician for providing the account expected of him and making the interviewer give up his own standpoint.

In his second question, the interviewer realizes through his topical choice the analytically relevant move of casting doubt on the politician's standpoint. The expression of doubt is intended to make the politician retract his standpoint so that the difference of opinion concerning the consistency of the politician and his party on the issue of the introduction of biometric identity cards ends in favor of the interviewer. In reply, the politician makes an ultimate attempt at maintaining his standpoint, which gives him the opportunity to have another try at giving a positive account of his decision.

The strategic choices involved in the analytically relevant moves of expressing and maintaining a standpoint and casting doubt on it are reinforced by how the interlocutors adapt their argumentative contributions to each other – and to their wider audience, but this is not the focus of Andone's analysis. In accordance with the constraints imposed by the rules of the game, the interviewer tries to steer the discussion into the desired direction by referring to shared background knowledge. He reminds Hague that less than two years earlier he advanced the opposite standpoint concerning biometric identity cards, and this reminder allows the interviewer to once again accuse the politician of an inconsistency. The politician is held to account in view of background information he cannot easily reject.

The strategic function of the various moves is reinforced too by the presentational devices that are chosen to convey these moves. In accordance with the preconditions for argumentative exchanges in a political interview, the interviewer advances his standpoint and doubt by means of questions. In the two cases discussed here he selects a "polar" (or "propositional") question aimed at limiting the politician's options for a response to either an explicit acceptance or a rejection. In the context of a political interview, such a choice for a polar question is part of an effort to make the politician account for his decision. If the politician avoids answering the question, a sub-discussion can be initiated in which the interviewer holds him to account for failing to provide an answer. The relevance of this sub-discussion would be that it shows the audience that the politician does indeed make an attempt to escape from giving an account.

If the politician accepts the expected answer implied in the interviewer's first question, he thereby admits that his party flip-flopped on the issue. If the politician rejects the expected answer, which is in fact what he does, he acquires the difficult job of defending the opposite standpoint. While the use of the adverb "well" in his reply is not the most helpful presentational choice, the politician steers the discussion toward a favorable outcome by making a dissociation (van Rees, 2009) between the principle and the practice of introducing biometric identity cards. This dissociation allows him to maintain his standpoint in a reading he presents as vital, related immediately to the terrible quality of the details of how the idea of introducing biometric identity cards is put into practice. Because the politician's stance had always been connected with the details, in fact, no change of position has occurred. If this perspective is accepted, the difference of opinion ends in favor of the politician.

CHAPTER 6 第六章

论辩话步策略功能的界定
Determining the strategic function of argumentative moves

策略操控的四个分析维度
6.1 Four factors serving as parameters

In analyzing the strategic maneuvering carried out in argumentative discourse taking place in a certain domain of communicative activity, the same parameters are to be considered for each category of strategic maneuvering – confrontational maneuvering, opening maneuvering, argumentational maneuvering, and concluding maneuvering. The parameters that must be considered in every case of strategic maneuvering for determining the strategic function of the argumentative moves that are made can be identified by taking account of the following factors in the analysis (van Eemeren & Houtlosser, 2009):

1. the *results* that can be achieved by making the moves concerned;
2. the *routes* that can be taken to achieve these results;
3. the *constraints* imposed on the discourse by the institutional context;
4. the *commitments* of the parties defining the argumentative situation.

Strategic maneuvering may be presumed to be aimed at achieving a specific result, so it is worth considering what kind of outcome may be aimed at by engaging in a certain mode of strategic maneuvering. Hence, the first factor to be taken into account in determining the strategic function of a particular argumentative move made at a particular stage of the resolution process concerns the results that can be achieved by carrying out that move ("strategic maneuver"). The spectrum of options available in the component of the analytic overview that is pertinent at that point of the resolution process is a theoretical tool that can be of help in this m endeavor. The second factor to be taken into account in the analysis of an argumentative move concerns the reasonable options that were available to choose from when the argumentative move was made. The route taken in carrying out a particular strategic maneuver needs to be determined. The dialectical profile for the moves that are analytically relevant at this juncture in the resolution process can be a helpful theoretical tool here. The third factor to be taken into account consists of the institutional constraints imposed on the argumentative discourse in the macro-context in which it is carried out. Taking these constraints into account is necessary in order to track the institutional preconditions that the strategic maneuvering carried out must meet in this type of communicative activity. An account of the communicative activity type in which the strategic maneuvering takes place and the argumentative characteristics of this activity type can be helpful theoretical tools in this endeavor. The fourth factor to be taken into account in determining the strategic function of an argumentative move is the current state of affairs in the resolution process – the positions of the parties resulting from their discursive activities during the discussion – at the point where the strategic maneuvering takes place. Taking this state of affairs into account is necessary in order to determine under what situational conditions the strategic maneuvering must operate. An overview of the contracted mutual commitments that define the argumentative situation can be a helpful theoretical tool here. Only if these four parameters are all duly taken into account in analyzing the strategic maneuvering manifesting itself in the discourse at the point the analyst is focusing on, can the strategic function that may be fulfilled by a particular argumentative move – characterized by a specific combination of topical choice, audience orientation and presentational design – be determined.

The four factors just discussed allow for taking account of a finite set of considerations pertinent to determining the strategic function of the moves made in a specific case of argumentative discourse. When taken together, the results of the considerations concerning each of these parameters constitute a useful basis for getting to the strategic function of the various modes of maneuvering in each of the four categories of strategic maneuvering distinguished in Chapter 2.6. As a matter of course, the analysis starts from the way in which the strategic maneuvering manifests itself in the discourse, i.e. in a particular choice that is made from the available topical potential, a particular way in which the opportunities for adapting to the audience are used, and a particular way in which the presentational possibilities are exploited. In each case the attribution of a particular strategic function to an argumentative move needs to be accounted for by relating the characterizing properties of each of the three aspects of the strategic maneuvering carried out in that move in a plausible way to the joint results of the consideration of the four parameters.

In response to a positive standpoint, for instance, the other party may have decided to advance a negative standpoint, anticipating that his position is so strong that, in addition to challenging the positive standpoint, he will be capable of defending the opposite standpoint. To the analyst this mode of strategic maneuvering would seem to amount primarily to making an expedient choice of the "confrontational" topical potential. If, to give another example, someone who is confronted with a standpoint he does not want to discuss attempts to turn a potential difference of opinion about this standpoint into a non-difference, the mode of strategic maneuvering involved would, to the analyst, in the first place appear to be an adaptation to the audience. And if, to mention one last example, at the argumentation stage an arguer attempts to avoid a commitment to a premise left unexpressed in his argumentation by presenting the argumentation as if it were complete as it stands, the presentational aspect of the maneuvering would foremost catch the analyst's eye. The analyst must relate the various modes of strategic maneuvering used in argumentative discourse to all three aspects of strategic maneuvering. He can do so by making clear that all argumentative moves concerned are, viewed in the perspective of the institutional mission ensuing from the macro-context of the communicative activity type in which they are made, realized in such a way that the topical choice, the audience adaptation, and the presentational choice (1) all allow for reaching an outcome of the discussion stage concerned that fits into an analytic overview, (2) agree with an analytically relevant continuation of the argumentative discourse represented by a certain dialectical route, and (3) connect well with the state of mutual commitments defining the argumentative situation at the specific juncture in the exchange.

Although in argumentative practice the three aspects of strategic maneuvering distinguished analytically always go together, and are in principle intrinsically connected with each other, in particular cases one particular aspect may be more prominently manifested than the others. The strategic maneuvering may, for instance, come primarily to the fore in the topical choice that is made, say by the conspicuous use of an argument from authority (*ex autoritate*), or in the way audience adaptation is realized, say by explicitly adopting the other party's arguments (*conciliatio*), or in the use of presentational techniques, say by the emphatic repetition of the standpoint (*repetitio*). This is why, at this point in the development of the study of strategic maneuvering, I recommend naming the mode of strategic maneuvering at issue for the present by referring to its most conspicuous manifestation in either of the three aspects: maneuvering by argument from authority, maneuvering by conciliation, maneuvering by repetition, etc.[1] The four parameters I have discussed can then be used to determine the strategic function the particular mode of maneuvering referred to in this way may have in the case at issue.

社论式广告个案分析：壳牌公司在尼日利亚的角色
6.2 A case in point: Shell's advertorial about its role in Nigeria

In order to illustrate how analyzing strategic maneuvering in argumentative discourse by determining the strategic function of the moves that are made in the discourse works, and what it adds to a pragma-dialectical analysis, I will reconstruct an "advertorial" published by Shell in the *Observer* of November 19, 1995. Because this advertorial has been analyzed before, independently, by Tindale (1999) and van Eemeren and Houtlosser (1999a, 2002a), the argumentative text concerned and its peculiarities may be familiar already to some readers.[2] This time I want to concentrate on showing how the theoretical tools discussed in Section 6.1 can be helpful in achieving an insightful analysis. Accordingly, I shall not try to present a complete analysis, but rather focus on those properties of the text that are enlightening for my present purposes.

---

1. It only makes sense to speak of a "type" of strategic maneuvering if a classification of types of strategic maneuvering has been developed that can serve as a typology to refer to. In the theorizing this point has not yet been reached.

2. For a comparison between Tindale's analysis and that of van Eemeren and Houtlosser, see Leff (2006). See also Fahnestock (2009, pp. 198–203).

Although one might wonder why exactly Shell considered it necessary to publish this costly advertorial, at first sight the text appears to be pretty straightforward: the oil company appears to simply inform the public about the exact nature of its involvement in Nigeria. However, if one takes into account that the advertorial was published at a time when Shell was widely accused of lending support to the dictatorial Nigerian regime and having a bad influence on the environment, and if one assumes that Shell must have felt the need to respond reasonably and effectively to these accusations, it becomes clear that the advertorial constitutes a defense of Shell's actions as well as an attempt to convince the public of the superiority of its policies in Nigeria. Having only just recovered from the damage inflicted by the Brent Spar case, which brought Shell into conflict with Greenpeace,[3] the company presumably wants to respond as strongly as possible to the massive, worldwide protests inflamed by the conviction and execution by the Nigerian regime of the writer, dissident critic, and environmental activist Ken Saro-Wiwa. Although it may seem as if in the advertorial Shell just explains what its political and economic role in Nigeria involves, the advertorial is in fact a sophisticated example of strategic maneuvering *in vivo*, because the oil company's argumentative moves in favor of its own position are well hidden in its account of its involvement in Nigeria.[4]

Clear thinking in troubled times

In the great wave of understandable emotion over the death of Ken Saro-Wiwa, it's very easy for the facts to be swamped by anger and recriminations. But people have the right to the truth. Unvarnished. Even uncomfortable. But never subjugated to a cause, however noble or well-meaning. They have the right to clear thinking.

---

3. The Brent Spar was a North Sea oil storage and tanker loading buoy in the Brent Group, operated by Shell. In 1991, Shell decided to put the Brent Spar out of operation. In June 1995, however, the Brent Spar station became a subject of public concern, when the British Government announced its support for Shell's application for disposal of the station in the Atlantic waters, approximately 250 kilometers away from the Scottish west coast. In reaction to this plan, Greenpeace initiated a world-wide campaign to stop the sinking of the Brent Spar. Greenpeace activists occupied the filling station for weeks and Shell was forced to abandon its plans to dispose of the Brent Spar at sea, although it continued to stand by its claim that this was the safest option from the perspectives of the environment, industrial health, and safety. Although Greenpeace's reputation suffered from the campaign as well – as it had to acknowledge that its assessment of the oil remaining in Brent Spar's storage tanks had been grossly overshooting the mark – Shell's reputation was considerably damaged as a result of the Brent Spar case and the widespread boycott that was issued against Shell's service stations.

4. Ken Saro-Wiwa was hanged on November 10, 1995. In New York, in 2009, his son and other relatives started proceedings against Shell, in which the company was accused of crimes against humanity based on the various kinds of involvement in Nigeria Shell had denied in the advertorial published in 1995. Without admitting guilt, Shell paid a large amount of money in compensation, thus preventing the case from being carried through.

5   The situation in Nigeria has no easy solutions. Slogans, protests and boycotts don't offer answers. There are difficult issues to consider.
    First, did discreet diplomacy fail? Perhaps we should ask instead why the worldwide protests failed. Our experience suggests that quiet diplomacy offered the very best hope for Ken Saro-Wiwa. But as worldwide threats and protests increased,
10 the Government position appeared to harden. As Wura Abiola, daughter of the imprisoned unofficial winner of the last Nigerian presidential election said on Newsnight "The regime does not react well to threats. I believe that this is the way of showing that they will not listen to threats." Did the protesters understand the risk they were taking? Did the campaign become more important than the cause?
15 There have also been charges of environmental devastation. But the facts of the situation have often been distorted or ignored. The public – who rightly care deeply about these issues – have too often been manipulated and misled.
    There are certainly environmental problems in the area, but as the World Bank Survey has confirmed, in addition to the oil industry, population growth, deforestation,
20 soil erosion and over-farming are also major environmental problems there.
    In fact, Shell and its partners are spending US$100 million this year alone on environment-related projects, and US$20 million on roads, health clinics, schools, scholarships, water schemes and agricultural support projects to help the people of the region. And, recognizing that solutions need to be based on facts, they are sponsoring
25 a $4.5 million independent environmental survey of the Niger Delta.
    But another problem is sabotage. In the Ogoni area – where Shell has not operated since January 1993 – over 60% of oil spills were caused by sabotage, usually linked to claims for compensation. And when contractors have tried to deal with these problems, they have been forcibly denied access.
30 It has also been suggested that Shell should pull out of Nigeria's Liquefied Natural Gas project. But if we do so now, the project will collapse. Maybe for ever. So let's be clear who gets hurt if the project is cancelled. A cancellation would certainly hurt the thousands of Nigerians who will be working on the project, and the tens of thousands more benefiting in the local economy. The environment, too, would suffer,
35 with the plant expected to cut greatly the need for gas flaring in the oil industry. The plant will take four years to build. Revenues won't start flowing until early next century. It's only the people and the Nigerian Government of that time who will pay the price.
    And what would happen if Shell pulled out of Nigeria altogether? The oil would
40 certainly continue flowing. The business would continue operating. The vast majority of employees would remain in place. But the sound and ethical business practices synonymous with Shell, the environmental investment, and the tens of millions of dollars spent on community programs would all be lost. Again, it's the people of Nigeria that you would hurt.

45 It's easy enough to sit in our comfortable homes in the West, calling for sanctions and boycotts against a developing country. But you have to be sure that knee-jerk reactions won't do more harm than good.
   Some campaigning groups say we should intervene in the political process in Nigeria. But even if we could, we must never do so. Politics is the business of
50 governments and politicians. The world where companies use their economic influence to prop up or bring down governments would be a frightening and bleak one indeed.

Shell. We'll keep you in touch with the facts.

In my analysis of this argumentative text I shall show how, at each of the four stages of its argumentative discourse, Shell strategically uses the available topical potential, adapts its message to the views and preferences of the audience, and exploits certain presentational devices. I determine the strategic function of the argumentative moves pertinent to my analysis by concentrating first on the components of an analytic overview as a source for considering the results that Shell may aspire to (Section 6.3); second, on the relevant dialectical profiles as a source for considering the available routes toward achieving a certain result (Section 6.4); third, on the properties of the argumentative activity type concerned as a source for considering the institutional constraints imposed on the strategic maneuvering (Section 6.5); and fourth, on the argumentative situation in which an argumentative move is made as a source for considering the mutual commitments that have accumulated at that point in the discourse (Section 6.6). I conclude this chapter by providing an illustrating analysis of the argumentation structure of Shell's advertorial (Section 6.7).

从分析概览中考察论辩的预期结果
6.3 The analytic overview as a source for results aspired to

Theoretical insight into the various components of the analytic overview ensuing from reconstructing a piece of argumentative discourse pragma-dialectically as a critical discussion provides an analytic instrument for substantiating the first parameter. Because each discussion stage has its own distinctive constitutive components (see Figure 1.1), insight into the options available for each component in an analytic overview enables the analyst to track down systematically the kinds of results that can be aimed for in each category of strategic maneuvering. The outcomes that can be reached in a particular discussion stage consist of the various options for filling out the components of the analytic overview applying to the stage concerned.

At the confrontation stage, which is aimed at defining the difference of opinion, if the difference of opinion is indeed maintained, the results can be a non-mixed single, a mixed single, a non-mixed multiple or a mixed multiple difference of opinion, depending on the number of propositions involved in the difference of opinion and the positions assumed by the parties. In the same vein, the results that can be reached in

Chapter 6. Determining the strategic function of argumentative moves

the other stages can be determined. At the opening stage, which is aimed at establishing the point of departure, the procedural and material starting points can vary from explicit concessions and agreements to implicitly assumed "endoxa" and contextual commitments. The argumentation stage is aimed at having a systematic exchange of doubt or criticisms and arguments, explicitly or implicitly (and – as a reconstruction may reveal – even indirectly). At this stage, various arguments can be advanced: various kinds of criticism can be leveled; various kinds of premises can be left unexpressed; various types of argument schemes based on causal, symptomatic or comparison relationships can be used; and various kinds of argumentation structures consisting of (some combination of) multiple, coordinative and subordinative argumentation structures can develop. At the concluding stage, which is aimed at determining the outcome of the discussion, the results can vary from accepting and upholding to non-accepting and retracting the standpoints at issue.

In the case I have chosen to illuminate my views on reconstructing strategic maneuvering, Shell is confronted with the silent claim of its opponents ("the protesters") that it is to be blamed for its role in Nigeria, supported by three accusations that had been made against the oil company regarding its involvement in Nigeria at the time when Shell published its advertorial. All three accusations seem to fall under the general umbrella of "blame:" Shell's opponents blame the company for being responsible for the death of Ken Saro-Wiwa, for polluting the environment, and for supporting the Nigerian regime. The opposition Shell is faced with when it begins its defense can be reconstructed in the following argumentation structure of the justification of the blame claim by Shell's opponents:

Shell's opponents

(1)   (Shell is to be blamed for its role in Nigeria)

| (1.1a) (Shell is responsible for the death of Ken Saro-Wiwa) | (1.1b) (Shell pollutes the environment in Nigeria) | (1.1c) (Shell supports the Nigerian regime) |

The accusations represented in parentheses (because they are not explicit in the advertorial) in the description of the (cumulative[5]) coordinative argumentation structure define the composite indictment that Shell is to address to the full if it wishes to clear itself from all blame.

A crucial element in Shell's strategic maneuvering at the confrontation stage of the argumentative discourse in this advertorial consists of the moves the company makes to have the confrontation stage result in a non-mixed difference of opinion with their primary audience, the general public, instead of a mixed difference of opinion. Shell tries to achieve this result in its handling of audience demand by dissociating the

---

5.   For cumulative coordinative argumentation, see Snoeck Henkemans (1997, pp. 96–97).

general public that is reading the advertorial from the campaigners who reacted against Shell's involvement in Nigeria. Not the general public but the campaigners are presented – with the passive voice used as a presentational device to create distance between them and the general public[6] – as Shell's real opponents, who have a mixed difference of opinion with Shell about its involvement in Nigeria. By maneuvering as if the general public is not really in opposition to Shell's position, but only has some doubts (resulting from ignorance rather than careful reflection), Shell suggests that it merely has a non-mixed difference of opinion with the public – or perhaps even no difference of opinion at all. This strategic separation between the public and the campaigners has the advantage to Shell that the company can treat the public as a possible ally. The blame accusations can now be dealt with as being open to a straightforward, quasi-informative defense. In the process, the naïve but well-meaning public that "rightly care[s] deeply" about "noble and well-meaning causes," but is easily "manipulated and misled" (lines 16–17), can be contrasted with the cunning campaigners. The campaigners are portrayed as unrealistic idealists, sloganeers who distort or ignore the facts, and irresponsible egocentrics who do not understand the risk they are taking and for whom "the campaign [has become] more important than the cause" (line 14). Goodwill is invoked by flattering the public at this stage, suggesting that they are sensible people who are concerned about the same problems as Shell. They are entitled to clear thinking and can cope with the unvarnished truth (lines 2–4). In addition, Shell appeals to the public's responsibility: because rights imply duties, it is the public's duty to think clearly and accept only what is objectively true, however unsettling the truth may be (lines 2–4, 45–47, 52).

Here are the results of Shell's strategic maneuvering with the difference of opinion at the confrontation stage:

Shell's opponents
(1)   (Shell is to be blamed for its role in Nigeria)

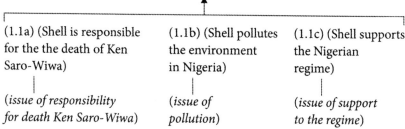

(1.1a) (Shell is responsible for the the death of Ken Saro-Wiwa)

(1.1b) (Shell pollutes the environment in Nigeria)

(1.1c) (Shell supports the Nigerian regime)

(issue of responsibility for death Ken Saro-Wiwa)

(issue of pollution)

(issue of support to the regime)

---

6. Among the passages in which Shell employs the passive voice to widen the dissociation between the campaigners and the public are: "there have [...] been charges" (line 15), "the facts [have] been distorted" (line 16), and "it has also been suggested" (line 30). In this way, the campaigners are portrayed as anonymous accusers.

Chapter 6. Determining the strategic function of argumentative moves 171

```
        Shell                    Shell                     Shell
        -/1.1a                   -/1.1b                    (-/1.1c)
   Shell is not responsible   Shell does not pollute    (Shell does not
   (but the campaigners are)  (but others do)           support the regime)

   Campaigners   Public     Campaigners   Public     Campaigners   Public
   (+/1.1a)      (?/1.1a)   (+/1.1b)      (?/1.1b)   (+/1.1c)      (?/1.1c)
```

However, this analysis does not yet give a full account of Shell's strategic maneuvering in the confrontation stage. By leaving the main claims addressed at the confrontation stage implicit in its presentation, Shell is able to make a topical selection from the available disagreement space that consists of the issues that are easiest for the company to cope with. One of the three accusations directed at Shell was that it indirectly supported the regime (1.1c). Shell was, of course, expected to address this difficult issue, but refrains from doing so, at least explicitly. Instead, the advertorial expands about a related issue: the justification of Shell's involvement in Nigeria. Only at the very end of the text Shell declares that the company will not intervene in Nigerian politics (lines 48–51) and adds (in line 51) that it rejects *propping up* a government as much as bringing it down – thus implicating that, in addition to not intervening, it does not support the regime either. In this way, Shell adapts to audience demand by addressing the issue of support without explicitly answering the accusation involved. This reconstruction makes clear that Shell's manipulation of the "intervention" issue calls in fact for a slightly different analysis of the confrontation stage, based on Shell's strategic maneuvering at the argumentation stage regarding the issues that are to be addressed:

(1) **Shell is not to be blamed**
    1.1a   *Shell is not to be blamed for the death of Ken Saro-Wiwa*
    1.1b   Shell is not to be blamed for any environmental devastation
    (1.1c) (Shell is not propping up the Nigerian regime)
(2) **Shell's involvement in Nigeria is justified**
    2.1a   Shell should not pull out of the NLG-project
    2.1b   Shell should not pull out of Nigeria

This amendment to the reconstruction of the difference of opinion that is dealt with in Shell's advertorial clearly illustrates that taking the result aimed for in strategic maneuvering into account can have real consequences for the analysis.

从论辩轮廓中考察论辩的可选路径
6.4 Dialectical profiles as a source for available routes

The theoretical notion of a dialectical profile discussed in Chapter 4.2 provides an analytic instrument for substantiating the second parameter. Dialectical profiles represent the concurrent sequential patterns of the analytically relevant moves that the participants can make in (an empirical approximation of) a critical discussion to achieve an outcome of a particular stage of the discussion. At the opening stage, for instance, the profile of the "explicitization procedure for unexpressed premises" defines the procedural ways to be pursued for making implicit premises used at the argumentation stage explicit. The dialectical profile of the explicitization procedure represents the possible routes the participants can take in the argumentation stage in the process that starts with the "production" of a supposedly incomplete argument and ends with an agreement about the unexpressed premise that is to be attributed to the protagonist. Because, in practice, the route that is actually followed is also determined by the interaction between the parties, it is not fully predictable in what way exactly the participants will go through the procedure. What next step they can take depends on the earlier steps they have made themselves, but also on the steps made by the other party. Nevertheless, the set of alternatives to choose from is finite; they are indicated by the dialectical profile.

The topical choices that Shell could have made in the confrontation stage in response to the accusations by its opponents I discussed in Section 6.3 can be represented in dialectical profiles of the analytically relevant routes, with a different profile for each accusation. The available choices in case of the first two accusations are shown below, where boldface type indicates which choices the company actually made. Shell chose to attempt to refute these accusations instead of merely casting doubt on them (elements not explicitly present in the advertorial are represented in parentheses):

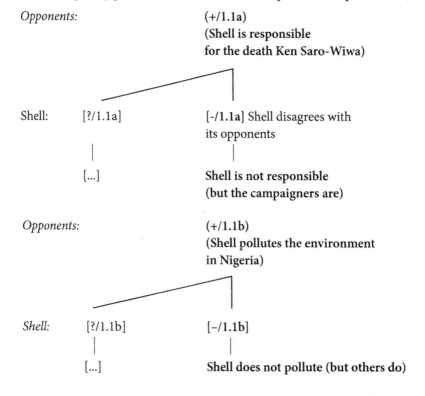

Chapter 6. Determining the strategic function of argumentative moves

In the opening stage of the advertorial, Shell seeks to create a solid basis for its case by advancing certain factual propositions as a starting point for the discussion that contrasts sharply with the emotionally-based starting point of the campaigners. In Shell's strategic maneuvering, the public's acceptance of its proposed starting point is simply presupposed. Especially in the case of the standpoint that Shell's involvement in Nigeria is justified, the company's strategic maneuvering is clever, because the propositions Shell proposes to accept are crafted so that they will be taken to be part of the starting point of the opponents, as is indicated in bold in the following dialectical profiles:

Shell: (Proposal 1: We should care about the environment)

Opponents: **Yes, we should care about the environment** (No, we should not care about the environment) (OK, we should care about the environment, provided that …)

Shell: (Proposal 2: We should care about the Nigerians)

Opponents: **Yes, we should care about the Nigerians** (No, we should not care about the Nigerians) (OK, we should care about the Nigerians, provided that …)

Given the campaigners' declared political preferences, Shell's opponents may be assumed to be in favor of a non-polluted environment and a prospering native Nigerian population, so Shell can be sure of their acceptance of these propositions as starting points and the company can make use of them in the argumentation stage.

When trying to create a solid starting point for its case by contrasting the factual basis of its views with the alleged emotional basis of the opinions of its opponents, Shell makes it clear that in its opinion its position is only based on objective facts. Some facts are known due to the company's own experience (lines 8–9), some other facts are provided by authorities such as Wura Abiola – the daughter of the then imprisoned winner of the last election (lines 10–13) – and the World Bank (lines 18–20). Shell even makes a few concessions which strengthen its image of objectivity. One of these is the undeniable fact that there are indeed environmental problems in the Nigeria region (line 18).

Shell further enhances its credibility as an objective, disinterested and rational protagonist by emphasizing its knowledge of Nigerian affairs (lines 7–9, 21–25, 32–44), its reliance on genuine data and respect for the truth (lines 2–6, 15–20, 24–25, 45–47, 52). In its presentation, Shell sustains this image by labeling the issues as "difficult" (line 6), eluding "easy solutions" (line 5), and having to do with "unvarnished truth" (line 3) rather than being "subjugated to a cause" (line 3). To enhance its humanitarian ethos, Shell shifts the focus of attention from its own problems to a concern with the problems of Nigeria: Shell helps! (lines 2–4, 21–25, 32–35, 41–44). This is the perspective Shell is going to exploit thoroughly in its argumentation, elaborating extensively on its "development aid."

In contradistinction to Shell, the public is portrayed as allowing its judgments to be clouded by emotions (lines 1–2). The campaigners are even worse. They are people whose perceptions are suffused with anger and recriminations (line 2), who utter nothing but "slogans, protests and boycotts" (line 5) and for whom the campaign has become more important than the cause (line 14). One of the presentational means used to strengthen Shell's communion with the public consists in addressing them patronizingly in the way a father speaks to his children: although the emotions they feel are "understandable" (line 1), they should learn the truth. But if they take sides with Shell, all will end well. On the other hand, if they don't, chances are that they end up in the same bad position as the campaigners. Cloaked in a warning, the public is put on a par with those it was initially, together with Shell, supposed to ridicule (lines 45–47). Shell's repeated use of antithesis serves to put even more emphasis on the contrast between its own purported clear thinking and rational attitude and the alleged irrational attitude and muddled thinking of the campaigners (and sometimes the public). It is "facts" versus "emotions" (lines 1–4), "discreet diplomacy" versus "threats and protests" (lines 7–13), "clear thinking" versus "troubled times" (title), etc.

从交际活动类型中考察论辩的机构性制约因素
6.5 Communicative activity types as a source for institutional constraints

The notion of communicative activity types discussed in Chapter 5 constitutes an analytic instrument for substantiating the third parameter pertinent to determining the strategic function of argumentative moves. Communicative activity types are more or less institutionalized communicative practices that have become conventionalized in a certain domain of communicative activity. Identifying the macro-context of the communicative activity type in which the argumentative discourse takes place therefore provides an indispensable source for tracking down the institutional constraints imposed on the strategic maneuvering. In some cases, communicative activity types are strongly institutionalized and have conventions that are defined formally in explicit institutional rules and customs, as is the case in the communicative activity type of a criminal trial in the domain of legal communication. In other cases, communicative activity types are only lightly institutionalized and have conventions that are defined informally in implicit institutional requirements, as is the case in the communicative activity type of a chat in the domain of personal communication. The institutional conventions of a communicative activity type constitute institutional preconditions that impose constraints on the argumentative discourse which involve limitations on, as well as opportunities for, strategic maneuvering. In a Dutch criminal trial, for instance, it is an institutional precondition that argumentation from analogy referring to other cases is not allowed, so that certain strategic possibilities for the parties are closed off and, at the same time, other strategic possibilities open up. In a chat, on the other hand, it is an "institutional" precondition that no type of argumentation may be excluded in advance, so that in this respect the strategic possibilities are unrestricted.[7] In all cases, depending on the institutional conventionalization of a communicative activity type and the prevailing institutional preconditions, various constraints apply to the strategic maneuvering.

Shell presents its defense of its role in Nigeria in the general framework of the communicative activity type of an advertorial that offers an apologia to its adjudicators.[8] Such an advertorial presenting an apologia is a conventionalized communicative practice that has been institutionalized in the domain of commercial communication; it exploits both the promotional genre used in advertising and the adjudicatory genre used in an apologia. In analyzing "Clear Thinking in Troubled Times" it is worthwhile to notice that within the general framework of the communicative activity type of an advertorial providing an adjudicatory apologia, a remarkable change takes place in the defense of Shell's standpoint that its involvement in Nigeria is justified. First, as is customary in advertorials responding to blame cast on the company or organization concerned (Ware & Linkugel, 1973; Benoit & Lindsey, 1987), Shell engages in the adjudicatory activity type of an apologia to fight the multiple accusations that it deserves blame (lines 5–29). Second, however, the company counters the vigorous incitements to get out of Nigeria in the deliberative activity type of a *policy discussion* (lines 30–51).[9] Shell thus pretends that the issue of its support for the regime is to be treated as a policy issue instead of a quasi-juridical blame issue, thereby moving the accusation it has to face from an adjudicatory apologia to a deliberative policy discussion.

In the analysis I gave in Section 6.3, I did not fully account for Shell's strategic maneuvering at the confrontation stage. But now, taking into consideration the parameter of communicative activity type and the change of discourse genre taking place in the advertorial, I can do so. One of the three accusations directed at Shell by its opponents was that the company had indirectly supported the Nigerian regime (1.1c),

---

7. Occasionally, however, it may happen that the parties agree for some reason or other to exclude a certain type of argumentation from being used (e.g. "Don't give me what these professors think. We're friends; I am interested in hearing what *you* think"). Of course, there may be other restrictions, such as politeness conditions, that do not regard the *type* of argumentation.

8. *Apologia* is the term Aristotle uses for speeches of defense that are about wrongdoing, that is in legal terms causing harm and committing crime. According to the Aristotle scholar Hill (1994), harm is said to be voluntary if it is due to reasoned choice, habit, anger and even to irrational desire.

9. For the communicative activity type of an advertorial providing an adjudicatory apologia see van Eemeren and Houtlosser (1999b, 2000b), Ware and Linkugel (1973), and Benoit and Lindsey (1987). For the communicative activity type of a deliberative policy discussion see Freeley (1993).

and Shell was expected to address this difficult issue in its apologia, but refrains – as explained in Section 6.3 – from doing so explicitly. The amended analysis of the argumentation structure that is required because of Shell's manipulation of the intervention issue takes account of the fact that Shell gives the impression that at a certain point the discourse has changed from an advertorial providing an adjudicatory apologia into a deliberative policy discussion, which makes it only natural that the last paragraph of the text reads as a justification of Shell's policy. Nevertheless, Shell is in fact back to its apologetic endeavor: the issue is not really whether Shell should adopt a certain policy, but whether the company is to *blame* for its policy.

This analysis of the strategic maneuvering in Shell's advertorial illustrates that taking account of the communicative activity type in which the discourse takes place can have real consequences for determining the strategic function of argumentative moves and, as a consequence, for the reconstruction of the argumentation structure:

Quasi-juridical: (1) Shell is not to be blamed
1.1a Shell is not to be blamed for the death of Ken Saro-Wiwa
    (1.1a.1a) (Shell has made efforts to help Ken Saro-Wiwa)[10]
    (1.1a.1b) (These efforts were frustrated by the campaigners)
        (1.1a.1a-b).1a Shell's experience suggested that quiet diplomacy offered the very best hope for Ken Saro-Wiwa
        (1.1.a.1a-b).1b Yet the Government position hardened as the result of threats and protests increased
            (1.1.a.1a-b).1.b.1 The regime does not react well to threats
            (1.1.a.1a-b).1.b.1.1 Wura Abiola confirmed this
1.1b Shell is not to be blamed for any environmental devastation
    1.1b.1a There are other (environmental) problems in the area
        1.1b.1a.1 The World Bank confirms this
    (1.1b.1b) (Shell is in fact contributing to saving the environment)
    (1.1b.1b).1a They are substantially subsidizing environment-related projects
    (1.1b.1b).1b They are substantially subsidizing other "good" projects
    (1.1b.1b).1c They are substantially subsidizing an environment survey
    (1.1b.1c) (A substantial component of environmental devastation is not caused by Shell)
    (1.1b.1c).1a In the Ogoni area 60 % of the environmental devastation is caused by sabotage
    (1.1b.1c).1b The contractors have been denied access when they tried to deal with these problems
    (1.1b.1c).2 Shell has not been operative in the Ogoni area since 1993

---

10. Shell's efforts to help Ken Saro-Wiwa consisted in the first place in its "discreet" and "quiet" diplomacy mentioned in the advertorial.

Chapter 6. Determining the strategic function of argumentative moves

(1.1c) (Shell is not propping up the Nigerian regime)
    (1.1c).1 Shell should not intervene in Nigerian politics (even if it could)
        (1.1c).1.1a   Politics is the business of governments and politicians
        (1.1c).1.1b   A world in which companies use their influence to prop up or bring down governments would be a frightening and bleak world

Policy: (2) Shell's involvement in Nigeria is justified
2.1a Shell should not pull out of the Natural Liquefied Gas (NLG)-project
    2.1a.1a The people would suffer
    2.1a.1b The environment would suffer
    2.1a.1c The future Nigerian government would suffer
        2.1a.1a-c.1   If Shell would pull out of the NLG-project, the project would collapse
2.1b Shell should not pull out of Nigeria
    2.1b.1 The people of Nigeria would get hurt
    2.1b.1.1 All kinds of advantages for the Nigerian people would be lost

In justifying its position in the argumentation stage of the advertorial, Shell makes strategic use of symptomatic argumentation (in particular, argumentation from authority referring to Wura Abiola, the World Bank, and Shell itself) and pragmatic causal argumentation. The response that is thus evoked – and is anticipated in Shell's argumentation – consists of the critical questions associated with the argument schemes characterizing these two types of argumentation.

    In its policy discussion, Shell exploits the factual basis it has created in the opening stage by means of the use of *conciliatio*. The propositions safeguarded in this strategic maneuver, however, are not used here to support the opponents' position, but to support Shell's own position (lines 32–34). Because through the use of *conciliatio* the opponents' adherence is secured, this part of Shell's strategic maneuvering is rhetorically strong. And because the argument proceeds *ex concessis*, it is also pre-eminently dialectical. The danger of fallaciousness in strategic maneuvering by means of *conciliatio* stems from the fact that although the opponent may be assumed to agree with the propositional content of the argument, he may not automatically be assumed to agree with the way in which the argument is used to support a standpoint that is precisely the opposite of his own standpoint. In the case of argumentation by means of *conciliatio*, the propositional content of a starting point is typically granted, but not its justificatory force for the standpoint at issue.

The following dialectical profile distinguishes the critical questions that Shell should be able to answer in its argumentation for its use of *conciliatio* to be sound:

Shell: Given that neither the Nigerian people nor the environment should suffer, Shell should not pull out of Nigeria

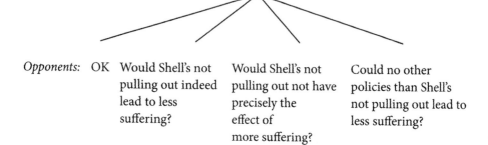

Opponents: OK   Would Shell's not pulling out indeed lead to less suffering?   Would Shell's not pulling out not have precisely the effect of more suffering?   Could no other policies than Shell's not pulling out lead to less suffering?

6.6 The argumentative situation as a source for commitment sets

The state of affairs in the resolution process at the point in the discourse where the maneuvering the analyst focuses on takes place is the fourth factor to be taken into account in analyzing the strategic function of argumentative moves. At this point – like at any other such point – the parties involved in the discourse may be assumed to try to handle the argumentative situation in an opportune way. The sets of commitments they have contracted in the argumentative discourse up until that point constitute an analytic instrument for substantiating this fourth parameter.[11] The argumentative situations the arguers are in at a specific juncture in the exchange are eventually defined by the sets of mutually recognized commitments the parties have obtained. Due to the various types of speech acts the parties have performed in the argumentative discourse preceding that juncture, including their responses to each other's speech acts, each of the parties has compiled a certain set of commitments, which can be specified pragmatically with the help of the identity and correctness conditions of these speech acts. In the follow-up of the discourse the parties may keep each other to their commitments and they may exploit these commitments in their strategic maneuvering. For this reason it is imperative to take the meso-context of the argumentative situation into consideration in determining the strategic function that argumentative moves may have.

For instance, in an argumentative situation in which the protagonist's standpoint has been contradicted, rather than just called into question, by the antagonist at the confrontation stage, he can hold the antagonist to account for being the protagonist of the opposite standpoint, and then the antagonist is committed to defend his opposing standpoint

---

11. This analytic instrument for describing the commitments that are argumentative was first proposed in Hamblin (1970),

at the argumentation stage when challenged to do so. Also, if the antagonist has made certain concessions at the opening stage when establishing the material starting point of the discussion, the argumentative situation entitles the protagonist to make use of these concessions when defending his standpoint at the argumentation stage. If at that stage the antagonist starts criticizing a certain part of the protagonist's argumentation, he cannot do so without ending up in problems if he is already committed as a starting point to the proposition that is used as a premise in the argument. And if – to give one final example – the parties are about to conclude their discussion at the concluding stage, neither of them can ignore the commitments they have made during the preceding discussion. In fact, in their strategic maneuvering both parties are bound at every point in the discourse by the mutual commitments defining the argumentative situation at the point the discourse has reached. This is not to say, however, that their commitment sets are merely limitations on the parties' subsequent strategic maneuvering in the discussion; the commitment sets defining the argumentative situation also open up genuine opportunities to use the other party's commitments to the advantage of one's own cause.[12]

When considering the role played by the argumentative situation in determining the strategic function of argumentative moves it is good policy to distinguish between the argumentative situation as a "dialectical situation" and the argumentative situation as a "rhetorical situation." The advantage of making this distinction is that by considering the dialectical situation and the rhetorical situation separately it becomes easier to take into account both the exploitation of the mutual commitments in maintaining the reasonableness of the discourse and the exploitation of the mutual commitments in securing the effectiveness of the discourse. In line with my general view of strategic maneuvering, the point of departure in this endeavor is the dialectical situation, which is defined pragmatically by the sets of commitments accumulated by the protagonist and the antagonist in the process of resolving a difference of opinion on the merits at the point in the discourse the analysis is focusing on. The rhetorical situation is, as it were, the complement of the dialectical situation in which the argumentative situation is viewed from the rhetorical perspective of aiming for effectiveness. Just as the dialectical aims of the various discussion stages may be assumed to have their rhetorical counterparts, so it is presumed that the dialectical dimension of the argumentative situation always has its rhetorical counterpart. In this rhetorical counterpart the prevailing perspective of the argumentative situation is not primarily concerned with the opportunities for making *reasonable* moves the argumentative situation allows in view of the pattern of commitments that has been established, but rather with the opportunities the argumentative situation allows in view of this pattern of commitments for making *effective* argumentative moves in promoting the arguer's cause.[13]

---

12. In addition, the argumentative situation is not an inescapable fact of life but a state of affairs that comes about as a result of decisions made by the arguers about the argumentative moves they make, so that it is in fact at any point defined by the intentional mutual interaction of the arguers.

13. A rhetorical definition of the situation may, for instance, involve presenting a party's interpretation of the state of affairs at that particular point in the discussion as a "crisis" or viewing it in a similarly "biased" perspective furthering the interests of the party concerned.

In "The rhetorical situation" Bitzer explains that a particular discourse comes into being because of "some specific condition or situation" (1968, p. 4): "Rhetorical discourse is called into existence by situation; the situation which the rhetor perceives amounts to an invitation to create and present discourse" (p. 9).[14] Just like a dialectical situation invites a response that fits with the dialectical state of affairs at that specific point in the dialectical procedure, according to Bitzer, a rhetorical situation "invites a fitting response, a response that fits the situation" (p. 10). To say that "a rhetorical response fits a situation" is to say that it meets the requirements established by the situation. Bitzer adds that "one might say metaphorically that every situation prescribes its *fitting* response" (p. 11). If a rhetorical situation is "strong and clear," it affects all aspects of strategic maneuvering, dictating "the purpose, theme, matter, and style" of the response that an audience will get (p. 10).[15]

A "real or genuine" rhetorical situation is objective, publicly observable, and historic (Bitzer, 1968, p. 11).[16] According to Bitzer, three constituents comprise "everything relevant in a rhetorical situation:" "exigence," "audience," and "constraint" (p. 8). Each exigency is something waiting to be done, "an imperfection marked by urgency" (p. 6). Exigencies which cannot be modified and exigencies which can be modified only by means other than discourse are not rhetorical, because "an exigence is rhetorical when it is capable of positive modification and when positive modification requires discourse or can be assisted by discourse" (p. 7). In any rhetorical situation, Bitzer observes, "there will be at least one controlling exigence which functions as the organizing principle: it specifies the audience to be addressed and the change to be effected" (p. 7). A rhetorical audience, he adds, "consists only of those persons who are capable of being influenced by discourse and of being mediators of change" (p. 8).[17] This is the audience "to be

---

14. According to Bitzer, "a work of rhetoric is pragmatic; it comes into existence for the sake of something beyond itself; it functions ultimately to produce action or change in the world; it performs some task" (1968, pp. 3–4).

15. To say that "rhetoric is situational," means for Bitzer that "(1) rhetorical discourse comes into existence as a response to situation, in the same sense that an answer comes into existence in response to a question, or a solution in response to a problem; (2) a speech is given *rhetorical* significance by the situation, just as a unit of discourse is given significance *as* answer or *as* solution by the question or problem; (3) a rhetorical situation must exist as a necessary condition of rhetorical discourse, just as a question must exist as a necessary condition of an answer; (4) many questions go unanswered and many problems remain unsolved; similarly, many rhetorical situations mature and decay without giving birth to rhetorical utterance; (5) a situation is rhetorical insofar as it needs and invites discourse capable of participating with situation and thereby altering its reality; (6) discourse is rhetorical insofar as it functions (or seeks to function) as a fitting response to a situation which needs and invites it. (7) Finally, the situation controls the rhetorical response in the same sense that the question controls the answer and the problem controls the solution" (pp. 5–6).

16. A problem of the way in which Bitzer and many other rhetoricians deal with the rhetorical situation is that they often do not seem to refer to types of situations but to contingent individual situations.

17. In pragma-dialectical terms, Bitzer requires that the audience is in a particular state of mind, which implies that the second order conditions have been fulfilled.

constrained in decision and action" (p. 6). Besides exigency and audience, every rhetorical situation contains, in Bitzer's view, a set of constraints that influence the rhetoric and that can be brought to bear upon the audience and modify the exigency.[18] Constraints such as existing traditions, past events, recognized facts and values, authorative sources (e.g. the law), and physical, social, and cultural conditions, are circumstances the arguer has to take into account when trying to resolve the exigency because they may hinder the resolution process. According to Bitzer, there are two general classes of constraints: those "managed by the rhetor and his method" which Aristotle called "artistic proofs," and those "other constraints, in the situation, which may be operative" which Aristotle called "inartistic proofs" (p. 8).[19] Some constraints belonging to the latter category do not belong to what I regard as the rhetorical situation, but are part of the macro-context of the communicative activity type or the starting points of the discourse (or both).[20]

A rhetorical situation may be defined as "a complex of persons, events, objects, and relations presenting an actual or potential exigence which can be completely or partially removed if discourse, introduced into the situation, can so constrain human decision or action as to bring about the significant modification of the exigence" (Bitzer, 1968, p. 6). Rhetorical situations exhibit structures which are simple or complex, and are more or less organized. "A situation's structure is simple," says Bitzer, "when there are relatively few elements which must be made to interact" (p. 11).[21] A rhetorical situation, whether simple or complex, can be highly structured or loosely structured. Bitzer calls the rhetorical situation "highly structured" when, as is often the case in courtroom situations, "all of its elements are located and readied for the task to be performed" (p. 12).[22] Some situations recur, in a great many cases due to convention, so that they prompt comparable responses (such as the speech of accusation and the speech of

---

18. It is striking that constraints impose restrictions on the arguer as well as the audience.

19. "Artistic" is a very obscure translation of Aristotle's ʼἔντεχνος (entechnos), which means according to the art of rhetoric; "inartistic" is a translation of ʼἄτεχνος (atechnos), which means outside the art of rhetoric (*Rhet.* I.2, 1355b 37–38).

20. Standard sources of constraint mentioned by Bitzer include beliefs, attitudes, documents, facts, traditions, images, interests, motives and the like. When the orator enters the situation, Bitzer adds, "his discourse not only harnesses constraints given by situation but provides additional important constraints – for example his personal character, his logical proofs, and his style" (1968, p. 8).

21. Situations may become weakened in structure, Bitzer observes, due to complexity or disconnectedness. The list of causes he mentions includes these: (a) a single situation may involve numerous exigencies; (b) exigencies in the same situation may be incompatible; (c) two or more simultaneous rhetorical situations may compete for our attention; (d) at a given moment, persons comprising the audience of situation A may also be the audience of situations B, C, and D; (e) the rhetorical audience my be scattered, uneducated regarding its duties and powers, or it may dissipate; (f) constraints may be limited in number and force, and they may be incompatible (1968, p. 12).

22. I use the term (dialectical and rhetorical) *situation* in a more specific way than Bitzer, excluding from the situation proper the starting points of the discourse and the macro-context of the communicative activity type in which the discourse takes place.

defense in a courtroom).[23] In determining in a pragma-dialectical reconstruction the commitment sets defining a particular argumentative situation, it is necessary to include an account of the joint impact of the factors of exigency, audience and constraint, identified by Bitzer, that define in their mutual interaction the rhetorical situation – whether conventionalized or not – complementing the dialectical situation.

Let us return to the Shell advertorial for some illustrations of the role of the argumentative situation in strategic maneuvering. When dealing, in its advertorial, with the three blame accusations that were at the time made against Shell, the company silently prepares the ground for the change from the apologia it is expected to issue (in agreement with the quasi-juridical institutional conventions of an adjudicatory activity type) to the deliberative activity type of a policy discussion. Shell does so, at the point at which it has to deal with the third blame issue (*Shell supports the regime*), by strategically presenting the argumentative situation in policy terms, so that the dialectical commitments the company has to take into account are put in a new perspective and the rhetorical situation shifts accordingly in the way enforced by Shell. The opposition Shell is confronted with, which was part of the rhetorical situation at the time being hinted at in the advertorial (lines 48–51), is the following:

(1.1c) (Shell supports the Nigerian regime)

In order to clear Shell of all blame, the company has to address not only the two issues (1.1a and 1.1b) it explicitly presents as blame issues (Shell's responsibility for the death of Ken Saro-Wiwa and Shell's polluting the environment), but also the blame issue it treats as a policy issue (1.1c), namely Shell's supporting the Nigerian regime. In the advertorial, Shell chooses to address only the first two accusations directly. The third accusation the company was expected to deal with is addressed only implicitly and indirectly by reacting to the accusation in a non-conspicuous way. The support issue, which belongs dialectically to the confrontation stage, Shell does not address at the beginning of the advertorial together with the other blame issues belonging to the confrontation stage. It is addressed only after Shell's strategic maneuvering in the other stages is calculated to have taken its effect at the end of the advertorial (lines 48–51), where one expects the concluding stage to be carried through. In the process, Shell transcends the accusation by referring, not specifically to support, but to intervention in general ("prop up or bring down governments"), thus counterbalancing the negative side of the issue expressed in the accusation of "propping up" the government with the opposite side of bringing down the regime, a course that would be valued positively by the opponents. In this way, Shell creates a rhetorical perspective on the argumentative situation that is instrumental in effecting a change in the communicative activity type to which the standpoint of support belongs. By pretending that its support for the regime is to be treated as a policy issue instead of a quasi-juridical issue, Shell moves the support accusation away

---

23. "Hence," Bitzer concludes, "rhetorical forms are born" (1968, p. 13).

from the semi-legal domain of an adjudicatory apologia to a deliberative discussion on policy in the political domain, suggesting that Shell never supported the regime.

The reconstruction of Shell's manipulation of the third accusation in its strategic maneuvering in the confrontation stage illustrates that taking the argumentative situation into account when considering the strategic function of argumentative moves can be of real consequence to the analysis. Another example is Shell's dissociation, in the confrontation stage, of the general public from the campaigners. The campaigners are presented as Shell's real opponents, who have a mixed difference of opinion with the company, while the general public is presumed to be not really in opposition to Shell but to have only some doubts resulting from ignorance or lack of careful reflection. By maneuvering in this way, Shell suggests an argumentative situation in which it merely has a non-mixed difference of opinion with the general public or perhaps even no difference at all, which is contrary to what in reality the argumentative situation was like at the time. As I explained in Section 6.3, the advantage of this strategic dissociation is that Shell can now present the general public as a possible ally and treat the blame accusations as being open to a straightforward, quasi-informative defense – contrasting in the process the naïve but well-meaning public with the cunning campaigners.

A remarkable feature of Shell's strategic maneuvering with regard to the argumentative situation in the concluding stage is that the company presupposes that it is obvious, both in the apologia part and in the policy part of the advertorial, that the facts speak for themselves, so that an explicit concluding stage can be left out altogether. In this way, Shell claims implicitly that after the company provided its argumentation the argumentative situation is now such that it is evident that Shell can neither be blamed for Ken Saro-Wiwa's death nor for environmental pollution and that Shell should stay in Nigeria.

论辩话步的策略功能分析
6.7 Analyzing an argumentative move for its strategic function

As I have shown in the preceding sections, Shell's possibilities for strategic maneuvering are constrained by preconditions imposed on the discourse by the communicative activity type in which the maneuvering takes place and by particulars of the argumentative situation at the point at which the argumentative move is made. Summarizing, it can be said that the combination of factors that need to be taken into account in determining the strategic function of argumentative moves generally includes: the kind of communicative activity type, the dialectical and rhetorical characteristics of the argumentative situation, the kind of result aimed for in the appropriate component of the analytic overview, and the particular route that is chosen from the possible routes of analytically relevant moves that can be distinguished in the appropriate dialectical profile. Making use of these analytic instruments, I shall now, as a preliminary to my continued analysis of Shell's strategic maneuvering, give an exemplifying analysis of the strategic function of some argumentative moves made in another illustrative case of argumentative discourse.

I shall first concentrate on the concluding stage of a one-sided argumentative exchange that took place in Bosnia on July 11, 1995, between commander Karremans of a Dutch battalion of United Nations blue helmets, who were stationed in Srebrenica, and general Mladić of the Bosnian Serb Army (BSA/VRS). It was the eve of the Srebrenica massacre and Karremans, confronted by Mladić and his troops, was trying to convince Mladić that he should not be killed. This is what Karremans said:

> [...] I am only the piano player. And we have a saying, "Don't shoot the piano player ..."

According to the options available in an analytic overview of such an argumentative discourse for the concluding stage, the argumentative process may end in a conclusion that is to the advantage of the protagonist, Karremans, or in a conclusion that is to the advantage of the antagonist that Karremans is out to convince, Mladić. In the first case, the difference of opinion would end in Mladić's withdrawing his projected doubt concerning the acceptability of Karremans' unexpressed standpoint that Mladić should not shoot him, so that Karremans may maintain the standpoint inherent in the implied conclusion of his argumentation. In the second case, the difference of opinion would end in Karremans' withdrawing his implied conclusion, i.e. his standpoint that Mladić should not shoot him, and Mladić's maintaining his projected doubt. The first possibility is, of course, the option favored by Karremans and aimed for in his argumentation.

The dialectical profile of the argumentative moves that are analytically relevant in the concluding stage of the argumentative process aimed at resolving a non-mixed difference of opinion about a negative standpoint such as *You should not shoot me* reads as follows (van Eemeren *et al.* 2007, p. 225):[24]

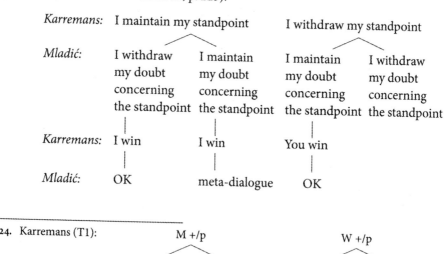

24.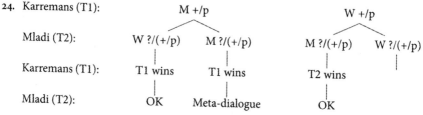

In the threatening circumstances in which this argumentative process takes place, Karremans engages in the communicative activity type of an adjudicatory apologia. As protagonist of the unexpressed standpoint *You should not shoot me*, he addresses his antagonist Mladić not just as an ordinary listener but as a listener who is to act as an adjudicator. Although Karremans' words cannot be taken literally, they should certainly be taken seriously because they involve a self-serving justificatory appeal to Mladić's adjudicative power to release Karremans from his predicament. Only when analyzed within the framework of the activity type of adjudicatory apologia do the argumentative moves made by Karremans acquire their proper meaning.

By saying "I am only the piano player," Karremans creates a material starting point in the opening stage, but the strategic function of this starting point, which is meant metaphorically, becomes clear only when it is associated with the introduction of the saying "don't shoot the piano player" in Karremans' next utterance. The remarkable topical, audience-oriented and presentational choice made by Karremans in this argumentative move[25] makes sense only because it transforms the statement "I am only the piano player" – with the help of the connective "and" – into a minor premise in the argumentation in which "Don't shoot the piano player" (after having been reconstructed as "The piano player should never be shot") serves as a major premise. At this point in the discourse the argumentation stage seems completed and the argumentative process enters the concluding stage. Because any explicit standpoint is lacking, the argumentative situation defined by the dialectical and rhetorical commitments of the parties as projected in the discourse leaves room for only one conclusion: *You should not shoot me*.

This analytic reconstruction of the unexpressed argumentative move *You should not shoot me* depends on all four factors that need to be taken into account in combination to determine the strategic function of argumentative moves. First, the options distinguished in the analytic overview with regard to the concluding stage include this possibility. Second, the routes of analytically relevant moves distinguished in the dialectical profile for the concluding stage allow for this possibility. Third, the communicative activity type of an adjudicatory apologia points to this option. Fourth, the dialectical and rhetorical commitments defining together the argumentative situation at the point concerned in the argumentative discourse confirm that this option is implied and should therefore be preferred in the analysis.

However great the differences, a similar mode of strategic maneuvering toward an advantageous outcome takes place in Shell's advertorial. By leaving the general

---

25. The topical choice made in this argumentative move is remarkable because one would not expect someone who is in such a dangerous situation to come up with this wild west metaphor, the audience-oriented choice because it assumes that rough guys such as Mladić *cum suis* will be inclined to agree with a wild west wisdom that "we" are supposed to accept, and the presentational choice because, instead of begging on his knees or resorting to some other humiliating move, Karremans tries to reach the desired outcome by making general Mladić draw the desired conclusion himself from the argument he has put forward.

conclusion of the discussion concerning its involvement in Nigeria implicit, Shell suggests that it has said all there is to say and that the conclusion is obvious. What else can the readers conclude than that Shell is neither to be blamed for the killing of Ken Saro-Wiwa nor for any environmental disaster? On the contrary, Shell is a great help to the people of Nigeria and should stay there to prolong its generous "development aid." To ensure that the public reaches this favorable view, Shell again makes an appeal to the public's responsibility. Having paved the way by its repeated warnings that the fate of the Nigerian people is in their hands, Shell strikes a final blow at the end of the text, when the company starts lecturing the general public about their attitude ("It's easy enough to sit in our comfortable homes in the West, calling for sanctions and boycotts" etc.). The public acts irresponsibly: their opinions of the Nigerian problems amount to empty slogans, and their response is nothing but a knee-jerk reaction that can only harm this poor developing country (lines 46–47). They do indeed need Shell to put them straight.

Shell's crucial strategic move at the argumentation stage of the discussion is to evoke a straightforward image of doom and horror (lines 31–44). Using the presentational device of sketching a looming disaster that Shell's actions have prevented is aimed at eradicating at the concluding stage any idea that the company could be doing a thing so evil as supporting the Nigerian regime (lines 50–51). The implication of this move for the concluding stage of the discussion is clear: if it is evident to all what horrific consequences supporting the Nigerian regime will have, Shell can only be accused of such misbehavior by extreme malevolents whose sole aim is to destroy Shell's political and moral ethos. The final words, "We'll keep you in touch with the facts" (line 52), are not just a slogan, but should reassure the public that Shell will prevent the menacing perspective of a frightening and bleak world from becoming a reality – clear thinking will prevail. These words, however, also convey a veiled counter-accusation: "You, the public, are not capable of keeping in touch with the facts." This is why Shell will do it for you.

A strategic maneuver, finally, that is crucial to the concluding stage is Shell's invoking of a catastrophic scenario that would become reality should the campaigners' wishes be fulfilled (lines 31–44). In making this dramatic maneuver Shell confronts the general public with a *false dilemma*. Instead of pointing out other possibilities, the company suggests that the public should either support Shell or will be just as guilty as the campaigners. This dilemma can only have persuasive force because it relies on Shell's perpetual personal attacks on the campaigners earlier on in the advertorial. Had the campaigners been portrayed as sensible people, the choice presented here would not have been a realistic dilemma to the public.

CHAPTER 7 第七章

谬误：脱轨的策略操控
Fallacies as derailments of strategic maneuvering

谬误逻辑学标准处理方法的批评
7.1 Hamblin's criticism of the logical standard treatment

Scholars of argumentation, dialecticians and rhetoricians alike, are often attracted to studying argumentation because they are not entirely satisfied with certain aspects of the quality of argumentative practice as they encounter it.[1] They would like to develop designs and methods for improving argumentative practice – if possible in a systematic way – in agreement with their critical ideal (van Eemeren & Grootendorst, 2004, Chapter 2). In this endeavor, finding a theoretically-based method for dealing with the fallacies that may occur in argumentative discourse plays a crucial role, because fallacies are generally seen as argumentative moves that are in one way or another not acceptable when argumentative discourse is evaluated from a critical point of view. Therefore developing adequate tools for dealing with the fallacies is a vital component of any normative theory of argumentation. In my view, the treatment of the fallacies can even be seen as the acid test for any normative theory of argumentation: is the theory capable of dealing in a satisfactory way with all fallacies?

For an example of a fallacy of the kind that the evaluative tools provided by an adequate normative theory of argumentation should enable us to deal with, I turn to the "Nigeria Spam Letters" analyzed by Kienpointner (2006).[2] These are e-mail messages that were sent in recent years to a great many people to ask them for their financial assistance in making it possible to transfer enormous amounts of money to the sender. Referring to the number of the section of the Nigerian law that forbids these fraudulent practices, these messages are now usually called "419 letters." In one of these 419 letters, a barrister, who calls himself Michael Chris, presents himself as the legal adviser to an American couple called Mr. and Mrs. Brown. Mr. Chris informs the addressee that the

---

1. This chapter is an extended and revised version of van Eemeren and Houtlosser (2008), which was based on the Van Zelst lecture I presented at Northwestern University on November 10, 2006.

2. For didactic reasons, in teaching students about the fallacies most of the time clear cases of fallacies are used so that the students easily understand what is wrong. Often these examples present caricatures of certain types of fallacies or cases of fallacious argumentative discourse that are embedded in a context that makes their fallaciousness obvious. In the more obscure cases one is confronted with in ordinary argumentative discourse, fallacies are often much harder to detect and such fallacies are therefore much trickier. In this chapter, I want to move away from the clear cases to the more obscure ones.

Browns had lived in Nigeria for 30 years before they died in 2002 in a plane crash – the kind of story that is usually told in 419 letters. The Browns, says Mr. Chris, had no children and were good Christians. In his last will, Mr. Brown had asked Mr. Chris to sell all his property and give it to a ministry "for the work of God." Mr. Chris confesses that first he had wanted to embezzle the money (US$13,800,000), but later had "an encounter with Christ," and, "as a born again Christian," started to read the Bible. He now wants to fulfill Mr. Brown's last will. Looking for a good Christian, Mr. Chris took refuge to the Internet and experienced what could be called a miracle: "after my fervent prayer over it, [...] you were nominated to me through divine revelation from God." The addressee was then asked to send some money in order to finance the release of the much larger sum that was allegedly constituting the inheritance. Although 419 letters such as this one first of all appeal to greed and have had a (considerable) impact only on people who wanted to have a share in the money and therefore sent money of their own to set the African capital free, it will be clear that it is not just an intellectual challenge but also an important social task to unmask the fallacies upon which the success of these letters is based – in this case, a profane appeal to God that amounts here to an abuse of authority known as the *argumentum ad verecundiam*. Although in most other cases it will not be possible to calculate so precisely how many dollars a fallacy costs, in view of the need to protect the quality of argumentative discourse in the various domains of communication detecting them in other domains than that of 419 letters may be even more important.

Given the combination of their treacherous nature and their negative role, it is both understandable and fortunate that from antiquity onwards the fallacies have been an important object of study. Aristotle, for one, examined them extensively in his dialectical writings and also deals with them in his rhetorical study. In the *Topics* (Aristotle, 1960, Trans.), his treatise on dialectic, Aristotle placed the fallacies in the context of a debate between a questioner and an answerer in which the questioner attacks a thesis which the answerer tries to uphold. The questioner can win the debate first of all by refuting the answerer's thesis (see Chapter 3.2). Aristotle discusses correct moves the questioner can make to refute the answerer's thesis as well as incorrect moves that he considers fallacious. Among the fallacious moves, for instance, are various circular ways of reasoning known as "begging the question" or *petitio principii*. Viewed from Aristotle's dialectical perspective on the fallacies, they are false moves employed in the questioner's efforts to refute the answerer's thesis. In *Sophistical refutations*, Aristotle (1928c, Trans.) deals systematically with all possible false ways of refuting a thesis (which he ascribed, according to some scholars, to the prominent debate experts known as the Sophists – hence the epithet "sophism"). In his *Rhetoric*, Aristotle (1991, Trans.) discusses from a rhetorical perspective some fallacious refutations that are only apparent refutations.

Fallacies have remained a popular subject of study and in the course of time a number of "new" fallacies were distinguished, such as the *"ad"* fallacies *argumentum ad hominem* and *argumentum ad verecundiam*. Although in the nineteenth century the dialectical perspective was, largely due to the influence of bishop Whateley, replaced by a much broader logical perspective, the newly discovered fallacies were just added to the Aristotelian list, so that the list lost more and more of its original coherence. The Latin names that were given to many of the "new" fallacies may suggest that they stem from the classical tradition, but this is generally not the case.[3]

In 1970, Charles Hamblin caused a revolution in the treatment of the fallacies through the publication of his book *Fallacies*. After having studied the leading logical textbooks, Hamblin was struck by the similarity of their treatments of the fallacies. Each of them presented more or less the same list of fallacies and the fallacies were always explained in more or less the same way. Often even the same examples were used. These commonalities may seem to be a sign of general agreement among the various authors but, because of the many incongruities in the treatment of the fallacies and the remarkable lack of clarity, Hamblin suspected that the one author was just, without any further reflection, copying the other.[4]

Hamblin observed that the logical "Standard Treatment" he had detected in the textbooks started from a logical "Standard Definition" in which the fallacies were described as *arguments that seem valid but are in fact not valid*. Strangely, however, the treatment of the fallacies that was actually given in the logical textbooks was inconsistent with this definition. A great many of the fallacies that were treated were in fact not arguments, such as the fallacy of many questions, or they were arguments that were by no means invalid, such as "circular reasoning" or *petitio principii*; there were also various cases, such as the *argumentum ad verecundiam*, in which the fallacy described was a defective argumentative move for a different reason than invalidity.

It will be no surprise that these observations caused a lot of turmoil among those interested in the study of fallacies, although open-minded argumentation theorists saw that Hamblin was basically right. Gradually they came to share virtually all his objections against the logical Standard Definition of the fallacies. Nowadays, most argumentation theorists no longer consider "logical invalidity" the sole criterion for fallaciousness. Also they tend to agree that including a word like "seems" in the definition of fallacies, as in the logical Standard Definition, brings in an undesirable amount of psychologistic subjectivity. A certain argument may seem sound to you, but why would it seem sound to me if I know (because of my training in logic or due to some other insight) that it is invalid or otherwise unacceptable?

In spite of the pertinence of Hamblin's criticisms, they were not always effective in practice. Let me first mention two extremely unproductive reactions. First, there were the leading logic textbooks. They were in most cases reprinted without any attempt being made to deal seriously with Hamblin's objections. Perhaps – one might suspect – the authors or their publishers thought that the textbooks were selling well as they

---

3. See Nuchelmans (1993).

4. Hansen (2007), for one, questions whether the choice of material on which Hamblin based his observations was indeed representative.

were: and what did the students know about Hamblin?[5] Another extreme reaction to Hamblin consists of expunging the treatment of the fallacies altogether from the textbook (e.g. Lambert and Ulrich, 1980). Assuming that Hamblin is right, from an ethical perspective the second kind of reaction may be preferable to the first, but it is clear that from the perspective of an argumentation theorist interested in having the fallacies carefully studied neither of these reactions is really constructive. Fortunately, most argumentation theorists do not seem prepared to throw the baby out with the bath water and to leave the problem of dealing with the fallacies unresolved.

谬误综合研究路径的必要性
7.2 The need for a comprehensive approach to the fallacies

Hamblin's book *Fallacies* did not only lead to unhelpful reactions as those mentioned in Section 7.1, but also provided an important source of inspiration for argumentation scholars who wanted to develop a constructive alternative to the way in which the fallacies were dealt with in the logical Standard Treatment. Twenty-five years after Hamblin's epoch-making study was published, another volume titled *Fallacies* appeared to honor Hamblin with a collection of classical and contemporary readings (Hansen & Pinto, 1995). The contemporary essays made clear that since Hamblin's publication several argumentation theorists had made a serious effort to meet the challenge posed by his work. Among the prominent modern fallacy theorists taking part in this enterprise are both North-Americans and Europeans (see van Eemeren, Ed., 2001).

The most continuous and extensive post-Hamblin contribution to the study of the fallacies coming from North-America was made by the Canadian logicians Woods and Walton, who substantiated in a series of co-authored articles and books their remedy for the logical Standard Treatment, namely calling on more sophisticated logics (see Woods & Walton, 1989).[6] Woods and Walton's first starting point is that fallacies can generally be analyzed with the help of logical systems in a broad sense, so that successful analyses of a great many fallacies will have features that qualify those analyses as "formal" in the sense that they make use of concepts described by employing the technical vocabulary or the formal structures of a system of logic or some other sort of formal theory. This preoccupation with formality characterizing the Woods-Walton approach was not maintained in the studies of the fallacies that were later on undertaken independently by Walton (1987, 1995, 1998b, 2008).

---

5. This suspicion is justified in particular when the author makes clear that he is aware of Hamblin's criticisms (if he is not, his credentials as an argumentation theorist may be doubted), and even claims to agree with them, but nevertheless leaves parts of the text to which these criticisms apply unmodified (Copi, 1986).

6. Rhetoricians felt for various reasons less inspired to theorize about the fallacies, a noteworthy exception in North-America being Brinton (1995), who developed a normative rhetorical perspective.

A second typical feature of the Woods-Walton approach is that it is "pluralistic," because in Woods and Walton's view each fallacy must be treated in its own way. It demands, as it were, its own (formal) theory. In my opinion, a major disadvantage of this theoretical starting point is that it makes the Woods-Walton approach *ad hoc* in several ways. First, because Woods and Walton take the more or less arbitrary list of fallacies that happens to have been handed down by history and recorded in the literature as the point of departure of their theorizing, in spite of the fact that the list is not systematic, let alone theoretically motivated – a point of departure maintained by Walton in his independent studies. Second, the Woods-Walton approach to the fallacies is *ad hoc* because each individual fallacy is given its own idiosyncratic theoretical treatment that is independent of the treatment of other fallacies. A negative consequence of the *ad hoc* nature of the Woods-Walton approach in this second sense is that the various treatments of the fallacies can easily be at variance with each other. It is clear that passing these criticisms on such a constructive and productive response to Hamblin's critique of the logical Standard Treatment as Woods and Walton's obliges me to sketch an alternative that does not display these drawbacks.

Prompted by Hamblin's challenge, in Europe two theories of argumentation were developed around 1980 that relate the fallacies systematically to standards or rules for sound argumentation. Both argumentation theories are dialectical theories that share a "critical rationalist" perspective on argumentative discourse in which the fallibility of all human thought is the fundamental starting point. First there was formal dialectic, developed by Barth and Krabbe (1982), second came the pragma-dialectical theory of argumentation that constitutes the theoretical framework of my present study (van Eemeren & Grootendorst, 1984, 1992a, 2004). Barth and Krabbe's formal dialectic provides formal systems for conducting critical dialogues and regards the fallacies as moves that cannot be generated by these formal systems. The pragma-dialectical theory of argumentation links up with formal dialectic, but concentrates on ordinary argumentative discourse and starts from the conviction that fallacies can be properly understood only if argumentative discourse is viewed pragmatically in a communicative and interactional perspective.

In examining the communicative interaction taking place in argumentative discourse between the speech acts performed by the protagonist of a standpoint and the speech acts performed by the antagonist who is in doubt about the acceptability of this standpoint, pragma-dialectics starts from the ideal model of a critical discussion and the rules for critical discussion that specify in which cases the performance of certain speech acts contributes to the resolution of the difference of opinion. As already explained in Chapter 2.2, the rules for critical discussion proposed in pragma-dialectics when taken together constitute a discussion procedure that is claimed to be problem-valid and has the potential of being recognized as conventionally valid. The claim to problem-validity is based on the fact that each rule makes a specific contribution to solving certain problems inherent in the process of resolving a difference of opinion on the merits; the conventional validity of the rules has been largely confirmed by experimental research regarding their intersubjective acceptability (van Eemeren, Garssen & Meuffels, 2009).

Before turning to the pragma-dialectical treatment of the fallacies, I need to clarify how I shall forestall the criticisms I raised against the Woods-Walton treatment of the fallacies. My view is that the theorizing about fallacies has to start, first of all, from a general and coherent perspective on argumentative discourse that provides a common rationale for the study of all fallacies.[7] In the case of the pragma-dialectical theory, the general and coherent perspective will be that each part of argumentative discourse that is judged for its soundness or fallaciousness is always considered as being aimed at resolving a difference of opinion on the merits. This perspective is general and coherent: it serves as an umbrella covering the study of argumentative discourse and guarantees a unified view of all fallacies. It provides a common rationale to the study of the fallacies because in each particular case the reason to consider an argumentative move as fallacious is its being in some way or other prejudicial or harmful for the realization of the general goal of resolving a difference of opinion on the merits. Viewing fallacies in this way means concentrating on the soundness norms for argumentation rather than on the fallacies as such, taking neither individual cases of fallacies nor the somewhat arbitrary list of fallacies that has come down to us from history as the starting point of theorizing.

The unified theory of the fallacies that pragma-dialectics aspires to offer is as a matter of course an integral part of a normative theory of argumentation. As de Morgan (1847) and Massey (1975) have observed (from different perspectives), a theory of errors cannot be constructed independently of a theory of correctness.[8] A theory of fallacies must therefore be incorporated in a normative theory of argumentation that provides the standards or rules for sound argumentative discourse. Only in this way can it be made clear in what sense a fallacy represents a kind of wrongness and can all

---

7. A fundamental problem that threatens fallacy theory, in particular when each fallacy gets its own theoretical treatment, is that not only the treatments of the various fallacies are at variance with each other, but also the general perspectives from which these treatments start. Although in principle giving each fallacy its own treatment does not prevent the theorist from making all fallacy judgments from the same perspective (say a formal perspective as favored by Woods (1992) or an epistemological perspective as favored by Biro and Siegel (1992)), in practice often one perspective is used in one case and another in an other case, and different perspectives may even get mixed up. In such cases, ethical or moral considerations, for instance, all of a sudden get the upper hand over logical (or other) considerations relating to the perspective claimed to have been chosen. Wagemans (2003) provides a good illustration when he discusses Walton's (1999a) treatment of the *argumentum ad ignorantiam*. In his analysis, Walton introduces an epistemic norm to condemn such "arguments." Next, however, he starts classifying exceptions to this norm, and mentions, instead of epistemic considerations, practical considerations relating to the consequences of applying the norm.

8. Jacobs (2002, p. 122) correctly observes that "no list of categories will ever exhaustively enumerate all the ways in which argumentation can go wrong."

fallacies be related to the observation of certain general norms of soundness. In the pragma-dialectical theory of argumentation, this requirement is realized by relating all fallacies systematically to the standards expressed in the rules for critical discussion. Ideally, in this way it can be indicated for each fallacy which norm inherent in a rule for critical discussion is contravened by the argumentative move concerned (although in everyday practice the identification is often rather troublesome). This means that in the pragma-dialectical treatment the fallacies are immediately connected with a coherent set of norms serving a common general goal and that the rationale for calling an argumentative move fallacious is invariably the same. In addition, the theoretical tools that pragma-dialectics provides for distinguishing between non-fallacious and fallacious argumentative moves are the same for all fallacies and apply equally to all cases of argumentative discourse.

谬误：批判性讨论规则的违反
7.3 Fallacies as violations of rules for critical discussion

In our efforts to offer an alternative to the logical Standard Treatment, Grootendorst and I started from the consideration that there is no reason to assume from the outset that all fallacies are essentially logical errors. In our view, the fallacies could be better understood if they were treated as *faux pas* of communication – as argumentative moves whose wrongness consists in the fact that they are a hindrance or impediment to the resolution of a difference of opinion on the merits. The specific nature of each of the fallacies depends on exactly where and how it interferes with the resolution process. Therefore, rather than considering all fallacies to be violations of one and the same validity norm, as in the logicocentric approaches, or considering the fallacies as belonging to an unstructured list of nominal categories inherited from the past, as in the logical Standard Treatment, the pragma-dialectical approach distinguishes a variety of functional norms (van Eemeren & Grootendorst, 1984, 1992a, 2004).

The rules for critical discussion developed in pragma-dialectics cover the argumentative discourse entirely by stating all the norms pertinent to resolving a difference of opinion on the merits. In all stages of a critical discussion the protagonist and the antagonist of the standpoint at issue must observe all the rules for the performance of speech acts instrumental in resolving the difference. In principle, each of the rules constitutes a distinct standard for critical discussion. Any argumentative move that is an infringement of any of the rules, whichever party performs it and at whatever stage in the discussion, is a possible threat to the resolution of the difference of opinion and must therefore (and in this particular sense) be regarded as fallacious. In this way the use of the term *fallacy* is systematically connected with the rules for critical discussion and a fallacy is defined as a speech act that prejudices or frustrates efforts to resolve a difference of opinion on the merits. The rules for critical discussion can be recapitulated in a code of conduct for conducting a critical discussion (van Eemeren &

Grootendorst, 2004, pp. 187–190). This code of conduct thus constitutes a theoretical tool for identifying fallacies in argumentative discourse.

The pragma-dialectical approach to the fallacies is not only broader than the logical Standard Treatment, but also much more specific. Since according to pragma-dialectics each fallacy is a violation of one or more of the rules for critical discussion, it follows on the one hand that the category of fallacies includes much more than just logical errors, and on the other hand that an argumentative move is only considered a fallacy if it constitutes an obstacle to resolving a difference of opinion on the merits. A comparison between the classification of fallacies made in the pragma-dialectical approach and the list of fallacies provided in the logical Standard Treatment shows that several fallacies which were traditionally only nominally lumped together are now either shown to have something in common or clearly distinguished, whereas genuinely related fallacies that were separated are brought together. For instance, according to the logical Standard Treatment there are two distinct versions of the *argumentum ad populum*: (1) the fallacy of appeal to popular passions, and (2) the fallacy of regarding something acceptable because it is considered acceptable by a great many people. However (in pragma-dialectical terminology), the first version is a violation of the Relevance Rule (that a party may defend its standpoint only by advancing argumentation relevant to that standpoint) whereas the other version is a violation of the Argument Scheme Rule (that a standpoint may not be regarded conclusively defended if the defense does not take place by means of an appropriate argument scheme that is used correctly). Thus, it turns out that these two "versions" of the *argumentum ad populum* must really be two completely different fallacies.

The pragma-dialectical approach also makes possible the analysis of thus far unrecognized and unnamed "new" obstacles to resolving a difference of opinion on the merits.[9] Examples are: *declaring a standpoint sacrosanct*, which is a violation of the Freedom Rule (that parties must not prevent each other from putting forward standpoints or casting doubt on standpoints); *evading* or *shifting the burden of proof*, both violations of the Obligation-to-Defend Rule (that a party who puts forward a standpoint is obliged to defend that standpoint if asked to do so); *denying an unexpressed premise*, which is a violation of the Unexpressed Premise Rule (that a party may not falsely present something as a premise that has been left unexpressed or deny a premise that has been left implicit); and *making an absolute of the success of the defense*, which is a violation of the Concluding Rule (that a failed defense must result in the protagonist retracting the standpoint and a successful defense in the antagonist retracting the doubt) (van Eemeren, 2001, pp. 135–164). At the same time, the pragma-dialectical approach to fallacies as violations of rules for critical discussion is much more systematic than the traditional approach because all fallacies are explained in terms of violations of rules for critical discussion and none of the individual fallacies is explained in an *ad hoc* way. This is, in fact, why it becomes clear what certain fallacies

---

9. In this specific sense, the pragma-dialectical discussion rules "generate" new kinds of fallacies.

have in common that are on first sight very different from each other and what makes fallacies different from each other that have traditionally been taken as belonging to the same group.

The way in which the fallacies are treated plays a part in substantiating both the claimed problem-validity and the claimed entitlement to conventional validity of the pragma-dialectical rules for critical discussion. As explained in Chapter 2.2, the problem-validity of the rules depends on their instrumentality in resolving differences of opinion on the merits and the conventional validity of the rules on their acceptability to the discussants. The two parts of the validity requirement are ordered in the sense that it is pointless to examine their conventional validity if it is still unknown whether they are instrumental in reaching the resolution goal. Whereas problem-validity is an analytic-theoretical matter, conventional validity is ultimately an empirical matter. Both the problem-validity and the conventional validity of the pragma-dialectical rules for critical discussion have been discussed elsewhere in more detail.[10] Therefore, I restrict my illustration of the role the treatment of the fallacies plays in this endeavor to discussing the problem-validity of rule 1, the Freedom Rule, by pointing out the specific contribution that this rule makes to solving certain problems inherent in the confrontation stage of a critical discussion by preventing the fallacies of *ad baculum*, *ad misericordiam* and *ad hominem* from being allowed as acceptable argumentative moves in this stage of the resolution process.

Resolving a difference of opinion on the merits by carrying out a critical testing procedure is possible only if the protagonist is free to express any standpoint he wishes to express, and the standpoints at issue (as well as the argumentation put forward in their defense) can be exposed to all criticisms the antagonist may wish to advance. In other words, a difference of opinion can only be resolved on the merits if it is completely brought out into the open. This means that neither of the parties in the discussion may limit the other party's freedom to put forward standpoints, arguments, expressions of doubt or other criticisms (nor their right to request language usage declaratives or to provide them[11]). This is exactly what the Freedom Rule, which pertains to the confrontation stage, states. The Freedom Rule can be violated by both the protagonist and the antagonist, and the consequence of such a violation can be that the difference of opinion comes to light only partly, which makes it impossible to resolve the full difference of opinion on the merits.

The Freedom Rule can be violated in various ways. A party can impose certain restrictions on the standpoints that may be advanced or called into question, and he can also deny a certain opponent the right to advance a standpoint this opponent would like to advance or the right to criticize a standpoint he would like to criticize. In

---

10. *Problem-validity* is discussed in van Eemeren and Grootendorst (1994, pp. 20–21 & 25–26, and 2004, pp. 16–17, 56–57, 132–134 & 187). For a detailed discussion of *conventional validity*, see van Eemeren, Garssen & Meuffels (2009).

11. For the concept of usage declaratives, see van Eemeren and Grootendorst (1984, pp. 109–112).

the first case, restrictions as to the contents of the standpoints are imposed. That means that certain standpoints are in fact excluded from the discussion. This may, for instance, happen by declaring a particular standpoint sacrosanct, so that the opponent is prohibited from casting doubt on it and the standpoint is rendered immune to criticism. The result is that the discussion never gets off the ground. In the second case, the denial of the right to advance or criticize a standpoint is an infringement of the other party's personal liberty. Such rule violations are attempts to eliminate the opponent as a serious discussion partner by putting pressure on him to refrain from advancing a particular standpoint or from casting doubt on a particular standpoint. This may happen by putting pressure on the opponent by threatening him with physical violence or – more subtly – by threatening him implicitly with sanctions. In both cases the arguer commits the fallacy of *argumentum ad baculum* ("Of course, you can hold that view, but then you should realize that it will be very hard for me to control my men in their response to you"). Another way of putting pressure on the opponent is to work on his emotions. For example, the opponent is made to understand that if questions will be asked about the standpoint he will be held responsible for hurting or disappointing the person who advanced the standpoint. Because the technique of restricting the other party's freedom to advance or criticize a standpoint plays on their feelings or compassion, this particular type of violation of the Freedom Rule is called *argumentum ad misericordiam* ("How can you ask me to discuss this when I am still so upset about my low grade for your class?"). Infringing the opponent's personal liberty by denying him the right to advance a standpoint may also be accomplished by discrediting his expertise, impartiality, integrity or credibility. In these cases, we speak of a personal attack that constitutes an *argumentum ad hominem*.

策略操控与谬误的欺诈性
7.4 Strategic maneuvering and the deceptiveness of fallacies

As soon as fallacies in argumentative discourse are conceived pragma-dialectically, the discourse is treated as if it were aimed at resolving a difference of opinion on the merits. In practice, of course, hardly any discourse will ever be completely resolution-oriented – or completely non-resolution-oriented, for that matter. For a realistic appreciation of the scope of the pragma-dialectical approach to the fallacies, it is important to note that the norms provided by the rules for critical discussion apply only *where and insofar as* the discourse concerned can be assumed to be aimed at resolving a difference of opinion on the merits. Although it is often clear that the discourse – in line with its argumentative character – may indeed be treated as being to a great extent aimed at resolving a difference of opinion between the speaker or writer and the intended listeners or readers, in practice it is not always obvious that this is the case. Sometimes it may even be clear that this is *not* the case. This is one of the reasons why a piece of discourse can only be fully and methodically screened for fallacies if the discourse as a whole or the part of it that is being evaluated is first adequately analyzed as a genuine piece of argumentative discourse.

Even a piece of discourse that is clearly argumentative will in many respects not correspond to the ideal model of a critical discussion – certainly not explicitly, completely, and immediately. In many cases, the hows and whys of divergent forms of argumentative reality can be easily explained with the help of empirical insight concerning ordinary discourse and its natural characteristics, such as the usual underexposure of what is already considered evident or known, the overexposure of what is considered significant or important, the expedient structuring according to what is considered topical or relevant at a particular point, and the lack of definition when more precision or elaboration is not considered necessary. The differences can easily be explained by referring, in a great many cases to such natural characteristics, and occasionally to indolence or sloppiness. In any case, it would certainly not do to simply declare all verbal behavior that does not seem to agree with the model of critical discussion automatically defective; the discourse as it has been brought to the fore can be evaluated adequately only if it has first been accurately determined what it actually conveys, by means of a pragma-dialectical reconstruction (see Chapter 1).[12]

When it comes to the identification of fallacies in the evaluation of argumentative discourse, the pragma-dialectical evaluation procedure starts with identifying the moves made in the discourse as particular kinds of speech acts creating certain sets of commitments for the participants. Next it is to be determined whether the performance of these speech acts agrees in every particular case with the rules for critical discussion. If a (reconstructed) speech act proves to violate any of these pragma-dialectical rules, it must be determined precisely what kind of norm violation this entails. In practice, this determination can be achieved only if it is clear exactly which soundness criteria for satisfying the critical norm pertain to the case concerned in that particular stage of the resolution process. The implementation of these criteria may vary to some extent depending on the macro-context in which the argumentative discourse takes place. It is therefore important to establish, first, of which communicative activity type the speech event concerned is a token, and what the specific criteria are that are pertinent to checking whether in this particular communicative activity type the general criteria for reasonable argumentative discourse have been fulfilled.[13] Only then can it be determined whether or not a fallacy has been committed and, if this is indeed the case, which fallacy. As I shall explain in Section 7.5 and Section 7.6, fallacy

---

12. Such a reconstruction in terms of a critical discussion should be theoretically justified and empirically faithful to the commitments that may be ascribed to the actors on the basis of their contributions. In order not to "over-interpret" the argumentative potential of the discourse, sensitivity must be maintained to the details of the presentation, the general rules for communication, and the contextual constraints inherent in the speech event concerned (van Eemeren, Grootendorst, Jackson, & Jacobs., 1993, pp. 38–50).

13. It is important to emphasize that the relationship between general and specific criteria needs further examination. In my view, specific criteria are not completely different criteria, or even new criteria, but different implementations of the general criteria which may vary among different communicative activity types.

judgments are, on the pragma-dialectical view, in the end always contextual judgments and the decision as to whether a certain argumentative move is to be regarded as fallacious is to some extent context-dependent.

The concept of strategic maneuvering can be of help in explaining why in practice sound and fallacious argumentative moves are sometimes hard to distinguish, and in developing additional conceptual tools for distinguishing them. The view that strategic maneuvering is aimed at alleviating the potential tension between arguing reasonably and effectively at the same time implies that all moves that are made in argumentative discourse can be regarded as being designed to serve simultaneously both objectives. However, this implication does not mean that in practice the pursuit of these two objectives will always be in perfect balance. On the one hand, arguers may at times neglect their interest in effectiveness for fear of being perceived as unreasonable; on the other hand, they may at times neglect their commitment to reasonableness in their zeal to promote their case effectively. Neglect of effectiveness can result in bad strategy,[14] but because such ineffective moves are not "condemnable" for being fallacious and harm merely the interests of the arguer himself, not the adversary, this case does not need to be discussed here.[15] If, however, arguers allow their commitment to having a reasonable exchange to be overruled by their eagerness for achieving effectiveness, their strategic maneuvering has got "derailed." By violating the rules for critical discussion, the argumentative move they have made prejudices or hinders the process of resolving a difference of opinion on the merits and so their strategic maneuvering must be condemned as fallacious. *All derailments of strategic maneuvering are fallacies in the sense that they violate one or more of the rules for critical discussion and all fallacies can be viewed as derailments of strategic maneuvering.*

In my view, the various modes of strategic maneuvering that can be distinguished in argumentative reality can be imagined as representing a continuum running from evidently sound to evidently fallacious strategic maneuvering. This continuum may vary from pointing out inconsistencies to wrongly accusing someone of being inconsistent in one case and from correctly referring to an authority to appealing improperly to an authority in another case, with a whole area of rather more obscure cases in between.[16] In practice it is not always crystal clear where precisely the boundaries are to be found between sound and

---

14. Walton and Krabbe (1995, p. 25) even speak of "blunders," but I consider this term too strong for general use.

15. Talking about the effectiveness of strategic maneuvering gives me the opportunity to remark that the optimal utilization of the opportunities for being effective will be an important topic at the next stage of the development of the pragma-dialectical research program. I agree with Jacobs that "to get beyond a categorical analysis of fallacies requires a refocus on the notion of argumentative *effectiveness* (Jacobs, 1999, 2000)" (2002, p. 123).

16. Jacobs observes that "what makes for the difference between a tactic being obstructive or constructive is not the tactic per se, but the way in which the tactic in text functions in its context of use" (2002, p. 125).

fallacious strategic maneuvering and it might be the case that in different macro-contexts these boundaries are not to be drawn in exactly the same way. This account of fallacies as derailments of modes of strategic maneuvering that could also have been sound explains, together with some other observations that I shall presently discuss, why in argumentative practice it may not be immediately apparent to all concerned that a fallacy has been committed, so that fallacies may pass unnoticed. Because each fallacy has, in principle, sound counterparts that are manifestations of the same mode of strategic maneuvering, the fallacies do not distinguish themselves as "different animals" that have certain distinctive features other than their fallaciousness which are shared by all of them and distinguish all of them from their sound counterparts (like dogs are distinguished from cats).

Deviations from the rules for critical discussion are often also hard to detect since none of the parties will be keen on portraying themselves as being unreasonable, if only because this will make their discussion moves less effective in the end. Therefore, rather than resorting to completely different means, they will most likely try to stick to the established dialectical means for achieving rhetorical objectives which are possibly at odds with the dialectical rationale of a certain discussion rule, and "stretch" the use of these means so much that the fallacious maneuvering is also covered. As Jackson (1995) has pointed out, it is an assumption of reasonableness in argumentative discourse that both parties will normally uphold a commitment to the rules for critical discussion. A presumption of reasonableness conferred on every discussion move will therefore also be operative when a particular strategic maneuver is in fact fallacious. Echoing the logical Standard Definition of the fallacies used in the logical Standard Treatment, we can complement our theoretical definition of the fallacies as violations of a rules for critical discussion with the empirical observation that in argumentative practice the fallacies will often manifest themselves as strategic maneuvers that seem to comply with the critical discussion rules but in fact do not. The undesirable element of subjectivity that, according to Hamblin (1970, pp. 253–254), is brought into the logical Standard Definition of the fallacies by the using the word "seem" is then avoided by sticking to a definition of the fallacies as violations of rules for critical discussion, thus keeping the word "seem" outside the definition, while linking the occurrence of the fallacies in argumentative practice immediately to modes of strategic maneuvering that can also be non-fallacious, so that the potentially treacherous character of the fallacies expressed in the word "seem" is acknowledged.

The treacherous character of the fallacies conveyed in the Latin word *fallax*, which means deceptive or deceitful, must not be ignored in the study of the fallacies, and the search for an explanation of the deceptiveness should not be abandoned, as happened after Hamblin mentioned the drawback of subjectivity in his list of criticisms against the logical Standard Treatment. Even if we can claim, as I think we can, that Hamblin's criticisms no longer apply to our theory of fallacies, this theory is in my view still not entirely satisfactory if it ignores the intriguing problem of the alleged persuasiveness of the fallacies. O'Keefe's (2006) "meta-analyses" of experimental persuasion studies may suggest that sound argumentation is generally speaking more likely to be persuasive than fallacious argumentation, but even if this suggestion were proven true in experimental research geared to checking in sufficient detail the claim involved, we need nevertheless to find out why in argumentative practice the fallacies go so often unnoticed.[17] Jackson (1995), for one, urges us to pay attention to the (sneaky) persuasiveness – which I would like to broaden to effectiveness – of the fallacies in argumentative practice. I think that, thanks to the systematic incorporation of rhetorical insights, the extended pragma-dialectical theory of strategic maneuvering in argumentative discourse proposed in this volume enables us to explain more satisfactorily how fallacies "work" and can be effective in argumentative practice.

脱离语境的谬误识别标准
7.5 Context-independent criteria for judging fallaciousness

In tackling the "demarcation problem" of how to distinguish in actual argumentative discourse between sound and fallacious moves I have proposed to view fallacious moves as derailments of strategic maneuvering in which a rule for critical discussion has been violated. This means in practice that in such cases the pursuit of rhetorical interests has gained the upper hand and the dialectical criteria pertaining to carrying out the mode of strategic maneuvering concerned have not been satisfied. This approach differs considerably from how the demarcation problem is dealt with by other argumentation theorists. On the one hand, there are argumentation theorists, such as Biro and Siegel (1992) and Johnson (2000), who give precedence to epistemological considerations and view fallacies as argumentative moves that obstruct in some way or other the search for the truth. On the other hand, there are rhetorically-minded theorists such as Willard (1995) and Leff (2000) who go primarily by empirical standards and view the fallacies in a more relativistic way as argumentative moves that are not accepted in a certain communicative community. Although in some cases the results of the theorizing may be virtually the same, these perspectives from which the fallacies are approached are fundamentally different from each other and from ours.

A speaker who goes against a rule of communication (or Gricean maxim) might in principle still be regarded as maintaining the Principle of Communication, which is the pragma-dialectical counterpart of the Gricean Principle of Cooperation (van Eemeren & Grootendorst, 1992a, pp. 49–55). Similarly, a party that commits a fallacy in argumentative discourse might in principle still be regarded as upholding a general commitment to reasonableness that involves an obligation to obey the rules for critical discussion, so that the rule violation would be viewed as just an incidental offense against the dialectical standards of reasonableness. Even if the rule violation is a deliberate one, it will in the context of strategic maneuvering be imperative for the guilty party to emphasize that his general commitment to reasonableness still stands; if it

---

17. This is the more remarkable because when they are presented in clear cases these moves prove to be disapproved of. See van Eemeren, Garssen & Meuffels (2009, pp. 205–208).

were clear that he has withdrawn this commitment, the intended persuasive effect of his move would be lost immediately. If the rule violation is unintentional – the unreasonable move is simply a mistake – the strategic maneuver still constitutes a fallacy in the pragma-dialectical sense, because the move is not reasonable, even if it may seem rhetorically strong as well as dialectically acceptable to the offender. In practice, such an infringement is not irreversible. Once it has been pointed out by the other party that an offense against reasonableness has been committed, the derailment of strategic maneuvering can be instantly repaired. However, the fact that it may be possible to repair derailments of strategic maneuvering does not diminish the importance of making a sharp distinction between sound and fallacious argumentative moves. Consequently, unlike other authors, who use the same labels indiscriminately to refer to both fallacious and non-fallacious moves, I would insist on restricting the use of traditional (often Latinized) names of the fallacies, such as *argumentum ad hominem*, to the fallacious cases of strategic maneuvering.[18]

We have characterized the fallacies as violations of rules for critical discussion which manifest themselves in derailments of strategic maneuvering that may easily escape attention because the derailments can be very similar to sound instances of strategic maneuvering. It now becomes necessary to reflect upon the criteria that can be brought to bear to distinguish between sound and fallacious strategic maneuvering. In this endeavor I make a distinction between general criteria for judging fallaciousness that are context-independent and more specific criteria that may be dependent on the macro-context in which the strategic maneuvering takes place, because this specific context requires a well-adapted implementation of the general criteria. In practice the identification of general and specific criteria for judging fallaciousness in argumentative discourse often meets with considerable problems. Our view of fallacies as derailments of strategic maneuvering can be helpful in making it clear why it is so difficult to establish clear-cut criteria for all cases of fallacious argumentative behavior. Because, in principle, each mode of strategic maneuvering brings about its own continuum of sound and fallacious acting, which is structured in its own particular way, there is no generally established set of considerations that enable the analyst to predict *a priori* when strategic maneuvers will go astray in fallacious ways.

---

18. More confusing than the labeling, by the way, is the fact that, when characterizing fallacies, authors such as Walton (e.g. 1998a) take as their starting point a certain argumentative phenomenon, say a personal attack, and call each argumentative move *ad hominem* in which this phenomenon occurs. Next they observe that these moves are not always fallacious and decide on an *ad hoc* basis whether or not a specific manifestation of *ad hominem* is fallacious. In contradistinction, in the pragma-dialectical approach fallacies are systematically viewed as violations of one or more rules for critical discussion that hinder the process of resolving a difference of opinion on the merits in a certain stage of the resolution process. In the case of an *argumentum ad hominem* fallacy, for instance, a violation is committed of the Freedom Rule by hindering the expression of a standpoint or doubt in the confrontation stage through a personal attack that prevents the other party from fulfilling his role in a critical discussion.

Although no fixed criteria can be provided in advance for deciding at the same time between fallaciousness and non-fallaciousness for all strategic maneuvers, this does not mean that fallacy judgments are ultimately always *ad hoc* – or that in practice there must necessarily be a grey (or dark) zone of argumentative moves whose soundness or fallaciousness is always dubious. It rather means that, in principle, the soundness or fallaciousness of argumentative moves must be determined by first examining clear cases of sound maneuvering and fallacious maneuvering by means of a particular mode of strategic maneuvering whose fitting in or not fitting in with the relevant pragma-dialectical norms is evident. Only based on these findings can general soundness criteria for that particular mode of strategic maneuvering be established that can subsequently be appropriated for application to the more obscure cases that are causing problems. It will next be necessary to examine whether in the macro-context of specific communicative activity types the context-independent general soundness criteria for using a certain mode of strategic maneuvering need to be further specified, amended or supplemented with context-dependent specific soundness criteria in order to do justice to pertinent macro-contextual differences.

As a case in point, I would like to discuss the demarcation of non-fallacious and fallacious moves in one particular mode of strategic maneuvering: defending a standpoint by appealing to an authority. The argument from authority is a subtype of the general type of argumentation known as "symptomatic argumentation," which is also called "sign argumentation." Argumentation of this general type is based on an argument scheme that presents the acceptability of the reason (premise) that is advanced as a sign that the standpoint at issue (conclusion) is acceptable by establishing a relationship of concomitance between the property mentioned in the premise and the property mentioned in the conclusion. Such a fixed association is suggested, for instance, in argumentation such as "Paul must be a cheese lover, because he is Dutch" [and we all know that loving cheese goes together with being Dutch]. In the case of the subtype of symptomatic argumentation consisting of an argument from authority, the transition of acceptance is (aimed to be) brought about by referring in the premise to a source who has the knowledge or expertise required for drawing the conclusion. This happens, for instance, in "The competence for learning a language is innate – Noam Chomsky says so (and Noam Chomsky is an authoritative linguist)," but also in the Nigeria Spam Letter quoted in Section 7.1: "My choosing you for helping me solve this problem is the right choice because God told me to make this choice (and God is a sacrosanct/ultimate guide)."

Like using other arguments from sign, using arguments from authority is potentially a sound mode of strategic maneuvering. In a great many cases, we are fully justified in supporting our claims by referring to an authority who is supposed to know – in argumentative practice this is in fact often the only sensible thing we can do. However, a prerequisite for appealing to an authority in supporting one's standpoint is that the general soundness conditions pertaining to this particular mode of strategic maneuvering are fulfilled. Among the general soundness conditions for an argument from authority mentioned in the literature are, for instance, that the authority referred to does indeed have the professed authority, that his authority is recognized as pertinent to the topic at issue in the difference of opinion, that the parties in the difference of opinion in principle agree on appealing to the authority in the discussion,[19] that the authority is quoted regarding a subject-matter within the area of his expertise, and that the authority is quoted correctly at a point where this is relevant (cf. Woods & Walton, 1989, pp. 15–24; van Eemeren & Grootendorst, 1992a, pp. 136–137). If there are good reasons to think that the source referred to is indeed a good source to rely on in the case concerned and has to be taken seriously when making the observation referred to, an appeal to authority can be unproblematic and may even be conclusive.[20] In argumentative practice, however, strategic maneuvering by means of arguments from authority can also derail.[21] An appeal to authority might not be justified in a particular case because one or more of the "critical questions" that need to be asked to check if the criteria for assessing arguments from authority have been fulfilled cannot be answered satisfactorily. Then the argument violates the Argument Scheme Rule and must be viewed as an *argumentum ad verecundiam*. In the next section I will discuss how these general criteria for arguments from authority can be refined by special considerations in a given context.

基于语境的谬误识别标准
7.6 Context-dependent criteria for judging fallaciousness

More often than not, fallacy judgments are (or should be) in the end contextual judgments that depend on the specific circumstances of situated argumentative acting. In fact, fallacy judgments always relate to strategic maneuvering in specific circumstances of argumentative acting. However, in some cases – as in a great many textbook examples and other clear-cut cases of fallacious acting – there is no real need to take the macro-context into account because it is already clear that one or more of the

---

19. In argumentative practice it may happen that one of the parties does not agree with appealing to an authority or with appealing to this particular authority because, for instance, this party is interested only in learning what the other party himself has to say on the matter ("Why do you refer to Professor Schama? You said yourself that this is such a beautiful painting and now I would like to hear what *your* arguments are for giving such a positive judgment").

20. Woods and Walton (1989, pp. 17–21) formulated, for instance, the following general "adequacy conditions" for the argument from authority: (1) "The authority must be interpreted correctly"; (2) "The authority must actually have special competence in an area and not simply glamour, prestige, or popularity"; (3) "The judgment of authority must actually be within the special field of competence"; (4) "Direct evidence must be available in principle"; (5) "A consensus technique is required for adjudicating disagreements among equally qualified authorities."

21. For the development of a pragma-dialectical view of an evaluative procedure and soundness conditions regarding strategic maneuvering with arguments from authority, see van Eemeren and Houtlosser (2003b).

context-independent general soundness criteria that pertain to the mode of strategic maneuvering concerned have not been satisfied. This is, for example, the case when the authoritative source is misquoted in an argument from authority. In other cases, however, it may be necessary for determining whether or not a dialectical norm incorporated in the rules for critical discussion has been violated to appeal to specific soundness criteria that depend on the institutionalized conventions of the communicative activity type in which the argumentative move concerned is made. Basically, the specific soundness criteria indicate how the general soundness criteria need to be interpreted, amended or supplemented in the macro-context of a specific communicative activity type. By the way, the fact that the specific soundness criteria, as context-dependent precizations of the context-independent general soundness criteria, may vary to some extent from one communicative activity type to another does not automatically mean that there are no clear soundness criteria available for judging fallaciousness. It only means that the implementation of the general soundness criteria for strategic maneuvering is, in principle, context-dependent.[22]

Let us return to the argument from authority to illustrate the case I am making. Imagine that you and I are playing a game of scrabble together and we have decided to do this in English. You know that I am a Dutchman who cannot be trusted with the English language. On top of that, you also know that I am always most eager to win such inconsequential games. At a certain moment I claim to have compiled a *word*, but you doubt that the combination of letters I have laid out really constitutes an English word. Now I use an argument from authority to defend my claim: "This is an English word, because it is in the dictionary." Whether my appeal to authority is in this case a legitimate strategic maneuver depends in the first place on the agreement that exists, or that the players – you and I – have made prior to playing the game, as to the testing procedure for deciding whether or not a combination of letters that is claimed to be an English word does indeed count as an English word. There are several possibilities for answering this question, depending on which starting point regarding the decision concerning English words we agreed on when we started our game of scrabble.

If you and I had agreed that a combination of letters would be regarded as an English word if both of us recognized it as an English word, it would be hard for me to defend my claim that the combination of letters I laid out constitutes an English word by means of an argument from authority if you did not recognize the combination as an English word. It might have been the case, however, that we had both realized that such an agreement would not really solve our problem in the best possible way, so that we had come to a different agreement. If we had agreed that in case of doubt we let a specific dictionary decide, which seems an appropriate (problem-valid) decision

---

22. Because the general soundness criteria need to be applied in widely diverging macro-contexts in which different institutional needs must be satisfied, the exact meaning of the general criteria and the ways in which their fulfillment can be checked may vary. Who or what counts as an authority, for instance, will be different in a scientific debate than in a political interview.

criterion, and I cite the dictionary correctly in appealing to its authority to defend my claim, then there is nothing wrong with my argumentative move. The move "This is an English word, because it is in this dictionary" would even be a strong one, unless you and I had also agreed in advance that the *Concise Oxford Dictionary* would be the ultimate judge while in my argument I am referring to *Webster's*. If I were to appeal to the dictionary while you and I had in fact agreed that a combination of letters would get recognition as an English word *only* if the word and its meaning are known to both of us, then my appeal to the authority of the dictionary would be irrelevant – whichever dictionary I was referring to – and therefore fallacious. If, finally, nothing had been agreed upon between the two of us concerning how to decide in these cases, my appeal to the dictionary's authority could not be considered "fallacious," because in that case there would be no decision criterion that could be applied – or, for that matter, ignored. In such a case – if there is no decision criterion available that we explicitly or implicitly agree upon – it has to be decided in the second instance whether, in appealing to the dictionary, I refer to an admissible source of expertise, or whether this would only be so if I referred (correctly) to the *Concise Oxford Dictionary*. If we failed to agree that this particular dictionary is an admissible source of expertise, or that the *Concise Oxford Dictionary* is, my appeal would not count as a conclusive defense. My appeal to authority would be fallacious if we had agreed on a specific source of expertise and I referred to a different source or if I would use this source wrongly.[23]

In the scenarios I have just sketched, different criteria are agreed for complying with the soundness norm incorporated in the argument-from-authority variant of the Argument Scheme Rule. This means that the specific soundness criteria for judging arguments from authority, in a specific macro-context, may vary depending on the agreements reached (or implicitly confirmed) in the opening stage of the discussion that constitutes the accepted starting point of the discussion. Three main cases can be distinguished. In the first case (1a) the parties in the discussion have agreed beforehand that an appeal to authority is legitimate and (1b) the agreement allows an appeal to precisely the authority that is actually (correctly) appealed to. If conditions (1a) and (1b) are met, no *argumentum ad verecundiam* has been committed, and using the argument from authority may be regarded as sound strategic maneuvering. In the second case (2a), the parties in the discussion have agreed in the second instance that an appeal to authority is legitimate and (2b) the agreement allows a (correct) appeal to precisely the authority that is actually appealed to. If the conditions (2a) and (2b) are met, again, no *argumentum ad verecundiam* has been committed and using the argument from authority may be regarded as sound strategic maneuvering. In the third case (3), the parties in the discussion have not come to any agreement about the legitimacy of an appeal to authority. If (3) is the case, no rule for critical discussion has

---

23. A precondition for being allowed to consider this appeal to authority (and the other appeals to authority I have mentioned) fallacious is, of course, that the criterion applied may be considered problem-valid in the first place.

as yet been violated, but the use of the argument from authority may very well introduce a (new) discussion concerning the legitimacy of this appeal.

It is not hard to imagine that when other modes of strategic maneuvering than those I have discussed here are used, similar cases can be distinguished and similar differences between the soundness criteria may occur. The examples I have given all concern explicit agreements made between the parties in the opening stage of the discussion, but it could just as well be the case that such agreements between the parties that play a decisive role in judging the fallaciousness of argumentative moves remain implicit. In fact, in actual practice it is often the case that the agreements concerned are not so much made between the parties but are already given when the parties engage in a particular communicative activity type. This means that the specific soundness criteria pertaining to the strategic maneuvering in a particular communicative activity type are supposed to be familiar to those engaging in it. For some communicative activity types, such as a chat or an apology, the soundness criteria for the argumentative discourse will have been largely acquired when getting to know these communicative activity types in primary socialization, while for others, such as a summoning or arbitration, the soundness criteria will only be known to those who have learned them when encountering these specific communicative activity types in their further education in secondary socialization.

In the various specific communicative activity types constituting the context of strategic maneuvers carried out in argumentative discourse, different implementations of the general soundness criteria have been developed that are designed to create the conditions necessary to realize the institutional point of the communicative activity type concerned in an optimal way. These different implementations can be articulated in distinct sets of specific soundness criteria, each set appropriate to a particular communicative activity type.[24] The specific soundness criteria pertaining to strategic maneuvering by appealing to an authority in the macro-context of a criminal trial in the legal domain, for instance, may be in some respects different from the specific soundness criteria pertaining to strategic maneuvering by appealing to an authority in the macro-context of a scientific paper in the scholarly domain. Starting from the adequacy conditions formulated by Woods and Walton (1989, pp. 17–21), the condition, for instance, that a consensus technique is required for adjudicating disagreements among equally qualified authorities will, in a criminal trial, be implemented with different specific adequacy conditions compared to what happens in a scientific paper. In a criminal trial the final decision may be obtained by appealing to a designated higher court whereas in a scientific paper no such court of appeal exists and a (temporary)

---

24. Jacobs nicely sums up this position, which I share, "What is necessary is an analysis of [the use in context of – addition FHvE] the functional design of any message property under study, and this together with some standard of proper functioning allows us to assess the fallacious potential of an argumentative move" (2002, p. 123).

decision is sought by appealing to all fellow scientists with the required expertise in the area concerned.[25]

策略操控的合理性评判实例
7.7 Evaluating the soundness of strategic maneuvers: An example

To illustrate how the pragma-dialectical evaluation of the reasonableness of strategic maneuvering is supposed to proceed, I will discuss the use of one specific mode of strategic maneuvering, *conciliatio*, by concentrating on an example taken from the Shell advertorial analyzed in Chapter 6. *Conciliatio* is a mode of strategic maneuvering – named after its most conspicuous aspect – in which a party uses a proposition the other party is explicitly committed to in order to support his own standpoint (van Eemeren & Houtlosser, 1999a, p. 485). When the figure of *conciliatio* is used, a proposition advanced by the first party to defend his standpoint is, for instance, used by the second party in an argument to defend a different (and perhaps contradictory) standpoint of his own by "borrowing" this proposition, as it were, from the first party.

In terms of strategic maneuvering, making use of a *conciliatio* amounts to making a topical selection from the available argumentative potential that is expedient and involves an argumentative choice that is optimally adapted to audience demand because it exploits a proposition the other party is committed to. A presentational device that is particularly well-suited to making it obvious that the argument used is in fact already part of the other party's commitments, is the use of a rhetorical question. Using such a presentational device is certainly no prerequisite for strategic maneuvering by means of *conciliatio*, but doing so may add to its effectiveness, especially when the strategic maneuvering is directed primarily at convincing a third party audience consisting of other listeners or readers.

Because the other party's adherence is claimed in advance on clear grounds, this mode of strategic maneuvering is, in principle, rhetorically strong. It is at the same time pre-eminently dialectical, because in his strategic maneuvering the arguer proceeds by arguing *ex concessis*. The danger of derailment stems from the fact that although the other party may safely be assumed to agree with the propositional content of the argument, he may *not just like that* be assumed to agree with the way in which this content is used to support an entirely different standpoint, which could even be precisely the opposite of his own standpoint. The discrepancy can be illuminated with the help of the pragma-dialectical analysis of the speech act of advancing argumentation, which makes it clear that in order for an argument to count as a felicitous attempt

---

25. According to de Groot (1984), ideally, the Scientific Forum will keep considering the decision and may eventually come to a different decision in the future. See also de Groot (1969). Together with the problem-validity requirement this continuity of the assessment process is to protect scientific and scholarly claims to truth from being based merely on a temporary consensus of a momentary collection of experts.

to convince the other party both parties must not only accept the propositional content of the argument but also accept the justificatory function the proposition has for the standpoint at issue (van Eemeren & Grootendorst, 1984, pp. 47–74). Typically, in a *conciliatio* the propositional content of the argument used by the arguer is indeed accepted by the other party, but its justificatory potential for the arguer's standpoint is by no means accepted – and certainly not automatically.

This speech act analysis points to a condition that can be of help in evaluating actual manifestations of *conciliatio*. Such manifestations can be regarded as sound only if the arguer offers sufficient support for his view that the proposition taken over from the other party has an overriding justificatory potential with regard to his standpoint, and leaves it eventually to the other party to decide whether he agrees that this is indeed the case. Strategic maneuvering by means of *conciliatio* can be said to derail if the arguer just presupposes that the adopted argument has an unquestionable justificatory potential for his standpoint and leaves the opponent no room to question this presupposition. When a *conciliatio* derails in this way, the arguer who makes use of this mode of strategic maneuvering relies on a starting point as if it were a common starting point, although it is not yet accepted by the other party. In so doing, he violates the pragma-dialectical Starting Point Rule (rule 6) (van Eemeren & Grootendorst, 2004, p. 193). Additional conditions that need to be fulfilled for strategic maneuvering by means of *conciliatio* to be sound are that the proposition that is exploited in the *conciliatio* really be part of the other party's commitments and that the arguer who makes use of *conciliatio* be himself prepared to live up to the commitments involved.

In his novel *A Perfect Spy*, John LeCarré provides an interesting example of *conciliatio*. The boy who is the central character in the book is raised by everyone but his father, who is a real, albeit amiable, charlatan who loves cars and gambling. The boy is fond of his father, who comes to visit him only now and again. Every time the father gets ready to leave again the boy is about to cry. At a certain moment the father wants to prevent his son from crying and tries to achieve the desired effect by saying this:

> Do you love your old man? Well then ...

Even in such a short argumentative discourse, all the constitutive stages of a critical discussion can be recognized and reconstructed. The confrontation stage consisting of the clash between the father's standpoint that the boy should not cry and his son's ambivalence about this is clear from the context but is wisely left implicit by the father (if he externalized his standpoint the effect would likely be that the son would start crying). The opening stage consists of the father's observation that the son loves his father, which is presented by way of a rhetorical question. By using the expression "well then" the father starts the argumentation stage and turns the uncontested starting point that the son loves his father into an argument in favor of his standpoint. The concluding stage is clearly marked by "...," but the conclusion itself (the son should not cry) is, again, left unexpressed. Briefly put, the strategic maneuvering by means of *conciliatio* that is going on here works as follows. First, the father attributes to the boy by means of a rhetorical question a proposition the boy will agree with ("I love my old man"). By adding "well then ...," he then implies that *given that* the boy adheres to the proposition that he loves his old man, he should also accept the unexpressed standpoint that he should not cry. In this case, however, from an evaluative point of view the father's strategic maneuvering by means of *conciliatio* has got derailed because he suggests that this is all there is to be said and does not support his argumentation any further, without giving his son, who is subjected to great emotional pressure, a fair chance to reflect independently upon the argumentation and draw his own conclusion. The derailment of this strategic use of *conciliatio* is due in part to the fact that the son is more or less forced to accept his father's standpoint. Although in this implicit case of *conciliatio* he could theoretically protest that loving his father is not something he has explicitly conceded as a starting point, the objection would be a weak one because implicitly it is obvious that he does accept this starting point. Even more important in this case is that the father acts as if the son accepts the unexpressed premise "Someone who loves a person does not start crying when this person leaves," which he clearly does not do.

In Shell's advertorial "Clear thinking in troubled times," published to defend its involvement in Nigeria and discussed in Chapter 6.7, the oil company also makes use of a *conciliatio* when it justifies not pulling out of Nigeria's Liquified Natural Gas project by pointing out that not Shell but the Nigerian people and the environment would suffer if Shell pulled out (lines 31–35):

> But if we do so now, the project will collapse. [...] A cancellation would certainly hurt the thousands of Nigerians who will be working on the project, and the tens of thousands more benefiting in the local economy. The environment, too, would suffer, with the plant expected to cut greatly the need for gas flaring in the oil industry.

These arguments for not pulling out of the project are clearly derived from Shell's opponents' avowed concerns for the people and the environment. Given their political preferences, Shell's opponents may be assumed to be in favor of a prospering native population and a non-polluted environment. At the propositional level, Shell can therefore be sure that acceptance is certain. But how does the oil company proceed to ensure the opponents' acceptance of the justificatory potential of these two points for its standpoint that Shell should not pull out of the project? Shell does so by claiming that there is a causal relation between its pulling out of the project and a deterioration of the human and environmental circumstances. In this way, Shell lends direct support to the view that its opponents' propositions have an overriding justificatory potential for its standpoint. Although the addition of "certainly" suggests that the harmful effects are obvious, Shell does not actually deter the reader from questioning the supposed causal link. Therefore, no actual derailment of strategic maneuvering with *conciliatio* has taken place and Shell cannot rightfully be accused of derailed strategic maneuvering.

This part of Shell's strategic maneuvering in "Clear thinking in troubled times" is in fact rather strong, both dialectically, because argumentation by *conciliatio* proceeds *ex concessis*, and rhetorically, because it entitles Shell in the eyes of its primary audience, the general public reading their advertorial, to the adherence of its opponents. Shell's use of *conciliatio* also fits in very well with its dominant opening strategy of involving the readers as closely as possible in its views concerning Nigeria.[26] In the first instance, this is aimed for by acting, in the part of the advertorial that is genuinely an apologia, as if the public is not really in opposition to Shell, but has merely some doubts – doubts resulting from ignorance or lack of careful reflection. Leading on the readers in this way, Shell presents the public as a possible ally rather than a potential opponent. Near the end of the text that is professedly an apologia even though the advertorial has in fact become a policy statement, the public's comfortable position is suddenly made questionable and the final consequence of the inclusion strategy becomes apparent, because the readers are told that a public that does not take sides with Shell distances itself from this reasonable position and joins the campaigners – which has by then become a highly unattractive perspective.

How is this strategic maneuvering by Shell regarding its primary audience to be evaluated? First, we should notice that Shell offers the public an unrealistic alternative when it confronts it at the end of the text – in line with the institutional point of the deliberative communicative activity type of a policy statement rather than an apologia – with the need to make a choice. In times when the need of support is overwhelmingly urgent, forcing the public into an "either you are with us or you're against us" situation could be acceptable in the disputational communicative activity type of a policy statement. In an adjudicatory communicative activity type of an apologia aimed at proving one's innocence, however, such strategic maneuvering is clearly inadmissible, because establishing the facts is not a matter of making choices, let alone of

---

26. The circumvention strategy used by Shell in the confrontation stage consists in manipulating the difference of opinion and changing its focus by highlighting and addressing selectively only those issues that Shell can cope with and dealing only indirectly with the main issue Shell is expected to address. The inclusion strategy, dominant in the opening stage, amounts to involving the public as closely as possible in Shell's view of the case by presenting them as a possible ally rather than an opponent. In the argumentation stage, Shell's strategic maneuvering combines "certification" and "humanization." While demeaning its opponents as not knowledgeable and irresponsible, Shell resorts to causal reasoning based on "authorized" facts (certification) put in a perspective attractive to the public (humanization), while establishing at the same time its own image as a social conscience company. Shell's concluding strategy appeals to the public's common sense through rubbing in facts that are at variance with the public's present unrealistic attitude and remind the public emphatically (and rather unexpectedly) of its responsibilities. Several argumentative moves Shell makes are derailments of strategic maneuvering that are fallacious because they violate a rule for critical discussion. Shell's advertorial is, in fact, a good illustration of how supposedly clever strategic maneuvering can become rhetorically inappropriate when it is dialectically not acceptable. See for a more detailed evaluation of Shell's advertorial van Eemeren and Houtlosser (2002a, pp. 143–157).

confirming the choices made by Shell. Here Shell is guilty of maneuvering fallaciously by creating implicitly a *false dilemma*. Second, it should be noticed that this (false) dilemma can only have persuasive force because it is based on Shell's perpetual *ad hominem* attacks against the campaigners. Most of these attacks are abusive (the campaigners are unrealistic idealists, sloganeers who distort or ignore facts, irresponsible egocentrics who do not understand the risk they are taking); some are just circumstantial (the campaign became more important than the cause). Had the campaigners been portrayed as sensible people, the dilemma could not have been created and therefore these *ad hominem* fallacies are a constitutive part of the fallacious maneuvering aimed at involving the general public.

To add some more considerations to these observations: Shell's strategic maneuvering cannot be evaluated as positively as its clever use of *conciliatio* may have suggested. From the confrontation stage onward, Shell slyly manipulates the issues of the discussion by addressing the crucial issue of its involvement in Nigeria only in an implicit way. As emerged in the analysis, Shell emphasizes in what can be reconstructed as the opening stage that it is undesirable that companies use their economic influence to prop up or bring down governments in order to support its standpoint that the company should not intervene in Nigeria. To defend this standpoint, however, it suffices to argue that it is wrong for companies to use their economic influence *to bring down* governments. Adding that the company's influence may also never be used *to prop up* governments is only relevant if Shell implicitly also attempts to convey the idea that *it does not support the Nigerian regime*. In fact, this is precisely the point Shell should get across, because when the advertorial was published the primary accusation was that Shell kept the Nigerian regime going.[27] Shell is apparently unwilling to confront this accusation outright, but needs to deny it all the same. The company does this implicitly by providing an argument from which the denial can be deduced.

Shell engages in a confrontational strategy of circumvention to evade the crucial issue in the difference of opinion. One of the dialectical standards incorporated in the rules for critical discussion is that arguments should be relevant to the standpoint at issue. This rule is violated in Shell's argument in support of the (reconstructed) standpoint that Shell does not support the Nigerian regime, starting from the proposition that it is undesirable for companies to use their economic influence to prop up or bring down governments. Although this proposition is analytically relevant to the standpoint – in fact, it is precisely because of this analytic relevance that the standpoint could be reconstructed – it lacks any evaluative relevance.[28] For while the fact that it is undesirable to use economic influence to prop up or bring down governments may lend support to the *political* standpoint that Shell *should not* intervene in Nigeria's

---

27. There were cries for intervention after Ken Saro-Wiwa had been sentenced to death and had not yet been executed, but no such cries were heard *after* the execution, i.e. at the time when Shell published its advertorial. By then, the only demand was that Shell should get out of Nigeria.

28. For analytic and evaluative relevance, see van Eemeren and Grootendorst (1992b).

political situation, that fact could never support the *factual* standpoint that Shell *does not* support the Nigerian regime.[29] In the process, Shell not only violates the Relevance Rule for critical discussion, but also the Language Use Rule. What has become apparent only after a radical reconstruction would have been immediately clear if Shell had advanced the standpoint explicitly, so Shell is guilty of being misleadingly vague.[30]

---

29. Even for the standpoint that Shell should not intervene, this argument offers only very weak support, but because this explicit standpoint is much less controversial than the implicit standpoint, this support might suffice.

30. For the sake of clarity, I refer again to my earlier overview of the argumention in Chapter 6.5:
   1 Shell is not to be blamed
       1.1a Shell is not to be blamed for the death of Ken Saro-Wiwa
           (1.1a.1a)(Shell has made efforts to help Ken Saro-Wiwa)
           (1.1a.1b)(These efforts were frustrated by the campaigners)
       1.1b Shell is not to be blamed for any environmental devastation
           1.1b.1a There are other (environmental) problems in the area
                1.1b.1a.1   The World Bank confirms this
           (1.1b.1b)(Shell is in fact contributing to saving the environment)
               (1.1b.1b).1a They are substantially subsidizing environment-related projects
               (1.1b.1b).1b They are substantially subsidizing other "good" projects
               (1.1b.1b).1c They are substantially subsidizing an environment survey
           (1.1b.1c)(A substantial component of environmental devastation is not caused by Shell)
               (1.1b.1c).1a In the Ogoni area 60 % of the environmental devastation is caused by sabotage
               (1.1b.1c).1b The contractors have been denied access when they tried to deal with these problems
               (1.1b.1c).2   Shell has not been operative in the Ogoni area since 1993
       (1.1c) (Shell is not propping up the Nigerian regime)
           (1.1c).1 Shell should not intervene in Nigerian politics (even if it could)
               (1.1c).1.1a Politics is the business of governments and politicians
               (1.1c).1.1b A world in which oil companies use their influence to prop up or bring down governments would be a frightening and bleak world
       2.1a Shell should not pull out of the Natural Liquefied Gas (NLG) project
           2.1a.1a The people would suffer
           2.1a.1b The environment would suffer
           2.1a.1c The future Nigerian government would suffer

CHAPTER 8   第八章

对举证责任的策略操控
Strategic maneuvering with the burden of proof

作为程序性概念的举证责任
8.1 The burden of proof as a procedural concept

As a case of disciplining argumentative conduct, I am going to discuss the demarcation of non-fallacious and fallacious instances of a mode of strategic maneuvering that takes place in the empirical counterpart of the opening stage of a critical discussion[1] – strategic maneuvering with the burden of proof. Strategic maneuvering with the burden of proof can be done in a way that is perfectly legitimate, but it can also derail in shifting or evading the burden of proof.[2] Because the way in which the burden of proof is divided in an argumentative exchange sets the stage for the various interactional patterns that may develop in the discourse, the concept of burden of proof is crucial to the conduct of argumentative discourse. Therefore it is not surprising that it has received a great deal of attention, especially since Bishop Whately became involved.[3] I shall explain the pragma-dialectical perspective, starting by answering the fundamental question of why a division of the burden of proof is necessary.

In the pragma-dialectical view, a division of the burden of proof is in the first place necessary for dialectical reasons. Like Rescher (1977), I regard the burden of proof as a procedural concept. In my approach, this concept serves the critical rationalist purpose of testing the tenability of a standpoint by carrying through the appropriate testing procedures as systematically, thoroughly, efficiently, and perspicuously as required. A difference of opinion concerning the acceptability of a standpoint on the merits can only be resolved if the burden of proof is divided in a transparent way and the parties comply with this division. Grootendorst and I therefore introduced the Obligation-to-Defend Rule (also called Burden of Proof Rule) when implementing the principles of socialization and dialectification in the opening stage of a critical discussion to regulate

---

1. To avoid any misunderstanding I would like to emphasize in this context that the model of a critical discussion pertains both to non-mixed and mixed differences of opinion. For systematic reasons van Eemeren and Grootendorst (1984) started their theorizing about what a critical discussion involves from the least complex case, a non-mixed difference of opinion.

2. See for experimental research concerning ordinary arguers' judgments of reasonableness regarding the management of the burden of proof van Eemeren, Garssen, and Meuffels (2009, pp. 111–162).

3. Whately (1846/1963) is widely regarded as having introduced the concept of burden of proof into the study of argumentation.

the mutual coordination of the completion of the critical procedure (van Eemeren & Grootendorst, 2004, pp. 138–141, p. 191). The Obligation-to-Defend Rule regulates how the *onus probandi* with regard to a standpoint is distributed:

> Discussants who advance a standpoint may not refuse to defend this standpoint when requested to do so.

The concept of burden of proof thus conceived serves the "division of labor of argumentation" (Rescher, 1977, p. 25). In terms of formal dialectic, one could say that this division of labor stimulates the progress of critical exchanges because the dialogue can move forward only if the participants are taking on commitments in a collaborative way (Walton & Krabbe, 1995, p. 9). In attributing in this way a purely dialectical status to the concept of burden of proof, we differ from others who attribute epistemological, ideological, ethical (or even moral) qualities to assuming the burden of proof.[4]

If it is clear why a division of the burden of proof is necessary, the next question is: when is a burden of proof incurred? In answering this question, it is helpful to remember that pragma-dialectics regards argumentative discourse as consisting of the performance of speech acts, each type of speech act creating its own commitments. Only some specific commitments constitute a burden of proof. From the perspective of a critical discussion, among the assertive speech acts – or the speech acts that are to be reconstructed as assertives – two types are to be distinguished, because each type leads to commitments with distinct procedural consequences. First, there are assertives used to advance a standpoint or to advance a reason (premise) that in the course of the discussion becomes a substandpoint because it is not accepted right away and needs to be defended itself. These assertives create the commitment at the opening stage constituting a burden of proof. Second, there are assertives performed to establish a starting point for the discussion. These assertives create commitments that can be used in the argumentation stage of the discussion but do not create a burden of proof. They have the same function as the formal dialectical concessions, albeit that in a critical discussion such concessions can be made by both parties and the commitments they create can be used both in defending and in attacking a standpoint by counterarguments. Since these assertives can only serve as starting points when – and because – they are, at least for the duration of the discussion, accepted as mutually agreed upon, they do not carry a burden of proof.

What does having a burden of proof involve? In the pragma-dialectical perspective the burden of proof for a (sub)standpoint involves the obligation to defend the standpoint once challenged to do so, i.e. to justify or refute the proposition(s) expressed in the standpoint. This regulation implies an obligation to give an adequate rejoinder to the critical response of the other party, i.e. to argue the case concerned as

---

4. See, for instance, Rescher (1977) for an epistemological foundation of this concept, Whately (1846/1963) for an ideological point of view, and Kauffeld (1998) for an ethical definition of the burden of proof.

thoroughly and extensively as the antagonist's criticisms require. Where Johnson (1998, 1999) includes dealing with contradictory or otherwise alternative standpoints in the protagonist's burden of proof, the presence of such alternative standpoints makes the difference of opinion in our approach "mixed" – or "multiple" and "mixed" – and then similar conditions for a burden of proof apply to the other party. According to the principle of externalization, however, the protagonist only needs to deal with those doubts and objections that are advanced in the discussion, whether explicitly, implicitly or indirectly, and not with objections that could be raised in theory but are not raised in fact.

Under which conditions is there a burden of proof? The obligation to defend a standpoint when asked to do so does always apply, and it holds fully until the protagonist has complied with his obligation to defend his standpoint or has retracted the standpoint. Nevertheless there are some general practical restrictions (and in specific communicative activity types more specific restrictions may apply). Both in a non-mixed and in a mixed difference of opinion, holding on to the burden of proof does not make sense when the protagonist has earlier defended the same standpoint successfully against the same antagonist starting from the same point of departure. Having a critical discussion is also a waste of time when no joint point of departure can be established.[5]

Who has the burden of proof? In a critical discussion, which task is assigned to whom is a matter of procedural agreement concerning the division of labor. Unless it has been explicitly agreed otherwise, the burden of proof is on the side of those whose standpoints have been challenged by the other party. During the discussion, the division of the burden of proof can become more diversified. As Walton and Krabbe observe, "some commitments are initially set or undertaken, and other commitments are [...] incurred along the way" (1995, p. 50). In the pragma-dialectical approach, the latter comprise both the commitment to defend the reasons advanced in defense of the standpoint that have been challenged and have become substandpoints, and the commitment to reply to the critical reactions advanced in challenging the applications of argument schemes that connect these reasons with the standpoint at issue.[6] Rescher (1977) and Walton (1988) contend that the protagonist's advancing a *prima facie* argument for his initial standpoint shifts the burden of proof to the other party. In the pragma-dialectical view, this shift amounts to a specific transfer of argumentative duties from one party to the other, a "shift of initiative" rather than a "shift of burden of

---

5. I agree with Rescher (1977) that it should always be possible to refer to a "common ground" that determines "what is to count as evidence." I do not agree, however, that this common ground is necessarily "impartially fixed." I leave it to the parties involved to choose their own point of departure.

6. For the pragma-dialectical notion of argument scheme see van Eemeren and Grootendorst (1992a, pp. 94–102) and Garssen (2001, pp. 91–92).

proof;"[7] it is now up to the antagonist to either give up or to maintain his doubt. In a non-mixed difference of opinion it is the antagonist's task to ask pertinent critical questions regarding the protagonist's argumentation; in a mixed difference of opinion there are two antagonists, so that the situation becomes more complex.

通过论辩承担举证责任
8.2 Meeting the burden of proof by means of argumentation

Another important question to be answered is: what means can be used to meet the burden of proof? According to the pragma-dialectical approach, the only means of meeting the burden of proof is by advancing argumentation. The argumentation advanced can be single, but, depending on the (anticipated) critical reactions to the use of a particular argument scheme and the other party's counter-arguments, it may also become multiple, coordinatively compound, or subordinatively compound (or display some combination of those structures).

The protagonist's argumentation must, in the end, always rest upon the starting points that have been established in the opening stage of the discussion (including those added as a result of a successful defense of substandpoints in the argumentation stage). Two kinds of distinction need to be made with respect to these starting points. First, there is a distinction between starting points consisting of material commitments ("premises") and starting points consisting of formal commitments ("discussion rules"). Second, there is a distinction between explicit starting points and implicit starting points. The explicit starting points are mutually agreed upon; as avowed commitments, they may not simply be revoked. The explicit starting points have a status similar to that of the propositional commitments that Hamblin (1970), Barth and Krabbe (1982), and Walton and Krabbe (1995) call "concessions." The implicit starting points are assumed to be inherent in the discussion context as "contextual commitments" (see also Chapter 9.2). They are liable to rejection but must be maintained if they (may be assumed to) successfully pass the appropriate "intersubjective identification procedure" instigated by the party who does not accept them at face value (van Eemeren & Grootendorst, 2004, pp. 145–148).[8]

The rationale for allowing particular starting points is in the pragma-dialectical approach viewed philosophically and practically as a pragmatic one.[9] A starting point

---

7. Here we connect with Hamblin (1970). In his system for dealing with what pragma-dialecticians call (mixed) differences of opinion, Hamblin relies solely on the "somewhat simpler concept of initiative" (p. 274).

8. Our contextual commitments are akin to Walton and Krabbe's (1995) "veiled" or dark-side commitments, albeit that the latter are associated with non-externalized states of mind and are not related to any speech acts (cf. Mackenzie & Staines, 1999).

9. In argumentative practice, too, the arguers' orientation seems pragmatic rather than epistemological. Gaskins (1992, 25–26) observes that "for pragmatists truth is 'the evolving product of

is acceptable if it is in agreement with the rules for critical discussion and is by intersubjective agreement accepted as a starting point by the parties, irrespective of whether the reason for their acceptance is epistemological, ethical, ideological, juridical, esthetical or other. As I have emphasized in Chapter 1, argumentation does not deal only with descriptive matters of truth and plausibility but also (for instance) with evaluative moral matters and practical policy matters. An epistemological perspective such as Rescher's can therefore at best cover only part of argumentative reality, thus excluding an abundance of important issues from "argumentative space."

When has the burden of proof been discharged? In practice, one can sometimes get rid of the burden of proof because of incidental circumstances such as the antagonist abandoning his doubt without any further critical consideration – or the death of the protagonist. In fact, the burden of proof has only really been discharged when the standpoint has been conclusively defended in a critical discussion so that it can be maintained whereas the opposition has to be withdrawn. A well-defined procedure has to spell out how this result can be achieved in an orderly fashion and in a practicable number of steps.

As in Rescher's approach, in the pragma-dialectical approach the parties determine (in the opening stage of the discussion) what the rules are to which they are committed.[10] Unlike Rescher's approach, the pragma-dialectical approach views the rationale for accepting the rules – which include also rules for the use and the correct application of argument schemes and for critically responding to argumentation in which a certain argument scheme is used – as lying in their "problem-validity" for critically testing the acceptability of standpoints. However complex the structure of the argumentation may be – due to the need to deal with (anticipated) critical reactions – every separate argument is by means of a certain logical scheme or argument scheme connected with the main standpoint or with a substandpoint, and needs to be tested on its own merits. In pragma-dialectics, this testing takes place in accordance with a fixed procedure.

A crucial role in the testing procedure is given to the critical questions associated with the argument scheme that is used by the protagonist. These critical questions differ for causal argumentation, comparison argumentation, and symptomatic argumentation. Only by responding to all relevant critical questions – thus providing extensions

---

a properly constituted research community' and that, in a similar spirit, the authority and legitimacy of the (American) judicial process is based on the integrity of its procedures rather than any privileged access to truth."

10. Walton and Krabbe (1995, p. 46) point out a favorable consequence of spelling out the rules of dialogue in the opening stage of the discussion: "[...] your commitment tends to be made more specific as well, for when precise rules of argument are spelled out, the means you can use to defend your point of view are narrowed down." This favorable consequence, by the way, can only materialize when, in the argumentative reality of ordinary argumentative discourse, the empirical counterparts of the stages happen to be ordered in the same way as the stages in the ideal model of a critical discussion.

to his argumentation – can the protagonist discharge his (possibly accumulated) burden of proof.[11] The burden of proof has been discharged only when all the antagonist's relevant critical questions have been answered in a way that the antagonist deems sufficiently thorough, and no unanswered critical questions remain. The required constellation of arguments has then been advanced completely in the argumentation and the argumentation has to be accepted.

混合意见分歧中的辩护顺序
8.3 The order of defense in a mixed difference of opinion

In a non-mixed difference of opinion only one party has advanced an initial standpoint and this party is also the only party who has an obligation to defend. In a mixed difference of opinion, where two parties have advanced contradictory standpoints, each party has an obligation to defend his own standpoint.[12] The problem is: in which order are the standpoints to be defended? For resolving the difference of opinion on the merits, it is not essential who starts the defense but in strategic maneuvering it can make a difference to the chances of success of the defense or the attack. The order in which the standpoints are defended can have a strategic importance, if only because it is advantageous, when defending one's standpoint, to know what arguments have been advanced to defend the opposite standpoint.

In Whately's (1846/1963, p. 112) view, the burden of proof in such a case lies on the side of he who would dispute a "presumption," so that the issue of who should start the defense is decided in favor of the party whose standpoint has the highest degree of presumption.[13] The presumptive status of a standpoint depends, in this approach, on

---

11. The pragma-dialectical critical questions, which are systematically associated with the use of particular argument schemes, agree to some extent with the Standard Objections distinguished by Johnstone Jr., which refer to a class of objections "typically or frequently found in the neighborhood of prominent issues," but, due to their association with particular argument schemes, the critical questions are more general and more systematic. The critical questions are not identical with "objections" that an arguer, according to Johnson (1998), should respond to. As a matter of course, critical questions are not equal to counter-arguments and they do not involve any burden of proof, however "serious" they may be.

12. In practice, this is as a rule also the case when the standpoints advanced are *contrary*. The other party responding to the standpoint "X is blue" with the counterstandpoint "X is red" implies "X is not blue, as it was claimed to be."

13. Whately claims that "according to the most correct use of the term a 'Presumption' in favor of any supposition, means, not (as has been sometimes erroneously imagined) a preponderance of probability in its favor, but a *pre-occupation* of the ground, as implies that it must stand good till some sufficient reason is adduced against it; in short, that the *Burden of Proof* lies on the side of him who would dispute it" (1846/1963, p. 112). He treats the problem of the division of the burden of proof in fact as a problem of choice, changing a mixed difference of opinion into a non-mixed difference of opinion in which only one party has a burden of proof.

the extent to which it is in line with the *status quo*. In epistemological approaches, such as Rescher's (1977, p. 39), the crucial issue is "how readily the thesis in view could make its peace within the overall framework of our cognitive commitments." Presumption is then conceived as a cognitive and epistemic category: one assertion has presumption because it is more plausible than another. In Rescher's (1977, p. 31) opinion, "in most probative contexts, there is a standing presumption in favor of the usual, normal, customary course of things," which he characterizes as "the cognitive *status quo*." When Rescher refers to "the usual course of things" in plausibility assessment, his words seem to echo those of Perelman and Olbrechts-Tyteca in *The New Rhetoric* (1958/1969).

In mixed differences of opinion the fallacy of evading the burden of proof appeals to the presumption principle from which our criminal law starts: as long as the guilt of a suspect is unproven, he will be treated as innocent. The suspect himself does not need to defend his innocence, but it is up to the district attorney to prove his guilt. Similarly, the perpetrator of this fallacy pretends that it is not up to him to prove his "innocence." Even though in certain cases the presumption principle can offer a solution to the sequential problem, it cannot be generally applied: if the one wishes to go to the movies and the other wishes to go to a bar, or when the one wishes to invest their extra bonus and the other prefers to put it into a savings account, the presumption principle offers no solution. Whately's opinion about the role of presumption and the burden of proof attached to it is not only rather conservative but it basically breaches the pragma-dialectical Obligation-to-Defend Rule: whether or not someone has presumption on his side is irrelevant to whether that person has the burden of proof – in order to determine where the status of presumption can be awarded it does not matter if in the standpoint a generally accepted opinion is proclaimed or a completely new plan which involves a radical break with the *status quo*; in either case the discussant has, in accordance with Obligation-to-Defend Rule, the whole burden of proof for his own standpoint.

According to the pragmatic view of Ullman-Margalit (1983), the issue is not so much concerned with "ascertaining the facts" as with "proceeding on them." Her procedural consideration concerning the "comparative convenience with which the parties can be expected to produce pertinent evidence" has to do with the question "of what presumption will be the most useful to adopt as an initial step in the process of deliberation [...], quite apart from the question whether the conclusion to which [this] adoption [...] points is likely to be true."[14] In a similar pragmatic vein, Houtlosser and I have developed the solution to the problem of the order of defense in a mixed

---

14. Although adopting a presumption can prejudge an issue, in Ullman-Margalit's view it may be seen as rational in a twofold sense: in any particular instance the presumption is open to rebuttal, and the bias it promotes is independently justifiable. In pragma-dialectical terms, the former would mean that a starting point can be revoked; this, however, is only allowed when it can be shown by offering counter-evidence that this starting point is, after all, not acceptable. The latter would mean that institutional or other contextual support must be available.

difference of opinion that I am going to explain.[15] However, before doing so in section 8.5, I have to prepare the ground for this pragmatic solution.

In relying on establishing commitments that have ensued in argumentative discourse from what has been explicitly or implicitly said, pragma-dialectics finds itself in agreement with Mackenzie and Staines, who argue that an argument "directly affects, not belief or opinion, but public commitment" (1999, p. 35). As Hamblin observed much earlier (1970, p. 264), our saying something commits us, whether we believe what we say or not. I also agree with Hamblin (1970, pp. 16–17) that commitments can be incurred simply by putting on the appropriate linguistic performance – in pragma-dialectical terms, by performing the appropriate speech act. In the critical discussion I envisage, the participants' aims are to convince the other by making use of one's own commitments and the other party's commitments.[16]

Walton and Krabbe (1995, p. 9) note that a dialogue is enabled to move forward because the participants are willing to take on commitments in a collaborative way. This observation is captured in pragma-dialectics by situating the performance of speech acts in a dialogical context where the discourse progresses by anticipating and responding to (presumed) reactions of the other party. By indicating "agreement or disagreement with a preceding remark of the other speaker" (Hamblin, 1970, p. 256), the participants build up their commitment sets. As Walton and Krabbe rightly observe, to know what a party is committed to should be equal to knowing what that party should or should not do, to live up to this commitment (1995, p. 17). Therefore there must be rules of procedure for performing speech acts in a critical discussion that specify for each discussion stage the conditions under which certain commitments are incurred or deleted from a participant's commitment store – from the beginning of the discussion in the confrontation stage to the termination of the discussion in the concluding stage. In establishing procedural rules for resolving a difference of opinion, following the principle of dialectification, pragma-dialecticians provide standards for the conduct of argumentative discourse that regulate critical interaction (van Eemeren & Grootendorst, 1984, 1992a).

In this way, we are in perfect agreement with Rescher's (1977, p. 40) recommendation to move "from the plane of the [...] descriptive and ontological to that of the [...] regulative and methodological." It is worth noting that the dialectical standards of pragma-dialectics are more inclusive and also more differentiated than the logical standard of formal validity and the preservation of truth (van Eemeren & Grootendorst, 1992a). With Barth and Krabbe (1982), pragma-dialecticians are among those who speak of a reasonable result of a discussion when this result has been reached by

---

15. My explanation is in the first place based on van Eemeren and Houtlosser (2003a).
16. Hamblin's idea of a *commitment store*, which is similar to Lorenzen's *set of concessions*, and the accompanying *commitment rules*, are an invaluable addition to this way of theorizing. They make it possible to determine what each participant is committed to at each particular point in the discussion. This is exactly the kind of externalization pragma-dialecticians are aiming for.

arguing *ex concessis*. In other words, they opt for a pragmatic way out of the Münchhausen trilemma (Albert, 1975): the pragmatic angle of pragma-dialectics warrants the arguer to stop the discussion process at the point where acceptance by the other party is assured.[17]

I shall now explain how I think the pragma-dialectical analysis of the burden of proof can be completed with a pragmatic solution of the problem concerning the order in which two opposing standpoints regarding the same proposition are to be defended in a mixed difference of opinion. I first describe the argumentative situation in which the problem arises. The dialectical profile pertaining to this argumentative situation specifies the moves that are admissible when dividing the burden of proof in a mixed difference of opinion in the empirical counterpart of the opening stage of a critical discussion applying to this dialectical situation. This dialectical profile starts from the point that a mixed difference of opinion has come into being in the confrontation stage between two parties. It includes both possibilities that are available, the one in which the party that has advanced a positive standpoint is challenged to defend this positive standpoint first and the one in which the party that has advanced a negative standpoint is challenged to defend this negative standpoint first:[18]

Result of the confrontation stage: S1: +/p,?/(-/p); S2:?/(+/p), -/p
(speaker 1 (S1) advances a positive standpoint with respect to proposition p; speaker 2 (S2) doubts S1's positive standpoint with respect to proposition p and advances a negative standpoint with respect to p; S1 doubts S2's negative standpoint with respect to p)[19]

---

17. It should be noted here that *truth finding discussions* ("inquiries"), in which the aim is not to resolve a difference of opinion but to determine which standpoint is *true*, are in their purest form not argumentative discussions (there is no standpoint and no difference of opinion). Discussions in which the aims of resolving a difference of opinion and truth preservation are combined (ensuing, for instance, from differences of opinion arising within truth finding discussions) constitute a special category of argumentative discussions in which the starting points have to meet certain extra demands, rather than just being shared by both discussion parties. If this were not the case, it could happen that the prevailing standpoint in a discussion is not to be accepted as correct from a scientific point of view although it is agreed upon by the discussion parties, which would contradict the aim of a truth-preserving argumentative discussion. The extra demands the starting points in such a discussion have to meet are expressed in criteria such as "being in accordance with current scientific insights" and "meeting the appropriate standards of epistemological correctness." These specific criteria, however, are not to be set by argumentation theorists, but can only be determined within the relevant scientific or scholarly community.

18. I restrict myself here to the part of the dialectical profile that concerns the positive standpoint. The part of the dialectical profile that concerns the negative standpoint is, *mutatis mutandis*, the same.

19. The ideal procedure for going through the confrontation stage of a critical discussion makes clear that it must be externalized in the analysis that S2's negative standpoint implies doubt about S1's positive standpoint and that S1's positive standpoint in turn implies doubt about S2's negative standpoint. If a critical discussion is to be conducted about the tenability of the positive

Opening stage:

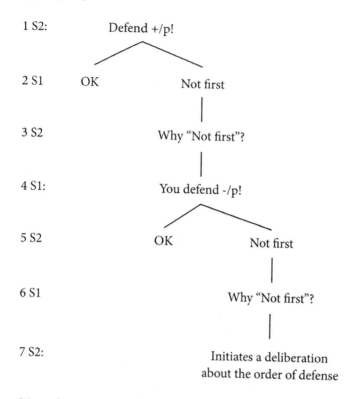

We are here concerned with a dialectical situation that comes into being when a party, S1, in response to the other party's challenge (in turn 1), refuses (in turn 2) to defend his standpoint first. When asked (in turn 3) why he does not want to defend his standpoint first, S1 can (in turn 4) challenge the other party, S2, to defend his opposing standpoint. As the profile specifies, in such a situation S2 has (in turn 5) two possibilities: either he concedes that he should begin defending his own standpoint or he rejects the challenge. If he rejects the challenge, S1 may (in turn 6) require an explanation why

---

standpoint advanced by S1, the only move S2 is allowed to make is reacting to this standpoint; this reaction should either be one of acceptance or one of non-acceptance. Advancing the opposite (negative) standpoint by S2 is not a dialectically relevant move, because it does not further *the present* critical discussion, but initiates a *new* discussion, i.e. a critical discussion about the tenability of S2's negative standpoint. Viewed dialectically, the latter discussion is a new discussion because its result has not necessarily any bearing on the outcome of the discussion about the tenability of S1's positive standpoint. Consequently, if a positive standpoint is in practice directly opposed by a negative standpoint, the ensuing *mixed* difference of opinion should be decomposed into two *simple* differences of opinion, which need to be separately resolved, i.e. one by one, thus avoiding the occurrence of argumentative moves in which the two discussions get confused, such as the *argumentum ad ignorantiam*.

he does not want to defend his standpoint. At this point, S2 may (in turn 7) no longer return the challenge, because he would then be repeating the challenge that he issued in his very first move (turn 1). If the dialogue is to continue, he should therefore initiate a deliberation about the order in which the standpoints at issue are to be defended.

Thus the dialectical profile makes it clear that the problem of establishing the order in which two opposing standpoints are to be defended amounts to a procedural problem concerning who will be the first to try to discharge the burden of proof in a mixed difference of opinion. In the opening stage of a critical discussion, a deliberation may be started over the order in which the defenses should take place, and this deliberation is to be initiated by the party that has started the process of challenging. The dialectical profile also makes it clear why this procedure is so. It is only after the party that has been challenged initially (in turn 1) has returned this challenge (in turn 4) that the order of defense can become pertinent. The order of defense can be made an issue by the other party only in the subsequent turns (turn 5–7).

The dialectical profile clearly specifies how and when the order of defense can become an issue in a mixed difference of opinion, but it does not specify how it can be decided what the order should be. As was also the case with the problems concerning the burden of proof that I discussed in the previous section, various kinds of solutions have been proposed in the various treatments of this particular burden of proof problem – epistemological, juridical, ethical, etc. The pragma-dialectical approach opts for a more general stance. I think that the way in which the problem is to be resolved depends in the first place on the institutional practice or macro-context in which the discussion takes place. The opening stage of a critical discussion is designed precisely to accommodate the specific kinds of procedures and conventions that are operative in the various institutional practices and contexts. As I observed in Chapter 5, there are practices that are formally institutionalized, such as criminal court procedures and parliamentary debates, which have fixed procedures to determine how issues of order should be decided. There are also practices where no such fixed procedures exist, but where nevertheless certain conventional rules are operative that are in agreement with the goals of the communicative activity type concerned.[20] If no formalized institutional procedures are operative in the communicative macro-context in which a discussion takes place, then specific kinds of conventions of the latter type provide a *pragmatic rationale* for deciding on issues such as order of defense.

---

20. In the broader perspective I adhere to, all everyday verbal interaction can be regarded as institutional in the sense that performing speech acts is a form of conventionalized rule-governed behavior and specific types of speech acts in specific kinds of exchanges are subject to specific kinds of (institutional) preconditions.

决定辩护顺序的语用原则
8.4 A pragmatic rationale for deciding on the order of defense

What does the pragmatic rationale for deciding on the order of defense in mixed differences of opinion consist of and how can it account for a decision on the order of defense when two opposite standpoints are advanced? In answering these questions I start by presenting two dialogues in which the parties advance opposing standpoints and the first speaker requires the second speaker to defend his opposite standpoint first. The standpoint that introduces the issue is represented in italics. In the first dialogue, this standpoint involves an implicit accusation:

(8.1)   1   S1: *My purple vase!*
        2   S2: Yes, what a pity, isn't it?
        3   S1: *You dropped it!*
        4   S2: I did not!
        5   S1: Make me believe you didn't.
        6   S2: I beg your pardon?!

In the second dialogue, the standpoint is an informative assertive:

(8.2)   1   S1: *Jan is leaving for Warsaw tomorrow.*
        2   S2: When exactly?
        3   S1: *Ten a.m.*
        4   S2: I shouldn't think so …
        5   S1: Why not?
        6   S2: As far as I know, the train departs every odd hour.

In a pragma-dialectical reconstruction of these dialogues in terms of a critical discussion, in both cases the difference of opinion can be characterized as *mixed* because the parties take opposite positions in regard of an issue: in dialogue (8.1), the issue is whether S2 has dropped the vase; in (8.2), the issue is whether the train leaves at ten a.m. In both differences of opinion each party has a standpoint of its own. Consequently, in both cases each party has an obligation to defend its standpoint.[21] There is a problem, however. Temporarily or definitively – we cannot tell which – the party who puts forward his standpoint first shifts the burden of proof to the other party. This shift seems more or less legitimate in case (8.2), but certainly not in case (8.1).[22] By examining how in ordinary argumentative discourse a burden of proof is acquired and what the pragmatic rationale for attributing such a burden of proof can be, an explanation can be given for this difference.

---

21. It may be a useful reminder here that in a critical discussion advancing a standpoint implies assuming a conditional obligation to defend the position expressed in that standpoint. When two opposing standpoints are advanced by different parties, each party is required to defend its position.

22. In (8.2) it would indeed have been odd if S2 had said in turn 6 that S1 should first prove that the train leaves at ten a.m.

Reconstructing what people say and intend to convey in argumentative discourse as a series of moves in a critical discussion, as is aimed for in pragma-dialectics, amounts to giving an explicit analysis of these people's "dialectical" commitments to certain propositions. Such an analysis can only be achieved if the dialectical commitments of the parties involved in the discussion can be derived from the "pragmatic" commitments inherent in the way in which they have expressed themselves in the discourse, whether explicitly or implicitly. These pragmatic commitments can be traced by making use of insights provided by theories of language use that focus on how mutual obligations are incurred and acquitted in verbal communication and interaction, such as Searlean speech act theory and Gricean theory of rational exchanges.

Indeed, Searlean speech act theory and Gricean theory of rational exchanges can be called upon in the first place to explain the rationale for attributing certain pragmatic commitments to the participants in argumentative discourse. As Jackson (1995) observes, the Gricean maxims, in particular the Maxim of Quality ("Do not say what you believe to be false or that for which you lack adequate evidence"), support the general presumption that an assertion advanced in the discourse is acceptable – and I reckon this goes for other types of speech acts too. According to Jackson, this presumption is cancelled only if (1) the interlocutor has independent reason to doubt that the assertion is indeed acceptable, or (2) has independent reason to doubt that the speaker is indeed behaving in a cooperative way, or (3) the context indicates that the speaker himself deems his assertion less acceptable to the interlocutor (1995, p. 258). Ullman-Margalit (1983) expresses basically the same idea when she says that viewed in a legal perspective an assertion's being "presumptively acceptable" means that the interlocutor *is entitled to regard it as acceptable.*[23]

In our view, the presumption of acceptability needs to be grounded even more fundamentally in a genuinely normative principle, such as the Interaction Principle postulated by van Eemeren and Grootendorst (1991). The Interaction Principle involves a general prohibition against the performance of any speech act that cannot be made acceptable to the interlocutor. Unlike the Gricean maxims, the Interaction Principle involves a real requirement. A violation of this principle does not encourage alternative interpretations of what is said. On the contrary, such a violation obstructs the

---

23. In the law, the notion of presumption is applied to situations in which something is an "impending issue." What to do, for example, when someone has been absent for more than seven years: should this person be declared dead or not? For legal purposes, it is then presumed that this person is dead. Ullman-Margalit (1983, p. 148) emphasizes this feature when she says that "presumption entitles deliberators to make an assumption *that they are otherwise not entitled to make.*" Jackson's use of the notion of presumption conforms to the legal use on the condition that the acceptability of a speaker's assertion can be considered an impending issue. What to do when someone has said something: accept it or not? The presumption is then acceptance, unless there is something that weighs against it.

normal course of the interaction, and can even lead to sanctions.[24] Anyone who performs a speech act is committed to complying with the requirement involved in the Interaction Principle, and this commitment gives rise to the presumption that the speech act that was performed is indeed acceptable. This presumption is similar to the presumption that motorists who approach a red traffic light will obey the traffic rule and stop their cars.

Until there are clear indications of the opposite, the interlocutor is thus entitled to regard the speech act performed by the speaker or writer as acceptable. If, however, there *are* indications that the speaker or writer *has not committed himself* to the requirement involved in the Interaction Principle, the situation is different. When, for instance, a speaker makes it known in advance that he anticipates opposition from his interlocutor, or – following up on this – the interlocutor does indeed express opposition to the speech act concerned, then the proposition involved is not (or no longer) a presumption. To regain the presumption of acceptability the speaker has to adduce evidence that his proposition is acceptable after all. In other words, he has acquired a burden of proof. Only when the speaker has succeeded in acquitting himself of this burden does the burden of initiative shift away from his position. If the interlocutor intends to maintain his opposition, then he, in turn, should acquit himself of the burden of proof for his opposite position. This is the only way he can get rid of the "burden of initiative" (see Rescher, 1977).[25]

I think that this analysis can be taken a step further by observing that it is reasonable to let the exemption from having to take the initiative remain with a speaker as long as the speaker's speech act does not go against the prevailing pragmatic *status quo*. This means that his speech act should not be at odds with the set of premises that are mutually shared by the parties involved in the interaction. This set of premises represents the *pragmatic status quo* because it does not necessarily refer to warranted beliefs or the general state of knowledge in a certain field, as the "cognitive" and "epistemic" *status quo* do, but to the list of premises that the parties involved in the discourse explicitly or implicitly accept and that define their interactional relationship in the

---

24. The Gricean maxims, which are Jackson's basis for the presumption of acceptability, are not rules in the same sense. Unlike violating a "real" rule, violating a maxim does not lead to any sanctions but to an interpretation of the speaker's meaning that is different from the literal "utterance meaning" (assuming that the Cooperation Principle still applies). Thus, in a Gricean perspective, the fact that the Maxim of Quality is *not* obviously violated does not warrant the conclusion that what the speaker asserts is presumptively acceptable. Given that none of the other maxims are violated either, and, again, that the Cooperation Principle still holds, it is only warranted to conclude that nothing else was meant than was literally said.

25. In a discussion, a presumption serves as a common starting point that applies *pro tempore*, i.e. until sufficient evidence has been produced that makes revision necessary and as a *prima facie* accepted starting point that in the course of the discussion can be revised or falsified.

argumentative situation at hand.[26] The pragmatic *status quo* is challenged as soon as one of the parties involved performs a speech act that is obviously inconsistent with the shared premises, for example because the state of affairs presupposed by the correctness conditions of the speech act conflicts with one or more jointly accepted premises.

语用现状与辩护顺序
8.5 The pragmatic *status quo* and the order of defense

When may a speech act be assumed to be inconsistent with one or more mutually shared premises? I think that Kauffeld's (1998, 2002) analyses of the way a burden of proof is incurred in everyday verbal interaction can be of help in answering this question. In Kauffeld's view, at what point exactly people engaged in verbal interaction incur a burden of proof and what the burden of proof involves depend primarily on the nature of the speech acts concerned. This means that the illocutionary point of a speech act and the implications of having made this point in a felicitous way are of decisive importance. In my view, Kauffeld's account has the merit of complementing a dialectical concern with obligations in ideal situations with a pragmatic concern with the way in which a burden of proof is assumed in everyday verbal interaction. He achieves this complementation by showing how the performance of certain speech acts, namely proposing and accusing, can endow the speaker with certain *probative obligations*.[27]

I think that Kauffeld's approach can be generalized and applied to all verbal interaction by means of speech acts. In my outline of how I think such a generalization can be realized, I adapt Kauffeld's idea that certain speech acts may have implications that – possibly or presumably – go against the interlocutor's views.[28] My adaptation amounts to taking Kauffeld's idea to mean that a speech act may have implications that go against the interlocutor's view of the interactional relationship between the speaker and the interlocutor encompassed in the present pragmatic *status quo*. According to my adapted account, a proposal would invite an adjustment of what the interlocutor until then took to be the shared expectation of the interactional relationship between

---

26. What Rescher (1977) and others have called a "cognitive *status quo*" (or "epistemic *status quo*") is in fact subsumed in our concept of "pragmatic *status quo*." The concept bears some relation to Walton and Krabbe's (dialectical) concept of "dark-side commitments."

27. "In many kinds of illocutionary act, S does not, at least not typically, engage a larger obligation to provide, on demand, reason and evidence vindicating the truth and adequacy of her primary utterance. [...] But, other things being equal, where S makes a proposal or levels an accusation, she cannot responsibly dismiss an addressee's demand for proof" (Kauffeld, 2002).

28. In his analysis of proposing, Kauffeld claims that the major reason for having to justify an act of proposing is that the one who proposes something is supposed to have good reasons for what he proposes and if he aims at having his proposal accepted he should inform the interlocutor of these reasons. In his analysis of accusing, Kauffeld suggests that a major reason for having to justify an act of accusing is that the accused party has a right to deny the accusation and can only do so properly if the accuser has provided reasons for his accusation.

the communicators; also, an accusation invites an adjustment of what the interlocutor so far regarded as the shared view of the relationship between them. In my conception of a pragmatic *status quo* this would mean that both a proposal and an accusation have implications that are likely to be inconsistent with the list of mutually shared premises – or at least with what the interlocutor supposed the list to be.

Searle's taxonomy of speech acts can be of help in determining which types of speech acts can have implications that run counter to the interlocutor's view of his current interactional relationship with the speaker. "Commissives," for instance, can generally be expected to have implications that agree with the interlocutor's view of the interactional relationship between the speaker and the interlocutor. "Directives," on the contrary, can easily have implications that are in disagreement with the interlocutor's view. Prototypical commissives such as promises do not, as a rule, introduce actions that the interlocutor will think inconsistent with agreed-upon desirables, but with prototypical directives such as requests this may quite well be the case. There is at least one class of speech acts in Searle's taxonomy that contains *both* kinds of speech acts. This is the class consisting of the "assertives." Some assertives are designed to provide the interlocutor with information that he did not possess before, but that is expected to be consistent with what he already knows, such as "informing" and "explaining." There are also assertives, however, that aim to make the interlocutor accept a view that he did *not* accept before and that can often *not* be expected to be consistent with what he already accepts, such as "claiming" and "accusing."[29] (A view may be surprising, and such that one can *not* expect the other to agree with it at once, yet it can be expected to be consistent with what the other accepts (but often it can not). In both cases argument is required.)

Now that I have explained what I mean by a pragmatic *status quo* and how we can determine whether or not a speech act may be considered to violate this *status quo*, I return to the problem of the order in which two opposing standpoints are to be defended in a mixed difference of opinion. In the pragma-dialectical view of argumentative confrontation, the speech act that initially introduces the issue can acquire the status of a standpoint in a difference of opinion when the person who performed that speech act makes it clear (e.g. by advancing an argument) that he anticipates that the interlocutor will not accept this speech act at face value or the interlocutor makes it known that he is not prepared to accept the speech act at face value by performing a counter speech act (see van Eemeren, 1987b; Houtlosser, 2002). In the former case, the speech act does not result in a presumption because the speaker or writer makes it clear from the start that it may *go against the prevailing pragmatic status quo* between him and the interlocutor. In the latter case, the speech act concerned initially *has* a presumptive status, because for all the speaker or writer knows – and also for all we know – it *does not violate the prevailing pragmatic status quo*. This presumptive

---

29. The declaratives, in particular "language declaratives" such as definitions and specifications, are likely to be open to the same problem, just as the "expressives."

status is, of course, canceled when the interlocutor opposes the speech act with a counter speech act.

Returning to cases (8.1) and (8.2) above, it will be clear that we may assume that in (8.2) move 4 by S2 opposes the preceding move by S1. Also in (8.1) we may assume this for the corresponding moves. Thus, we assume that the interlocutor opposes the speaker's initial speech act with a counter (assertive) speech act, also in the case (8.1) in which the speaker has made it clear that he anticipates such opposition. The interlocutor's reaction then agrees completely with this anticipation. Both cases can now be regarded as involving the kind of interactional situation of maximal opposition that can be reconstructed pragma-dialectically as a mixed difference of opinion: the two parties have assumed contradictory standpoints and each party has a duty to defend its own standpoint. All the same, there is an important difference between the two argumentative situations. In the first case, the standpoint that initiated the difference of opinion has no presumptive status from the start, whereas in the second case it has. And the interlocutor's opposition has a presumptive status in the first case, but not in the second. In the second case it is, after all, precisely the interlocutor's opposition that first challenges the pragmatic *status quo* that is up to then supposed to prevail.

What are the implications for handling the burden of proof of this discrepancy between argumentative situations in a mixed difference of opinion? Earlier I have argued that the burden of proof consists in an obligation for a party in a difference of opinion to defend his standpoint if challenged to do so, but I have also mentioned an additional, procedural obligation that Hamblin (1970) pointed out and referred to as the *burden of initiative*. Besides having an obligation to defend a standpoint, having a burden of initiative implies in the pragma-dialectical perspective an obligation to defend this standpoint *at this particular juncture* of the discussion. Distinguishing the obligation to defend a standpoint from the obligation to defend the standpoint at this particular junction of the discussion allows for the existence of an argumentative situation in which a certain party has an obligation to defend a standpoint, but is not required to acquit himself of this obligation now. That is, a party who has advanced a particular standpoint might, at a particular juncture, have the burden of proof, but not the burden of initiative.[30]

It is precisely the additional obligation of having the burden of initiative that makes for the difference in the burden of the parties in the two cases I just discussed. In the first case (8.1), the speaker has both a pragmatic and dialectical obligation to defend his standpoint and a merely pragmatic obligation to start the defense. In the second case (8.2), he does have an obligation to defend his standpoint, but not a pragmatic obligation to defend it immediately. He is only required to defend his standpoint after the interlocutor has defended *his* standpoint. Whereas the *order* in which the two standpoints are to be defended coincides in the first case with the order in which they have

---

30. This is, in fact, a different way of making Rescher's well-known distinction between an I(nitial)-burden of proof and an E(vidential) burden of proof.

been put forward, in the second case it does not. In the second case (8.2), the first speaker's assertion (in turn 3) has acquired the status of a standpoint because of the second speaker's opposition (in turn 4). Nevertheless, the presumptive status of the first speaker's assertion is preserved, because at the stage in which it was performed there were no indications that he performed a speech act that could be regarded as going against the prevailing pragmatic *status quo*; consequently, this speech act cannot bestow a burden of initiative on the speaker. First, the interlocutor should justify his opposition. Once he has done so, the first speaker's assertive loses its presumptive status and this speaker is obliged to accept the burden of initiative. At that juncture he cannot escape any longer from defending his assertive against the interlocutor's opposition.

基于举证责任的阶段性操控
8.6 Stage-bound maneuvering with the burden of proof

How about strategic maneuvering with the burden of proof? The strategic maneuvering by the parties will be aimed at strengthening their position as much as possible in all stages of the resolution process. Besides non-fallacious maneuvering, there can also be fallacious manipulation of the burden of proof.[31] As Walton (1988) rightly observes, some fallacies "reflect subtle shifts in the burden of proof that can be powerfully effective, yet often go unnoticed." In view of the difficulty of determining whether the criteria for complying with the dialectical norms are in fact fulfilled, it is necessary to have a clear view of the various kinds of manifestations of strategic maneuvering with the burden of proof.

In the confrontation stage, the dialectical objective of the parties is to achieve clarity concerning the specific issues that are at stake in the difference of opinion and the positions of the parties involved. Viewed rhetorically, the parties aim to direct the confrontation in the way that is most beneficial from their own perspective. Both parties will attempt to achieve a definition of the disagreement that highlights the issues they want to discuss and will attempt to create the positions they would like to see assumed. As far as the burden of proof is concerned, this means that their strategic maneuvering will concentrate on acquiring the most expedient burden of proof – but this maneuvering in the confrontation stage is preparatory to the actual assumption and division of the burden proof in the opening stage. In the confrontation stage, both parties can play a constructive part and also a not so constructive part. In the first case, their strategic maneuvering results in a clear view of the preconditions for assuming and dividing the burden of proof; in the second case, it prejudges these matters.

---

31. Of course, there is no fallacy of evading the burden of proof in mixed differences of opinion if in the opening stage both parties agree to follow the sequence of defense according to the presumption principle. Whether this or some other principle for making an agreement about the order of defense can be chosen depends in argumentative practice upon the communicative activity type in which the argumentative discourse takes place, among other things.

The party having taken up a standpoint can act constructively in acquiring an expedient burden of proof by stating as precisely as possible what his position amounts to, thus avoiding any confusion about what exactly he is prepared to defend. One way of doing this is to make, in the presentation of the standpoint, unequivocally clear that its scope is limited in a specific way, so that no burden of proof can ensue for anything that exceeds this scope. The same effect can be achieved by leaving aside any issues that are known to be controversial in the present context of discussion and would interfere with the (piecemeal) engineering of the resolution process when taken into account. The admissibility of using such a technique in strategic maneuvering may depend on the communicative activity type involved. In the case of a communicative activity type involving an apologia, for instance, it seems clear that specific accusations need to be responded to – if not for dialectical reasons, then at least for social or moral reasons. The party that doubts the acceptability of the standpoint, or is inclined to contradict it, can play a constructive strategic part in construing the burden of proof by articulating in a way favorable to his interests what the nature of his criticisms is and to exactly which aspect(s) of the standpoint they pertain. He can also articulate a strategic position in the discussion. An obvious way of achieving this is to state immediately that he does not take a counter-standpoint on the topic, but is only interested in hearing reasons for the standpoint of the other party, so that he "plays it safe" and no burden of proof can be attached to his position.

Strategic maneuvering with regard to the burden of proof in the confrontation stage can also be fallacious. This is the case when the party who advances a standpoint tries to escape from acquiring a burden of proof. He can, for instance, do so by pretending that there is no real difference of opinion, thus avoiding a critical treatment of his standpoint. Techniques that can be used are: phrasing the standpoint "hermetically" ("The Frenchman is essentially intolerant"), making it immune to criticism; presenting something as a point of departure rather than a standpoint; presenting the standpoint as self-evident ("It is clear that") or guaranteeing its acceptability in another way ("I assure you that"); and declaring the standpoint sacrosanct ("this is an undeniable truth") so that there can presumably be no difference of opinion about it that lends itself to discussion. The party who is critical maneuvers fallaciously when he attempts to saddle the other party with an extra burden of proof. He can do so by attributing a burden of proof to the other party for a standpoint that the other party may be expected to adhere to but has not explicitly or implicitly expressed and that he obviously cannot properly defend, exploiting what Gaskins (1992, p. 21) calls the "risk of non-persuasion." Another technique is making the other party prove that he does not have a personal interest in the standpoint he has advanced (circumstantial *ad hominem*) or that his standpoint is not inconsistent with a view he has expressed earlier (*tu quoque*).

In the opening stage, the dialectical objective is to establish an unambiguous point of departure for the discussion. This point of departure consists of intersubjectively accepted procedural and material starting points – the mutual "concessions" – and includes a division of the discussion roles. The rhetorical aim of each of the parties is to arrive at a point of departure that serves that party's interest best. Since it depends on the allocation of discussion roles and the choice of procedural and material starting points how expedient the division of the burden of proof will be and how easy it is to discharge, both parties' strategic maneuvering will be aimed at establishing the most opportune allocation of discussion roles and the most workable procedural and material starting points. Which allocation of discussion roles counts as most opportune, and which starting points are most workable, are interrelated questions. The answers depend to a great extent on the argumentative duties each party is prepared to assume in view of the argumentative duties the other party is prepared to assume.

With respect to the material starting points, the parties' constructive strategic maneuvering will amount to making a rhetorically advantageous choice that allows them to defend or attack exactly those points they see fit to defend or attack. For instance, if a party intends to take on the role of protagonist, this would-be protagonist's constructive maneuvering regarding the starting points will be aimed at establishing the strongest possible basis for defending his standpoint. To this end, he might attempt to highlight those concessions of the would-be antagonist that suit him best. As Pinto correctly maintains, "questions of reasonableness of premises are intimately connected with questions about the suitability of the inferences that can be made from them" (Hansen in the introduction to Pinto, 2001, p. xii).[32] A way of achieving this emphasis is to make the other party's commitments, including the contextual commitments that can be attributed to him, transparent in the presentation, thus making those starting points explicit in the process that would otherwise remain obscure and, because of their obscurity, could lead to an avoidable discussion.

Strategic maneuvering on the part of the would-be protagonist becomes fallacious when he declines, without a valid reason, to take on the role of protagonist of a standpoint that he has advanced ("evading the burden of proof"). His maneuvering is also fallacious when he plays down his burden of proof, weakens it in his final presentation of the standpoint in the opening stage, or even "shifts" the burden of proof to the other party by acting as if the antagonist in expressing his doubt has acquired a burden of proof for the negation of the standpoint – or by acting as if the antagonist is in fact even the only one who has a burden of proof. Conversely, a party who acts as a would-be antagonist maneuvers fallaciously if he ignores a burden of proof for a contradictory standpoint that he has advanced (so that he has become the protagonist of that contradictory standpoint). He can do so by presenting a negative standpoint as merely an expression of doubt. He also acts fallaciously if he exaggerates the scope of the protagonist's standpoint, thus attributing a stronger burden of proof to the protagonist than is justified ("straw man"). A protagonist gets an easy opportunity to act fallaciously as a would-be antagonist when in a mixed difference of opinion it is not clear

---

32. In this connection it is noteworthy that in law "inadmissible evidence" does not automatically mean that a certain "fact" is not correct but rather that the consequences that follow from this fact for the case at hand may not be drawn. Cf. Rescher (1977).

what precisely the criteria are for applying such principles as the principle of presumption (i.e. what is the prevailing *status quo*?) or the principle of fairness. Then he can act as if it is only the other party who has a burden of proof by changing the problem of order of defenses into a problem of choice of defendants, thus messing about with the burden of proof and the pragmatic *status quo*.

In the argumentation stage, the dialectical objective is to advance arguments in defense of the standpoints that have been made an issue in the confrontation stage and to test the tenability of these standpoints starting from the point of departure established in the opening stage.[33] Viewed from a rhetorical perspective, the parties aim to make the strongest case and to launch the most effective attack. This means that the strategic maneuvering of the protagonist in regard of discharging the burden of proof will consist in bringing forward the argumentation that resolves the difference of opinion as quickly and thoroughly as possible. One way of doing this constructively is by construing an argumentation that reacts to or anticipates optimally the antagonist's opposition, responding first to those real or anticipated objections against his standpoint or against the arguments advanced in its defense that Govier (1998) calls "the most telling" objections and that Krabbe (2001) specifies as those serious objections that would utterly refute the protagonist's position.[34] In practice, the protagonist can also maneuver constructively by acknowledging objections (other than he himself deems unanswerable) and advance multiple argumentation to accommodate these objections by separate lines of arguments, making the abundance of his defense manifest in his presentation.[35] Conversely, by advancing multiple argumentation he can also make clear that, even if a certain argument he himself finds convincing is not accepted as convincing, there are still other sufficient reasons to accept the standpoint. The constructive maneuvering of the antagonist can amount to creating kinds of opposition, including those that the protagonist is likely to find hardest to deal with. When the difference of opinion is non-mixed, this can be done by asking all critical questions that are pertinent; when the difference of opinion is mixed, by doing the same as well as persistently advancing refuting objections and by arguing for the opposite point of view. In the first case, the antagonist can critically question either both the reasons that are advanced and the argument scheme that connects these reasons to the standpoint at issue, or he may concentrate on the aspect of the argument he expects the protagonist will find hardest to support, again taking advantage of the protagonist's obligation

---

33. The decision about the tenability of the standpoints that have shaped the difference of opinion in the confrontation stage is taken in the concluding stage.

34. See the notion of "dialectical power" introduced in Chapter 10.5.

35. This is Whately's observation: "It may often be expedient to bring forward more proofs than can be fairly *demanded* of you. It is always desirable, when this is the case, that it should be *known*, and that the strength of the cause should be estimated accordingly" (1846/1963, III, 2, part I, p. 112).

to produce such support and exploiting the protagonist's risk that providing inconclusive support will count against him.³⁶

The protagonist may maneuver fallaciously in various ways. He can, for instance, anticipate irrelevant doubts or objections that are only of his own invention, address relevant objections only partly, put forward irrelevant argumentation (*ignoratio elenchi*), and appeal to sources that are only seemingly authoritative (*argumentum ad verecundiam*). The antagonist, on his part, maneuvers fallaciously when, pretending to be a radical critic, he keeps repeating critical questions that have been answered already and for which the burden of proof has already been discharged (see van Eemeren & Grootendorst, 2004, p. 154, Rule 13a).

In the concluding stage, the dialectical objective of the parties is to establish the result of the critical testing procedure and to decide jointly to what extent the burden of proof has been met. Can the protagonist maintain his standpoint in the light of the criticisms advanced by the antagonist? Or can the antagonist maintain his position of doubt even considering the arguments advanced by the protagonist? Viewed rhetorically, each party will attempt to claim victory and their strategic maneuvering will be designed accordingly. Constructive maneuvering by the protagonist may at this stage consist of emphasizing the elements that are part of the burden of proof that have been satisfactorily dealt with. The antagonist may maneuver constructively by emphasizing the points where some doubt can be maintained. A fallacious move by the protagonist would, for example, be to act as if his standpoint had been adequately defended while ignoring certain obvious shortcomings in his defense. He can also hyperbolize the success of his defense by claiming that his standpoint is true instead of only proven tenable in the light of the antagonist's concessions and criticisms. The antagonist, for his part, would make a fallacious move if he acted as if the standpoint of the protagonist had been refuted while ignoring the protagonist's adequate responses. He would also maneuver fallaciously if he claimed that the protagonist's failure to defend his standpoint conclusively automatically proves the opposite standpoint to be correct (*argumentum ad ignorantiam*). Although concluding from a failed defense that the opposite standpoint is true is not a reasonable move in a critical discussion, in some communicative activity types belonging to institutional contexts where a final decision or immediate action is required, due to the institutional circumstances, it can be the only morally, practically, or otherwise justified way to proceed.³⁷ It could be the case that the *ad ignorantiam* move derives its rhetorical force from its use in these specific macro-contexts.

---

36. In elaborating this analysis the notion of "dialectical power," introduced in Chapter 10.5, and the analogous notion of "rhetorical power," may play a role.

37. An example of an institutional context where such a final decision is required is a legal case, in which one of the parties must be proven right and the other must be proven wrong. Concluding from a failed defense of a standpoint that the opposite standpoint is to be accepted is only justified if the parties have agreed, or the institutional point of departure binds them to agree, as in the juridical context, that exactly one of two alternatives is to be

举证责任策略操控的广告案例
8.7 A case of managing the burden of proof in advertisements

For some months in the 1990s the following advertisement was published in American and British magazines:[38] "Carlsberg, probably the best beer in the world." In the same period, the advertisers of the Dutch morning paper *Trouw* [Loyalty][39] treated Dutch radio listeners to the following announcement, which has been repeated *ad nauseam* ever since: "*Trouw*, perhaps the best newspaper in the Netherlands."[40] It is not difficult to notice that there is something awkward about these two slogans. But what is it? Is it the firm and at the same time surprisingly cautious wording that makes one wonder whether Carlsberg is indeed the best beer in the world and *Trouw* indeed the best newspaper of the Netherlands? Or is it the fact that a qualifier has been added to the appraisal that is wholly out of tune with the convention of advertising that products are recommended only in the boldest terms ("*Durex*, the best there is")? Or is it yet something else?

In a pragma-dialectical analysis advertisements are, just like other specimens of argumentative discourse, viewed as contributions to a critical discussion.[41] In an advertisement, the difference of opinion that is to be resolved is whether or not the appraised product should be purchased. The advertiser is the protagonist who makes an attempt to convince the antagonist – the reader or listener – of the acceptability of the standpoint that the product should be purchased. In the advertiser's message, however, this *inciting* (prescriptive) standpoint usually remains implicit. As a rule, advertisers restrict themselves to advancing – and justifying – an *evaluative* standpoint in which the product they want to sell is positively assessed. It is merely implied that this positive assessment provides at the same time the justification for the implicit *prescriptive* standpoint that this product should be purchased.

---

accepted: (p1 V p2) & ~(p1 & p2). By the way, presumption plays a role here too: institutional presumption should be such that standpoint A must be defended (~A has presumption).

38. This section is based on van Eemeren and Houtlosser (2006).

39. *Trouw* was established as an illegal, underground Dutch newspaper during the Second World War on 30 January 1943. Its founders were four members of the resistance movement, some of whom had worked for the illegal underground resistance paper *Vrij Nederland* (literally "Liberated Netherlands"). The Dutch word "trouw" denotes "loyalty" or "allegiance," but also "dedication."

40. The Dutch version is: "*Trouw*, misschien wel de beste krant van Nederland." The addition of the word "wel" (which does not translate well) makes it sound colloquial but suggests at the same time a refutation of contrary expectations. Because this element does not affect the point of my analysis, I have left it out of consideration.

41. A dialectical analysis of the advertisement is certainly relevant because listeners and readers will demand faithful information and good reasons for buying the advertised product, even if the advertisers cannot be expected to make an attempt at critical dispute resolution.

In the Carlsberg and *Trouw* slogans, evaluative standpoints are expressed.[42] In a pragma-dialectical analysis these standpoints must be situated in the confrontation stage of a critical discussion in which, ideally, the standpoint is presented that is at issue in the discussion. At the same time, the nature and the force of the standpoint are specified. Is the standpoint descriptive, evaluative, or prescriptive? Is it upheld firmly or cautiously? In the confrontation stage, the presented standpoint meets with doubt on the part of the presenter's interlocutor, so that a difference of opinion develops. In the cases of Carlsberg and *Trouw*, there is, of course, no question of an explicit expression of doubt. There is no antagonist who responds and the discussion remains implicit; the standpoint is presented and that is all. The way in which Carlsberg's and *Trouw's* standpoints are phrased, however, causes the problem we are dealing with here. For one thing, it is not exactly clear what dialectical positions Carlsberg and *Trouw* have assumed. On the one hand, the force of their standpoints is rather weak ("probably," "perhaps"); on the other hand, the evaluation expressed in these standpoints is quite strong ("the *best* beer," "the *best* newspaper"). This makes it hard to determine what the burden of proof is that Carlsberg and *Trouw* would have to discharge in order to justify their standpoints in the argumentation stage of the discussion. The question, however, is whether it is really the combination of a weak force and a strong evaluation in one and the same standpoint that leads to these problems of interpretation.

My analysis of the Carlsberg and *Trouw* standpoints (based on van Eemeren and Houtlosser, 2006) starts from the assumption that a standpoint is to be viewed as resulting from the performance of the speech act of advancing a standpoint. Like any other speech act, this speech act has certain felicity conditions: identity conditions and correctness conditions (van Eemeren & Grootendorst, 1984, 1992a). The most significant of the correctness conditions of the speech act of advancing a standpoint is the preparatory condition that a speaker or writer who advances a standpoint must assume that the listener or reader does not already accept the proposition expressed in the standpoint at face value (Houtlosser, 1995, 2002). This condition provides a useful clue for a more precise analysis of the standpoints advanced by Carlsberg and *Trouw*: it leads straight to the question why the speaker or writer expects the listener or reader not to accept the proposition expressed in the standpoint at face value.

What kind of answer can be given to this question generally depends on the nature of the standpoint at issue. If this standpoint is descriptive, the speaker or writer will expect the listener or reader not to consider the state of affairs represented in the proposition to be the case at face value. If the standpoint is evaluative, it will be assumed that the listener or reader will not regard the value judgment represented in the standpoint as necessarily shared by both parties. If the standpoint is inciting, the speaker or

---

42. The standpoints are, of course, elliptically phrased. In full they would read: "Carlsberg is probably the best beer in the world" and "*Trouw* is perhaps the best newspaper in the Netherlands," or even "You should buy Carlsberg beer" and "You should buy *Trouw*." In the last reconstructions the inciting standpoints have been made explicit.

writer will expect the listener or reader not to be immediately prepared to perform the action represented in the standpoint. Therefore, the nature of the standpoint has consequences for the type of justification that is to be given in defense of that standpoint. In the case of a descriptive standpoint, argumentation is called for that makes it credible (to the extent claimed in the standpoint) that the state of affairs represented in the standpoint does indeed pertain. In the case of an evaluative standpoint, argumentation is required that shows that the value judgment expressed in the standpoint is rooted in some normative common ground. In the case of an inciting standpoint, argumentation should be advanced that underlines the urgency for the listener or reader to perform the action represented in the standpoint.

The standpoints expressed in Carlsberg's and *Trouw*'s slogans are both evaluative. More precisely, in each standpoint a proposition is expressed that represents a subjective value judgment that must be assessed with the help of commonly shared assessment criteria and on the basis of some normative common ground for its intersubjective validity, not for its truth. Going by the nature of the propositions expressed in their standpoints, Carlsberg and *Trouw* have taken on, as it were, the obligation to show, with the help of a set of intersubjectively shared assessment criteria and on the basis of a normative common ground, that their value judgments on the beer and the newspaper can claim intersubjective validity – in other words, that these judgments can – and should – be shared by their listeners and readers.

If a standpoint is advanced in its complete form, it expresses not just a proposition but also some specifications of the nature and the force of the speaker's or writer's commitment (van Eemeren & Grootendorst, 1984; Houtlosser, 1995; Snoeck Henkemans, 1997). Some of these specifications are not related to the nature of the standpoint. This applies for example to the specification of the speaker's or writer's commitment to the standpoint as being positive or negative: "It *is* imperative to buy new shoes first and then a new pair of trousers, instead of the other way around" and "It *is not* imperative to buy new shoes first and then a new pair of trousers, instead of the other way around." Other specifications, however, *are* closely related to the nature of the standpoint. Examples are the speaker's or writer's indication of his propositional attitude vis-à-vis the expressed proposition and the modal qualifications of his commitment to the standpoint. Both indications of propositional attitudes and modal qualifications of commitments have to be congruous with the nature of the standpoint. Some combinations are "allowed," other combinations are not. A descriptive standpoint, for example, may not be combined with an indication of an "evaluative" propositional attitude such as "in my view." For instance, normally the statement "In my view it is four o'clock" is unacceptable. This is so because by definition "in my view" introduces a personal opinion and "It is four o'clock" normally does not represent a personal opinion.[43]

---

43. One can, of course, claim that "In my view it is four o'clock" is an acceptable statement provided that it is meant to be, or interpreted as, an *interpretation* (in a discussion, for instance, on whether it is now four o'clock when the seconds hand nears the top of the clock but has not

Conversely, an evaluative standpoint expressing a value judgment may not be introduced by a descriptive modal qualification that specifies the extent to which the factualness of the state of affairs represented in the standpoint is conceivable, such as "it is possible that," or knowable, such as "it is certain that." Even if in colloquial speech such combinations of value judgments and descriptive modal qualifications may merely sound a little odd, they are conceptually quite absurd. Value judgments pertaining to taste and personal preferences *cannot* "be the case" or "not the case." Whether something is the case or not is in principle an objective issue that is determined by the extent to which it can (conceivably or according to our knowledge) be considered a fact. The value judgments we are dealing with here are merely "valid" or not, i.e. valid for a particular person or a particular group of persons. Whether such a value judgment is valid or not is not an objective but a subjective – or at most an inter-subjective – matter.

The Carlsberg and *Trouw* standpoints manifest precisely that combination which we have just diagnosed as conceptually absurd, an evaluative proposition along with a descriptive modal qualification. In Carlsberg's standpoint the evaluative proposition that Carlsberg is the best beer in the world is introduced by the modality "probably;" in *Trouw*'s standpoint the evaluative proposition that *Trouw* is the best newspaper in the Netherlands is preceded by the modality "maybe." Part of the answer to the question about what makes Carlsberg's and *Trouw*'s standpoints so awkward is therefore that these standpoints are at the same time evaluative and descriptive. They sound odd because they are absurd in this very sense.[44]

Should we now conclude that the advertisers of Carlsberg and *Trouw* are not in command of their own language? Or should we assume that they know very well what they are doing and that the reason why they are advancing an absurdity is that they try to gain a certain advantage that outweighs the "disadvantage" of advancing an absurdity? My analysis already indicates the direction in which this advantage could be sought. After all, just as expressing an "evaluative" propositional attitude such as "in my view" seems to turn a descriptive proposition into an evaluative proposition, expressing a descriptive modality such as "probably" or "perhaps" seems to make an evaluative proposition descriptive. It is quite plausible that this is the very reason why these modal words are added. At the same time, it is obvious that neither Carlsberg nor *Trouw* is interested in presenting a claim that is merely descriptive. They want the public to agree that this beer is the best beer and this newspaper the best newspaper – and that this consent will incite them to dash to the shop where these products are

---

reached it). Then, however, the expressed proposition would be no longer descriptive but rather (implicitly) evaluative (see Ducrot, Bourcier, & Bruxelles, 1980; Houtlosser, 1995; Labov & Fanshel, 1977).

44. All the same, the tension between being at the same time firm and cautious also plays a part. "Trouw, *certainly* the best paper in the Netherlands" is after all less awkward than the real slogan, and the same goes for "Carlsberg, *certainly* the best beer in the world."

for sale. I think that the reasons why the advertisers nevertheless use a descriptive modality can be explained if the analysis is situated in the framework of strategic maneuvering that combines the dialectical perspective of a critical discussion with a rhetorical perspective on the effects that are pursued in the presentation of a standpoint.

If we put our analysis of Carlsberg's and *Trouw*'s standpoints in the framework of extended pragma-dialectics, we can advance the hypothesis that the conceptual absurdities noted in these standpoints are the result of a deliberate attempt at strategic maneuvering, in this case a form of strategic maneuvering that utilizes a certain presentational device. The next question is precisely in what way the presentational device used in presenting these (sub)standpoints is a strategic device. A strategic presentation of a standpoint consists in phrasing the standpoint in such a way that it can be justified effectively by the protagonist. Obviously, it cannot be predicted what will be an effective justification in practice. In a concrete case, this ultimately depends on the concessions the other party is prepared to make in the opening stage of the discussion. The *nature* of the standpoint that is to be justified, however, plays an important role on a more abstract level. In the best case, standpoints of the descriptive type can be "proven" whereas evaluative and prescriptive standpoints cannot. In principle, it could after all be decided objectively whether or not something is the case, but it cannot be decided objectively in the same sense whether something should be valued in a particular way or whether a certain action should be performed.

If it is not clear beforehand which concessions the other party will make, the protagonist of a standpoint cannot know for certain whether he will be able to give an effective justification of it. In such cases it is difficult to create a solid point of departure for the discussion in the opening stage. One thing the protagonist can do is to try and attribute concessions to the antagonist that can be used effectively in the justification of the standpoint. Another possibility is to suggest that such concessions will be granted because the standpoint at issue can be justified on the basis of *factual* arguments, i.e. putting forward the standpoint as an objectively justifiable standpoint. The last strategic maneuver is precisely the strategic way of proceeding that Carlsberg and *Trouw* employ. By using the modalities "probably" and "maybe," they imply that their standpoints can be justified objectively. By using "probably," Carlsberg suggests that it can be determined objectively whether Carlsberg beer is the best beer in the world and that chances are high that this is the case. By using "perhaps," *Trouw* gives the impression that it could be an objective fact that *Trouw* is the best newspaper in the Netherlands and that it is not so silly to think that this may indeed be the case.

Instead of advancing one ambiguous statement, both Carlsberg and *Trouw* make in fact two strategically motivated discussion moves. The first move consists in advancing the evaluative standpoint that Carlsberg is the best beer in the world and *Trouw* the best newspaper of the Netherlands. The second move consists in suggesting by means of "probably" and "perhaps" that these standpoints can be objectively justified. While the first move is really confrontational, the second move belongs to the opening stage of the discussion. It serves to suggest that there is agreement about the burden of proof that has to be discharged for the standpoints at issue to be defended satisfactorily.[45]

It will be clear that this way of strategic maneuvering amounts to a manipulation of the burden of proof that is dialectically unacceptable. What would an objective justification of such an evaluative standpoint amount to? Carlsberg and *Trouw* give the impression that it will be sufficient to make an inventory of the entities that are to be compared in the domain concerned and the criteria that are to be applied in the evaluation. They act as if such an inventory automatically yields the result that they suggest: "We have not yet tested *all* the existing brands of beer, but as soon as that has been done Carlsberg will (probably) turn out to be the best beer in the world," and "We do not yet know *exactly* what makes a newspaper a good newspaper, but once we have found out it will appear that *Trouw* is (perhaps) the best." Yet, there is ample reason left for doubt. If it can indeed be established by means of a test that Carlsberg is the best beer in the world, why then has such a test not yet been run? And should we really assume that the editors of *Trouw* have not yet found out what a good newspaper is, but will do so soon?[46]

My analysis makes clear that in both advertisements a standpoint is presented that might seem ambivalent because it is upheld at the same time both firmly and cautiously, or even absurd because it is both evaluative and descriptive. In fact, it concerns in both cases a firmly upheld evaluative standpoint that is presented in a way that suggests that it can be objectively justified. When evaluated critically, this presentational way of strategic maneuvering involves a burden of proof manipulation because an objective justification of such evaluative standpoints cannot be given.[47] As I have shown, an integrated pragma-dialectical analysis is a sound basis for detecting such (amusing or not) derailments of strategic maneuvering when they occur.

---

45. Another rhetorical function of this phrasing could, of course, be raising Carlsberg's and *Trouw*'s ethos. The cautious descriptive formula conveys that the firms do not skate on thin ice and want their standpoints to be founded on facts.

46. It is implausible, though, that Carlsberg and *Trouw* intend to conduct this type of consumers' guide appraisal: "the best" would in such an interpretation mean no more than "the best in the test." This qualification would turn "the best" into a merely descriptive indication of the fulfillment of certain criteria (see Hare, 1952; Toulmin, 1958/2003; Mackie, 1977). An undesirable consequence of this interpretation is that it invites follow-ups such as "*Trouw* has emerged as the best from the test, but in the office we all prefer *de Volkskrant*" (the People's Paper, another Dutch newspaper).

47. Remarkably, both Trouw and Carlsberg undertake a heavy burden of proof (for a descriptive standpoint). The second part of their strategy is to suggest that this burden could be met rather than meeting it.

CHAPTER 9　第九章

回应"前后不一"或谬误指责中的策略操控
Strategic maneuvering in response to presumed inconsistency or fallaciousness

一方公开承诺中的逻辑与语用不一致
9.1 Logical and pragmatic inconsistencies in a party's avowed commitments

As another case of how argumentative conduct in strategic maneuvering is disciplined, I will discuss the demarcation between non-fallacious and fallacious maneuvering when one party attacks another party by accusing the other party of an inconsistency between something he says or does now and something he said or did earlier.[1] The inconsistency the other party is accused of may manifest itself at any moment in the discussion, but always relates to that party's standpoint or starting points. The inconsistency may be a purely logical inconsistency, i.e. a contradiction, or a pragmatic inconsistency involving an incompatibility (van Eemeren & Grootendorst, 1992a, p. 65). In the case of a logical contradiction between two starting points, the commitments undertaken by the party maintaining these starting points exclude each other on logical grounds. This happens when someone maintains that something is the case after having asserted earlier that it is not, so that both *p* and not-*p* are among his avowed commitments. In the case of a pragmatic inconsistency involving an incompatibility, the two starting points cannot both be accepted because one involves a commitment that cannot be combined with a commitment involved in the other. In such a case the party's avowed commitments cannot go together in practice, as when a party promises to do something but also says that he does not intend to do it or is incapable of doing it.[2] Pointing out an inconsistency can be a perfectly legitimate strategic maneuver;[3] this maneuver can even be very strong, but it can also derail and result in a fallacy.

When considering inconsistencies between starting points we must distinguish between two kinds of starting points: (explicit or implicit) *procedural* starting points, and (explicit or implicit) *material* starting points. Ideally, both kinds of starting points

---

1. This discussion of the strategic use of pointing to inconsistency is in the first place based on van Eemeren and Houtlosser (2005a).

2. In principle, pragmatic inconsistencies can always be brought back to logical inconsistencies, but they are not inherently contradictory and in order to reduce them to logical inconsistencies a complicated process of reduction may be required. Cf. Bonevac (2003, pp. 31–32), who considers not only a set of sentences that contains a logical contradiction inconsistent, but also a set of sentences that implies a contradiction.

3. Pointing out an inconsistency is here not looked upon and analyzed as a type of fallacy accusation, but as a mode of strategic maneuvering that can be sound or derail.

are fully clear, so that the parties involved in the discussion know how the discussion is going to be conducted and what propositions they can safely bring to bear. In order to conduct a proper critical discussion, the parties must agree in the opening stage about the division of the burden of proof, the discussion rules, and the propositions that may be used in the argumentation stage to defend and challenge the standpoints at issue. In argumentative practice, in some institutionally conventionalized macro-contexts agreement about certain procedural and material starting points is presupposed. This is true, for instance, for the procedural starting points in the communicative activity type of parliamentary debate. The admissions of the accused in a police interrogation preceding the actual trial are an example of recognized material starting points in a criminal trial. In both cases their status of a starting point is due to institutional conventions pertaining to the activity type concerned.

In informal argumentative activity types there are usually no explicitly established agreements as to the procedural or material starting points. There is no need for such a thing and it would be highly inefficient, if not superfluous, if all procedural agreements and all propositions the parties agree upon in this type of context had to be listed in advance. The need to avoid logical and pragmatic inconsistencies is for similar reasons taken for granted – both in formal and in informal argumentative activity types. In informal argumentative activity types the parties generally assume – rightly or wrongly – that certain procedural and material starting points are shared by the other party, without asking for the other party's consent. All the same, there are also a lot of cases in which it is explicitly discussed between the parties whether or not a particular proposition or way of proceeding may serve as a common starting point. When such deliberations take place during the discussion they can, in the case of material starting points, be viewed as *sub-discussions*, and in the case of procedural starting points, as *meta-discussions* that are to be situated in the opening stage of the main discussion. It is characteristic of such sub-discussions and meta-discussions that they result in a conclusion as to whether or not the proposition or the procedural proposal at issue may be used as a starting point.

In sub-discussions about material starting points the dialectical profile of the initial exchange of moves is as follows. The protagonist aiming at securing a basis for his defense initiates the sub-discussion by proposing to consider a specific proposition as a common starting point. He can, for instance, claim that the proposition concerned is a good point of departure for the discussion and invite the antagonist to accept it as a starting point: "Let's see if we cannot agree after all. Would you agree to the following points to start with?" Alternatively, the protagonist can boldly attribute the proposition to the antagonist, as in "You do think that we need to take certain measures now, don't you?" followed by "Well, why don't you just start considering them then?" In all such cases one tries to elicit a proposition as a concession from the antagonist. And in all these cases, it is up to the antagonist to react. The antagonist may accept the protagonist's proposal, so that the deliberation comes to an end, but he can also reject it. In the latter case, the antagonist may make either of two moves. He can deny the proposed proposition the status of a common starting point just like that: "I do not agree with that" or he can also give reasons why the proposition should not be treated as a common starting point: "You cannot just assume that. That's one of the things to be discussed."[4]

Viewed dialectically, the antagonist is under no obligation to provide a reason for not admitting a particular proposition as a starting point (see van Eemeren & Grootendorst, 2004, pp. 123–157). There is a dialectical obligation, however, to determine whether there is any common ground between the parties. Viewed rhetorically, it is most advantageous to the antagonist to admit as few propositions as possible. Explaining why a certain proposition is denied the status of a common starting point can thus be regarded as a germane form of antagonistic strategic maneuvering. This mode of maneuvering is aimed at reconciling the rhetorical aim of admitting only those starting points that are consonant with the antagonist's own position and the dialectical objective of achieving sufficient common ground for having a critical discussion. By refusing to accept a particular proposition as a starting point, the antagonist seems to go against this dialectical objective. He therefore has to show that his refusal is not gratuitous, so that it is at least clear that he has not violated the higher order condition (see Chapter 2.2) for conducting a critical discussion that the participants should be prepared to attempt to look for common ground.

Giving reasons for a refusal to admit a proposition as a starting point can be a perfectly sound way of strategic maneuvering, but it can also derail into fallaciousness. In one subtype of the *tu quoque* fallacy,[5] the reason-giving amounts to saying that the protagonist's proposal to treat a proposition as a starting point is not acceptable because the proposition is inconsistent with something the protagonist has said or done, or with something implied by what he said or did, *on another occasion*.[6] If, for example,

---

4. It may make a difference to deliberations about the starting points what type of difference of opinion initiated the main discussion. For instance, when two consecutive attempts are made to resolve two non-mixed discussions ensuing from a mixed difference of opinion, a particular proposition cannot be accepted as a common starting point in the first discussion and not accepted in the second discussion. In the case of a non-mixed discussion ensuing from a non-mixed difference of opinion, no such restrictions apply.

5. Van Laar (2008) discusses another subtype of the *tu quoque* fallacy that is a derailment of the kind of strategic maneuvering in which a critic shows that an arguer lacks credibility as a sincere and capable protagonist when appealing to the higher order conditions for critical discussion by pointing at a pragmatic inconsistency between the standpoint the arguer puts forward and his former behavior.

6. A rhetorical technique that comes close to this mode of strategic maneuvering is in classical rhetoric described as the adversarial technique of *anticategoria* ("counter charge," "accusing in turn," Latin: *accusatio adversa, translatio in adversarium, incidens quaestio*, meaning "a retort in which one turns the very accusation made by one's adversary back against him"). Lausberg (1973/1998, Section 197) describes the objective of *anticategoria* as compromising the prosecutor, in this way proving his lack of jurisdiction. *Anticategoria* is divided into two *genera*. In reply

a protagonist suggests starting the discussion from the assumption that all promises should be kept at all times, the antagonist may point out that the protagonist never keeps his promises or earlier on advocated a less strict moral view.[7] What are the soundness criteria that make it possible to decide whether or not an antagonist maneuvers in an admissible way when he refuses to admit a proposition as a starting point because of a proclaimed inconsistency between the proposed proposition and the protagonist's (verbal or non-verbal) behavior on a previous occasion? This will be discussed in the section that follows.

"你也一样"谬误：脱轨的"前后不一"指责
9.2 *Tu quoque* fallacies as derailments of pointing out inconsistencies

When discussing the soundness conditions for the mode of strategic maneuvering described at the end of the preceding section, it is important to note that they hinge on three points: (1) how inconsistency must be defined in order to make it possible to determine whether two propositions are logically or pragmatically inconsistent (a logico-pragmatic point of definition); (2) how an accusation by the antagonist can be brought to bear in considerations pertaining to an inconsistency between the proposition presently proposed as a starting point and something that was *done* earlier by the protagonist (a matter of scope); and (3) what, in practice, is to be understood by "on a different occasion" – a question that needs to be answered in order to be able to

---

to the prosecutor's accusation, the defendant charges the prosecutor with having committed (1) the same particular crime, or (2) another crime; the other crime is in different ways related to the crime of which the defendant is accused. In the second case, the relationship can be one of similarity [with any other crime], one of causality [*remotio*, as in "Befehl ist Befehl"] or one between the crime and the act of prosecution itself [as in a *dépit amoureux*]. In today's law courts, the admissibility of this type of technique is not undisputed. In its decision of February 3, 1999, the Trial Chamber of the International Criminal Tribunal for the former Yugoslavia, for instance, ruled that "the principle of *tu quoque* does not apply to international humanitarian law since that body of law creates obligations *erga omnes (contractantes)* and not obligations based on reciprocity." The Chamber found, however, that "evidence of events beyond the main geographical focus of the indictment may be admissible insofar as it is not repetitious and is duly circumscribed and intended to rebut the allegations, explain the behavior of the accused or provide information concerning the organization and activities of the armies involved." The Chamber added that "before adducing such evidence, the defense should state its purpose" (http://www.un.org/icty/rappannu-e/1999/index.htm).

7. In pragma-dialectics, *tu quoque* is primarily discussed as a violation of the Freedom Rule for the confrontation stage, but this fallacy can, unlike the other variants of the *argumentum ad hominem*, also be committed in a later stage of the discussion (van Eemeren & Grootendorst, 2004, pp. 123–157). Then, the *tu quoque* is not aimed at preventing the other party from maintaining a certain standpoint, but from founding the case for a certain standpoint on a particular starting point.

determine in a specific case whether from a dialectical perspective it makes sense to point at an inconsistency (a quasi-empirical issue). I shall address all three issues.

First, an adequate argumentation theory should make clear how the parties engaged in an argumentative exchange, or an analyst dealing with the discourse, can make use of logical and pragmatic insights to arrive at a proper understanding of (undesired) inconsistency. Because logical as well as pragmatic insights may be derived from a variety of logical systems and theories of language use, it would be helpful if a coherent choice could be made from these theoretical instruments that is based on a well-considered and mutually agreed upon philosophy of reasonableness and rationality. The pragma-dialectical theory of argumentation as it is externalized in the model for conducting a critical discussion offers an opportunity to do so. If the parties engaged in a critical discussion have come to an agreement about which logical and pragmatic views of inconsistency they will rely on, a decision about whether or not two propositions are actually logically or pragmatically inconsistent eventually depends on the result of the relevant "intersubjective inference procedure" they need to go through (van Eemeren & Grootendorst, 2004, p. 148).

Second, the question of how a person who has performed a certain (non-linguistic) action can be held committed to a certain proposition falls, strictly speaking, within the domain of action theory. However, the current state of affairs in action theory is such that no decisive criteria are available for determining univocally in all cases whether or not a certain action implies a commitment to a particular proposition (see, among others, Walton, 1998b, p. 31). By making a distinction between *avowed* commitments and *contextual* commitments, Houtlosser and I have made a contribution to solving this problem (van Eemeren & Houtlosser, 2002b, p.20). "Avowed" commitments are propositional commitments explicitly assumed by a speaker or writer through the performance of speech acts of the assertive type; they resemble the commitments that Walton and Krabbe (1995) call "concessions." In our conception, "contextual" commitments are commitments that may be assumed to be inherent in the actual context of the exchange.[8] Obviously, the propositional commitments that might be implied by the protagonist's actions belong to the latter category. Because contextual commitments are open to rejection and can eventually only be of real consequence for the discussion if they stand up to an appropriate intersubjective identification procedure, having performed a certain action can commit a party to a certain proposition only if the parties engaged in the dialogue agree that the action implies, or can be "translated into," the proposition concerned.[9] This may not seem very helpful, but it must be borne in mind that in argumentative practice all kinds of agreements are presupposed as a result of actions that give rise to propositional commitments, so that the basic idea is familiar. Some of these agreements apply to the institutional or

---

8. See Chapter 1.5.
9. Cf. van Laar (2008).

semi-institutional practices conducted in a particular communicative activity type; others apply perhaps to all communicative activity types (cf. Walton, 1998a, p. 285).[10]

The last issue to address is about what is to be understood by "on a previous occasion." This seems a purely empirical issue, but from a pragma-dialectical point of view it is not entirely so. In pragma-dialectics, "on a previous occasion" is defined as meaning "in an argumentative discussion that is to be reconstructed as a different critical discussion than the present one." From a pragma-dialectical point of view, an inconsistency between something that is presently said or done and something that was said or done on a previous occasion matters only if it involves an inconsistency in *one and the same critical discussion*. When dealing with a proclaimed inconsistency between a party's starting points this proviso is particularly important. The starting points assumed in a critical discussion are always assumed *for the sake of having a constructive critical discussion in a specific argumentative context*. This implies that the participants in such a discussion cannot automatically be held committed to having accepted these starting points, as it were forever, *in their own right and for their own sake*. In a different critical discussion the same persons are fully entitled to assume other starting points – or even starting points that are precisely opposed. The only thing they are not allowed to do is to accept *and* deny a starting point in one and the same critical discussion.

The-one-and-the-same-critical-discussion criterion may seem hard to apply to argumentative discourse as it is conducted in practice. A critical discussion in the pragma-dialectical sense is after all an idealization of a resolution-oriented argumentative exchange and not a real-life discussion. However, it is precisely this discrepancy that makes it possible to solve the problem of what is to be understood by "on a previous occasion:" by approaching the problem first in a theoretical way, instead of in a purely empirical way. Because real-life discussions never fully coincide with a critical discussion, an evaluation of a piece of actual argumentative discourse by means of the model of critical discussion always requires a certain amount of methodical reconstruction taking account of those and only those (explicit and implicit) elements of the (piece of) discourse concerned that can have a constructive function in the process of resolving a difference of opinion on the merits. In such a reconstruction, contributions to the resolution process that are in practice distributed over time or different texts may be assigned to one and the same critical discussion. A letter to the editor, for instance, which reacts to a newspaper article published a week earlier and the article itself will then be reconstructed as two contributions to the same critical discussion. In some cases, pieces of argumentative discourse can only be properly understood if they are first reconstructed as belonging to one and the same critical discussion. This implies that the answer to the question of what should count as "one and the same critical

---

10. When turned around to mean that one should not say things that are at odds with what one practices, maxims such as "Practice what you preach" might even be taken to point to the existence of a general agreement that carrying out certain actions precludes undertaking commitments that are inconsistent with these actions.

discussion" ultimately depends on whether it is theoretically as well as empirically justified to reconstruct different pieces of argumentative discourse as being part of one and the same critical discussion.

How can a reconstruction of two or more pieces of argumentative discourse in which material starting points are proposed or established as belonging to the same critical discussion be justified? I think that in case of an accusation of inconsistency between starting points such a reconstruction is justified if the following four conditions are fulfilled:

1. All the pieces of argumentative discourse concerned are aimed at resolving the same difference of opinion;
2. All the pieces of argumentative discourse concerned have the same procedural starting points;
3. All the pieces of argumentative discourse concerned can be placed in an order so that they build up the same material starting points;
4. The party whose proposal to use a certain proposition as a starting point was rejected assumed the same dialectical position and the same discussion role in the preceding pieces of discourse under consideration.

The first condition excludes cases from being considered as one and the same critical discussion in which the *issues* that are discussed in the various pieces of argumentative discourse are not identical. The second condition excludes cases in which different *procedural starting points*, i.e. discussion rules, are followed. The third condition excludes cases in which the *material starting points* do not contribute to one and the same collection of such starting points. The fourth condition excludes cases in which the protagonist who proposed the starting point at issue made this proposal while being in a different *dialectical position* (e.g. acting in a dialectical situation characterized by a crucially different division of commitments) or while having a different *discussion role* (e.g. as protagonist and defender of the opposite standpoint) than before.[11] When they are taken together, the fulfillment of these conditions guarantees that the proclaimed inconsistency between a starting point that a protagonist presently proposes and a starting point he proposed on a previous occasion is an inconsistency in the opening stage of one and the same critical discussion. These four conditions constitute general criteria for judging strategic maneuvering by pointing out an inconsistency in the other party's starting points. If one or more of these conditions have not been fulfilled, the

---

11. In the classification of types of outcome of an argumentative dialogue proposed by Barth and Martens (1977), our conditions apply to the case of a thesis T claimed to be *tenable ex concessis against opponent O* because it can be successfully defended against this opponent on the basis of a set of concessions C. Barth and Martens also distinguish outcomes less dependent on the opponent and his concessions: (1) a thesis *tenable ex concessis* ("follows logically from a set of concessions C") because it can be successfully defended against any opponent O on the basis of a set of concessions C, and (2) a thesis is *tenable* ("logically true") because it can be successfully defended against any opponent O on the basis of any set of concessions.

strategic maneuvering has derailed and the person making the accusation of inconsistency is guilty of committing the *ad hominem* fallacy known as *tu quoque*.[12]

In argumentative practice there may be more specific criteria for determining whether or not an argumentative move made by the other party has derailed that are to some extent dependent on the communicative domain and the macro-context of the communicative activity type in which the discourse takes place. This applies in particular to accusations of pragmatic inconsistency where the macro-context of the communicative activity type in which the argumentative discourse takes place plays a decisive role in defining what is meant by pragmatically consistent and inconsistent. Whether certain pieces of argumentative discourse are regarded as aimed at resolving the same difference of opinion (criterion 1), may be judged differently, for instance, in the context of a personal chat than in the context of a court case or an ongoing political debate, so that more specific criteria must be applied in each of these contexts. Our judgments regarding such diverging communicative activity types may, moreover, differ with respect to the following points: whether all pieces of argumentative discourse are to be regarded as having the same procedural starting points (criterion 2); whether all pieces of argumentative discourse are regarded as building up the same set of material starting points (criterion 3); whether the party that is criticized is considered to have assumed the same dialectical position and the same discussion role on the occasions that are being compared (criterion 4). For such diverging activity types we need specific assessment criteria.

In addition to the context-dependency just mentioned, whether different persons may be regarded as representing the same party on previous occasions (and even on physically the same occasion) will be judged differently, for instance, in the context of the communicative activity type of a plenary parliamentary debate (where the answer will in principle be "Yes" if these persons are representing the same political party when inconsistencies between them are disapproved of) than in the context of a legal case (where each person's individual integrity will be protected so that the answer will in principle be "No"). Another factor that can make a difference to the assessment of accusations of inconsistency is whether or not the inconsistency occurs in a communicative activity type that involves an audience consisting of a third party that is in fact the primary addressee, as is the case in a public political debate. As I shall explain later on in this chapter, the communicative activity type in which an accusation of inconsistency occurs may even affect the impact the commitment of a *tu quoque* fallacy will have on the argumentative exchange as regards the continuation of the discourse and, as a consequence, as regards the way it might be responded to.

---

12. For experimental research concerning the judgments of ordinary arguers with regard to the (un)reasonableness of the use of the *tu quoque* fallacy, see van Eemeren, Garssen and Meuffels (2009, pp. 51–82).

Chapter 9. Strategic maneuvering in response to presumed inconsistency or fallaciousness 249

荷兰政坛"前后不一"指责的个案分析
9.3 An accusation of inconsistency case from Dutch politics

How does the approach I have just proposed work in practice? How can the soundness conditions for strategic maneuvering be applied in cases where an inconsistency is pointed out between a starting point a party proposes for the present discourse and some other assumed commitment of this party? As an illustration, I shall give an analysis of a case of an accusation of inconsistency that played an important role in Dutch politics at the beginning of the 21st century.[13] A brief introduction to the context of this accusation is needed. By the end of 2001, the "purple" coalition between the Social Democrats (PvdA), the Conservative Liberal Democrats (VVD) and the Progressive Liberal Democrats (D'66), which had ruled the Netherlands for eight years, resigned.[14] In the election campaign that followed, the country witnessed the spectacular rise of the populist politician Pim Fortuyn, followed by a sudden hardening of the political climate which culminated, most tragically, in the assassination of Fortuyn in 2002. Despite Fortuyn's death – or perhaps because of it – his party, the so-called "List Pim Fortuyn" (LPF), achieved an enormous electoral success, and became the second largest party in Parliament after the Christian Democrats (CDA), the champions of "Norms and Values." The results of the elections led to the formation of a new coalition government between the Christian Democrats, the Fortuynists, and the Conservative Liberal Democrats (VVD), which the Fortuynists managed to blow up through internal struggles in less than half a year.

After the new elections following the resignation of the government the Social Democrats returned unexpectedly to center stage because they had become the second biggest political party after the Christian Democrats, who had managed to keep their newly-acquired electorate and were once more in the leading position in the new coalition negotiations. Although they would have liked to, in these negotiations the Christian Democrats could not ignore the Social Democrats. In the final stage of the negotiations, however, they succeeded in getting rid of them, so that they were free again to select new negotiation partners. They then invited the Conservative Liberals and the Progressive Liberals to join in. On the eve of the elections, however, the leader of the Progressive Liberals had explicitly and definitively precluded his party, in case it were to suffer a severe loss of votes, from taking part in any coalition government. In fact, the loss of the Progressive Liberals had been so dramatic that its leader resigned on the spot, but his "no participation" stance was the next day reconfirmed by his successor. When three months later this new leader was invited to enter the second round of coalition talks, he was therefore expected to reject the invitation out of hand. This, however, is not what happened. Arguing that the situation had changed in the meantime, and that at least part of the "purple heritage" could be saved by taking part

---

13. This section is based on van Eemeren and Houtlosser (2005a).

14. The coalition is called *purple* because it involves a coalition of "red" (social democrats) and "blue" (conservative liberals and progressive liberals) parties, PvdA, VVD and D'66 respectively.

in the new government, the Progressive Liberals accepted the invitation to join the coalition negotiations and, as a result, ended up in the awkward, and in the eyes of many dubious, position of being in government together with the right wing Conservative Liberals and the Christian Democrats, despite the election promises they had made earlier. The question now is whether the Progressive Liberals were acting in a dialectically inconsistent way by first precluding *any* participation in any coalition government and subsequently accepting the invitation to become the third party to participate in the new Dutch government beside the Christian Democrats and the Conservative Liberals. Or can the accusation that they were inconsistent be dismissed as a *tu quoque* fallacy?

Against the background I have just outlined, three observations seem relevant to judging an accusation of inconsistency against the Progressive Liberals. First, although the new leader maintained that in no case the Progressive Liberals would take part in any coalition, more than two months had passed between this decision and the moment at which he agreed to take part in the coalition negotiations. Second, the Progressive Liberals confirmed their decision that they would in no case take part in any coalition when they still expected the Christian Democrats to form a government together with the Social Democrats. Third, although there had been a silent agreement between all other parties that this time the Fortuynists would be left out of the coalition talks, all of a sudden the Christian Democrats and the Conservative Liberals had started portraying them as a viable third party. To check whether these observations are indeed relevant to the accusation of inconsistency, one has to examine whether they relate, and if so in what way, to the dialectical conditions for a sound accusation that there is an inconsistency between the party's starting points.

The observation that there was a time span of more than two months between when, right after the elections, the decision not to participate was confirmed and the moment that the progressive liberals joined the negotiation talks may be considered relevant to determining whether or not the Progressive Liberals may indeed be assumed to have the same dialectical position in the first and the second discussion. The position of (conditionally) not being prepared to take part in any coalition that the Progressive Liberals assumed before and confirmed (unconditionally) right after the elections could be justifiably reconstructed as a statement to their voters and to the general public that they were taking the outcome of the elections really seriously, which was a big issue in the discussion taking place at the time about the reliability of politicians. Several months later, however, their priority was no longer to show that they took the outcome of the elections seriously but to convince their voters that they were out to save whatever could be saved of the purple heritage. This means that in the time that had passed the issue – and hence their position and even the difference of opinion that they aimed to resolve – had changed. Originally, the issue was whether not taking part in the coalition negotiations would show sufficiently clearly that the Progressive Liberals took their voters seriously. In the later discussion, the projected difference with the electorate was whether entering the coalition talks would ensure that the

Chapter 9. Strategic maneuvering in response to presumed inconsistency or fallaciousness

Progressive Liberals could save crucial parts of the purple heritage. If both the party's position and the difference they aimed to resolve have indeed changed in this way, according to the condition that was set in my approach, the accusation of inconsistency would not be justified. On second inspection, however, these changes of positions and difference of opinion appear to be changes that merely take place on the surface, as a result of a (voluntary and deliberate) change of perspective. In fact, the Progressive Liberals had *not explicitly given up* their standpoint that they were serious about the outcome of the elections. Therefore, their later standpoint that they should save crucial parts of the purple inheritance can certainly not be regarded as a replacement or nullification of their original standpoint. At best, it could be viewed as an *additional* standpoint in an *additional* difference of opinion, which would make the difference of opinion multiple. Then this additional standpoint should have been (although it was not) shown to be consistent with the initial (unretracted) standpoint at the center of the still unresolved difference of opinion about taking the voters seriously.

The observation that the Progressive Liberals initially expected the Christian Democrats to form a government with the Social Democrats, and the observation that in the second round of negations the Fortuynist party was unexpectedly viewed as a viable third party alternative, relate both to the condition I earlier formulated that, apart from the starting point at issue, the first and the second discussion should build up the same set of commitments to material starting points. It turns out that in this case this condition is in fact *not* fulfilled. After all, considerations such as the prospect of a joint government of Christian Democrats and Social Democrats (so that a third coalition partner was not needed) and the *a priori* exclusion of the Fortuynists were precisely the conditions that earlier gave the Progressive Liberals the confidence to take their firm stance and provided them with an easy chance to show the public that they took the outcome of the elections seriously. However, as soon as the prospect of a government consisting of the Christian Democrats ruling together with the Conservative Liberals *and* the Fortuynists became a realistic prospect, this confidence was lost. Viewed dialectically, their original starting point ceased to be a viable starting point for the Progressive Liberals. This shows that, while the Progressive Liberal position that the electorate should be taken seriously had still to be maintained, the starting points of the critical discussion to resolve the difference really did change – and this change caused a new critical discussion to be started. As a consequence, the condition required for an accusation of inconsistency to be a sound strategic maneuver – that the first and second critical discussion build up the same set of material starting points – is not fulfilled. It is by referring to the non-fulfillment of this soundness condition that the accusation that the Progressive Liberals are guilty of inconsistency can be disputed. In providing this analysis I have shown how the conditions formulated in Section 9.2 provide criteria that can help to identify a potential occurrence of the fallacy of *tu quoque* and decide whether the accusation that a fallacy of inconsistency has been committed is correct.

谬误出现的现实影响
9.4 The practical impact of the occurrence of fallacies

It is inevitable that in argumentative discourse, just like in other forms of communication, now and then something goes wrong. Even the occurrence of fallacies such as shifting or evading the burden of proof or wrongly accusing the other party of an inconsistency is an unavoidable fact of life. In practice, the occurrence of a fallacy need not always have a disastrous impact on the proceeding of the discourse. Fallacies may go unnoticed, so that they have their undesired consequences without the "offended" party being aware of it, but they can also be deliberately ignored, without having had any practical negative impact on the process of resolving the difference of opinion on the merits. For instance, it may be the case that the listener or reader realizes that the fallaciousness of an argumentative move is of no real importance to a serious evaluation because it was made unknowingly without the speaker or writer really endorsing it – as in the case of a mere slip of the tongue or the mind, which can be corrected right away if required. And if it is clear that the would-be fallacious move is only made as a joke, the commitment of a fallacy may not be of any real importance to an undisturbed progress of the discourse either (and should perhaps not be called a *fallacy*). The latter can be the case when the speaker or writer makes fun of someone's position by blowing it up in a way that is hilariously out of all proportion and plainly so to all concerned. In such a case – and there are a great many similar cases – the matter can usually be put right without any negative consequences for the resolution process (although there may be rhetorical effects that harm the resolution process indirectly).

At times, fallacies can even be so witty that we all like them. All the same, our sense of humor should not keep us from remaining critical, because basically fallacies prevent or hinder the resolution of a difference of opinion on the merits. Since in practice more often than not they really do so, we cannot afford to take a lenient attitude toward fallacies. A nice example, taken from an exchange that took place forty years ago in the Canadian House of Commons between Prime Minister Trudeau and George Hees, an opposition Member of Parliament who had been Minister of Transport and Minister of Trade and Commerce in an earlier government, is provided by Walton (1985). In 1970, Mr. Trudeau responded negatively to a request to consider using a Jet-star government plane to send an information-gathering team to Biafra in Africa by saying:

> It would have to refuel in the middle of the Atlantic Ocean . . .

Whereupon Mr. Hees (who was well known for liking his drink), responded by raising a point of order:

> On a point of order, Mr. Speaker, I bought the plane for the government and I know it can make the flight with the proper stops on the way . . .

Mr. Trudeau then finished off the exchange by remarking:

> I do not think it would have to stop if the hon. Member went along and breathed into the [fuel] tank.

By insinuating that Mr. Hees was habitually drunk, Mr. Trudeau gave a textbook example of the fallacious personal attack known as the *argumentum ad hominem*, here appearing in its *abusive* variant. The ad hominem attack was in this case lethal, because Mr. Hees kept silent after the rebuke. This example nicely illustrates how humor can be brought to bear not only to enliven the discussion and make it more relaxed, but also to get away with fallacies.

It is obvious that Mr. Trudeau did not allude to Mr. Hees' drinking habits in order to show that the conclusion of the MP's argument does not follow from its premises. The Prime Minister had expressed a standpoint, and his diversionary allusion to his challenger's drinking habits enabled him to evade defending that standpoint. Mr. Trudeau's allusion is a strategic maneuver that violates the pragma-dialectical Freedom Rule (rule 1) by putting Mr. Hees in a position that makes it practically impossible for him to maintain his opposition. "If Trudeau had not ridiculed his challenger," observed Hitchcock later, "he would have had to admit that his challenger was correct and that Trudeau was wrong" (2006, p. 114).

Basically, fallacies are always distortions of the progress of an argumentative exchange because, even if they do not obstruct the resolution process completely, they at least distract from a sound resolution process. In order for us to protect the maintenance of reasonableness, they therefore deserve our undivided attention. The crucial question to be answered here is what needs to be done when a fallacy has been committed in the discourse and the fallacious move is to be taken seriously in the sense that it is not just a joke or an inconsequential mistake. Does the commission of such a fallacious move automatically mean that the reasonable exchange is over and that the discussion is brought to an untimely end? Or do the participants in the discussion still have a duty, or perhaps even a dialectical obligation, to look for ways to continue the discussion? I think that the answer to these questions depends on the practical *impact* the fallacy concerned has, in the argumentative circumstances the parties are in, on the possibilities for having a reasonable discussion. Is the occurrence of the fallacious move just an isolated case of unreasonable strategic maneuvering that does not really disrupt the discussion or does it imply that in the current discussion the idea of reasonableness has gone by the board? In my view, only if the commitment of a fallacy signals a fundamental rejection of the very Principle of Reasonableness does it not make sense to continue the discussion.

尚存合理性的脱轨论辩修复
9.5 Repairing derailments that do not cancel reasonableness

In argumentative discourse fallacious strategic maneuvers occur that hinder the process of resolving a difference of opinion on the merits but even so do not block the discussion completely by abandoning the Principle of Reasonableness. Concentrating on such fallacious moves, which could be *tu quoque* fallacies, specimens of shifting the burden of proof, or any other kind of derailment of strategic maneuvering, it must now be examined how they are to be dealt with. My point of departure is that it remains worthwhile to make an effort to maintain dialectical reasonableness as long as this seems feasible in practice. That effort, however, must not lead to a vindication of a disturbance of the resolution process that would transform a willingness to overlook some local disturbance into a permanent indulgence. Starting in the present section from the pragma-dialectical view of what it means to regard an argumentative move as fallacious, I shall, in the section that follows, discuss the pieces of advice for responding to alledgedly fallacious moves given by two prominent argumentation theorists, Erik C. W. Krabbe (2003) and Scott Jacobs (2000). Based on this discussion, and benefitting from the insights developed by these authors, I shall next explain my own view on the matter.[15]

As mentioned in Chapter 7, in the study of argumentation various theoretical models have been developed to create a suitable framework for evaluating argumentative discourse and tracking down fallacies. In their extremes, these models vary from abstract models that regulate the discourse by formal rules which cannot be violated without destroying the game, to functional models treating argumentative discourse as a methodical exchange of moves instrumental in realizing the argumentative purposes of the arguers. Depending on the kind of model that is applied, the assessment of the argumentative moves and their potential fallaciousness will proceed differently, because the theoretical perspective of the model determines the way in which the assessment takes place. If the assessment takes place within a formal perspective that is precisely delineated, the evaluation will be strict and essentially unequivocal. In such a formal perspective, an argumentative discussion is usually treated as a rule-bound game and all moves that cannot be generated by the rules of the game are, by definition, inadmissible.[16] Like in chess, when such an inadmissible move is made the game is over, because by making the move the guilty party has moved outside the system – and this most probably means that the game is lost by this party. Quintessentially, formal dialectic as developed by Barth and Krabbe in *From Axiom to Dialogue* (1982) proposes a formal model of argumentation of this type.

If the assessment of argumentation takes place within a functional perspective, the evaluation will be less rigid and there is more room for interpretation. This last observation also applies to the pragma-dialectical theory of argumentation. However close the pragma-dialectical model of a critical discussion is to formal dialectic as far as the dialectical dimension is concerned, due to its pragmatic dimension, the model of a critical discussion is a functional model. By viewing the argumentative moves in resolving a difference of opinion on the merits as performances of speech acts that are instrumental in realizing the dialectical aims of the various discussion stages, the model is a pragmatic model designed to take account of the communicative and

---

15. This explanation is based on considerations first expressed in van Eemeren and Houtlosser (2007b).

16. However, some theorists attempt to provide a formal account of rule-violations and repair (Mackenzie, 1990; Krabbe, 2003; van Laar, 2003).

interactional functions of these moves. In this way, the commitments the parties incur in the resolution process as a consequence of their dialectical rights and obligations, can be duly considered in the analysis and evaluation of the discourse. The model of a critical discussion includes all speech acts instrumental in resolving a difference of opinion on the merits, whether these speech acts are performed explicitly, implicitly, directly or indirectly. In this way, speech acts that do not play a constructive role in the resolution process are not excluded from the actual discourse but pronounced inadmissible based on the rules for critical discussion. Both formal dialectic and pragma-dialectics have in fact their own strictness, but in each of the two cases this strictness has a different source and rationale. In the case of formal dialectic, the strictness is determined by formal criteria, in the case of pragma-dialectics, by functional criteria.

According to Grice (1975), the interlocutors in informal exchanges are supposed to obey the Principle of Cooperation, which Grootendorst and I adapted in our integration of Searlean and Gricean insights and renamed the *Principle of Communication* (van Eemeren & Grootendorst, 1992a, p. 50). If any of the interlocutors makes a contribution to the exchange that cannot be interpreted as conforming directly or indirectly (by way of an "implicature") to the maxims subsumed under this Principle, the person who has made this move is regarded as behaving non-cooperatively (in the Gricean sense). In ordinary argumentative communication, however, the "game" is usually not over when one of the rules known as the pragma-dialectical rules for critical discussion has been violated and the violating move cannot be sensibly interpreted as a constructive contribution to the resolution process, even by being given some indirect (implicature-like) interpretation. What usually happens instead is that the people engaged in the argumentative communication attempt to "repair" their dialogue in such a way that the purpose the exchange is deemed to serve can still be achieved. If in a conversation an irrelevant remark is made that cannot be interpreted with the help of the Gricean inferential mechanisms as having any relevant implicature, rather than giving up the conversation altogether, the interlocutors will try to make it clear to the "offender" that his contribution was off the mark, and continue the conversation. In principle, the same applies when a party has violated a rule for critical discussion in argumentative discourse. Rather than assuming right away that the party who violated the rule has completely abandoned the aim of resolving the difference of opinion that initiated the discussion, the other party will – provided that the effect of the violation is not completely destructive – usually make an attempt to repair the violating party's contribution in such a way that the discussion can still remain on track to achieving its resolution-oriented aim.

Unlike the Gricean approach to cooperative informal exchanges, the pragma-dialectical approach takes the possibility of making such repairs emphatically into account, relying where this is practicable on the Principle of Communication and the "rules for communication" (van Eemeren & Grootendorst, 1992a, pp. 49–55). In this endeavor it is not only acknowledged that every speech act that is part of the resolution process may be performed implicitly or indirectly, but also that these speech acts will be performed in a way that serves both the aim of resolving the difference of opinion on the merits as defined in the discussion stage concerned and the aim of furthering the position of the party concerned. In this way this "liberal" approach does justice to the fact that in the confrontation stage of an argumentative discussion a party is not only free to advance his standpoint implicitly or indirectly, but also to opt for the standpoint that is most suitable to his general stance, best adapted to the other party's actual position, and phrased in the most effective way.[17]

The question now is, of course, how can it be established that a piece of strategic maneuvering derails? As I have explained in Chapter 7, this question is hard to answer in a general way. To some extent the criteria for deciding whether a particular argumentative move goes against a basic norm of dialectical reasonableness incorporated in a rule for critical discussion may be dependent on the context of the communicative activity type in which this move is made. The concept of strategic maneuvering can be of help in tackling this problem, because it enables us to specify in a relevant way the context in which the derailments may occur. Every macro-context in which strategic maneuvering takes place, whether it is strongly or only weakly dependent on institutional conventions, determines to some extent the opportunities that are available for managing the topics at issue in a certain discussion stage, the argumentative conduct that is acceptable to the parties, and the presentation that is appropriate.

In this way, the concept of strategic maneuvering helps us to specify the relevant features of the contextual environment in which the strategic maneuvering takes place and thus to establish the criteria for determining whether or not a rule for critical discussion has been violated and a fallacious derailment has occurred. In addition, the concept of strategic maneuvering enables us to give a theoretical explanation of why the discussion need not be abandoned as soon as a fallacy has allegedly been committed. Whether the accusation that a party has committed a fallacy is correct depends, first of all, on the interpretation of the context. With the exception of those blatant offences that are, for didactic reasons, often cited as clear-cut examples in textbooks, in cases of potentially fallacious strategic maneuvering the "offended" party's margins for assuming that the "offending" party is still (if only in principle) set on resolving the difference of opinion between them on the merits, are often sufficiently wide to allow

---

17. It must be remembered that any argumentative move the parties have to make according to the procedure for conducting a critical discussion will manifest itself – in the pragma-dialectical view – in the argumentative discourse as a piece of strategic maneuvering designed to maintain a balance between pursuing the aims of fulfilling one's dialectical obligations and completing the discussion stage concerned as much as possible to one's rhetorical heart's content. Another (practice-oriented) starting point assumes that more often than not it is difficult to find the right balance and this balance can sometimes be distorted, deliberately or unconsciously. If the distortion stems from the fact that rhetorical considerations concerning the effectiveness of the argumentative moves have gained the upper hand over the dialectical commitment of reasonably playing the game by the rules, the strategic maneuvering violates a rule for critical discussion and derails into fallaciousness.

the parties to find a way out. This explains why the offended party, if he is indeed motivated to resolve the difference of opinion on the merits, usually remains motivated to regard the exchange as an "open" discussion and tries to have the fallacious moves repaired in such a way that the aim of resolving the difference of opinion on the merits can still be achieved. By showing his reasonableness in this way he may at the same time increase his effectiveness, because the other party is likely to feel forced to contain his maneuvering by toning down his attacking or defending moves.

公认谬误的两种处理方案
9.6 Two diverging proposals for dealing with perceived fallacies

On the basis of the explanation just offered for the offended party's presumed inclination to continue the discussion in spite of presumed fallacious strategic maneuvering by the other party, the question I am interested in can be summarized in the following way. What moves should parties confronted with an argumentative move they perceive as fallacious make to ensure that the aim of resolving the difference of opinion on the merits can still be reached? In my view, the most pertinent positions articulated in the literature in response to this question are Krabbe's "immanent" dialectical proposal to react to a fallacy by initiating a "meta-dialogue" and Jacobs' "pragma-rhetorical" proposal [my characterization] to counter a move perceived as fallacious by making a move that helps to put the process back on the right track, even if this may involve making a move that gives the impression of being a counter-fallacy.[18] Let me consider these two alternatives.

In most formal dialectical systems there is no room for strategic maneuvering, and, strictly speaking, in discussions within these systems fallacies cannot occur. Krabbe, however, views the argumentative dialogues conducted in practice as "approximations" of a formal dialectical discussion and in these approximations fallacies are possible.[19] Formal dialectic, he claims, aims to provide the participants in such all-but-formal dialogues with the tools to respond to the occurrence of fallacies. According to Krabbe, "the status of a [discussion] move or argument must be decided in

---

18. Jacobs seems to be driven by a concern for the higher order conditions that need to be fulfilled to be able to resolve a difference of opinion on the merits (cf. also Jacobs, 2002, pp. 124–125). "You have to take seriously the idea that rhetorical strategy can function to improve dialectical functioning and not just function to persuade," Jacobs says (2002, p. 128). The same intentions can be ascribed to Battistelli (2009), who states: "Once argumentation has derailed, rhetoric can provide the means for opening up solidified attitudes through appeal to the ambiguity and plurality of opinion existing in a given rhetorical setting." Battistelli's observations resemble those of Jacobs; rhetoric as he views it has an important role to play in indicating how to promote reasonableness in argumentative reality.

19. The approximations are partly formalized. In formal dialectic there are therefore two strategies: formalizing discussions in which fallacies occur, and considering discussions with fallacies as approximations of formal dialogues.

discussion, by the participants themselves" (2002b, p. 162), and responding to a fallacy consists in "fallacy criticism" or, as Hamblin (1970, pp. 283-284) would have it, making a "point of order." In this way, in Krabbe's (2003) terminology, a "meta-dialogue" is initiated in which the party who thinks that a move made by the other party is fallacious aims to make that party retract this move. If the initiator of the meta-dialogue successfully sustains his accusation, according to the rules of such meta-dialogues, the party that was rightly accused of committing a fallacy has to retract the disputed move – and pay the costs of the meta-dialogue (in Krabbe, 2002b, referred to as a "fine"). If the initiator cannot sustain his charge, he must retract his accusation – and pay the costs himself (Krabbe, 2003, p. 89).

In his approach to the fallacies, which he subsumes under the heading of "normative pragmatics," Jacobs (2000) advocates the view, which is in my appreciation basically rhetorical, that in practice arguers need not always act in conformity with dialectical rules, because in some circumstances doing so would damage their position in the discussion. According to Jacobs, in such circumstances they should "be adjusting otherwise bad deliberators to their best and making the best of an otherwise bad situation" (2000, p. 281), even if this would amount to making a move that has the appearance of being fallacious.[20] As an illustration, he discusses a response by pro-life activists (party B) to a statement by the National Organization for Women (party A) in the context of the continuing American discussion about abortion:

> *Party A (National Organization for Women):*
> Myth: The "partial-birth" abortion procedure is unnecessary.
> Fact: Medical experts state that the safest method of late pregnancy termination for some women is the intact dilation and extraction (D&X) procedure (Jacobs, 2000, p. 278).
>
> *Party B (The national conference of Catholic bishops, Secretariat for pro-life activities):*
> Killing a mostly-born infant with a pair of scissors. We're *debating* this? This is not a bad dream. It's real. Every year, thousands of infants are forcibly dragged from their mother's wombs, then killed. Brutally. And our nation is actually debating whether or not this should be allowed to continue (Jacobs, 2000, p. 276).

According to Jacobs, the pro-life activists' response to what they perceive as a fallacy is not a fallacy, but an attempt to "encourage full and open exploration of alternative standpoints," a "self-regulating procedure" by which "people adjust to the contingencies and complexities of actual situations" (Jacobs, 2000, pp. 278-279). Responding in this way is in Jacobs' view allowed if it serves to restore the balance between the parties. In the case at hand, this

---

20. In considering argumentation as reasonable if it "makes the best of the situation" Jacobs (2002, pp. 124-125) takes reasonableness much more loosely and broadly than pragma-dialecticians, who define reasonableness in terms of compliance with the rules for critical discussion (van Eemeren & Grootendorst, 1992a).

would mean that the anti-abortionists dispute the idea that the issue of the discussion is a purely medical one, as is (in the anti-abortionists' opinion) suggested by the terminology employed by the National Organization for Women (Jacobs, 2000, p. 277–279).

What are the advantages and disadvantages of each of the two approaches I have summarized with regard to the problem of how to respond to a (perceived) fallacy? One obvious advantage of the formal dialectical approach is that it leaves no room for confusion: a party who perceives a move made by the other party as a fallacy makes it explicitly clear to the other party that, in his view, a fallacy was committed and that the discussion cannot be continued unless the fallacious move has been retracted. Because it is eventually up to the parties to determine whether the alleged fallacy was indeed a fallacy, another advantage of the formal dialectical approach is that it provides the parties with the tool of conducting a regulated "meta-dialogue" to argue out this dispute in a civilized, i.e. reasonable, manner. What could be regarded as a disadvantage of the formal dialectical approach, however, is that it presupposes a permanent willingness in arguers to engage in meta-discussions over the things they are doing in the (ground-level) discussion. As Krabbe acknowledges, this approach allows the participants to hold up the discussion indefinitely by seizing any opportunity to initiate a meta-dialogue about a supposedly fallacious ground-level move. Krabbe's suggestion to attach a penalty to such obstructive behavior should perhaps not be seen merely as a joke. If it is a joke, then the problem is not solved; if it is not a joke, the problem is solved, but not in a theoretically motivated way.

Jacobs' pragma-rhetorical approach has the advantage of being utterly realistic – or giving at least the impression of being utterly realistic. What you do when you are offended is hit back and thereby restore the balance between the offender and yourself. Jacobs fails to explain, however, what balance is being restored. Is it the power balance, a psychological balance, or some other balance? And why exactly does this balance need to be maintained? What is also left out of this picture is the damage that may be caused in the process. Just as the boxers in a boxing match do not look particularly handsome anymore after ten rounds of "restoring the balance between them," in some cases making the move that may have the appearance of a counter-fallacy could indeed have the effect of setting the issue of the discussion straight, but in other cases the effect might be that the relation between the parties is damaged to such an extent that their appetite for continuing the critical debate is lost. In Jacobs' example, the move having the appearance of a counter-fallacy is supposed to work constructively because of the shock effect it brings about. Apart from the psychologistic flavor of this observation (and of Jacobs' approach in general), there is in fact no good reason to assume, let alone a guarantee, that the balance between the parties in the abortion debate will be restored. And even if the balance is regained this need not to have brought the parties any closer. They could just as well have become even further divided than they already were, as seems the most probable result in the case of the abortion debate.

Because in the pragma-dialectical perspective on argumentative discourse a fallacy is an inadmissible move, it is not very likely that in our treatment of the problem of how to respond to a supposedly fallacious move the advice would be to respond by means of a counter-fallacy or an argumentative move that has the appearance of being a counter-fallacy. Ever since pragma-dialectical theoreticians have reached the stage in which they take account of "rhetorical" aspirations of the discussants entering into the process of critically testing the tenability of a standpoint, they have considered the strategic maneuvering involved in combining the pursuit of rhetorical aims with the maintenance of dialectical obligations sound if and only if it stays within the boundaries set by the rules for critical discussion. In all other cases the strategic maneuvering is fallacious. The provision just mentioned applies equally to those moves that are perceived, rightly or wrongly, as violations of the rules for critical discussion, and to the moves that are made in response to them. This general provision, however, does not necessarily imply that a reply to a fallacy should always lead to either the complete withdrawal or the non-withdrawal of the ground-level move, as is suggested in Krabbe's approach.

I think that in responding to would-be fallacies the best option is to adopt a middle course and regard in the first instance every response to a supposedly fallacious move as a piece of strategic maneuvering in a sub-discussion (or, if one likes, a meta-dialogue) – one in which the responding party assumes that the other party still aims to resolve the difference between them by means of a critical test of the standpoints at issue, and at the same time tries to make it clear to the other party that this party's strategic maneuvering as regards *this issue*, in response to *this opponent*, and *presented in this way* has *in this case* derailed and does not bring the parties any closer to a resolution of the difference of opinion. Suppose a party encounters an argumentative move he considers fallacious. What can we do in response to the would-be fallacious move in order to make the other party "re-rail" the derailed move? Rather than stating right away that the denounced move must be withdrawn altogether, he may suggest to the other party that there is a need to readjust this move so as to undo the derailment and re-rail the maneuvering. Although this solution is not a turn of 180 degrees in comparison with Krabbe's solution, it is at any rate more subtle and realistic.

In my view, in the example provided by Jacobs the reaction should be neither the response given by the pro-life activists and tolerated by Jacobs, nor the response Krabbe would instigate by requiring the National Organization for Women to withdraw the move they have made. A more adequate reaction would be if the pro-life activists pointed out in a strategically opportune manner to the National Organization for Women that they need to readjust their move if they want to discuss the abortion issue in a way that is considered reasonable *by both parties*. The pro-life activists could do so, for instance, by pointing out that it is not the medical experts who should have the final say with regard to abortion or that the abortion issue should be discussed in ethical terms as well as in clinical medical terms. In tackling the problem in this way, I have chosen an approach that boils down to maintaining a balance between raising a procedural issue (Hamblin's "point of order"), thus making clear that the other party is still considered a reasonable discussion partner, and enhancing the chances that the other party will readjust its supposedly fallacious contribution to the discussion in such a way that the discussion can be continued constructively.

可修复脱轨策略操控的校正
9.7 Re-railing repairable derailments of strategic maneuvering

The question I am dealing with at this juncture is how to respond in a constructive way to a (perceived) fallacy in the other party's strategic maneuvering. Starting from the proposals made by Krabbe (2003) and Jacobs (2000), I have considered what possibilities there are for a constructive continuation of the argumentative exchange.[21] Since I view fallacies as derailments of strategic maneuvering that go against a norm for critical reasonableness, the question I have to answer is what is to happen if such a derailment is perceived to have taken place. Basically, I have argued that the party who observes that something has gone wrong in an argumentative discourse should start a sub-discussion in which he maneuvers so that not only is the alleged derailment recognized but also a re-railment is brought about that brings the discussion back on track.

Viewed analytically, strategic maneuvering in argumentative discourse manifests itself in topical choice, audience adaptation, and presentational design, the three aspects of strategic maneuvering distinguished in Chapter 4. Topical choice refers to the specific selection that is made from the set of dialectical options, the "topical potential," available at the point in the discussion stage the discourse has reached; audience adaptation involves adjusting one's moves to the perspective the audience has or is supposed to have; and presentational design concerns the selection that is made from the existing repertoire of presentational devices. What is involved in responding constructively to a fallacy charge by making a well-considered repair amounts, in my view, to trying to bring about a re-railment of the alleged derailment through the readjustment of precisely those aspects of the strategic maneuver in which the derailment manifested itself. In practice, this could amount to the following kinds of responses or to some combination of them:

a. Revising the topical choice that was made in the denounced move in such a way that the amended strategic maneuver no longer derails – as when an argumentative move that is according to accepted standards of evaluation a *tu quoque* or a "straw man" fallacy is replaced by a move containing a legitimate accusation of inconsistency or a legitimate reference to the other party's standpoint.
b. Revising the adaptation to audience demand that was made in the denounced move in such a way that the strategic maneuver no longer derails – as when an argumentative move that is in first instance perceived by the audience as a *tu quoque* or an *argumentum ad verecundiam* is put in a perspective that makes the audience recognize it as a legitimate accusation of inconsistency or appeal to authority.

---

21. I reported earlier on the results of these considerations at an argumentation conference in honor of Erik Krabbe in Groningen (van Eemeren, 2008).

c. Revising the presentational design of the denounced move in such a way that the strategic maneuver no longer derails – as when an argumentative move that is seemingly a *tu quoque* or an abusive *argumentum ad hominem* because of the way it is phrased is rephrased as an argumentative move that clearly constitutes a legitimate accusation of inconsistency or personal attack.

It can easily happen in argumentative practice that the process of resolving a difference of opinion on the merits is put back on track after a change has been made to an offender's argumentative move that removes the problem but does not require the offending party to withdraw the argumentative move altogether. In some cases changing the type of move that was made will do (as when a formerly causal argument is changed into a symptomatic one); in other cases changing the perspective from which the audience was stimulated to view the argumentative move might be enough (as when a perspective that creates distance is replaced by a more engaging one); and in still other cases changing the mode of expression that was used will do the trick (as when a denigrating term is replaced by a more politely negative one). Because the three aspects of strategic maneuvering hang together and are only analytically distinguished from each other, making changes to one aspect will automatically affect the others, but still this does not have to mean that the offending party has to retrace his steps altogether, let alone that his offending move automatically puts an end to the whole critical exchange.

Clearly, this method of readjustment, which I recommend for such cases that would admit it, can more easily be applied in an exchange that is (or resembles) a "real" discussion than in an argumentative exposition that is presented as a monologue or written text, but this does not mean that the possibility of such readjustments cannot be considered just as well in argumentative confrontations that are not explicitly dialogical. In any case, only after it has become clear in argumentative practice that these kinds of readjustments cannot be made, or do not lead to the repair of the resolution process that is aimed for, will it be necessary to follow Krabbe's proposal to discuss the need of a complete retraction of the denounced move. In such a case it might be necessary to check first whether perhaps the Principle of Communication has gone by the board, so that it does no longer make sense to continue the discussion. If the Principle of Communication is still being maintained, it is always worthwhile at least to check whether it is possible to comply with the proposed procedure for dealing constructively with fallacious moves, which aims to be the pragma-dialectical golden mean between Jacobs' pragmatic functional approach aimed at ensuring rhetorical effectiveness and Krabbe's formal approach aimed at maintaining dialectical reasonableness.

CHAPTER 10 第十章

后续研究计划设定
Setting up an agenda for further research

语用论辩学理论拓展中的重点回顾
10.1 Recapitulating the basics of the extended pragma-dialectical theory

In the preceding chapters I have outlined a general perspective on argumentative discourse that integrates rhetorical insights concerning the effectiveness of argumentative discourse into the theoretical framework of standard pragma-dialectics pertaining to the reasonableness of argumentative discourse. To bridge the gap between the dialectical perspective and the rhetorical perspective on argumentative discourse, I introduced "strategic maneuvering" as a theoretical notion covering the simultaneous pursuit of rhetorical effectiveness and dialectical reasonableness. In this way, an extended version of the pragma-dialectical theory is brought into being that makes it possible to enrich the analysis and evaluation of argumentative discourse by taking account of the strategic design of the argumentative moves that are made, so that the reconstruction of the discourse presented in the analysis can be more precise and better justified and fallacies can be more accurately identified in the evaluation.

Each of the four stages distinguished in pragma-dialectics in the process of resolving a difference of opinion by means of a critical discussion is characterized by having a specific dialectical objective. Because in extended pragma-dialectics the rhetorical aims of the participants are construed as being dependent on their dialectical goals in the resolution process, the specification of these rhetorical aims will run in all stages parallel to the specification of the dialectical goals. This presumed relationship of dependency is the methodological reason why, in the study of strategic maneuvering proposed in extended pragma-dialectics, rhetorical insights are systematically integrated in a dialectical framework of analysis – more in particular, the *pragma*-dialectical framework.

As a matter of course, analyzing strategic maneuvering starts from the way in which the strategic maneuvering manifests itself in the discourse, i.e. as a particular choice made from the topical potential available at that point in the discourse, as a particular way of exploiting the opportunities available for audience adaptation, and as a particular manner of utilizing the available presentational possibilities. Although in strategic maneuvering these three aspects always go together, and are dependent on each other, it is useful to distinguish them analytically in examining argumentative practices. This is because in a certain piece of strategic maneuvering one aspect may be more conspicuous than the others while all three aspects must be taken into account in the analysis.

In analyzing the strategic function of a piece of maneuvering, we have to consider, first, what kinds of results could be achieved by making that argumentative move, so that the outcome that may be aimed for in the maneuvering can be taken into account.

Of crucial assistance in this endeavor is the spectrum of relevant options that are available in the analytic overview. Second, we have to consider which reasonable options were available when the argumentative move was made, so that the route that is taken by carrying out this strategic maneuver can be taken into account. A crucial help here can be the dialectical profile for the moves that are both reasonable and analytically relevant at this juncture in the discussion. Third, we have to consider which institutional constraints were imposed on the argumentative discourse in which the strategic maneuvering takes place, so that the conventional preconditions the strategic maneuvering must meet can be taken into account. In order to bring these institutional constraints to light, an understanding of the institutional background of the communicative activity type is required in which the strategic maneuvering takes place. Fourth, we have to consider what was the actual state of affairs in the discourse when the strategic maneuvering took place, so that it can be taken into account which situational demands the strategic maneuvering must respond to. Of crucial assistance here can be an inventory of the dialectical commitment sets of the arguers and their rhetorical counterparts that define the argumentative situation. These four factors are parameters that together determine the strategic function a particular mode of maneuvering fulfills.

Although more often than not in strategic maneuvering aiming for dialectical objectives and trying to reach rhetorical aims go well together, it may happen that a party allows his commitment to a critical exchange to be overruled by his aim to persuade the opponent, so that his argumentative moves are no longer in agreement with the norms involved in the rules for critical discussion and the strategic maneuvering derails into fallaciousness. The difference between legitimate and fallacious strategic maneuvering is that in the latter case certain soundness criteria have not been met that apply in the communicative activity type concerned to the use of the mode of strategic maneuvering concerned. In the end, fallacy judgments are always contextual judgments that depend on the conventional constraints pertaining to a particular communicative activity type and the specific circumstances of situated argumentative acting.

Integrating rhetorical insights regarding the effectiveness of argumentative discourse in a dialectical framework is intended to bring argumentation theory closer to argumentative reality, so that the analysis and evaluation of argumentative discourse become more accurate and thorough, and can be more precisely accounted for. Rather than being the last word on the matter, however, my proposals are meant to be the starting point for further theorizing. It is just as clear to me as it will be to others that none of the theoretical propositions recapitulated in this section is final. More research has to be done to round out the theorizing concerning strategic maneuvering and to enhance its instrumentality in analyzing and evaluating argumentative discourse. In this concluding chapter, I limit myself to mentioning some of the most urgent challenges, preceded by a brief discussion of some prerequisites for carrying out the research program regarding strategic maneuvering successfully (Section 10.2). Depending on the kind of challenges involved, I will distinguish between philosophical

(Section 10.3), theoretical (Section 10.4), empirical (Section 10.5), analytical (Section 10.6), and practical (Section 10.7) research issues.

保持研究计划的连贯性和持续性
10.2 Maintaining coherence and vitality in the research program

The five types of research issues mentioned at the end of Section 10.1 correspond with the five components of the pragma-dialectical research program (van Eemeren, 1987a; van Eemeren and Grootendorst, 2004, pp. 9–41). This research program has been designed in such a way that the various components are clearly distinguished and the interdependency between the components is at the same time ensured. In the program, theoretical construction is based on philosophical reflection and guides, together with empirical observation, analytic reconstruction; the results of analytic reconstruction are the point of departure of the diagnosis of problems occurring in practice, and constitute the point of departure of interventions to solve these problems by means of an improved exchange format ("design") or improved argumentative skills. In order to maintain coherence in the pragma-dialectical research program, when carrying out a research project (or cluster of research projects), account must be taken not only of the way in which the project (or cluster of projects) is embedded in a specific component of the research program, but also of the way in which it relates to the research carried out in other components of the research program. Therefore, fine-tuning has to take place between the various research projects.

Another precondition for a successful continuation of the strategic maneuvering research addressed in this volume is that the research carried out in each project should always be informed by what is happening in other approaches by argumentation theorists of the same, or similar, problems, and in related fields of research relevant to the study of argumentation. Otherwise it will be deprived of the inspirational challenge of being confronted with alternative views and trains of thought, and having to point out the advantages and disadvantages of one's own approach compared with other approaches. Without having critical exchanges with proponents of other views the research would become seclusive and run the risk of getting sterile. Therefore, regular contacts need to be maintained with fellow argumentation theorists representing other approaches.

Among the approaches to argumentation that seem to me important to pragma-dialecticians interested in strategic maneuvering are: design engineering (see Jackson, 2002; Jacobs & Aakhus, 2002; Aakhus & Jackson, 2005),[1] formal dialectic (see Walton & Krabbe, 1995; Krabbe, 2003), informal logic (see Hitchcock, 2006; Blair, 2007; Johnson, 2008), and theory-minded rhetoric (see Kauffeld, 2002; Zarefsky, 2006; Tindale, 2009). Cooperative links should be entertained with scholars from related fields of interest, such as dialogue analysis (see Weigand, 2007; Rigotti, 2009), controversy studies (see Dascal &

---

1. Jackson introduced a broad understanding of "argumentation design" as "any negotiated method of dispute settlement" (1998, p. 184).

Chang, 2007; Dascal, 2008; van Eemeren & Garssen, 2008), critical discourse analysis (see Weiss & Wodak, 2003; Wodak & Chilton, 2005; Wodak & Meyer, 2009), and artificial intelligence and nonmonotonic logic (see Bench-Capon & Dunne, 2007; Prakken, 2000, 2006). Next to the need to secure the associations I have mentioned, the study of strategic maneuvering in argumentative discourse also requires to establish solid links with experts regarding the various kinds of institutionalized practices in which the maneuvering takes place. More in particular, it is necessary to work together with those specialists in the various communicative domains (e.g. political, legal, scholarly, medical, and financial communication) who share an interest in analyzing the characteristics and evaluating the quality of specific types of institutionalized argumentative discourse.

从哲学层面审视论辩与修辞视角
10.3 Reviewing dialectical and rhetorical perspectives philosophically

Further philosophical reflection is required on the relationship between dialectical theorizing and rhetorical theorizing. To what extent, and in what way, can the integration of the two perspectives on argumentative discourse be further implemented and intensified to extend the scope and enhance the quality of strategic maneuvering analysis and evaluation? The reflection that is required should take place against a well-considered and well-documented intellectual background of views and insights regarding these issues stemming from classical and modern dialectical and rhetorical scholarship supplemented by relevant philosophical ideas from other sources. In my view, reflection should concentrate in the first place on the philosophical problems involved in giving substance to the normative dimension of the study of argumentation and strategic maneuvering – with regard to the dimension of reasonableness, with regard to the dimension of effectiveness, and with regard to the combination of the two dimensions. To what extent, and in what way, can insights from classical and modern dialectics and insights from classical and modern rhetoric play a constructive role in this endeavor?

In my view it is of vital importance that the practice of argumentative discourse contributes optimally to realizing the normative goal of resolving a difference of opinion on the merits by critically testing the standpoints at issue for their acceptability before a rational and reasonable judge. Bringing the one kind of combination of dialectical and rhetorical insights to bear might be more instrumental to reaching this normative goal than relying on a different kind of combination. I can imagine that in light of this observation a case could be made for a (slightly or radically) different way of integrating insights from rhetoric into a dialectical framework of analysis and evaluation than the one here proposed. Although I have defended a different view, I can also imagine that those in favor of a purely anthropological philosophical perspective – in which the acceptability of the way argumentative discourse is conducted to the participants, or to the community to which the participants belong, is central – might consider a complete reversal of the methodological proceedings leading to an integration of dialectical insights into a rhetorical framework of analysis (and limiting the dialectical insights that are used perhaps to those accepted by the actual parties or by the community to which they belong).

It will be no surprise that the kind of philosophical reflection I am in favor of is directed at considering carefully how the relationship between dialectic and rhetoric in dealing with strategic maneuvering in argumentative discourse can be strengthened in line with the critical-rationalist testing procedure developed in pragma-dialectics. Important questions to be answered in this endeavor are which classical and modern dialectical views and insights, and which classical and modern rhetorical views and insights, are viewed philosophically best suited to connect the argumentative dimension of aiming for effectiveness in strategic maneuvering in argumentative discourse systematically with the argumentative dimension of aiming for reasonableness. My own philosophical starting point is that the relationship between the dialectical angle and the rhetorical angle should be strengthened in such a way that an integration is achieved that constitutes conceptually the best point of departure for developing analytical instruments for analyzing and evaluating strategic maneuvering that agree with a critical rationalist philosophy of reasonableness.

A philosophical issue relating to the contextualization of the dialectical framework for analysis and evaluation taking place in extended pragma-dialectics deserves special attention. This is the epistemological issue of the approximation of truth. It may seem as if an unwanted element of relativism is sneaking into pragma-dialectics if the criteria for deciding whether or not one of the norms involved in the rules for critical discussion has been violated are made to some extent dependent on the context. But does this danger really exist? Which extra or more specific soundness conditions must be formulated in pragma-dialectics for argumentative discourse in specific institutionalized contexts to prevent strategic maneuvering with regard to descriptive standpoints in which a claim to truth is made from derailing? And how about the soundness conditions for strategic maneuvering with regard to evaluative and prescriptive standpoints? A related philosophical issue deserving our immediate attention is the use of values and value hierarchies in strategic maneuvering and the role philosophy of action can play in dealing with this issue.

从理论层面确定策略操控类型与合理性条件
10.4 Defining types of strategic maneuvering and soundness conditions theoretically

On the theoretical level, continued research is needed. One important challenge is that of designing a theoretically motivated typology of modes of strategic maneuvering. Instead of providing a theoretically based classification of types of strategic maneuvering, distinguished on the basis of topical choice, audience adaptation, and presentational design, I have recommended naming each mode of strategic maneuvering provisionally after its most conspicuous aspect. Starting from the theoretical basis laid in this study, I think it should be possible to design a coherent typology in which the factors playing a part in determining the strategic function of specific modes of strategic maneuvering are systematically taken into account. A similar theoretical effort should be made with regard to the broader categories of confrontational strategies, opening strategies, argumentational strategies, concluding strategies, and discussion strategies extending over more discussion stages, which are characterized by a systematic "vertical" and "horizontal" coordination of the argumentative moves that are made.

Another theoretical *desideratum* is establishing general criteria for judging the soundness of the various modes – or types, if the previous project is successful – of strategic maneuvering, and the specific criteria applying to specific communicative contexts. This could be achieved by first determining the general soundness conditions applying in all cases to a particular mode of strategic maneuvering, and then specifying the specific soundness conditions applying to the use of particular modes of strategic maneuvering in specific argumentative activity types. On the basis of the general and specific soundness conditions general and specific soundness criteria for particular modes of strategic maneuvering can be formulated.[2]

Mohammed (2009a) made a start with this type of theoretical research, concentrating on responding to strategic maneuvering in which an inconsistency is pointed out in the other party's avowed commitments, and focusing in particular on the communicative activity type of Prime Minister's Question Time in the British parliament. Andone (2009b) concentrates on the same mode of strategic maneuvering, but focuses on its use in the communicative activity type of a political interview.[3] Against this background, it is to be expected that it will soon become clear exactly which soundness conditions for pointing out an inconsistency in the other party's avowed commitments are the same in both communicative activity types and which are (to some extent) different. This result will be of help in deciding in what way precisely contextual factors must be taken into account in specifying the soundness criteria of a particular mode of strategic maneuvering.

---

2. Soundness conditions constitute the theoretical basis for formulating systematic and workable criteria for determining whether the norms of reasonableness incorporated in the rules for critical discussion have been satisfied.

3. Andone (2009a) proposes a pragma-dialectical analysis of making an accusation of inconsistency as a mode of strategic maneuvering. She characterizes an accusation of inconsistency as an illocutionary act with certain identity and correctness conditions. The formulation of the essential condition that must be fulfilled for an utterance to count as an accusation of inconsistency connects the performance of the illocutionary act with the perlocutionary effect of securing a response that answers the charge raised by the speaker against the addressee. Maintaining a distinction between the inherent perlocutionary effect of acceptance and further consequences deriving from it, Andone interprets the response to an accusation of inconsistency as a continuation that the addressee is required to perform after the achievement of the inherent perlocutionary effect. Starting from the moves that speakers are obliged to perform or have the right to perform in the confrontation stage, she identifies a set of consecutive consequences that comprises retraction and maintenance of a standpoint. Finally, Andone analyzes an argumentative exchange reconstructed as part of the confrontation stage of a critical discussion in order to show how in a political interview the performance by an interviewer of an accusation of inconsistency constrains and opens up opportunities for the politician to respond by realizing the consecutive consequence of retraction.

从实证层面描述策略操控的模式与效果
10.5 Describing modes of strategic maneuvering and their effects empirically

The research projects that would be usefully carried out in the empirical component of the research program include both quantitative and qualitative research. O'Keefe's (2006, 2009) meta-analyses of persuasion research suggest that argumentation which complies more clearly with the model of a critical discussion generally tends to be more persuasive.[4] This is an interesting starting point for carrying out further quantitative empirical research, which should cover not just the argumentation stage but also the other stages. However, pragma-dialecticians need to carry out a somewhat different kind of empirical research than the traditional persuasion research O'Keefe reports about,[5] because they are not interested in persuasiveness just like that, but in rhetorical effectiveness within the boundaries of reasonableness. Starting from the notion of strategic maneuvering, empirical research can be undertaken to investigate rhetorical effectiveness that has a more solid theoretical basis.

Rhetorical effectiveness in strategic maneuvering is not necessarily equivalent to persuasiveness as conceptualized in persuasion research, because persuasiveness is not by definition subjected to the requirements of reasonableness. It goes without saying that argumentation theorists need to concentrate in the first place on factors having to do with the argumentative nature of the discourse, and on the dimension of reasonableness involved in argumentative discourse.[6] This calls for the use of an experimental design in the empirical research regarding strategic maneuvering that makes it possible

---

4. Persuasion research has brought to light a great many (mainly psychological) factors that should qualify this general conclusion. The leading models of processes that are claimed to yield persuasion are Petty and Cacioppo's (1986) Elaboration Likelihood Model and Eagly and Chaiken's (1993) Heuristic-Systematic Model. The latter model claims that in practice the Principle of Least Effort competes with the desire of having one's opinions well thought out that is central to the former model. In fact, only the "central route" within the Elaboration Likelihood Model is really argumentative.

5. O'Keefe (2009) reviews meta-analyses of the persuasive effects associated with various forms of manipulation, but does not, of course, concentrate on strategic maneuvering as it is introduced in my study. Both manipulations involving alternative ways of presenting the same arguments (e.g. the contrast between gain-framed and loss-framed appeals) and manipulations involving the presentation of substantively different arguments (e.g. the contrast between one-sided messages, which provide only supporting arguments, and two-sided messages, which present supporting arguments and also discuss opposing arguments) are found to make relatively little difference to persuasiveness. Across eight different manipulations, the average effect size corresponds roughly to a correlation of .07. O'Keefe's conclusion is that although there is little reason to fear that superficial presentational variations will deeply affect persuasive success, neither is there much reason to expect that substantive argumentative variation will have dramatic effects.

6. This means that the empirical research must exclude ("bracket off") effects caused by other factors than strategic maneuvering in argumentative discourse, such as the fact that the topic of discussion is emotionally loaded or that the speaker is a famous rock star.

to concentrate fully on effects caused by the selection made from the topical potential, the adaptation to audience demand, and the exploitation of presentational devices – in all cases in some combination. Persuasion research, on the other hand, is typically one-dimensional, focusing on only one aspect of maneuvering (or some other factor) at the time. This may explain why the effects that have been traced are rather minimal. Taking all three aspects into account may yield more interesting results.

In view of my earlier considerations, it seems sensible to concentrate the experimental research first on strategic maneuvering that is reasonable in principle, so that the complication of having to deal with rhetorical effects that might be due to an oversight with respect to the requirements of reasonableness can be avoided. When measuring the rhetorical effectiveness of particular modes of strategic maneuvering it seems a good idea to start from the contribution a particular argumentative type of move (or combination of moves) makes to the process of resolving a difference of opinion on the merits. In choosing the (sets of) argumentative moves to be included in the research, I would propose to select (sets of) moves that differ in "dialectical power," i.e. in critical efficiency,[7] so that sustained and falsifiable hypotheses can be formulated regarding the expected differences in rhetorical effectiveness that are pertinent to the theoretical study of argumentation.[8] For instance, combining an argument in support of a standpoint with a refutation of the other party's anticipated objection has, provided that the anticipation is correct, more dialectical power in resolving a difference of opinion on the merits than just giving argumentation in support of the standpoint. Therefore, the hypothesis can be developed that strategic maneuvering involving the former is rhetorically more effective than the latter way of strategic maneuvering (cf. Amjarso, 2008).[9] I think that it would be useful to carry out empirical research starting from this kind of hypotheses.

---

7. A reasonable argumentative move (or combination of moves) can be considered to be more critically efficient than another argumentative move (or combination of moves) aimed at making the same contribution to the resolution process in terms of choice from the topical potential if it brings the resolution closer than the other move (or combination of moves) does, because fewer moves are needed in the continuation of the critical exchange, so that the dialectical route that is taken is shorter. My notion of dialectical power may be similar to Johnson's (2008, p. 161) notion of dialectical strength, but I cannot be certain of this since Johnson has not defined this notion.

8. The general hypothesis underlying this cluster of research projects would be that, *ceteris paribus*, a strategic maneuver that is dialectically reasonable will be rhetorically more effective than a competing strategic maneuver if, all other things being equal, the former has more dialectical power than the latter.

9. Such a result would in fact be in agreement with Petty and Cacioppo's (1979) (confirmed) prediction regarding the "central route to persuasion" that messages with strong arguments are generally more effective than other messages when the judges' involvement increases. The crucial difference is that I am interested in the effect of the dialectical strength of arguments and other argumentative moves rather than in the effect of psychological factors.

Empirical research is also called for to reveal the factors that play a role in the deceptive practice I discussed in Chapter 7 of keeping the fallaciousness of derailed strategic maneuvering at bay. As I have explained, in principle each type of fallacy has a reasonable counterpart from which it departs. Because it may look very much like its reasonable counterpart, its fallaciousness can be hard to detect. A qualitative analysis of the various types of fallacies occurring in argumentative practice based on insights concerning strategic maneuvering will provide more insight in how these fallacies "work." Such qualitative research can lead to theoretically motivated hypotheses about the factors that make fallacies look reasonable that can be tested by way of systematic experimental research. I think of experimental research of the kind reported in *Fallacies and Judgments of Reasonableness* (van Eemeren *et al.*, 2009), in which fallacious instances of discussion moves are compared with their reasonable counterparts. In one of the experiments described in that volume the hypothesis has been tested and confirmed that ordinary arguers will regard evading the burden of proof in a mixed difference of opinion as more reasonable when the standpoint at issue has presumptive status than when it does not have this status (2009, pp. 151–157). In other words, the burden of proof for a standpoint can be evaded more easily when it concerns a standpoint that is in line with the (epistemological) *status quo*.

I recommend studying in a similar vein modes of strategic maneuvering such as the direct personal attack. When a direct personal attack derails into an abusive variant of the *argumentum ad hominem*, it involves a violation of the Freedom Rule concerning the expression of doubt in reaction to a standpoint put forward in the confrontation stage of the discussion. The fallacious character of an abusive *argumentum ad hominem* is sometimes hidden from sight because the personal attack that is made resembles a legitimate critical question that may be posed in the argumentation stage as a reaction to an argument from authority in which the arguer refers to himself as an expert (Garssen, 2009). This hypothesis can be checked in experimental research by presenting direct personal attacks in a context in which the protagonist might have used his authority but does not. In all cases examined in this type of research a contrast is to be made between fallacious cases that are strategically manipulated to make the fallacy seem closer to a reasonable discussion move and more or less clear cases of the same fallacy.

从分析层面重构策略操控具体形式及其构成的策略
10.6 Reconstructing strategic maneuvers and broader strategies analytically

A fourth area of research is covered by the analytical component of the research program. It concerns the reconstruction of argumentative discourse from the theoretical perspective of a critical discussion in light of empirical evidence. The inclusion of the strategic maneuvering going on in the discourse in the process of reconstruction is an addition typical of the extended pragma-dialectical approach. This addition requires for each strategic maneuver considering the spectrum of relevant options open to be filled out in the analytic overview, the analytically relevant moves available at the point when the maneuver is made in the relevant dialectical profile, the conventional preconditions imposed on the maneuvering by the institutional background of the communicative activity type in which the maneuvering takes place, and the dialectical commitment sets of the parties defining, together with their rhetorical interpretation the argumentative situation. By combining the results gained from considering each of these four factors, the strategic function of the maneuver that is analyzed is to be determined. In future research it must be examined in greater detail how exactly this can be properly done.

A related theme for analytic research (closely connected with theoretical research) concerns the way in which successive individual strategic maneuvers can be seen to combine in a confrontational strategy, an opening strategy, an argumentational strategy, a concluding strategy, or – if the coordination transcends the boundareis of a specific stage – a discussion strategy pertaining to the discussion as a whole.[10] In this analytic research, coordinated topical choices, coordinated adaptation to audience, and coordinated presentational choices need to be considered as well as coordination between the successive moves made in a particular discussion stage or throughout the discussion. The most promising angle to start from seems to me the analysis of the horizontal coordination of choices made regarding one particular aspect, if possible concentrating on a specific choice that is made regarding this aspect. For instance, Snoeck Henkemans' (2009) study of the strategic function of the use of the figure of *praeteritio* at different points in the various discussion stages may be a good point of departure for a more general analysis of the strategic function that exploiting this presentational device may have, in combination with other presentaion choices serving the same strategic purpose, in establishing the outcome of a particular discussion stage and the discussion as a whole. In principle, similar analyses of strategic maneuvering in a particular discussion stage and analyses of strategic maneuvering in the discussion as a whole can be made starting from specific analyses on the level of strategic maneuvers regarding particular ways of adapting to audience demand and particular ways of making topical choices.[11]

---

10. Although strategies may be "local" in the sense that they aim for a particular outcome, say a certain division of the burden of proof, in a specific discussion stage, so that they belong to a specific category of strategic maneuvering, say opening maneuvering, in principle they will also be intended to have consequences for the next stages and can be said to transcend the stage boundaries in this particular sense. See Tseronis (2009) for strategic maneuvering with the burden of proof that is aimed at having such further consequences.

11. Cf. Tindale (2009), who explores the rationale for and the role of rhetoric in the strategic maneuvering project of pragma-dialectics and compares it with his own implementation of rhetorical features. He makes a case for considering the active ways audiences influence the strategies of arguers and for seeing the role of rhetoric in argumentation as both fundamental and reasonable on its own terms.

从行为角度识别不同交际活动类型
10.7 Characterizing communicative activity types praxeologically

The fifth type of research projects to be considered is immediately related to the actual practice of argumentation in the various communicative domains. These projects belong to the "practical component" of the complex research program I envisage argumentation theorists to carry out. In this component, insights acquired in the other components of the research program are put to good use in dealing with argumentative discourse taking place in communicative activity types instrumental in specific institutional contexts. The conduct of strategic maneuvering in these activity types is always dependent on the constraints imposed on the discourse by the conventional preconditions of the argumentative activity type concerned. In order to deal well with contextual variety, it would be enlightening to make a comparison between the distinctive features of the prototypical modes of strategic maneuvering taking place in the various communicative activity types, so that these activity types can be characterized praxeologically, i.e. according to the argumentative conduct typical of a certain kind of communicative praxis. Such a comparison provides more insight into the commonalities and differences between similar modes of strategic maneuvering in institutionally motivated argumentative practices.

In my view, it would be worthwhile to focus on communicative activity types representing institutionally conventionalized argumentative practices that serve a broad variety of institutional goals and reflect different degrees of conventionalization. At the University of Amsterdam, we concentrate on communicative activity types from the political, the juridical,[12] the scholarly, and the medical domain, involving different kinds of institutional conventionalization and requiring different kinds of expertise. A cluster of recently completed research projects concentrating on the study of confrontational strategic maneuvering in the political domain prepares the ground for making a first systematic comparison.[13] Andone (2009a, 2009b) investigates the conventional

---

12. Feteris (2009), for one, gives a pragma-dialectical analysis of strategic maneuvering in the justification of judicial decisions by analyzing how a judge tried to reconcile dialectical and rhetorical aims in the famous Holy Trinity case dealt with by the US Supreme Court. She shows how the judge, to make an exception to a legal rule, tries to meet the dialectical reasonableness norm by seeing to it that his standpoint is sufficiently defended according to the requirements of the burden of proof of a judge in a rational critical discussion while trying at the same time to be rhetorically convincing by presenting the decision as a choice that agrees with argument schemes and starting points accepted by the legal community in the US and the US community as a whole.

13. In addition to the projects discussed here, Iețcu-Fairclough (2009) brings together a pragma-dialectical conception of argumentation, a sociological conception of legitimacy, and a sociological theory of the political field. In analyzing a political speech as an example of adjudication in the political field she explores the way in which strategic maneuvering is constrained by the logic of the political field, both in the sense that this logic restricts the possibilities of strategic maneuvering and in the sense that it offers field-specific rhetorical opportunities to the arguer. Zarefsky (2009) lists a number of common modes of strategic maneuvering in political

preconditions imposed on confrontational strategic maneuvering in the argumentative activity type of a political interview. She provides an analysis of the responses given by politicians to an accusation of inconsistency and distinguishes between reasonable responses and responses derailing into fallaciousness. Mohammed (2009a, 2009b) concentrates on the argumentative activity type of Prime Minister's Question Time in the British House of Commons. She makes clear how an analysis of strategic maneuvering in response to an accusation of inconsistency can benefit from an understanding of the specific institutional demands and conventional preconditions of the argumentative activity type. Tonnard (2009, forthcoming) analyzes how, in the General Debate in Dutch parliament, Geert Wilders, MP, manages to steer the discussion continually toward his favorite topic of "the dangers of Islam" by exploiting the conventional preconditions of this argumentative activity type. Wilders' choice of presentational means is shown to be the predominant aspect in which his topic-shifting and polarizing strategic maneuvering manifests itself.

---

argumentation: changing the subject, modifying the relevant audience, appealing to liberal and conservative presumptions, reframing the argument, using condensation symbols, employing the locus of the irreparable, and argumentative use of figures and tropes. In his view, evaluating strategic maneuvering in political argumentation is difficult, because the activity types concerned dictate wide latitude for the arguers, so that there are few cases of unquestionable derailment.

References 参考文献

Aakhus, M. (2003). Neither naïve nor critical reconstruction: Dispute mediators, impasse and the design of argumentation. *Argumentation, 17*(3), 265–290.

Aakhus, M., & Jackson, S. (2005). Technology, interaction, and design. In K. Fitch & R. Sanders (Eds.), *Handbook of language and social interaction* (pp. 411–436). Mahwah, NJ: Lawrence Erlbaum.

Agricola, R. (1967). *De inventione dialectica libri tres*. (Original work published in 1479)

Agricola, R. (1991). *Over dialectica en humanisme* [On dialectic and Humanism] (M. van der Poel, Ed.). Baarn: Ambo.

Albert, H. (1975). *Traktat über kritische Vernunft* [Treatise on critical reason] (3rd ed.). Tübingen: Mohr.

Alphen, E. van, Duyvendak, L., Meyer, M., & Peperkamp, B. (1996). *Op poëtische wijze. Een handleiding voor het lezen van poezie* [In a poetic way. A guidebook for reading poetry]. Bussum: Coutinho.

Amjarso, B. (2008). Addressing anticipated countermoves as a persuasive form of strategic manoeuvring. In F. H. van Eemeren, D. C. Williams & I. Z. Zagar (Eds.), *Understanding argumentation. Work in progress* (pp. 27–38). Amsterdam: Sic Sat.

Andone, C. (2009a). Accusing someone of an inconsistency as a confrontational way of strategic manoeuvring. In F. H. van Eemeren (Ed.), *Examining argumentation in context: Fifteen studies on strategic maneuvering* (pp. 153–170). Amsterdam: John Benjamins.

Andone, C. (2009b). Confrontational strategic maneuvers in a political interview. Unpublished doctoral dissertation, University of Amsterdam.

Anscombre, J. C. (1994). La nature des topoï [The nature of the topics]. In J. C. Anscombre (Ed.), *La théorie des topoï* (pp. 49–84). Paris: Éditions Kimé.

Anscombre, J. C., & Ducrot, O. (1983). *L'argumentation dans la langue* [Argumentation in language]. Brussels: Pierre Mardaga.

Aristotle (1928a). *Posterior analytics* (W. D. Ross, Ed.). Oxford: Clarendon Press.

Aristotle (1928b). *Prior analytics* (W. D. Ross, Ed.). Oxford: Clarendon Press.

Aristotle (1928c). *Sophistical refutations*. (W. D. Ross, Ed.). Oxford: Clarendon Press.

Aristotle (1960). *Topics* (E. S. Forster, Trans.). Cambridge, MA: Harvard University Press. (Loeb Classical Library)

Aristotle (1991). *On rhetoric*. In G. A. Kennedy, *Aristotle. On rhetoric: A theory of civic discourse* (pp. 23–282). New York, NY: Oxford University Press.

Aristotle (2002). *Nicomachean ethics* (S. Broadie & C. Rowe, Eds.). New York, NY: Oxford University Press.

Atkin, A., & Richardson, J. E. (2005). Constructing the (imagined) antagonist in advertising argumentation. In F. H. van Eemeren & P. Houtlosser, *Argumentation in practice* (pp. 163–180). Amsterdam: John Benjamins.

Atkinson, J. M., & Heritage, J. (Eds.) (1984). *Structures of social action: Studies in conversation analysis*. Cambridge: Cambridge University Press.

Auer, J. J. (1962). The counterfeit debates. In S. Kraus (Ed.), *The great debates: Background, perspective, effects* (pp. 142-150). Bloomington, IN: Indiana University Press.

Axelrod, R. (1977). Argumentation in foreign policy settings: Britain in 1918, Munich in 1938, and Japan in 1970. In W. Zartman (Ed.), *The negotiation process* (pp. 175-192). Beverly Hills, CA: Sage Publications.

Bakhtin, M. M. (1986). *Speech genres and other late* essays (V. W. McGee, Trans.; C. Emerson & M. Holquist, Eds.). Austin, TX: University of Texas Press.

Barth, E. M. (1972). *Evaluaties* (Evaluations). Inaugural address University of Utrecht, June 2. Assen: Van Gorcum.

Barth, E. M., & Krabbe, E. C. W. (1982). *From axiom to dialogue. A philosophical study of logics and argumentation.* Berlin: de Gruyter.

Barth, E. M., & Martens, J. L. (1977). Argumentum ad hominem: From chaos to formal dialectic. The method of dialogue tableaus as a tool in the theory of fallacy. *Logique et Analyse (NS), 20*, 76-96.

Bartley, W. W. (1984). *The retreat to commitment* (2nd ed.). LaSalle, IL: Open Court.

Battistelli, T. (2009). *Rhetoric, dialectic and derailment in church-state arguments.* Paper presented at the 2009 Conference of the Ontario Society for the Study of Argumentation, Windsor, Ontario.

Bell, A. (1984). Language style as audience design. *Language in Society, 13*, 145-204.

Bell, A. (2001). Back in style: Reworking audience design. In P. Eckert & J. R. Rickford (Eds.), *Style and sociolinguistic variation* (pp. 139-169). Cambridge: Cambridge University Press.

Bench-Capon, T. J. M., & Dunne, P. E. (2007). Argumentation in Artificial Intelligence. *Artificial Intelligence, 171*, 619-641.

Benoit, W. L., & D'Agostine, J. M. (1994). "The case of the midnight judges" and multiple audience discourse: Chief Justice Marshall and *Marbury v. Madison. Southern Communication Journal, 59*, 89-96.

Benoit, W. L., & Lindsey, J. J. (1987). Argument strategies: Antidote to Tylenol's poisoned image. Journal of the American Forensic Association, 23, 136-146.

Bentham, J. (1838-1843). *The works of Jeremy Bentham, published under the supervision of his executor, John Bowring.* Edinburgh: Tait.

Beth, E. W. (1955). Semantic entailment and formal derivability. *Mededelingen der Koninklijke Nederlandse Akademie van Wetenschappen, 18*, 309-342.

Bhatia, V. K. (1993). *Analysing genre. Language use in professional settings.* London: Longman.

Bhatia, V. K. (2004). *Worlds of written discourse. A genre-based view.* London: Continuum.

Bird, O. (1962). The tradition of the logical topics: Aristotle to Ockham. *Journal of the History of Ideas, 23*, 307-323.

Biro, J., & Siegel, H. (1992). Normativity, argumentation and an epistemic theory of fallacies. In F. H. van Eemeren, R. Grootendorst, J. A. Blair & C. A. Willard (Eds.), *Argumentation illuminated* (pp. 85-103). Amsterdam: Sic Sat.

Biro, J., & Siegel, H. (1995). Epistemic normativity, argumentation, and fallacies. In F. H. van Eemeren, R. Grootendorst, J. A. Blair & C. A. Willard (Eds.), *Analysis and Evaluation. Proceedings of the Third ISSA Conference on Argumentation (University of Amsterdam, June 21-24, 1994), Volume II* (pp. 286-299). Amsterdam: Sic Sat.

Biro, J., & Siegel, H. (2006). In defense of the objective epistemic approach to argumentation. *Informal Logic, 26*(1), 91-101.

Bitzer, L. (1968). The rhetorical situation. *Philosophy and Rhetoric, 1*, 1-14.

Bizzell, P. (Ed.) (2006). *Rhetorical agendas. Political, ethical, spiritual.* Mahwah, NJ: Lawrence Erlbaum.
Blair, J. A. (2007). The logic of informal logic. In H. V. Hansen, C. W. Tindale, R. H. Johnson & G. D. Godden (Eds.), *Dissensus and the Search for Common Ground. Proceedings of the Seventh OSSA Conference, University of Windsor* (CD-ROM). St. Catherines, ON: OSSA.
Blair, J. A., & Johnson, R. H. (1987). Argumentation as dialectical. *Argumentation, 1*(1), 41–56.
Bonevac, D. (2003). Pragma-dialectics and beyond. *Argumentation, 17*(4), 451–459.
Bons, J. A. E. (2002). Reasonable argument before Aristotle: The roots of the enthymeme. In F. H. van Eemeren & P. Houtlosser (Eds.), *Dialectic and rhetoric: The warp and woof of argumentation analysis* (pp. 13–28). Dordrecht: Kluwer Academic.
Braet, A. (1984). *De klassieke statusleer in een modern perspectief. Een historisch-systematische bijdrage tot de argumentatieleer* [The classical *stasis* theory in a modern perspective]. Groningen: Wolters-Noordhoff.
Braet, A. (2007a). *De redelijkheid van de klassieke retorica: De bijdrage van klassieke retorici aan de argumentatietheorie* [The reasonableness of classical rhetoric: The contribution of classical rhetoricians to argumentation theory]. Leiden: Leiden University Press.
Braet, A. (2007b). *Retorische kritiek. Overtuigingskracht van Cicero tot Balkenende* [Rhetorical criticism. Persuasive power from Cicero to Balkenende]. Den Haag: SDU.
Brinton, A. (1995). The ad hominem. In H. V. Hansen & R. C. Pinto (Eds.), *Fallacies. Contemporary and classical readings* (pp. 213–222). University Park, PA: Penn State Press.
Brummett, B. (2008). *A rhetoric of style.* Carbondale, IL: Southern Illinois University Press.
Burke, K. (1969a). *A grammar of motives.* Berkeley, CA: University of California Press (Original work published in 1945)
Burke, K. (1969b). *A rhetoric of motives.* Berkeley, CA: University of California Press. (Original work published in 1950)
Campbell, G. (1963). *The philosophy of rhetoric. Edited with a new introduction by L.F. Bitzer.* Carbondale and Edwardsville, IL: Southern Illinois University Press.
Ceaser, J. W., Thurow, G. E., Tulis, J. K., & Bessette, J. M. The rise of the rhetorical presidency. *Presidential Studies Quarterly, 11*, 158–71.
Cherwitz, R. A. (Ed.) (1990). The philosophical foundations of rhetoric. In R. A. Cherwitz (Ed.), *Rhetoric and Philosophy* (pp. 1–19). Hillsdale, NJ: Lawrence Erlbaum.
Cicero (1942). *De oratore* (E. W. Sutton & H. Rackham, Eds.). London: Heinemann.
Cicero (1949). *De inventione. De optimo genere oratorum. Topica* (M. Hubbell, Ed.). London: Heinemann.
Cicero (2001). *On the ideal orator* (J. M. May & J. Wisse, Trans.). New York, NY: Oxford University Press.
Clayman, S., & Heritage, J. (2002). *The news interview. Journalists and public figures on the air.* Cambridge: Cambridge University Press.
Cohen, T. (1973). Illocutions and perlocutions. *Foundations of Language, 9,* 492–503.
Conley, T. M. (1990). *Rhetoric in the European tradition.* Chicago, IL: The University of Chicago Press.
Cooper, L. (1932). *The rhetoric of Aristotle.* New York, NY: Prentice Hall.
Copi, I.M. (1986). *Introduction to logic* (7th ed.). New York, NY: Macmillan. (Original work published in 1976)
Crawshay-Williams, R. (1957). *Methods and criteria of reasoning. An inquiry into the structure of controversy.* London: Routledge & Kegan Paul.

Crosswhite, J. (1993). Being unreasonable: Perelman and the problem of fallacies. *Argumentation, 7*, 385–402.

Crosswhite, J. (1996). *The rhetoric of reason: Writing and the attractions of argument*. Madison, WI: University of Wisconsin Press.

Crosswhite, J. (2000). Nature and reason: Inertia and argumentation. In H. V. Hansen, C. W. Tindale & S. Raposo, *Argumentation at the Century's Turn* (CD-ROM). St. Catherines, ON: OSSA.

Dascal, M. (2001). How rational can a polemic across the analytic-continental 'divide' be? *International Journal of Philosophical Studies, 9*(3), 313–339.

Dascal, M. (2008). Dichotomies and types of debate. In F. H. van Eemeren & B. Garssen, *Controversy and confrontation. Relating controversy analysis with argumentation theory* (pp. 27–50). Amsterdam: John Benjamins.

Dascal, M., & Chang, H. (Eds.) (2007). *Traditions of controversy*. Amsterdam: John Benjamins.

Dascal, M., & Gross, A. G. (1999). The marriage of pragmatics and rhetoric. *Philosophy and Rhetoric, 32*(2), 107–130.

De Morgan, A. (1847). *Formal Logic*. London: Taylor and Walton.

Donohue, W. A., Allen, M., & Burrell, N. (1988). Mediator communicative competence. *Communication Monographs, 55*, 104–119.

Drake, L .E., & Donohue, W. A. (1996). Communication framing theory in conflict resolution. *Communication Research, 23*(3), 297–322.

Ducrot, O. (1988). Topoï et formes topiques [Topoi and topical forms]. *Bulletin d'Etudes de Linguistique Française, 22*, 1–14.

Ducrot, O., Bourcier, D., & Bruxelles, S. (1980). *Les mots du discours* [The words of discourse]. Paris: Les Éditions de Minuit.

Eagly, A. H., & Chaiken, S. (1993). *The psychology of attitudes*. Fort Worth, TX: Harcourt Brace Jovanovich.

Ede, L., & Lunsford, A. (1984). Audience addressed/audience invoked: The role of audience in composition theory and pedagogy. *College Composition and Communication, 35*(2), 155–171.

Eemeren, F. H. van (1986). Dialectical analysis as a normative reconstruction of argumentative discourse. *Text, 6*(1), 1–16.

Eemeren, F. H. van (1987a). Argumentation studies' five estates. In J.W. Wenzel (Ed.), *Argument and critical practices: Proceedings of the fifth SCA/AFA Conference on Argumentation* (pp 9–24). Annandale, VA: Speech Communication Association.

Eemeren, F. H. van (1987b). For reason's sake: Maximal argumentative analysis of discourse. In F. H. van Eemeren, R. Grootendorst, J. A. Blair & C. A. Willard (Eds.), *Argumentation: Across the Lines of Discipline. Proceedings of the Conference on Argumentation, 1986* (pp. 201–215). Dordrecht: Foris.

Eemeren, F. H. van (1990). The study of argumentation as normative pragmatics. *Text: An Interdisciplinary Journal for the Study of Discourse, 10*(1/2), 37–44.

Eemeren, F. H. van (Ed.) (2001). *Crucial concepts in argumentation theory*. Amsterdam: Amsterdam University Press.

Eemeren, F. H. van (2002). Democracy and argumentation. *Controversia 1*(1), 69–84.

Eemeren, F. H. van (2006). Argumentationstheorie nach der Neuen Rhetorik [Argumentation theory after the New Rhetoric]. In J. Kopperschmidt (Ed.), *Die neue Rhetorik – Studien zu Chaim Perelman* (pp. 345–382). Paderborn: Wilhelm Fink Verlag.

Eemeren, F. H. van (2008, February 14). *Countering fallacious moves*. Plenary speech at the Conference 'Strategies in Argumentation' at the University of Groningen organized on the occasion of the retirement of Professor Erik C. W. Krabbe. Groningen University.

Eemeren, F. H. van, & Garssen, B. (Eds.) (2008). *Controversy and confrontation. Relating controversy analysis with argumentation theory*. Amsterdam: John Benjamins.

Eemeren, F. H. van, & Garssen, B. (2010). Constraints on political deliberation: European parliamentary debate as an argumentative activity type. *Controversia, 1*(1), 13-32.

Eemeren, F. H. van, Garssen, B., & Meuffels, H. L. M. (2003). "I don't have anything to prove here": Judgements of the fallacy of shifting the burden of proof. In F. H. van Eemeren, A. F. Snoeck Henkemans, J. A. Blair & C. A. Willard, *Proceedings of the Fifth Conference of the International Society for the Study of Argumentation*. Amsterdam: Sic Sat.

Eemeren, F. H. van, Garssen, B., & Meuffels, H. L. M. (2008). Reasonableness in confrontation. Empirical evidence concerning the assessment of ad hominem fallacies. In F. H. van Eemeren & B. Garssen (Eds.), *Controversy and confrontation. Relating controversy analysis with argumentation theory* (pp. 181-195). Amsterdam: John Benjamins.

Eemeren, F. H. van, Garssen, B., & Meuffels, H. L. M. (2009). *Fallacies and judgments of reasonableness. Empirical research concerning the pragma-dialectical discussion rules*. Dordrecht: Springer.

Eemeren, F. H. van, & Grootendorst, R. (1984). *Speech acts in argumentative discussions. A theoretical model for the analysis of discussions directed towards solving conflicts of opinion*. Berlin: de Gruyter.

Eemeren, F. H. van, & Grootendorst, R. (1991). The study of argumentation from a speech act perspective. In J. Verschueren (Ed.), *Pragmatics at Issue. Selected Papers of the International Pragmatics Conference, Antwerp, August 17-22, 1987. Volume I* (pp. 151-170). Amsterdam: John Benjamins.

Eemeren, F. H. van, & Grootendorst, R. (1992a). *Argumentation, communication, and fallacies. A pragma-dialectical perspective*. Hillsdale, NJ: Lawrence Erlbaum.

Eemeren, F. H. van, & Grootendorst, R. (1992b). Relevance reviewed: The case of argumentum ad hominem. *Argumentation, 6*(2), 141-159.

Eemeren, F. H. van, & Grootendorst, R. (1994). Rationale for a pragma–dialectical perspective. In F. H. van Eemeren & R. Grootendorst (Eds.), *Studies in pragma-dialectics* (pp. 11-28). Amsterdam: Sic Sat.

Eemeren, F. H. van, & Grootendorst, R. (2004). *A systematic theory of argumentation: The pragma-dialectical approach*. Cambridge: Cambridge University Press.

Eemeren, F. H. van, Grootendorst, R., Jackson, S., & Jacobs, S. (1993). *Reconstructing argumentative discourse*. Tuscaloosa, AL: University of Alabama Press.

Eemeren, F. H. van, Grootendorst, Jackson, S, & Jacobs, S. (1997). Argumentation. In T. van Dijk (Ed.), *Discourse studies: A multidisciplinary introduction* (Vol. I: *Discourse as structure and process*) (pp 208-229). London: Sage.

Eemeren, F. H. van, Grootendorst, R., & Snoeck Henkemans, A. F. (2002). *Argumentation. Analysis, evaluation, presentation*. Mahwah, NJ: Lawrence Erlbaum.

Eemeren, F. H. van, Grootendorst, R., Snoeck Henkemans, A. F., Blair, J. A., Johnson, R. H., Krabbe, E. C. W., Plantin, C., Walton, D. N., Willard, C. A., Woods, J., & Zarefsky, D. (1996). *Fundamentals of argumentation theory. Handbook of historical backgrounds and contemporary developments*. Mahwah, NJ: Lawrence Erlbaum.

Eemeren, F. H. van, & Houtlosser, P. (1997). Rhetorical rationales for dialectical moves. In J. Klumpp (Ed.), *Proceedings of the Tenth NCA/AFA Conference on Argumentation* (pp. 51-56). Annandale, VA: Speech Communication Association.

Eemeren, F. H. van, & Houtlosser, P. (1998). Rhetoric in pragma-dialectics. *Armenian Mind, 2*(1), 24-44.

Eemeren, F. H. van, & Houtlosser, P. (1999a). Strategic manoeuvring in argumentative discourse. *Discourse Studies, 1*(4), 479–497.

Eemeren, F. H. van, & Houtlosser, P. (1999b). William the Silent's argumentative discourse. In F. H. van Eemeren, R. Grootendorst, J. A. Blair & C. A. Willard (Eds.), *Proceedings of the Fourth Conference of the International Society for the Study of Argumentation* (pp. 168–171). Amsterdam: Sic Sat.

Eemeren, F. H. van, & Houtlosser, P. (2000a). Rhetorical analysis within a pragma-dialectical framework. The case of R. J. Reynolds. *Argumentation, 14*(3), 293–305.

Eemeren, F. H. van, & Houtlosser, P. (2000b). The rhetoric of William the Silent's Apologie. A dialectical perspective. In T. Suzuki, Y. Yano & T. Kato (Eds.), *Proceedings of the First Tokyo Conference on Argumentation* (pp. 37–40). Tokyo: Japan Debate Association.

Eemeren, F. H. van, & Houtlosser, P. (Eds.) (2002). *Dialectic and Rhetoric: The warp and woof of argumentation analysis.* Dordrecht: Kluwer Academic.

Eemeren, F. H. van, & Houtlosser, P. (2002a). Strategic maneuvering in argumentative discourse: Maintaining a delicate balance. In F. H. van Eemeren & P. Houtlosser (Eds.), *Dialectic and rhetoric: The warp and woof of argumentation analysis* (pp. 131–159). Dordrecht: Kluwer Academic.

Eemeren, F. H. van, & Houtlosser, P. (2002b). Strategic maneuvering with the burden of proof. In F. H. van Eemeren (Ed.), *Advances in pragma-dialectics* (pp. 13–28). Amsterdam: Sic Sat.

Eemeren, F. H. van, & Houtlosser, P. (2003a). A pragmatic view of the burden of proof. In F. H. van Eemeren, J. A. Blair, C. A. Willard & A. F. Snoeck Henkemans (Eds.), *Anyone who has a view. Theoretical contributions to the study of argumentation* (pp. 123–132). Dordrecht: Kluwer Academic.

Eemeren, F. H. van, & Houtlosser, P. (2003b). Fallacies as derailments of strategic maneuvering: The *argumentum ad verecundiam*, a case in point. In F. H. van Eemeren, J. A. Blair, C. A. Willard, & A. F. Snoeck Henkemans (Eds.), *Proceedings of the Fifth Conference of the International Society for the Study of Argumentation* (pp. 289–292). Amsterdam: Sic Sat.

Eemeren, F. H. van, & Houtlosser, P. (2005a). More about an arranged marriage. In C. A. Willard (Ed.), *Critical Problems in Argumentation. Selected Papers from the Thirteenth Biennial Conference on Argumentation Sponsored by the American Forensics Association and National Communication Association August, 2003* (pp. 345–355). Washington, DC: National Communication Association.

Eemeren, F. H. van, & Houtlosser, P. (2005b). Theoretical construction and argumentative reality: An analytic model of critical discussion and conventionalised types of argumentative activity. In D. Hitchcock, & D. Farr (Eds.), *The Uses of Argument. Proceedings of a Conference at McMaster University, 18–21 May 2005* (pp. 75–84). Hamilton, ON: Ontario Society for the Study of Argumentation.

Eemeren, F. H. van, & Houtlosser, P. (2006). Flexible facts: A pragma-dialectical analysis of a burden of proof manipulation. In F. H. van Eemeren, M. Hazen, P. Houtlosser & D. C. Williams (Eds.), *Contemporary perspectives on argumentation: Views from the Venice Argumentation Conference* (pp. 37–46). Amsterdam: Sic Sat.

Eemeren, F. H. van, & Houtlosser, P. (2007a). The contextuality of fallacies. *Informal Logic, 27*(1), 59–67.

Eemeren, F. H. van, & Houtlosser, P. (2007b). Countering fallacious moves. *Argumentation, 21*(3), 243–252. (Special issue on metadialogues: Krabbe's immanent dialectic)

Eemeren, F. H. van, & Houtlosser, P. (2008). Rhetoric in a dialectical framework: Fallacies as derailments of strategic manoeuvring. In E. Weigand (Ed.), *Dialogue and rhetoric* (pp. 133–151). Amsterdam: John Benjamins.

Eemeren, F. H. van, & Houtlosser, P. (2009). Seizing the occasion: Parameters for analysing ways of strategic manoeuvring. In F. H. van Eemeren & B. Garssen (Eds.), *Pondering on problems of argumentation. Twenty essays on theoretical issues* (pp. 3–14). Amsterdam: Springer.

Eemeren, F. H. van, Houtlosser, P., Ihnen, C., & Lewinski, M. (to be published). Contextual considerations in the evaluation of argumentation.

Eemeren, F. H. van, Houtlosser, P. & Snoeck Henkemans, A. F. (2007). *Argumentative indicators in discourse. A pragma-dialectical study.* Dordrecht: Springer.

Eemeren, F. H. van, Houtlosser, P., & Snoeck Henkemans, A. F. (2008). Dialectical profiles and indicators of argumentative moves. *Journal of Pragmatics, 20*, 475–493.

Ehninger, D., & Brockriede, W. (1963). *Decision by debate.* New York, NY: Dodd, Mead and Company.

Fahnestock, J. (1999). *Rhetorical figures in science.* New York, NY: Oxford University Press.

Fahnestock, J. (2005). Rhetorical stylistics. *Language and Literature, 14*(3), 215–230.

Fahnestock, J. (2009). Quid pro nobis. Rhetorical stylistics for argument analysis. In F. H. van Eemeren (Ed.), *Examining argumentation in context. Fifteen studies on strategic maneuvering* (pp. 131–152). Amsterdam: John Benjamins.

Fahnestock, J., & Secor, M. J. (1983). Grounds for argument: Stasis theory and the topoi. In D. Zarefsky, M. O. Sillars & J. Rhodes (Eds.), *Argument in Transition: Proceedings of the Third Summer Conference on Argumentation* (pp. 135–146). Annandale, VA: Speech Communication Association.

Fairclough, N. (1995). *Critical discourse analysis: The critical study of language.* London: Longman.

Farrell, T. B. (1993). *Norms of rhetorical culture.* New Haven, CT: Yale University Press.

Feteris, E. T. (1987). The dialectical role of the judge in a Dutch legal process. In J. W. Wenzel (Ed.), *Argument and Critical Practices. Proceedings of the Fifth SCA/AFA Conference on Argumentation* (pp. 335–339). Annandale, VA: Speech Communication Association.

Feteris, E. T. (1993). The judge as a critical antagonist in a legal process: A pragma-dialectical perspective. In R. E. McKerrow (Ed.), *Argument and the Postmodern Challenge. Proceedings of the Eighth SCA/AFA Conference on Argumentation* (pp. 476–480). Annandale, VA: Speech Communication Association.

Feteris, E. T. (2009). Strategic maneuvering in the justification of judicial decisions. In F. H. van Eemeren (Ed.), *Examining argumentation in context: Fifteen studies on strategic maneuvering* (pp. 93–114). Amsterdam: John Benjamins.

Finocchiaro, M. (1980). *Galileo and the art of reasoning.* Dordrecht: Reidel.

Finocchiaro, M. (2005a). *Arguments about arguments. Systematic, critical, and historical essays in logical theory.* Cambridge: Cambridge University Press.

Finocchiaro, M. (2005b). Mill's On Liberty and argumentation theory. In D. Hitchcock (Ed.), *The Uses of Argument: Proceedings of a Conference at McMaster University, May 18–21 2005* (pp. 89–98). Hamilton, ON: Ontario Society for the Study of Argumentation.

Finocchiaro, M. (2006). Reflections on the hyper dialectical definition of argument. In P. Houtlosser & M. A. van Rees, *Considering pragma-dialectics: A festschrift for Frans H. van Eemeren on the occasion of his 60th birthday* (pp. 51–62). Mahwah, NJ: Lawrence Erlbaum.

Fisher, R., Ury, W., & Patton, B. (1991). *Getting to yes: Negotiating agreement without giving in* (2nd ed.). New York, NY: Penguin.

Foss, S. K. (2004). *Rhetorical criticism. Exploration & practice* (3rd ed). Long Grove, IL: Waveland.

Foss, S. K., Foss, K. A., & Trapp, R. (1985). *Contemporary perspectives on rhetoric*. Prospect Heights, IL: Waveland.

Foss, S. K., & Griffin, C. L. (1995). Beyond persuasion: A proposal for an invitational rhetoric. Communication Monographs, 62(1), 2–18.

Foucault, M. (1972). The archaeology of knowledge (A. M. Sheridan Smith, Trans.). New York, NY: Pantheon.

Freeley, A. J. (1993). *Argumentation and debate: Critical thinking for reasoned decision making*. Belmont, CA: Wadsworth.

Freeman, J. B. (1991). *Dialectics and the macrostructure of arguments*. Berlin: de Gruyter.

Gaonkar, D. P. (1990). Rhetoric and its double: Reflections on the rhetorical turn in the human sciences. In H. W. Simons, *The rhetorical turn: Invention and persuasion in the conduct of inquiry* (pp. 341–366). Chicago, IL: University of Chicago Press.

Garssen, B. (2001). Argument schemes. In F. H. van Eemeren (Ed.), *Crucial concepts in argumentation theory* (pp. 81–100). Amsterdam: Amsterdam University Press.

Garssen, B. (2009). *Ad hominem* in disguise: Strategic manoeuvring with direct personal attacks. *Argumentation and Advocacy, 45*(Spring), 207–213.

Gaskins, R. H. (1992). *Burdens of proof in modern discourse*. New Haven, CT: Yale University Press.

Giles, H., Coupland, J., & Coupland, N. (1991). Accomodation theory: Communication, context, and consequence. In H. Giles, J. Coupland & N. Coupland (Eds.), *Contexts of accomodation: Developments in applied sociolinguistics* (pp. 1–68). Cambridge: Cambridge University Press.

Goffman, E. (1970). *Strategic interaction*. Oxford: Blackwell.

Goffman, E. (1986). *Frame analysis. An essay on the organization of experience. With a foreword by B.M. Berger*. Boston, MA: Northeastern University Press. (Original work published in 1974)

Goldberg, S. B., Sander, F. E. A., Rogers, N. H., & Cole, S. R. (2007). *Dispute resolution: Negotiation, mediation and other processes* (5th ed.). Austin, TX: Wolters Kluwer.

Goodnight, G. T. (1982). The personal, technical, and public spheres of argument: A speculative inquiry into the art of public deliberation. *Journal of the American Forensic Association, 18*, 214–227.

Goodnight, G. T. (2009). Strategic maneuvering in direct-to-consumer drug advertising: Argument, contestation, and institutions. In F. H. van Eemeren (Ed.), *Examining argumentation in context: Fifteen studies on strategic maneuvering* (pp. 77–92). Amsterdam: John Benjamins.

Goodwin, J. (2002). Designing issues. In F. H. van Eemeren & P. Houtlosser (Eds.), *Dialectic and rhetoric: The warp and woof of argumentation analysis* (pp. 81–96). Dordrecht: Kluwer Academic.

Govier, T. (1998). Arguing forever? Or: Two tiers of argument appraisal. In H. V. Hansen, C. W. Tindale & A. V. Colman (Eds.), *Argumentation & Rhetoric* (CD-ROM). St. Catherines, ON: OSSA.

Govier, T. (1999). *The philosophy of argument*. Newport News, VA: Vale Press.

Govier, T. (2006). My interlocutor. In P. Houtlosser & M. A. van Rees (Eds.), *Considering pragma-dialectics: A festschrift for Frans H. van Eemeren on the occasion of his 60th birthday* (pp. 87–96). Mahwah, NJ: Lawrence Erlbaum.

Grassi, E. (1980). *Rhetoric as philosophy: The humanist tradition* (J. M. Krois & A. Azodi, Trans.). University Park, PA: Pennsylvania State University Press.

Gray, B. (2006). Mediation as framing and framing within mediation. In M. S. Herrman, (Ed.), *The Blackwell handbook of mediation: Bridging theory, research and practice* (pp. 193–216). Oxford: Blackwell.

Greco Morasso, S. (2009). *Argumentative and other communicative strategies of the mediation practice*. Unpublished doctoral dissertation, University of Lugano, Switzerland.

Green, L. D. (1990). Aristotelian rhetoric, dialectic, and the traditions of antistrophos. *Rhetorica, 8*(1), 5–27.

Grice, H. P. (1975). Logic and conversation. In P. Cole & J. L. Morgan (Eds.), *Syntax and semantics 3: Speech Acts* (pp. 43–58). New York, NY: Academic Press.

Grice, H. P. (1989). *Studies in the way of words*. Cambridge, MA: Harvard University Press.

Grimaldi, W. M. (1972). *Studies in the philosophy of Aristotle's Rhetoric*. Wiesbaden: Steiner.

Gronbeck, B. E. (Ed.) (1989). *Spheres of Argument. Proceedings of the Sixth SCA/AFA Conference on Argumentation*. Annandale, VA: SCA.

Groot, A. D. de (1969). *Methodology: Foundations of inference and research in the behavioral sciences*. The Hague: Mouton.

Groot, A. D. de (1984). The theory of science forum: Subject and purport. *Methodology and Science, 17*(4), 230–259.

Gross, A. G., & Dearin, R. D. (2002). *Chaim Perelman*. Albany, NY: SUNY Press.

Habermas, J. (1971). Vorbereitende Bemarkungen zu einer Theorie der kommunikativen Kompetenz [Preparatory remarks on a theory of communicative competence]. In J. Habermas & H. Luhmann, *Theorie der Gesellschaft oder Sozialtechnologie; Was leistet die Systemforschung?* (pp. 107–141). Frankfurt: Surkamp.

Habermas, J. (1981). *Theorie des kommunikativen Handelns* [Theory of communicative action]. Frankfurt: Surkamp.

Habermas, J. (1994). Postscript to Faktizität und Geltung [Postscript to between facts and norms]. *Philosophy & Social Criticism, 20*(4), 135–150.

Habermas, J. (1996). *Between facts and norms* (Trans., W. Rehg). Cambridge, MA: MIT Press.

Hall, P. A., & Taylor, R. C. R. (1996). Political science and the three new institutionalisms. *Political studies, 44*, 936–957.

Hamblin, C. L. (1970). *Fallacies*. London: Methuen.

Hamblin, C. L. (1971), Mathematical models of dialogue. *Theoria, 37*, 130–155.

Hansen, H. V. (2002). The straw thing of fallacy theory: The Standard Definition of 'fallacy'. *Argumentation, 16*(2), 133–155.

Hansen, H. V. (2006). Mill and pragma-dialectics. In P. Houtlosser & M. A. van Rees (Eds.), *Considering pragma-dialectics: A festschrift for Frans H. van Eemeren on the occasion of his 60th birthday* (pp. 97–107). Mahwah, NJ: Lawrence Erlbaum.

Hansen, H. V., & Pinto, R. C. (1995). *Fallacies: Classical and contemporary readings*. University Park, PA: Penn State Press.

Hare, R. M. (1952). *The language of morals*. London: Oxford University Press.

Havet, E. (1846). *Etude sur la rhétorique d'Aristote* [Studies on Aristotle's rhetoric]. Paris: Jules DelaLain.

Heritage, J. (1984). A change-of-state token and aspects of its sequential placement. In J. M. Atkinson & J. Heritage (Eds.), *Structures of social action. Studies in conversation analysis* (pp. 299–346). Cambridge: Cambridge University Press.

Hill, F. I. (1994). Aristotle's rhetorical theory. With a synopsis of Aristotle's Rhetoric. In J. J. Murphy & R. A. Katula, *A synoptic history or classical rhetoric* (2nd ed.) (pp. 51–110). Davis, CA: Hermagoras.

Hintikka, J. (1968). Language-games for quantifiers. In N. Rescher (Ed.), *Studies in logical theory* (pp. 46–76). Oxford: Blackwell.

Hitchcock, D. (2006). The pragma-dialectical analysis of the ad hominem fallacy. In P. Houtlosser & M. A. van Rees (Eds.), *Considering pragma-dialectics: A festschrift for Frans H. van Eemeren on the occasion of his 60th birthday* (pp. 109–120). Mahwah, NJ: Lawrence Erlbaum.

Hitchcock, D., & Verheij, B. (Eds.) (2006). *Arguing on the Toulmin model: New essays in argument analysis and evaluation*. Dordrecht: Springer.

Hohmann, H. (2002). In F. H. van Eemeren & P. Houtlosser, *Dialectic and rhetoric: The and woof of argumentation analysis* (pp. 41–52). Dordrecht: Kluwer Academic.

Hoppmann, M. J. (2008). *Argumentative Verteidigung. Grundlegung zu einer modernen Stasislehre*. Doctoral dissertation, Eberhard Karls Universität Tübingen, Germany.

Houtlosser, P. (1995). *Standpunten in een kritische discussie. Een pragma-dialectisch perspectief op de identificatie en reconstructie van standpunten*. [Standpoints in a critical discussion. A pragma-dialectical perspective on the identification and reconstruction of standpoints]. Doctoral dissertation, University of Amsterdam. Amsterdam: IFOTT.

Houtlosser, P. (2002). Indicators of a point of view. In F. H. van Eemeren (Ed.), *Advances in pragma-dialectics* (pp. 169–184). Amsterdam: Sic Sat.

Huseman, R. C. (1965). Aristotle's system of topics. *Southern Speech Journal, 30*, 243–252.

Hymes, D. (1972). *Foundations in sociolinguistics: An ethnographic approach*. Philadelphia, PA: University of Pennsylvania Press.

Iețcu-Fairclough, I. (2009). Legitimation and strategic maneuvering in the political field. In F. H. van Eemeren (Ed.), *Examining argumentation in context: Fifteen studies on strategic maneuvering* (pp. 131–152). Amsterdam: John Benjamins.

Ilie, C. (2009). Strategies of refutation by definition: A pragma-rhetorical approach to refutations in a public speech. In F. H. van Eemeren & B. Garssen (Eds.), *Pondering on problems of argumentation. Twenty essays on theoretical issues* (pp. 35–51). Dordrecht: Springer.

Irwin, T. (1988). *Aristotle's first principles*. Oxford: Clarendon Press.

Jackson, S. (1986). Building a case for claims about discourse structure. In D. G. Ellis & W. A. Donohue (Eds.), *Contemporary issues in language and discourse processes* (pp. 129–147). Hillsdale, NJ: Lawrence Erlbaum.

Jackson, S. (1992). 'Virtual standpoints' and the pragmatics of conversational argument. In F. H. van Eemeren, R. Grootendorst, J. A. Blair & C. A. Willard (Eds.). *Argumentation illuminated* (pp. 260–269). Amsterdam: Sic Sat.

Jackson, S. (1995). Fallacies and heuristics. In F. H. van Eemeren, R. Grootendorst, J. A. Blair & C. A. Willard (Eds.), *Analysis and Evaluation. Proceedings of the Third ISSA Conference on Argumentation, Volume II* (pp. 257–269). Amsterdam: Sic Sat.

Jackson, S. (1998). Argumentation by design. *Argumentation, 12*(1), 183–198.

Jackson, S., & Jacobs, S. (1980). Structure of conversational argument: Pragmatic bases for the enthymeme. *Quarterly Journal of Speech, 66*, 251–265.

Jackson, S., & Jacobs, S. (2006). Derailments of argumentation: It takes two to tango. In P. Houtlosser & M. A. van Rees (Eds.), *Considering pragma-dialectics: A festschrift for Frans H. van Eemeren on the occasion of his 60th birthday* (pp. 121–134). Mahwah, NJ: Lawrence Erlbaum.

Jacobs, S. (1999). Argumentation as normative pragmatics. In F. H. van Eemeren, R. Grootendorst, J. A. Blair & C. A. Willard (Eds.), *Proceedings of the Fourth International Conference of the International Society for the Study of Argumentation* (pp. 397–403). Amsterdam: Sic Sat.

Jacobs, S. (2000). Rhetoric and dialectic from the standpoint of normative pragmatics. *Argumentation, 14*(3), 261–286.

Jacobs, S. (2002). Messages, functional contexts, and categories of fallacy: Some dialectical and rhetorical considerations. In F. H. van Eemeren & P. Houtlosser (Eds.), *Dialectic and rhetoric: The warp and woof of argumentation analysis* (pp. 119–130). Dordrecht: Kluwer Academic.

Jacobs, S. (2005). Finding available means to put things right. In P. Riley (Ed.), *Engaging Argument: Selected Papers from the 2005 NCA/AFA Conference on Argumentation* (pp. 416–425). Washington, DC: National Communication Association.

Jacobs, S., & Aakhus, M. (2002). How to resolve a conflict: Two models of dispute resolution. In F. H. van Eemeren (Ed.), *Advances in pragma-dialectics* (pp. 29–44). Amsterdam: Sic Sat.

James, W. (1907). *Pragmatism: A new name for some old ways of thinking*. New York, NY: Longman Green.

Johnson, R. H. (1996). *The rise of Informal Logic. Essays on argumentation, critical thinking, reasoning and politics*. Newport News, VA: Vale Press.

Johnson, R. H. (1998). Argumentative space: Logical and rhetorical approaches. In H. V. Hansen, C. W. Tindale & A.V. Colman (Eds.), *Argumentation & Rhetoric* (CD-ROM). St. Catherines, ON: OSSA.

Johnson, R. H. (1999). More on arguers and dialectical obligations. In C. W. Tindale, H. V. Hansen & E. Sveda (Eds.), *Argumentation at the Century's Turn* (CD-ROM). St. Catharines, ON: OSSA.

Johnson, R. H. (2000). *Manifest rationality. A pragmatic theory of argument*. Mahwah, NJ: Lawrence Erlbaum.

Johnson, R. H. (2008). Responding to objections. In F. H. van Eemeren & B. Garssen (Eds.), *Controversy and confrontation: Relating controversy analysis with argumentation theory* (pp. 149–162). Amsterdam: John Benjamins.

Johnstone, H. W. (1959). *Philosophy and argument*. Philadelphia, PA: University of Pennsylvania Press.

Kahneman, D., & Tversky, A. (Eds.) (2000). *Choices, values and frames*. New York, NY: Cambridge University Press.

Kamlah, W. (1973). *Philosophische Anthropologie. Sprachkritische Grundlegung und Ethik* [Philosophical anthropology. Fundamentals of linguistic criticism and ethics]. Mannheim: Bibliographisches Institut.

Kamlah, W., & Lorenzen, P. (1967). *Logische Propädeutik. Vorschule des vernünftigen Redens* [Preparatory Logic. An introduction to speaking rationally] (2nd ed.). Mannheim: Bibliographisches Institut.

Katula, R. A., & Murphy, J. J. (1994). The sophists and rhetorical consciousness. In J. J. Murphy & R. A. Katula, *A synoptic history of classical rhetoric* (2nd ed.) (pp. 21–58). Davis, CA: Hermagoras.

Kauffeld, F. J. (1986). *Accusing, proposing, and advising: The strategic grounds for presumption and the assumption of probative responsibilities*. Madison, WI: University of Wisconsin Press.

Kauffeld, F. J. (1995). On the difference between assumptions and presumptions. In S. Jackson (Ed.), *Argumentation and Values: Proceedings of the Ninth SCA/AFA Conference on Argumentation* (pp. 509–515). Falls Church, VA: Speech Communication Association.

Kauffeld, F. J. (1998). Presumptions and the distribution of argumentative burdens in acts of proposing and accusing. *Argumentation, 12*(2), 245–266.

Kauffeld, F. J. (1999). Arguments on the dialectical tier as structured by proposing and advising. In H. V. Hansen, C. W. Tindale & S. Raposo, *Argumentation at the Century's Turn* (CD-ROM). St. Catherines, ON: OSSA.

Kauffeld, F. J. (2002). Pivotal issues and norms in rhetorical theories of argumentation. In F. H. van Eemeren & P. Houtlosser (Eds.), *Dialectic and rhetoric: The warp and woof of argumentation analysis* (pp. 97–118). Dordrecht: Kluwer Academic.

Kennedy, G. A. (1963). *The art of persuasion in Greece*. Princeton, NJ: Princeton University Press.

Kennedy, G. A. (1991). *Aristotle. On rhetoric: A theory of civic discourse. Newly translated with introduction, notes, and appendixes by G. A. Kennedy*. New York, NY: Oxford University Press.

Kennedy, G. A. (1994). *A new history of classical rhetoric*. Princeton, NJ: Princeton University Press.

Kennedy, G.A (2004). *Negotiation: An A-Z guide*. London: The Economist.

Kienpointner, M. (1999). Figures of speech: Definition, description and critical evaluation. In F. H. van Eemeren, R. Grootendorst, J. A. Blair & C. A. Willard (Eds.), *Proceedings of the Fourth International Conference of the International Society for the Study of Argumentation* (pp. 445–454). Amsterdam: Sic Sat.

Kienpointner, M. (2005). Aristotelische Rhetoriktradition im 20. Jahrhundert [The Aritotelian rhetoric tradition in the twentieth century]. In J. Knape & T. Schirren (Eds.), *Aristotelische Rhetoriktradition. Akten der 5. Tagung der Karl and Getrud Abel-Stiftung von 5.-6. Oktober 2001 in Tübingen* (pp. 363–387). Stuttgart: Franz Steiner Verlag.

Kienpointner, M. (2006). How to present fallacious messages persuasively. The case of the "Nigeria spam letters". In P. Houtlosser & M. A. van Rees (Eds.), *Considering pragma-dialectics: A festchrift for Frans H. van Eemeren on the occasion of his 60th birthday*. Mahwah, NJ: Lawrence Erlbaum.

Kienpointner, M. (2007). Figures of speech. In J. Verschueren & J. O. Östman (Eds.), *Handbook of pragmatics*. Amsterdam: John Benjamins.

Kock, C. (2007). The domain of rhetorical argumentation. In F. H. van Eemeren, J. A. Blair, C. A. Willard & B. Garssen (Eds.), *Proceedings of the Sixth Conference of the International Society of the Study of Argumentation* (pp. 785–788). Amsterdam: Sic Sat.

Kopperschmidt, J. (Ed.) (2006). *Die neue Rhetoric – Studien zu Chaim Perelman* [The New Rhetoric: Studies into Chaim Perelman]. Paderborn: Wilhelm Fink Verlag.

Krabbe, E. C. W. (1988). Creative reasoning in formal discussion, *Argumentation*, 2(4), 483–498.

Krabbe, E. C. W. (1992). So what? Profiles for relevance criticism in persuasion dialogues. *Argumentation*, 6(2), 271–283.

Krabbe, E. C. W. (1999). Profiles of dialogue. In J. Gerbrandy, M. Marx, M. de Rijke, & Y. Venema (Eds.), *JFAK. Essays dedicated to Johan van Benthem on the occasion of his 50th birthday, III* (pp. 26–36). Amsterdam: Amsterdam University Press.

Krabbe, E. C. W. (2001). In response to Ralph H. Johnson's 'More on arguers and dialectical obligations'. *Proceedings of the Ontario Society for the Study of Argumentation (OSSA) 1999*. CD Rom

Krabbe, E. C. W. (2002a). Meeting in the house of Callias. In F. H. van Eemeren & P. Houtlosser (Eds.), *Dialectic and rhetoric: The warp and woof of argumentation analysis* (pp. 29–40). Dordrecht: Kluwer Academic.

Krabbe, E. C. W. (2002b). Profiles of dialogue as a dialectical tool. In F. H. van Eemeren (Ed.), *Advances in pragma-dialectics* (pp. 153–167). Amsterdam: Sic Sat.

Krabbe, E. C. W. (2003). Metadialogues. In F. H. van Eemeren, J. A. Blair, C. A. Willard, & A. F. Snoeck Henkemans (Eds.), *Anyone who has a view. Theoretical contributions to the study of argumentation* (pp. 83–90). Dordrecht: Kluwer Academic.

Krabbe, E. C. W. (2004). Strategies in dialectic and rhetoric. In H. V. Hansen, C. W. Tindale, J. A. Blair, R. H. Johnson, & R. C. Pinto (Eds.), *Argumentation and its applications* (CD-ROM).

Laar, J. A. van (2003). *The dialectic of ambiguity: A contribution to the study of argumentation.* Doctoral dissertation, University of Groningen.
Laar, J. A. van (2008). Pragmatic inconsistency and credibility. In F. H. van Eemeren & B. Garssen (Eds.), *Controversy and confrontation: Relating controversy analysis with argumentation theory* (pp. 163–180). Amsterdam: John Benjamins.
Labov, W., & Fanshel, D. (1977). *Therapeutic discourse. Psychotherapy as conversation.* New York, NY: Academic Press.
Lambert, K., & Ulrich, W. (1980). *The nature of argument.* New York, NY: Macmillan.
Lauerbach, G. (2004). Political interviews as hybrid genre. *Text, 24*(3), 353–397.
Lausberg, H. (1998). *Handbook of literary rhetoric. A foundation for literary study* (D. E. Orton & R. D. Anderson, Eds.). Leiden: Brill. (Original work published in 1973)
Leff, M. (2000). Rhetoric and dialectic in the twenty-first century. *Argumentation, 14*(3), 241–254.
Leff, M. (2002). The relation between dialectic and rhetoric in a classical and a modern perspective. In F. H. van Eemeren & P. Houtlosser, *Dialectic and rhetoric: The warp and woof of argumentation analysis* (pp. 53–64). Dordrecht: Kluwer Academic.
Leff, M. (2003). Rhetoric and dialectic in Martin Luther King's 'Letter from Birmingham Jail'. In F. H. van Eemeren, J. A. Blair, C. A. Willard & A. F. Snoeck Henkemans, *Anyone who has a view* (pp. 255–268). Dordrecht: Kluwer Academic.
Leff, M. (2006). Rhetoric, dialectic, and the functions of argument. In P. Houtlosser & M. A. van Rees (Eds.), *Considering pragma-dialectics: A festschrift for Frans H. van Eemeren on the occasion of his 60th birthday* (pp. 199–210). Mahwah, NJ: Lawrence Erlbaum.
Levene, D. S. (2009). Introduction: Topoi in their rhetorical context. In S. Rubinelli, *Ars topica: The classical technique of constructing arguments from Aristotle to Cicero* (pp. i–xix). Dordrecht: Springer.
Levinson, S. C. (1983). *Pragmatics.* Cambridge: Cambridge University Press.
Levinson, S. C. (1992). Activity types and language. In P. Drew & J. Heritage (Eds.), *Talk at work: Interaction in institutional settings* (pp. 66–100). Cambridge: Cambridge University Press.
Lewinski, M. (2010). Internet political discussion forums as an argumentative activity type. A pragma-dialectical analysis of online forms of strategic manoeuvring with critical reactions. Unpublished doctoral dissertation, University of Amsterdam.
Lewis, D. K. (1977). *Convention. A philosophical study.* Cambridge, MA: Harvard University Press.
Lord, D. (1981). The intention of Aristotle's 'rhetoric'. *Hermes, 109,* 326–339.
Lorenzen, P., & Lorenz, K. (1978). *Dialogische Logik* [Dialogic logic]. Darmstadt: Wissenschaftliche Buchgesellschaft.
Lumer, C. (2007). An empirical theory of practical reasons and its use for practical philosophy. In S. Nannini & C. Lumer (Eds.), *Intentionality, deliberation and autonomy: The action-theoretic basis of practical philosophy* (pp. 157–186). Aldershot: Ashgate.
Lunsford, A. A., Wilson, K. H., & Eberly, R. A. (2009). Introduction: Rhetorics and roadmaps. In A. A. Lunsford, K. H. Wilson & R. A. Eberly, *The Sage handbook of rhetorical studies* (pp. xi–xxix). Los Angeles, CA: Sage.
Mack, P. (1993). *Renaissance argument: Valla and Agricola in the traditions of rhetoric and dialectic.* Leiden: Brill.
Mackenzie, J. D. (1979a). Question-begging in non-cumulative systems. *Journal of Philosophical Logic, 8,* 117–133.
Mackenzie, J. D. (1979b). How to stop talking to tortoises. *Notre Dame Journal of Formal Logic, 20,* 705–717.
Mackenzie, J. D. (1981). The dialectics of logic. *Logique et Analyse, 24,* 159–177.

Mackenzie, J. D. (1985). No logic before Friday. *Synthese, 63,* 329–341.
Mackenzie, J. D. (1989). Reasoning and logic. *Synthese, 79,* 99–117.
Mackenzie, J. D. (1990). Four dialogue systems. *Studia Logica, 49,* 567–583.
Mackenzie, J. D., & Staines, P. (1999). Hamblin's case for commitment: A reply to Johnson. *Philosophy & Rhetoric, 32,* 14–39.
Mackie, J. L. (1977). *Ethics. Inventing right and wrong.* Harmondsworth: Penguin Book.
Mansbridge, J. (1999). Everyday talk in the deliberative system. In S. Macedo (Ed.), *Deliberative politics: Essays on democracy and disagreement* (pp. 211–242). New York, NY: Oxford University Press.
March, J. G., & Olsen, J. P. (1984). The new institutionalism: Organizational factors in political life. *The American Political Science Review, 78*(3), 734–749.
Martel, M. (1983). *Political campaign debates: Images, strategies, tactics.* New York, NY: Longman.
Massey, G. (1975). Are there any good arguments that bad arguments are bad? *Philosophy in Context, 4,* 61–77.
McEvoy, S. (1999). The construction of issues: Pleading theory and practice, relevance in pragmatics, and the confrontation stage in the pragma-dialectical theory of argumentation. *Argumentation, 13*(1), 43–52.
McHugh, P. (1968). *Defining the situation. The organization of meaning in social interaction.* Indianapolis, IN: Bobbs-Merrill Company.
Meerhoff, C.G. (1988). Agricola et Ramus: Dialectique et rhétorique [Agricola and Ramus. Dialectic and rhetoric]. In F. Akkerman & A. J. Vanderjagt (Eds.), *Rodolphus Agricola Phrisius 1444–1485* (pp. 270–280). Leiden: Brill.
Memedi, V. (2007). Resolving deep disagreement: A case in point. In H. V. Hansen, C. W. Tindale, R. H. Johnson & J. A. Blair (Eds.), *Dissensus and the Search for Common Ground* (CD-ROM). Windsor, ON: OSSA.
Menashe, C., & Siegel, M. (1998). The power of a frame: an analysis of newspaper coverage of tobacco issues – United States, 1985–1996. *Journal of Health Communication, 3*(4), 307–326.
Menkel-Meadow, C. (2005). Roots and inspirations: A brief history of the foundations of dispute resolution. In M. L. Moffitt & R. C. Bordone (Eds.), *The handbook of dispute resolution* (pp. 13–32). San Francisco, CA: Jossey-Bass.
Meyer, M. (2008). *Principia Rhetorica.* Paris: Fayard.
Mill, J. S. (1863). *On Liberty.* London: Parker, Son, and Bourn.
Mitchell, G. R. (2000). *Strategic deception. Rhetoric, science, and politics in missile defense advocacy.* East Lansing, MI: Michigan State University Press.
Moffitt, M. L., & Bordone, R. C. (2005). Perspectives on dispute resolution: An introduction. In M. L. Moffitt & R. C. Bordone (Eds.), *The handbook of dispute resolution* (pp. 1–12). San Francisco: Jossey-Bass.
Mohammed, D. (2009a). "The honourable gentleman should make up his mind". Strategic manoeuvring with accusations of inconsistency in Prime Minister's Question Time. Unpublished doctoral dissertation, University of Amsterdam.
Mohammed, D. (2009b). Manoeuvring strategically in Prime Minister's Question Time. In F. H. van Eemeren (Ed.), *Examining argumentation in context: Fifteen studies on strategic maneuvering* (pp. 171–190). Amsterdam: John Benjamins.
Murphy, J. J. (1990). Topos and figura: Cause and effect? In G. L. Bursill-Hall, S. Ebbensen & K. Koerner, *De ortu grammaticae: Studies in medieval grammar and linguistics in memory of Jan Pinborg* (239–253). Amsterdam: John Benjamins.

Murphy, J. J., & Katula, R. A. (1994). *A synoptic history of classical rhetoric* (2nd ed.). Davis, CA: Hermagoras.

Myers, F. (1999). Political argumentation and the composite audience: A case study. *Quarterly Journal of Speech, 85*, 55–71.

Naess, A. (1966). *Communication and argument. Elements of applied semantics.* Oslo: Allen and Unwin.

Naess, A. (1992). How can the empirical movement be promoted today? A discussion of the empiricism of Otto Neurath and Rudolph Carnap. In E. M. Barth, J. Vandormeal & F. Vandamme (Eds.), *From an empirical point of view. The empirical turn in logic.* (pp. 107–155). Gent: Communication & Cognition, part II.

Natanson, M. (1955). The limits of rhetoric. Quarterly Journal of Speech, *41*(2), 133–139.

Nuchelmans, G. (1993). On the fourfold root of the *argumentum ad hominem*. In E. C. W. Krabbe, R. J. Dalitz, & P. A. Smit, *Empirical logic and public debate. Essays in honour of Else M. Barth.* Amsterdam: Rodopi.

Ochs, D. J (1969). Aristotle's concept of formal topics. *Speech Monographs, 36*, 419–425.

Ochs, D. J. (1994). Cicero's rhetorical theory. With synopses of Cicero's seven rhetorical works. In J. J. Murphy & R. A. Katula, *A synoptic history of classical rhetoric* (2nd ed.) (pp. 151–200). Davis, CA: Hermagoras.

O'Keefe, D. J. (2002). *Persuasion: Theory and research* (2nd ed.). Thousand Oaks, CA: Sage.

O'Keefe, D. J. (2003). The potential conflict between normatively-good argumentative practice and persuasive success: Evidence from persuasion effects research. In F. H. van Eemeren, J. A. Blair, C. A. Willard & A. F. Snoeck Henkemans (Eds.), *Anyone who has a view: Theoretical contributions to the study of argumentation* (pp. 309–318). Amsterdam: Kluwer Academic.

O'Keefe, D. J. (2006). Pragma-dialectics and persuasion effect research. In P. Houtlosser & M. A. van Rees (Eds.), *Considering pragma-dialectics: A festschrift for Frans H. van Eemeren on the occasion of his 60th birthday* (pp. 235–244). Mahwah, NJ: Lawrence Erlbaum.

O'Keefe, D. J. (2009). Persuasive effects of strategic maneuvering. Some findings from meta-analyses of experimental persuasion effects research. In F. H. van Eemeren (Ed.), *Examining argumentation in context: Fifteen studies on strategic maneuvering* (pp. 283–294). Amsterdam: John Benjamins.

Ong, W.J. (1983). *Ramus. Method, and the decay of dialogue. From the art of discourse to the art of reason.* Cambridge, MA: Harvard University Press. (Original work published in 1958)

Orr, C. J. (1990). Critical rationalism: Rhetoric and the voice of reason. In R. A. Cherwitz (Ed.), *Rhetoric and philosophy* (pp. 105–147). Hillsdale, NJ: Lawrence Erlbaum.

Pan, Z., & Kosicki, G. M. (1993). Framing analysis: An approach to news discourse. *Political Communication, 10*, 55–75.

Pareto, V. (1935). *The mind and society.* New York, NY: Harcourt, Brace and World.

Pater, W. A. de (1965). *Les topiques d'Aristote et la dialectique platonicienne* [The Aristotelian topics and platonic dialectics]. Fribourg: Éditions St.Paul.

Pater, W. A. de (1968). La fonction de lieu et de l'instrument dans les Topiques [The function of place and instrument in the *Topics*]. In G. E. L. Owen (Ed.), *Aristotle on dialectic. The Topics* (pp. 164–188). Oxford: Oxford University Press.

Patton, B. (2005). Negotiation. In M. L. Moffitt & R. C. Bordone (Eds.), *The handbook of dispute resolution* (pp. 279–303). San Francisco, CA: Jossey-Bass.

Perelman, C. (1980). *Justice, law, and argument: Essays on moral and legal reasoning.* Dordrecht: Reidel.

Perelman, C., & Olbrechts-Tyteca, L. (1969). *The new rhetoric. A treatise on argumentation* (Trans.). Notre Dame: University of Notre Dame Press. (Original work published in 1958)

Perlof, M. R. (1998). *Political communication, politics, press and public in America*. Mahwah, NJ: Lawrence Erlbaum.

Petty, R. E., & Cacioppo, J. T. (1979). Issue involvement can increase or decrease persuasion by enhancing message-relevant cognitive responses. *Journal of Personality and Social Psychology 37*, 1915–1926.

Petty, R. E., & Cacioppo, J. T. (1986). The elaboration likelihood model of persuasion. In L. Berkowitz (Ed.), *Advances in experimental social psychology* (Vol. 19, pp. 123–205). New York, NY: Academic Press.

Pike, K. L. (1967). Etic and emic standpoints for the description of behavior. In D. C. Hildum (Ed.), *Language and thought: An enduring problem in psychology* (pp. 32–39). Princeton, NJ: Van Norstrand.

Pinto, R. C. (2001). *Argument, inference and dialectic*. Dordrecht: Kluwer Academic.

Plato (1961). *The collected dialogues* (E. Hamilton, Ed.). Princeton, NJ: Princeton University Press.

Plug, H. J. (2010). Ad-hominem arguments in Dutch and European parliamentary debates: Strategic manoeuvring in an institutional context. In C. Ilie (Ed.), *Discourse and metadiscourse in parliamentary debates* (pp. 305–328). Amsterdam: John Benjamins.

Popper, K. R. (1962). *Conjectures and refutations*. London: Basic Books.

Popper, K. R. (1971a). *The open society and its enemies, 2*(5). Princeton, NJ: Princeton University Press.

Popper, K. R. (1971b). Oracular philosophy and the revolt against reason. In K. R. Popper, *The open society and its enemies, 2*(5) (pp. 224–258). Princeton, NJ: Princeton University Press.

Poster, C. (2000). Being, time, and definition: Toward a semiotics of figural rhetoric. *Philosophy and Rhetoric, 33*(2), 116–136.

Poulakos, J. (1997). The logic of Greek sophistry. In D. Walton & A. Brinton (Eds.), *Historical foundations of informal logic* (pp. 12–24). Brookfield, VT: Ashgate.

Prakken, H. (2000). On dialogue systems with speech acts, arguments and counterarguments. In M. Ojeda-Aciego, I. P. de Guzman, G. Brewka, & L. M. Pereira (Eds.), *Proceedings of JELIA 2000, the European Workshop on Logic /for Artificial Intelligence* (pp. 224–238). Berlin: Springer.

Prakken, H. (2006). Formal systems for persuasion dialogue. *The Knowledge Engineering Review, 21*, 163-188.

Putnam, L. L., & Poole, M. S. (1987). Conflict and negotiation. In K.H. Roberts & L. W. Porter (Eds.), *Handbook of organizational communication* (pp. 549–599). Newbury Park, CA: Sage.

Putnam, L. L., & Roloff, M. E. (1992). Communication perspectives on negotiation. In L. L. Putnam & M. E. Roloff (Eds.), *Communication and negotiation* (pp. 1–17). Newbury Park, CA: Sage.

Quintilian (1996). *Institutio oratoria* (1st ed.) (H. E. Butler, Trans.). Cambridge, MA: Harvard University Press.

Ray, J. W. (1978). Perelman's universal audience. *Quarterly Journal of Speech, 64*(4), 361–375.

Reboul, O. (1989). Relevance and argumentation: How bald can you get. *Argumentation, 3*(3), 285–302.

Reboul, O. (1991). *Introduction à la rhétorique: Théorie et pratique* [Introduction to rhetoric: Theory and practice]. Paris: Presses universitaires de France.

Rees, M. A. van (2001). Review of the book *Manifest rationality. A pragmatic theory of argument*. *Argumentation, 15*(2), 231–237.

Rees, M. A. van (2003). Within pragma-dialectics: Comments on Bonevac. *Argumentation*, *17*(4), 461–464.
Rees, M. A. van (2009). Strategic manoeuvring with dissociation. In F. H. van Eemeren (Ed.), *Examining argumentation in context* (pp. 25–40). Amsterdam: John Benjamins.
Rescher, N. (1977). *Dialectics: A controvery-oriented approach to the theory of knowledge*. Albany, NY: SUNY Press.
Richards, I. A. (1936). *The philosophy of rhetoric*. New York: Oxford University Press.
Rigotti, E. (2007). Can classical topics be revived within the contemporary theory of argumentation? In F. H. van Eemeren, B. Garssen, J. A. Blair & C. A. Willard (Eds.), *Proceedings of the Sixth Conference of the International Society for the Study of Argumentation* (pp. 1155–1164). Amsterdam: Sic Sat.
Rigotti, E. (2009). Whether and how classical topics can be revived within contemporary argumentation theory. In F. H. van Eemeren & B.Garssen, *Pondering on problems of argumentation* (pp. 157–178). Dordrecht: Springer.
Rigotti, E., & Rocci, A. (2006). Towards a definition of communicative context. Foundations of an interdisciplinary approach to communication. *Studies in Communication Sciences, 6*(2), 155–180.
Rocci, A. (2009). Manoeuvring with tropes. The case of the metaphorical polyphonic and framing of arguments. In F. H. van Eemeren (Ed.), *Examining argumentation in context. Fifteen studies on strategic maneuvering* (pp. 257–282). Amsterdam: John Benjamins.
Ross, W. H., & Conlon, D. E. (2000). Hybrid forms of third-party dispute resolution: Theoretical implications of combining mediation and arbitration. *Academy of Management Review, 25*(2), 416–427.
Rubinelli, S. (2009). *Ars topica: The classical technique of constructing arguments from Aristotle to Cicero*. Dordrecht: Springer.
Sawyer, J., & Guetzkow, H. (1965). Bargaining and negotiation in international relations. In H. C. Kelman (Ed.), *International behavior: A socio-psychological analysis* (pp. 466–520). New York, NY: Holt, Rinehart and Winston.
Schedler, A. (1999). Conceptualizing accountability. In A. Schedler, L. Diamond, & M. F. Plattner (Eds.), *The self-restraining state: Power and accountability in new democracies* (pp. 13-28). USA/UK: Lynne Rienner.
Schiappa, E. (1999). *The beginnings of rhetorical theory in classical Greece*. New Haven, CT: Yale University Press.
Schiappa, E. (2002). Evaluating argumentative discourse from a rhetorical perspective. In F. H. van Eemeren & P. Houtlosser, *Rhetoric and dialectic: The warp and woof of argumentation analysis* (pp. 65–80). Dordrecht: Kluwer Academic.
Schumpeter, J. A. (1950). *Capitalism, socialism, and democracy*. New York, NY: Harper.
Schütz, A. (1992). *Psychologie der Selbstdarstellung im Wahlkampf: Auftritte der Kanzlerkandidaten Helmut Kohl und Johannes Rau* [The psychology of self-portrayal in campaigns: The appearances of chancellor candidates Helmut Kohl and Johannes Rau]. Weinheim: Deutscher Studien Verlag.
Schütz, A. (1993). Self-presentational tactics used in a German election campaign. *Political Psychology, 14*(3), 469–491.
Scott, R. L. (1967). On viewing rhetoric as epistemic. *Central States Speech Journal, 18*, 9–17.
Searle, J. R. (1969). *Speech acts. An essay in the philosophy of language*. Cambridge: Cambridge University Press.

Searle, J. R. (1979). *Expression and meaning. Studies in the theory of speech acts.* Cambridge: Cambridge University Press.
Searle, J. R. (1995). *The construction of social reality.* London: Penguin.
Shapin, S. (1994). *A social history of truth.* Chicago, IL: University of Chicago Press.
Shapin, S (1996). *The scientific revolution.* Chicago, IL: University of Chicago Press.
Simons, H. W. (Ed.) (1990). *The rhetorical turn: Invention and persuasion in the conduct of inquiry.* Chicago, IL: University of Chicago Press.
Snoeck Henkemans, A. F. (1997). *Analysing complex argumentation: The reconstruction of multiple and coordinatively compound argumentation in a critical discussion.* Amsterdam: Sic Sat. (Original work published in 1992)
Snoeck Henkemans, A. F. (2009). The contribution of *praeteritio* to arguers' confrontational strategic manoeuvres. In F. H. van Eemeren (Ed.), *Examining argumentation in context. Fifteen studies on strategic maneuvering* (pp. 241–256). Amsterdam: John Benjamins.
Stump, E. (1978). *Boethius' de topicis differentiis.* Ithaca, NY: Cornell University Press.
Swales, J. M. (1990). *Genre analysis. English in academic research settings.* Cambridge: Cambridge University Press.
Swales, J. M. (2004). *Research genres. Exploration and application.* Cambridge: Cambridge University Press.
Swearingen, C. J., & Schiappa, E. (2009). Historical studies in rhetoric: Revisionist methods and new directions. In A. A. Lunsford, K. H. Wilson & R. A. Eberly, *The Sage handbook of rhetorical studies* (pp. 1–12). Los Angeles, CA: Sage.
Tindale, C. W. (1999). Case studies in rhetorical argumentation. In C. W. Tindale, *Acts of arguing: A rhetorical model of argument* (pp. 125–156). New York: SUNY Press.
Tindale, C. W. (2004). *Rhetorical argumentation: Principles of theory and practice.* London: Sage.
Tindale, C. W. (2009). Constrained maneuvering: Rhetoric as a rational enterprise. In F. H. van Eemeren (Ed.), *Examining argumentation in context: Fifteen studies on strategic maneuvering* (pp. 41–60). Amsterdam: John Benjamins.
Tonnard, Y. (2009). Shifting the topic in Dutch Parliament. How presentational choices can be instrumental in strategic manoeuvring. In F. H. van Eemeren (Ed.), *Examining argumentation in context: Fifteen studies on strategic maneuvering* (pp. 221–240). Amsterdam: John Benjamins.
Tonnard, Y. (forthcoming). Issue-influencing manoeuvres in Dutch parliamentary debate: A pragma-dialectical study on presentational choices of one-issue politicians in confrontational strategic manoeuvring. Unpublished doctoral dissertation, University of Amsterdam.
Toulmin, S. E. (1976). *Knowing and acting.* New York, NY: Macmillan.
Toulmin, S. E. (2001). *Return to reason.* Cambridge, MA: Harvard University Press.
Toulmin, S. E. (2003). *The uses of argument.* Cambridge: Cambridge University Press. (Original work published in 1958)
Tseronis, A. (2009). *Qualifying standpoints. Stance adverbs as a presentational device for managing the burden of proof.* Utrecht: LOT. Doctoral dissertation University of Leiden.
Tutzauer, F. (1992). The communication of offers in dyadic bargaining. In L. L. Putnam & M. E. Roloff (Eds.), *Communication and negotiation* (pp. 67–82). Newbury Park, CA: Sage Publications.
Ullmann-Margalit, E. (1983). On presumption. *Journal of Philosophy, 80,* 143–163.
Uzqueda, A., & Frediani, P. (2002). *La conciliazione. Guida per la soluzione negoziale delle controversie.* Milano: Giuffre.

Varga, K. (1983). Rhetoric: A story or a system? A challenge to historians of renaissance rhetoric. In J. J. Murphy (Ed.), *Renaissance eloquence* (pp. 84–91). Berkeley, CA: University of California Press.

Vuchinich, S. (1990). The sequential organization of closing in verbal family conflict. In A. D. Grimshaw (Ed.), *Conflict talk. Sociolinguistic investigations of Arguments in conversations* (pp. 118–138). Cambridge etc.: Cambridge University Press.

Wagemans, J. (2003). Conceptualizing fallacies: The informal logic and pragma-dialectical approaches to the argumentum ad ignorantiam. In F. H. van Eemeren, J. A. Blair, C. A. Willard & A. F. Snoeck Henkemans (Eds.), *Proceedings of the Fifth Conference of the International Society for the Study of Argumentation* (pp. 1049–1051). Amsterdam: SicSat.

Wagemans, J. H. M. (2009). Redelijkheid en overredingskracht van argumentatie: Een historisch-filosofische studie over de combinatie van het dialectische en het retorische perspectief op argumentatie in de pragma-dialectische argumentatietheorie [Reasonableness and persuasiveness of argumentation: A historical-philosophical study on the combination of the dialectical and the rhetorical perspective on argumentation in the pragma-dialectical theory of argumentation]. Unpublished doctoral dissertation, University of Amsterdam.

Wall Jr., J. A., Stark, J., & Standifer, R. L. (2001). Mediation: A current review and theory development. *Journal of Conflict Resolution, 45*(3), 370–391.

Walton, D. N. (1985). *Arguer's position: A pragmatic study of ad hominem attack, criticism, refutation, and fallacy*. Westport, CT: Greenwood Press.

Walton, D. N. (1987). *Informal fallacies: Towards a theory of argument criticisms*. Amsterdam: John Benjamins.

Walton, D. N. (1988). Burden of proof. *Argumentation, 2*(2), 233–254.

Walton, D. N. (1989). *Question-reply argumentation*. Westport, CT: Greenwood Press.

Walton, D. N. (1992). Types of dialogue, dialectical shifts and fallacies. In F. H. van Eemeren & R. Grootendorst (Eds.), *Argumentation illuminated* (pp. 134–147). Amsterdam: Sic Sat.

Walton, D. N. (1995). *A pragmatic theory of fallacy*. Tuscaloosa, AL: University of Alabama Press.

Walton, D. N. (1996). Plausible deniability and evasion of burden of proof. *Argumentation, 10*(1), 47–58.

Walton, D. N. (1998a). *Ad hominem arguments*. Tuscaloosa, AL: University of Alabama Press.

Walton, D. N. (1998b). *The new dialectic: Conversational contexts of argument*. Toronto: University of Toronto Press.

Walton, D. N. (1999a). The appeal to ignorance, or argumentum ad ignorantiam. *Argumentation, 13*(4), 367–377.

Walton, D. N. (1999b). Profiles of dialogue for evaluating arguments from ignorance. *Argumentation, 13*(1), 53–71.

Walton, D. N. (2008). *Informal logic: A pragmatic approach*. Cambridge: Cambridge University Press.

Walton, D. N., & Krabbe, E. C. W. (1995). *Commitment in dialogue: Basic concepts of interpersonal reasoning*. Albany, NY: SUNY Press.

Walton, D. N., & Macagno, F. (2007). The fallaciousness of threats: Character and ad baculum. *Argumentation, 21*(1), 63–81.

Ware, B. L., & Linkugel, W. A. (1973). They spoke in defense of themselves: On the generic criticism of apologia. *Quarterly Journal of Speech, 59*, 273–283.

Weaver, R. M. (1970). *Language is sermonic* (R. L. Johannesen, R. Strickland & R. T. Eubanks, Eds.). Baton Rouge, LA: Louisiana State University Press.

Weaver, R. M. (1985). *The ethics of rhetoric*. Davis, CA: Hermagoras. (Original work published in 1953)

Weigand, E. (2007). *Dialogue and culture*. Amsterdam: John Benjamins.

Weiss, G., & Wodak, R. (Eds.) (2003). *Critical discourse analysis. Theory and interdisciplinarity.* New York, NY: Palgrave Macmillan.

Wenzel, J. W. (1979). Jürgen Habermas and the dialectical perspective on argumentation. *Journal of the American Forensic Association, 16*(2), 83–94.

Wenzel, J. W. (1990). Three perspectives on argument: Rhetoric, dialectic, logic. In R. Trapp & J. Schuetz (Eds.), *Perspectives on argumentation: Essays in the honor of Wayne Brockriede* (pp. 9–26). Prospect Heights, IL: Waveland.

Wenzel, J.W. (1998). The rhetoric of argumentation: A rejoinder. In H. V. Hansen, C. W. Tindale & A.V. Colman (Eds.), *Argumentation & Rhetoric* (CD-ROM). St. Catherines, ON: OSSA.

Whately, R. (1963). *Elements of rhetoric: Comprising an analysis of the laws of moral evidence and of persuasion, with rules for argumentative composition and elocution* (D. Ehninger, Ed). Carbondale, IL: Southern Illinois University Press. (Original work published in 1846)

Willard, C. A. (1995). *Liberal alarms and rhetorical excursions. A new rhetoric for modern democracy.* Chicago, IL: University of Chicago Press.

Wisse, J. (1989). *Ethos and pathos from Aristotle to Cicero*. Amsterdam: Hakkert.

Wodak, R. (2009). *The discourse of politics in action. Politics as usual.* New York, NY: Palgrave Macmillan.

Wodak, R., & Chilton, P. (Eds.) (2005). *A new agenda in (critical) discourse analysis. Theory, methodology and interdisciplinarity.* Amsterdam: John Benjamins.

Wodak, R., & Meyer, M. (2009). *Methods for critical discourse analysis*. Los Angeles, CA: Sage.

Woods, J. (1992). Who cares about the fallacies? In F. H. van Eemeren, R. Grootendorst, J. A. Blair & C. A. Willard (Eds.), *Argumentation illuminated* (pp. 22–48). Amsterdam: Sic Sat.

Woods, J., & Walton, D. N. (1989). *Fallacies: Selected papers 1972-1982*. Berlin: de Gruyter.

Zarefsky, D. (2005). *President Johnson's war on poverty: Rhetoric and history.* Tuscaloosa, AL: University of Alabama Press. (Original work published in 1986)

Zarefsky, D. (2006). Strategic maneuvering through persuasive definitions: Implications for dialectic and rhetoric. *Argumentation, 20*(4), 399–416.

Zarefsky, D. (2009). Strategic maneuvering in political argumentation. In F. H. van Eemeren (Ed.), *Examining argumentation in context: Fifteen studies on strategic maneuvering* (pp. 115–130). Amsterdam: John Benjamins.

Index of names 人名索引

A
Aakhus, M. 132, 265
Abelard 106
Agricola 89
Albert, H. 5, 31–33, 41, 221
Allen, M. 127
Amjarso, B. 270
Anaximenes of Lampsacus 66
Andone, C. 159–162, 268, 273
Anscombre, J. C. 52, 120, 121
Aristotle 52–57, 59–60, 66–73,
    81–87, 90, 101–107, 111, 132, 141,
    175, 181, 188
Atkinson, J. M. 156
Auer, J. J. 142
Augustine 72
Axelrod, R. 150

B
Bakhtin, M. M. 113–118, 139
Barth, E. M. 5, 32–35, 62, 65, 191,
    216, 220, 247, 254
Bartley, W. W. 5, 33
Battistelli, T. 54, 80, 257
Bell, A. 112
Benoit, W. L. 175
Bentham, J. 34
Bessette, J. M. 78
Beth, E. W. 61
Bhatia, V. K. 139
Bird, O. 101
Bitzer, L. 51, 113, 180–182
Bizzell, P. 76
Blair, J. A. 63, 118, 265
Boethius 71, 82, 84, 87, 105–107
Bonevac, D. 109, 241
Bons, J. A. E. 67–68
Bordone, R. C. 149
Braet, A. 95, 104–105, 153
Brinton, A. 190
Broadie, S. 68
Brockriede, W. 75, 101
Brummett, B. 77
Burke, K. 52, 74–75, 113, 123–125
Burrell, N. 127

C
Cacioppo, J. T. 269–270
Campbell, G. 85
Carneades 60
Ceaser, J. W. 78
Chaiken, S. 269
Chang, H. 266
Charney, D. 131
Cherwitz, R. A. 51
Chilton, P. 266
Cicero 71
Clayman, S. 160
Cohen, T. 38
Conley, T. M. 52, 72
Conlon, D. E. 142
Cooper, L. 106
Crawshay-Williams, R. 32
Crosswhite, J. 114, 116–118

D
D'Agostine, J. M. 110
Dascal, M. 119, 145, 265–266
Dearin, R. D. 116
De Morgan, A. 192
Donohue, W. A. 126
Drake, L. E. 126
Ducrot, O. 52, 108, 120, 238

E
Eagly, A. H. 269
Ede, L. 110
Eemeren, F. H. van 1–3, 5–10,
    12–19, 22, 25–28, 31–38, 40, 46,
    50–51, 57, 60, 62–65, 75–76, 80,
    83–84, 86–87, 89–93, 98–102,
    107, 109, 113–114, 116–118,
    129–130, 132–133, 139, 145,
    149, 152–153, 163, 165, 175, 184,
    187, 190–195, 197, 200, 203,
    207–208, 210–211, 213–216,
    220, 225, 228, 234–237, 241,
    243–245, 248–249, 255, 258,
    261, 265–266, 271
Ehninger, D. 75, 101

F
Fahnestock, J. 95, 121, 123–125,
    153, 165
Fairclough, N. 139, 273
Fanshel, D. 238
Farrell, T. B. 77
Feteris, E. T. 109, 160, 273
Finocchiaro, M. 2, 65–66, 99
Fisher, R. 149
Foss, S. K. 73–74
Foucault, M. 73–74
Frediani, P. 142
Freeley, A. J. 175
Freeman, J. B. 64

G
Gaonkar, D. P. 74
Garssen, B. 35, 145, 152, 192, 195,
    200, 215, 248, 266, 271
Gaskins, R. H. 116, 216, 231
Goffman, E. 10, 41, 112, 119, 126
Goodnight, G. T. 130
Goodwin, J. 78–79
Gorgias 67–68
Govier, T. 65, 85, 109, 233
Grassi, E. 73
Gray, B. 127
Greco Morasso 126, 139, 149, 156
Green, L. D. 81
Grice, H. P. 7, 120, 255
Griffin, C. L. 51, 77
Grimaldi, W. M. 102
Gronbeck, B. E. 130
Groot, A. D. de 30, 207
Grootendorst, R. 1, 3, 5–10,
    12–17, 22, 26–28, 31–34, 36–38,
    50, 54, 57, 62, 65, 80, 86, 99,
    109, 113–114, 130, 153, 156, 187,
    191, 193–195, 197, 200, 203,
    208, 211, 213–216, 220, 225,
    234, 236–237, 241, 243–245,
    255, 258, 265
Gross, A. G. 116, 119
Guetzkow, H. 150

H
Habermas, J. 34–35, 74, 130, 140–141
Hall, P. A. 131
Hamblin, C. L. 23, 61–63, 67, 132, 178, 187, 189–191, 199, 216, 220, 229, 258, 260
Hansen, H. V. 189–190
Hare, R. M. 240
Havet, E. 69
Hegendorff, C. 84
Heritage, J. 13, 70, 156, 160, 249, 250–251
Hermagoras of Temnos 70, 102, 104, 108, 153
Hermogenes of Tarsos 70, 108
Hill, F. I. 69, 175
Hintikka, J. 61
Hitchcock, D. 75, 253, 265
Hohmann, H. 84
Hoppmann, M. J. 108
Houtlosser, P. 2, 13, 18, 22, 40, 42, 46, 63, 83–84, 86–87, 89–93, 98, 100, 129, 132–133, 139, 145, 163, 165, 175, 187, 203, 207, 210, 219–220, 228, 235–238, 241, 245, 249, 254
Huseman, R. C. 102
Hymes, D. 133, 140

I
Ieţcu-Fairclough, I. 273
Ihnen, C. 98, 160
Ilie, C. 76
Irwin, T. 111
Isocrates 67–68

J
Jackson, S. 14, 16, 28, 132, 136, 156, 197, 199–200, 225–226, 265
Jacobs, S. 14, 16, 40, 54, 80, 132, 136, 156, 192, 197–198, 206, 254, 257–262, 265
James, W. 34
Johnson, R. H. 15, 53, 63–65, 78, 85, 91, 118, 200, 215, 218, 265, 270
Johnstone, H. W. 65, 218

K
Kahneman, D. 126
Kamlah, W. 34
Kant, I. 116
Katula, R. A. 67, 87

Kauffeld, F. J. 77, 79, 108, 214, 227, 265
Kennedy, G. A. 26, 66–69, 101–102, 121–122, 131, 143
Kienpointner, M. 121, 187
Kock, C. 2, 76
Kopperschmidt, J. 76
Kosicki, G. M. 126
Krabbe, E. C. W. 5, 32–35, 40, 59, 61–63, 65–66, 69, 86–87, 90, 98–99, 130–135, 137–138, 142, 144–146, 191, 198, 214–217, 220, 227, 233, 245, 254, 257–262, 265

L
Laar, J. A. van 243, 245, 254
Labov, W. 238
Lambert, K. 190
Lauerbach, G. 160
Lausberg, H. 243
Leff, M. 52, 56, 65–66, 72, 77–79, 85–86, 88, 90, 165, 200
Levene, D. S. 101–102
Levinson, S. C. 13, 129
Lewinski, M. 98, 133, 136, 160
Lewis, D. K. 38
Lindsey, J. J. 175
Linkugel, W. A. 175
Locke, J. 52
Longinus 71
Lord, D. 68
Lorenzen, P. 62
Lorenz, K. 62
Lumer, C. 113
Lunsford, A. A. 109

M
Macagno, F. 133
Mack, J. L. 87
Mackenzie, J. D. 61, 99, 216, 220, 254
Mackie, J. L. 240
Mansbridge, J. 141
March, J. G. 131
Martel, M. 46, 142
Martens, J. L. 247
Massey, G. 192
McEvoy, S. 78
McHugh, P. 42
Meerhoff, C. G. 87–88
Melanchthon 89, 124
Memedi, V. 1
Menashe, C. 126
Menkel-Meadow, C. 149

Meuffels, H. L. M. 195, 200, 213, 248
Meyer, M. 95, 266
Mill, J. S. 2, 34
Mitchell, G. R. 46
Mohammed, D. 160, 268, 274
Murphy, J. J. 71–72, 125
Myers, F. 110

N
Naess, A. 29, 60–61
Natanson, M. 88
Nicolaus of Damascus 66
Nuchelmans, G. 189

O
Ochs, D. J. 71, 102
O'Keefe, D. J. 66, 199, 269
Olbrechts-Tyteca, L. 1, 31–32, 46, 75–76, 83, 88, 102, 107, 110–119, 121, 123, 219
Olsen, J. P. 131
Ong, W. J. 83
Orr, C. J. 77

P
Pan, Z. 126
Pareto, V. 118
Pater, W. A. de 103–104
Patton, B. 142, 149
Perelman, C. 1, 31–32, 46, 75–76, 83, 88, 102, 107, 110–114, 116–119, 121, 123, 219
Perlof, M. R. 142
Peter of Spain 105–106
Petty, R. E. 269–270
Phaedrus 68
Pike, K. L. 136
Pinto, R. C. 190, 232
Plato 52, 54–57, 59–60, 67–68, 81, 86–87
Plug, H. J. 61
Poole, M. S. 149
Popper, K. R. 5, 29, 31, 33–35
Poster, C. 121
Poulakos, J. 67
Prakken, H. 266
Putnam, L. L. 149, 157

Q
Quintilian 53

R
Rainolds, J. 81

Ramus 52, 83, 87
Ray, J. W. 117
Reboul, O. 81–82, 88, 121, 123
Rees, M. A. van 64–65, 109, 162
Rescher, N. 54, 63–64, 85, 213–215, 217, 219–220, 226–227, 229, 232
Richards, I. A. 52, 73
Rigotti, E. 70, 108, 130, 139, 265
Rijksbaron, A. 41
Rocci, A. 121, 130, 139
Rogers, N. H. 142
Roloff, M. E. 157
Ross, W. H. 142
Rowe, C. 68
Rubinelli, S. 58–59, 67, 95, 102–105

S
Sander, F. E. A. 142
Sapir, E. 25
Sawyer, J. 150
Schedler, A. 141
Schiappa, E. 52–53, 67, 73, 77–78
Schumpeter, J. A. 3
Schütz, A. 46
Scott, R. L. 74, 254
Searle, J. R. 2, 7, 10, 37, 129, 154, 228
Secor, M. J. 70, 105

Shapin, S. 88
Siegel, H. 2, 192, 200
Siegel, M. 126
Simons, H. W. 52–53
Slob, W. 54
Snoeck Henkemans, A. F. 12–13, 98, 100, 121, 169, 237, 272
Socrates 32, 68, 81, 101
Staines, P. 216, 220
Stump, E. 84, 102–103, 105–106
Swales, J. M. 139
Swearingen, C. J. 52–53, 73

T
Taylor, R. C. R. 131
Thurow, G. E. 78
Tindale, C. W. 1, 53, 91, 95, 114–116, 118, 125, 165, 272
Tonnard, Y. 155, 160, 274
Toulmin, S. E. 31, 54, 64, 75, 88, 101, 240
Trapp R. 51–52, 73–74, 88
Tseronis, A. 272
Tulis, J. K. 78
Tutzauer, F. 150, 158
Tversky, A. 126

U
Ullmann-Margalit, E. 225
Ulrich, W. 190
Uzqueda, A. 142

V
Varga, K. 125
Verheij, B. 75
Vuchinich, S. 10, 142, 152

W
Wagemans, J. H. M. 55–58, 72, 81, 90, 192
Wall Jr., J. A. 156
Walton, D. N. 63, 132, 134, 158, 190, 201, 203, 206, 214–215, 230, 252, 265
Ware, B. L. 175
Weaver, R. M. 73, 88
Weigand, E. 265
Weiss, G. 266
Wenzel, J. W. 31, 77, 88
Whately, R. 72–73, 213–214, 218–219, 233
Whorf, B. L. 25
Willard, C. A. 75, 200
William of Orange 18
Wilson, K. H. 52, 73
Wisse, I. 71
Wodak, R. 18, 266
Woods, J. 190–192, 203, 206

Z
Zarefsky, D. 78, 81, 85, 126, 265, 273
Zeno 55, 57–59

Index of terms 名词索引

A

academic debate *see* debate
acceptability 1, 5–6, 15–16, 26, 28–29, 31–32, 34, 39, 44, 57, 60, 65, 76, 80, 84, 89, 104, 109, 114, 137, 184, 191–192, 195, 202, 213, 217, 225–226, 231, 235, 266
accepted opinion 84, 219
accusation of inconsistency 160–161, 247–251, 261–262, 268, 274
actio 17, 87
activity type *see* communicative activity type
adaptation/adjustment to audience demand *see* audience demand/orientation
addition (transformation) 14–15
adequacy condition 203, 206
ad fallacy 188
ad hominem see argumentum ad hominem
adjacency pair 17
adjudication 139–140, 142–143, 146–147, 149, 151–153, 160, 273
advertisement 77, 235, 240
advertorial 20–21, 47, 49, 143, 165–177, 182–186, 207, 209–211
Alternative Dispute Resolution 142
American Presidential debate *see* debate
amplification 11
analogy argumentation *see* comparison argumentation/relation
analysis *see* reconstruction/reconstructive analysis
reconstructive, *see* reconstruction/reconstructive analysis
analytical component research program 5, 8, 271

analytic overview 10–17, 19, 163, 165, 168, 183–185, 264, 272
antagonist 3, 6–7, 10–11, 20, 28, 33–34, 44–45, 64, 99–100, 109, 178–179, 184–185, 191, 193–195, 215–216, 218, 232–236, 239, 242–244
  collective 109
  official 109
anticategoria 243
antimetabole 125
antique dialectical strategy 58
antistrophos 81, 84, 86
antithesis 125, 174
apologia 139, 175–176, 182–183, 185, 210, 231
apology 143, 206
appeal to authority *see* argument from authority
appropriateness 72, 85, 140
approximation of a critical/formal dialectical discussion 172, 257
approximation of truth 267
arbitration 140–143, 206
archeology *see* genealogy
argument 1, 4–5, 8, 11–13, 16, 20–21, 26, 29, 32, 44, 48, 53, 56–57, 59, 63–67, 72, 74–77, 85, 87, 91, 94, 101–106, 108–110, 114, 122–125, 132, 134, 150, 156–157, 165, 169, 172, 177, 179, 185, 189, 194, 202–208, 211–212, 215–218, 220, 228, 233, 253, 257, 262, 270–274
  based on the structure of reality 107
  creating a structure of reality 107
  from authority 165, 202–206, 271
  unexpressed *see* unexpressed premise
argumentatio 70–71, 96, 98, 107

argumentation 1–14, 18–22, 25–40, 43–47, 49–55, 57–60, 62–65, 67, 69–70, 72, 74–91, 94–95, 97, 99–100, 102–104, 106–110, 113–115, 117–118, 120, 122–123, 125, 129–138, 141, 145–146, 148, 150–152, 156–157, 164, 168–169, 171–179, 183–195, 199–200, 202, 207–210, 213–214, 216–218, 221, 233–234, 236–237, 242, 245, 254, 257–258, 261, 264–266, 269–274
argumentational strategy 46, 268, 272
argumentation stage 10–12, 20, 39, 44–47, 94, 97, 99–100, 108, 110, 113–115, 122, 151, 156, 164, 169, 171–173, 177, 179, 185–186, 208, 210, 214, 216, 233, 236, 242, 269, 271
argumentation structure 11–12, 19, 47, 168–169, 176
argumentative activity type 145–146, 152, 155, 159–161, 168, 242, 268, 273–274
argumentative attack 6–7, 28, 33, 41, 44–45, 56, 58–59, 61–62, 97, 100, 188, 214, 218, 232–233, 257
argumentative defense 6, 8, 41, 45, 58, 61–62, 70, 94, 97, 100, 102, 175, 194–195, 216, 218–219, 223–224, 227, 229–230, 232–234, 242
argumentative means and criticism 51, 69, 146–147, 151–152
argumentative move *see* move
argumentative practice/reality 4–5, 13, 22, 45, 64, 86, 93–94, 100, 111–112, 139, 165, 187, 199–200, 202–203, 216, 230, 242, 245, 248, 262–263, 271, 273

argumentative predicament 40–41
argumentative reality 5, 13, 17, 19–20, 22, 33, 35–36, 54, 63, 80, 89, 132, 197–198, 217, 257, 264
argumentative situation *see* situation argumentative
argument scheme 8, 11–12, 21, 44, 57, 76, 94, 101–105, 169, 177, 194, 202–205, 215–218, 233, 273
Argument Scheme Rule 8, 57, 194, 203, 205
argumentum
　ad baculum 196
　ad hominem 188, 195–196, 201, 211, 231, 244, 248, 253, 262, 271
　　abusive variant 253, 262, 271
　　circumstantial variant 231
　　tu quoque variant 231, 243–244, 248, 250–251, 253, 261–262
　ad ignorantiam 192, 222, 234
　ad misericordiam 196
　ad populum 194
　ad verecundiam 188–189, 203, 205, 234, 261
Aristotelian list of fallacies 189
Aristotle's dialectic(al discussion) 56–59
aspect of strategic maneuvering 93, 95–98
assertive 11, 15–16, 33, 214, 224, 228–230, 245
assessment criteria *see* soundness criteria
associated conditional 12
associated perlocution 37
atechnos 181
audience 1, 3, 15, 26–27, 32, 40, 42, 47, 52–53, 55, 66–67, 69–76, 80, 84, 89, 91, 94–97, 107–119, 121, 123–126, 142, 148, 151–152, 154, 157–158, 161–162, 164–165, 168–169, 171, 180–182, 185, 207, 210, 248, 261–263, 267, 270, 272, 274
　addressed 70, 84, 109, 113–114, 117, 180
　collective 109
　composite/heterogeneous 110
　　mixed 110
　　multiple 110

　constructed 115–116
　demand/orientation 94–97, 108, 112–115, 118–119, 125, 152, 164, 169, 171, 207, 261, 270, 272
　invoked 109
　multiple 110
　particular 76, 111, 116–118
　primary 109, 154, 169, 210
　secondary 109, 154
　third party *see* third party
　universal 32, 76, 116–118

B
background information/knowledge 18–19, 162
　general 18
　specific 18
bargaining 149–150
begging the question *see* fallacy of *petitio principii*
Begründung 31
black rhetoric 86
blunder 198
broadening the zone of agreement 46
burden of initiation/initiative 64, 226, 229–230
burden of proof 23, 44, 64, 99, 147, 194, 213–240, 242, 252–253, 271–273
Burden of Proof Rule *see* Obligation-to-Defend Rule
business communication *see* commercial communication/domain

C
Carlsberg case 235–240
causal argumentation/relation 12, 104, 177, 209, 217
central route (to persuasion) 270
chat 141–143, 174–175, 206, 248
circular reasoning *see* fallacy of *petitio principii*
classical dialectic(al system) 51, 54–55, 59–60, 81, 90, 122
cluster of communicative activity types 139, 144, 146–150, 154–157
code of conduct 3–4, 7, 193–194
commercial communication/domain 143, 175

commissive 11
commitment 6, 14, 16, 27–28, 33, 49, 64, 94, 108–112, 115–116, 137, 156–157, 163–165, 168–169, 178–179, 182, 185, 197–201, 207–208, 214–217, 219–220, 225–227, 232, 237, 241, 245–256, 264, 268, 272
　avowed 216, 241, 245, 268
　contextual 216, 226
　dark-side *see* commitment contextual
　descriptive 110
　dialectical 182, 225, 256, 264, 272
　formal (discussion rule) 49, 216
　generally accepted *see* accepted opinion
　material (premise) 216
　normative 110–111
　pragmatic 111, 225
　propositional 216, 245
　rule 220
　veiled *see* commitment contextual
commitment set 116
communication rule 17
communicative act complex *see* speech act complex
communicative act/effect 27–28, 36–39, 227, 268
communicative activity type 23, 112, 129–163, 165, 174–176, 181–183, 197, 202, 204, 206, 210, 215, 223, 230–231, 234, 242, 246, 248, 256, 264, 268, 272–274
　coincidentally argumentative 145
　essentially argumentative 145
　non-argumentative 146
　predominantly argumentative 145, 147
communicative domain 23, 130–131, 139–140, 142–143, 248, 266, 273
communicative sphere 4, 85, 113, 129–130, 139
communion 76, 108, 139, 142–143, 174
comparison argumentation/relation 12, 217

component of the *oratio* 71, 97, 105, 107
composite/heterogeneous audience *see* audience
compulsion 35
concession 33, 44, 48, 56–57, 59, 61–63, 85, 100–111, 120, 147–152, 154, 156–169, 173, 179, 214, 216, 220, 231–232, 234, 239, 242, 245, 247
conciliatio 121, 165, 177–178, 208–211
concluding maneuvering/strategy 46–47, 163, 210, 268, 272
Concluding Rule 7–8, 194
concluding stage 7, 10–12, 39, 44–46, 49, 97, 100, 110, 113, 122, 156, 169, 179, 182–186, 208, 220, 233–234
confirmatio 96
confrontational challenging 100
confrontational maneuvering/strategy 46, 163, 211, 268, 272
confrontation stage 7, 10–13, 20, 39, 43, 45–46, 94, 97, 99–100, 112, 115, 121, 151, 153, 156, 168–172, 175, 178, 182–183, 195, 201, 208, 210–211, 220–221, 230–231, 233, 236, 244, 256, 268, 271
consecutive/optimal perlocutionary consequence 36
consensus 10, 30–31, 34, 77–78, 89, 118, 203, 206–207
constraint *see* institutional constraint
constraint on audience adaptation 152
constraint on presentational choice/device 152
constraint on topical choice 152
consultation 139, 143, 160
context 1, 4, 6, 8, 13, 16–18, 20, 23, 28–29, 59, 63–64, 72, 74, 91, 101–102, 104–105, 115, 117–118, 120–121, 126, 129–136, 138, 142, 152, 155, 157, 159, 162–163, 165, 174, 178, 181, 187–188, 197–206, 208, 213, 216, 219–220, 223, 225, 231, 234, 242, 245–246, 248–249, 256, 258, 267–268, 271, 273
extralinguistic *see* mesocontext

contradiction *see* inconsistency logical
controversy studies 265
convention/conventionalization/conventionalized 23, 129–133, 135–136, 139, 141, 144–145, 148, 150, 152, 174–175, 182, 223, 242, 273
convention(al)/conventionalized communicative activity/practice 23, 129–130, 144–145, 175
conventional precondition *see* institutional precondition
conventional validity 32, 34–35, 137, 191, 195, 237
conversational context of argument 63, 132
conversational implicature *see* implicature
Cooperation Principle *see* Principle of Cooperation
coordinated strategic maneuvering 45–47, 272
coordinative argumentation (structure) 169
coordinative strategic maneuvers 47
correctness condition 6, 16–17, 28, 33, 111, 178, 227, 236, 268
countermove 64, 98
court case/proceedings 109, 131, 139–140, 147, 153, 234, 248, 253
criminal trial 147, 174–175, 206, 242
criteria *see* soundness criteria
critical discourse analysis 266
critical discussion 3–4, 6–7, 9–10, 12–14, 16–17, 23, 28, 30, 32–35, 42–43, 46, 49–50, 58–59, 61, 74, 80, 89, 96–99, 114, 129–130, 133–134, 144–147, 160, 168, 172, 191, 193–201, 204–205, 208, 210–215, 217, 220–225, 234–236, 239, 242–243, 245–247, 251, 254–256, 258, 260, 263–264, 267–269, 271, 273
model of a 7, 9–14, 16, 28, 74, 96, 98, 114, 129–130, 144–147, 191, 197, 213, 217, 254–255, 269
norm/standard for 4, 7, 15, 27, 31, 39, 63, 192–193, 200, 211, 220

rule for 50, 193, 200, 205, 210, 212, 255–256
critical question/reaction 3, 6, 12, 60, 64, 177–178, 203, 215–218, 233–234, 271
critical rationalism 33, 77
critical testing procedure *see* intersubjective testing procedure
cumulative coordinative argumentation (structure) 169

D
debate 26, 36, 57, 59–60, 101, 103, 109, 131, 134, 138–143, 145, 147–148, 152–155, 160, 188, 204, 223, 242, 248, 259, 274
academic/scientific 153, 204
parliamentary 140–141, 145, 154–155, 223, 242, 248
law-making 160
plenary 147, 152
general 141, 143, 155, 160, 274
political 109, 134, 138, 248
public 109, 141, 148, 154
Presidential 131, 139–141, 143, 148
American 139, 141, 148
public 109, 141, 148, 154
television 109, 131, 139, 141–143
deceptiveness of fallacies 196, 199, 271
declaring a standpoint sacrosanct *see* fallacy of declaring a standpoint sacrosanct
deep disagreement 1
definition 4, 11, 14, 25–29, 43, 45–46, 52–54, 62, 65–66, 69, 73, 75, 78–79, 85, 90, 97, 103, 115, 121, 125–126, 138, 142, 147, 150, 152, 179, 189, 197, 199, 214, 230, 237, 244, 254, 269
rhetorical 179
deletion (transformation) 14–15
deliberation 80, 99, 133, 138–142, 147–149, 151, 154, 159–160, 219, 223, 242
deliberative democracy 140
deliberative genre *see genus deliberativum*
demarcation problem 200
demonstration (proof) 1, 31, 70, 145

Index of terms 301

denying an unexpressed premise *see* fallacy of denying an unexpressed premise
derailment of strategic maneuvering 23, 41, 187, 198–201, 207, 209–210, 240, 243–244, 253, 256, 260–261, 274
descriptive dimension 5
design engineering 265
dialectical aim/goal/objective 42–45, 98, 179, 230–231, 233–234, 243, 254, 263–264
dialectical condition 250
dialectical dimension/ideal/perspective 3–4, 12, 42–43, 47, 51, 53, 60, 64, 80, 91–93, 97, 113, 179, 188, 213–214, 229, 239, 245, 254, 259, 263
dialectical position 236, 247–248, 250
dialectical power 233–234, 270
dialectical procedure 31–32, 34–35, 55, 58, 91, 99, 180
dialectical profile 18, 98–100, 145, 163, 168, 171–173, 178, 183–185, 221, 223, 242, 264, 272
dialectical reasoning 55, 58–59, 84
dialectical route 165, 270
dialectical rule 4, 7, 57–58, 82, 195, 197, 255, 258
dialectical shift 134–135
dialectical situation *see* situation
dialectical strength 270
dialectical system 61–63, 65, 132, 257
dialectical tier 53, 64–65, 85, 91
dialectification 28
dialogical tableaux 61
dialogue analysis 265
dialogue context 133
dialogue logic 61, 63, 132
dialogue type 63, 132–135, 137–138, 144
difference of opinion 1, 3, 6–14, 17, 26, 28–29, 32–34, 39–46, 51, 58, 60, 62, 89, 94, 96–99, 110, 112–113, 115, 121, 146–151, 156, 162, 164, 168–171, 179, 183–184, 191–196, 198, 201, 203, 210–211, 213, 215–216, 218, 220–224, 228–233, 235–236, 243, 246–248, 250–257, 260, 262–263, 266, 270–271

mixed 13, 94, 99, 112, 169–170, 183–184, 213, 215–216, 218–219, 221–223, 228–229, 232, 243, 271
multiple 168
non-mixed 99, 112, 169–170, 183–184, 213, 216, 218, 243
simple 222
single 94, 99, 168
type of 12, 243
differentia(e) 71, 103, 106
digressio 96
diplomatic communication/domain 130–131, 143
directive 11, 15
disagreement space 28, 46, 100, 171
discourse dialectic 5, 89
discursive formation 74
discussion 2–7, 9–14, 16–17, 23, 27–28, 30–36, 38, 42–50, 55–62, 64, 74, 80–81, 83, 85, 87, 89–90, 94, 96–100, 104–105, 107, 109, 111–116, 122, 129–130, 132, 133–134, 142, 144–148, 150–151, 156, 159–160, 162, 164–165, 168–169, 172–173, 175–177, 179, 182–183, 186, 191, 193–201, 203–206, 208, 210–217, 220–226, 229, 231–232, 234–237, 239, 241–248, 250–251, 253–264, 267–269, 271–274
discussion role 6, 13, 28, 56, 147, 231–232, 247–248
discussion stage *see* stage of critical discussion
discussion strategy 5–47, 268, 272
dispositio 71–72, 87
disputation (model) 63
dissociation 46, 162, 170, 183
distribution of speech acts 11
division of the burden of proof *see* burden of proof
domain of communicative activity 129–131, 138–144, 150, 153, 159–160, 174–175

E

effective(ness) 22, 25–36, 39–44, 49–51, 55, 66, 72–74, 77, 80, 84–85, 89–92, 95, 97, 102, 107–108, 112, 123, 179, 198, 200, 207, 256–257, 262–264, 266–267, 269–270

Elaboration Likelihood Model 269
elenchus 55–58
elocutio 71–72, 87
emic perspective 6, 136
empirical component research program 5, 8, 35–36, 269–270
empirical standard 32, 41, 200
endoxa see accepted opinion
entechnos 181
enthymeme 69–70, 104–105
epicheirema 70
epideictic genre *see genus demonstrativum*
epilogos see peroratio
episteme 74
epistemic/epistemological perspective 113, 192, 217
eristic discussion 58, 60, 133–134
Erlangen School 61
essential condition 39, 268
ethical perspective 190
ethnographic information *see* background information/knowledge specific
ethos 56, 66, 69, 71, 96, 174, 186, 240
etic perspective 6, 136
European predicament 152
evading the burden of proof *see* fallacy of evading the burden of proof
example 69
ex autoritate see argument from authority
ex concessis 61, 177, 207, 210, 221, 247
exordium 71, 96, 98, 107
experimental research *see* empirical component research program
expert information *see* background information/knowledge specific
explicitization procedure for unexpressed premises 172
expressive 27, 120
extended approach *see* pragma-dialectical approach/method/theory
externalization 6, 27–28, 215, 220
external perspective 32, 35, 105, 136–137

Index of terms

F
face-threatening act/move 13, 156
fallacy 7–8, 16, 23–34, 50, 80, 89, 92, 134–137, 187–203, 211, 219, 230, 241, 243–244, 248, 250–254, 256–261, 263–264, 271
  logical Standard Definition of *see* Standard Definition
  perceived *see* fallacy would-be
  would-be 252, 260
fallacy criticism 258
fallacy of declaring a standpoint sacrosanct 194
fallacy of denying an unexpressed premise 194
fallacy of evading the burden of proof 219, 230
fallacy of *ignoratio elenchi* 50, 234
fallacy of making an absolute of the success of the defense 194
fallacy of many questions 180, 189
fallacy of *petitio principii* 188–189
fallacy of shifting the burden of proof 253
fallacy of the straw man 8, 232, 261
fallacy of wrongly accusing the other party of an inconsistency 241, 252
false dilemma 186, 211
felicity condition *see* identity condition *and* correctness condition
field of argument *see* genre (of communicative activity)
figure of style *see* figures of speech and thought
figures of speech and thought 71, 121–122, 124
first order condition 35
forensic genre *see genus iudiciale*
formal dialectic 5, 61–63, 65, 89, 191, 214, 254–255, 257, 265
formal logic/model/perspective 32, 75–76, 101, 192, 254
forum *see* Science Forum
frame convergence 127
framing 112, 119, 126–127

framing device 126
Freedom Rule 7, 57, 194–196, 201, 244, 253, 271
functionalization 5, 27–28
functional perspective 254

G
game 10, 42, 59, 61, 63, 75, 132–133, 149, 162, 254–256
  non-zero-sum 149
  zero-sum 149
genealogy 74
general plenary parliamentary debate 141
genre (of communicative activity) 131, 139–145, 147–151, 154–157, 159–160, 175
genus deliberativum 69
genus demonstrativum 69
genus iudiciale 69, 153
good man *see vir bonus*
Gricean maxim 120, 200
Gricean maxim of manner 120
Gricean maxim of quality 225
Gricean theory of rational exchanges 225
guarantee function 104

H
Hellenistic rhetoric 70
Heuristic-Systematic Model 269
hidden dialogicality 115
higher order condition 35, 243, 257
horizontal convergence/coordination 47, 272
hyper dialectical definition of argument 65–66
hypothesis 55–56, 59

I
ideal speech situation 35, 74
identification 74–75
identity condition 6, 28, 111, 236
ideological analysis/perspective/point of view 77, 88–89, 91
idia *see topos (topoi)* special
ignoratio elenchi see fallacy of *ignoratio elenchi*
illative core/tier 64–65, 85
illicit shift 135
illocution(ary act/effect) *see* communicative act/effect
illocutionary perlocution 37–38

implicature 18, 120, 255
inclusion strategy 210
incompatibility 241
inconsistency 18, 23, 33, 48, 159–162, 198, 241–252, 261–262, 268, 274
  logical 241
  pragmatic 18, 33, 241–242
inference 18, 33, 82, 101–102, 107, 232, 245
  logical 33, 241
  pragmatic 18
informal logic 64, 88, 265
information-seeking dialogue 133–134, 138
ingenium 73
inherent/minimal perlocutionary effect 36
initial situation 62, 133, 146–147, 149–152, 154
inquiry 63, 73, 133, 138, 221
inside information *see* background information/knowledge specific
institution(alized) 5, 23, 77, 129–131, 136, 140–142, 147–148, 155, 174–175, 204, 223, 266–267
institutional constraint 4, 74, 80, 117, 129, 133, 142, 146, 148, 152–155, 159, 162–163, 168, 174–175, 181, 197, 264, 273
institutional convention 112, 141–142, 150, 174, 182, 242, 256
institutional demand *see* institutional requirement
institutional goal 139–141, 147, 159, 165, 273
institutionally determined convention 130–131, 140–141, 144–145, 150, 174–175, 204, 242
institutional mission 49, 139–140, 144, 146, 152, 154, 165
institutional point 129–131, 139–142, 144–146, 148, 152, 155, 159, 206, 210, 234
institutional precondition 23, 129–130, 146, 152–155, 159–161, 163, 174–175
  primary 152
  secondary 152
institutional requirement 274
integrated approach *see* pragma-dialectical approach/method/theory extended

interactional act complex *see* speech act complex
interactional act/effect 22, 27–28, 36–37, 38, 40, 108, 119–120, 268
interaction field 130, 139
Interaction Principle 225–226
interaction scheme 139
interdiscursive context *see* intertextual context
internal perspective 136–137
international communication/domain *see* diplomatic communication/domain
Internet communication 136
Internet forum discussion 147, 160
interpersonal communication/domain 130, 142–143
interpretation 8, 10, 19, 66, 79, 81, 89, 104, 118, 126, 138, 147, 179, 225–226, 236–237, 240, 254–256, 272
intersubjective explicitization procedure 33, 172
intersubjective identification procedure 216, 245
intersubjective inference procedure 245
intersubjective reasoning procedure 62
intersubjective testing procedure 5
intersubjective validity *see* conventional validity
intertextual context 18
inventio 71–72, 87, 96, 107
issue (design) 79
 procedural 260

J
John Sopel case 160–161
journalism 140
juridical perspective 139, 234, 273
justificationism 5, 31

K
Karremans case 184–185

L
language usage declarative *see* usage declarative
Language Use Rule 8, 57, 212

law-making debate *see* debate parliamentary
legal case/proceedings *see* court case/proceedings
legal communication/domain 108, 130–131, 143, 147, 153, 160, 183, 206
letter to the editor 246
licit shift 135
line of attack 97, 100
line of defense 94, 100, 102
locus (loci) see topos (topoi)
logic(al approach/dimension) 31, 53, 64, 85
logical minimum 12
logical perspective *see* formal logic/model/perspective
logical reasoning 18
logical Standard Definition of a fallacy *see* Standard Definition
logical Standard Treatment of the fallacies *see* Standard Treatment
logical validity 61, 87, 108
logos 56, 66–67, 69, 96

M
macro-context 18, 126, 129–131, 142, 152, 155, 159, 163, 165, 174, 181, 197, 199, 201–206, 223, 234, 242, 248, 256
Max Havelaar case 153
maxim *see* Gricean maxim
maximal proposition 106
maxim of manner *see* Gricean maxim of manner
maxim of quality *see* Gricean maxim of quality
mediation 126, 139–140, 142–143, 147–149, 151, 156–157
 custody 143, 148
medical communication/domain 143, 160, 273
memoria 71
meso-context 18, 178
meta-analysis 199, 269
meta-dialogue/discussion 184, 257–260
meta-discussion 242, 259
metalepsis 121
metaphor 41, 121–124, 185
meta-theoretical principle 5, 27–28, 108

method of collection and division 56
method of hypothesizing 55–57, 59
methodological starting point *see* meta-theoretical principle
metonymy 121
micro-context 17–18
minimal dialectic(al system) 62
misunderstanding 31, 66, 73, 213
mixed dialogue 134
mixed speech event 134
mode of strategic maneuvering 46–47, 152, 163–165, 185, 198–202, 204, 206–208, 213, 241, 243–244, 264, 267–268, 271, 273
modus ponens 104–105
move 3, 7, 9–10, 13, 16, 23, 28, 32, 47, 50, 89, 93–95, 99–101, 103, 106–112, 116, 118–120, 123, 137, 161, 163–164, 166, 168, 174, 176, 178–179, 183–185, 187, 193, 195, 198, 200–202, 206, 210, 222, 254, 256, 263–264, 268, 270
 direct 111, 120, 235, 255
 explicit 27, 120, 151, 215, 220, 225, 231, 241, 246, 255
 implicit 10, 12, 14, 26–27, 120, 151, 194, 196, 215–216, 220, 225, 231, 241, 246, 255–256
 indirect 9–10, 12, 14–16, 49, 109, 111, 120, 255–256
multiple argumentation (structure) 19, 110, 233
multiple audience *see* audience
multiple strategic maneuvers 47
Münchhausen trilemma 31, 221

N
narratio 71, 96, 98, 107
negotiation 26, 133–135, 139, 142–143, 147, 149–151, 157–158, 249–250
 distributive 149
 integrative 149
neo-classical approach 76, 102
New Institutionalism 130–131
new rhetoric 31, 75–76, 83, 88, 107, 113–114, 116, 123, 219
news bulletin 145
Nigeria spam case 187–188, 202
normative dimension 5, 29, 79, 266

normative pragmatics 4–5, 79, 258
norm of reasonableness *see* rule for critical discussion

O
Obligation-to-Defend Rule 7, 58, 194, 213–214, 219
officia oratoris see tasks of the orator
one-and-the-same-critical-discussion criterion 246
opening maneuvering/strategy 46, 163, 210, 268, 272
open society 34–35
opening stage 10–12, 39, 44–46, 94, 99–100, 110–111, 113–114, 120–121, 151, 156, 169, 172, 205–206, 210, 213–214, 216–217, 221–223, 230–233, 239, 242, 247
opponent 61–62, 64, 118, 169–170, 172–173, 177, 182–183, 195–196, 208–210, 247, 260, 264
opportunity 35, 162, 198, 232, 245, 259
order of defense 218–219, 223–224, 227, 230
ordinary arguer 6
orientation 4, 63, 79, 82, 95–96, 108, 115, 120, 164, 216
outcome/result of (stage of) argumentative discussion 4, 6, 11–14, 47, 100–101, 113, 122, 146, 148–152, 154, 157, 161–162, 165, 168–169, 172, 185, 222, 247, 250–251, 263, 272

P
package deal 158
partes orationis/parts of the *oratio* 96–97, 107
pathos 56, 66, 69, 71, 96
peace talks 142–143, 149–150
peitho 67
Perfect Spy case 208–209
perlocution(ary act/effect) *see* interactional act/effect
perlocution cube 37–38
permutation (transformation) 14–15
peroratio 71, 96, 98, 107
personal attack 186, 196, 201, 253, 262, 271

persuasion dialogue 63, 86–87, 133–134
persuasion research 66, 269–270
persuasive(ness) 39, 52, 58, 66, 76, 78–79, 85–87, 101–102, 123, 186, 199–201, 211, 269
petitio principii see fallacy of *petitio principii*
philosophical component research program 5, 266–267
philosophy of action 267
phronesis 68, 72
Plato's dialogues 54, 56–57, 67–68
plenary parliamentary debate *see* debate
pointing out an inconsistency 198, 241, 244, 247, 268
point of departure *see* starting point/premise
point of order 258, 260
policy statement 210
political communication/domain 4, 130–131, 140–141, 143, 159–160, 183, 273
political interview 131, 140–141, 145, 159–162, 204, 268, 274
polyptoton 125
practical component research program 5, 8, 273
practical impact fallacy 7, 248, 252–253
practice *see* argumentative practive/reality
praeteritio 121, 272
pragma-dialectical approach/method/theory 7, 16, 19–22, 27–28, 32–35, 51, 53–55, 57–58, 63–65, 72, 79–81, 86, 89–90, 94, 109, 113–115, 132–133, 191–194, 196, 200–201, 214–217, 220–221, 223, 225, 239, 244–246, 254–255, 263, 267, 271–272
extended 22–23, 49–50, 58, 200, 239, 263–264, 267, 271
standard 19, 21–22, 86, 263
pragmatic device 121
pragmatic optimum 12, 18
pragmatic perspective 63
pragmatics 4–5, 79, 119, 123, 258
normative *see* normative pragmatics
precization 60, 204

precondition for strategic maneuvering 23, 129–131, 152–156, 159–162, 174–175, 183, 223, 230, 264, 272–274
predicable 103, 106
premise *see* starting point/premise
preparatory condition 112, 236
presentational choice/device/means 94–97, 112, 118–123, 126, 152, 156–157, 162, 165, 168, 170, 174, 185–186, 207, 239, 261, 270, 272, 274
Presidential debate *see* debate
presumption 39, 64, 110, 116, 199, 218–219, 225–226, 228, 230, 233, 235, 274
primary audience *see* audience
Prime Minister's question time 140–141, 143, 152, 160, 268, 274
Principle of Communication 200, 255, 262
Principle of Cooperation 200, 255
Principle of Least Effort 269
Principle of Reasonableness 32, 253
pro-aut-contra survey 60–61
probative obligation 79, 227
problem of choice 96, 218, 233
problem of order 233
problem-solving communication/domain 142–143
problem (solving) validity 34
procedure *see* dialectical procedure
pro-et-contra survey 60–61
profile of dialogue 98
Progressive Liberals case 249–251
pro-life case 258–260
promotion 32, 139, 143
pronunciatio see actio
proponent 61–64
propositio 71, 96
propositional content condition 39
protagonist 3, 6–7, 10–11, 20, 28, 31, 33–34, 43–45, 59, 88, 99–100, 109, 121, 140, 148, 172–173, 178–179, 184–185, 191, 193–195, 215–218, 232–235, 239, 242–245, 247, 271
collective 109

protaseis 103
prudentia see phronesis

Q

qualitative analysis/research *see* empirical component research program 271
quantitative research *see* empirical component research program
quasi-discussion 3
quasi-logical argument 107

R

rational choice institutionalism 130–131
rational(ity) 29, 64, 72, 75, 77, 85–86, 91, 133, 245
readjusting derailment *see* repair of derailment
reasonable(ness) 1–7, 15, 17, 25–27, 29–36, 37, 39–45, 50–51, 54–55, 57–59, 63, 69, 76, 80, 89–92, 95, 97–98, 102, 104, 108, 113, 116–118, 133, 135, 137, 148–149, 152–153, 160, 163, 179, 197–201, 207, 210, 213, 220, 226, 232, 234, 245, 248, 253–254, 256–259, 260–264, 266–274
    assumption of *see* reasonable(ness) presumption of
    conception/philosophy of 5, 31–32, 34, 54, 245, 267
    anthropological 31–32, 54, 266
    critical (rationalist) 17, 35, 54, 89, 102, 261
    geometrical 31–32, 54
    dialectical 4, 22, 51, 90, 254, 256, 262–263, 273
    judge 26, 29, 32, 39, 266
    option *see* dialectical profile
    presumption of 39, 199
reconstruction/reconstructive analysis 9, 12–22, 42, 49, 56, 58, 103, 115, 163, 169, 171, 176, 182–183, 185, 197, 212, 224, 246–247, 263, 265–267, 271
refutatio 96
register 119
Relevance Rule 7, 43, 50, 194, 212
relevance/relevant 7, 9, 43, 50, 65, 73, 154, 162, 194, 211–212
analytical(ly) 9–10, 13, 98–99, 161–163, 165, 171–172, 183–185, 211, 272
evaluative(ly) 9, 211
repair 201, 254–255, 261–262
repair of derailment 23
repetitio 165
re-railing derailment *see* repair of derailment
research program 1, 4–6, 8, 54, 198, 264–265, 269, 271, 273
resolution process 9–10, 13–16, 33, 41, 43, 47, 62, 93, 98, 108, 110, 115, 146, 156, 163–164, 178, 181, 193, 195, 197, 201, 230–231, 246, 252–255, 262–263, 270
resolving a difference of opinion on the merits 1, 3, 5–7, 10–11, 13–14, 17, 26, 28, 32–35, 40–42, 44–45, 60, 89–90, 98, 107, 112, 126, 145–146, 179, 191–193, 201, 213, 217–218, 227, 246, 252–257, 262, 266, 270
responsibility condition *see* sincerity condition
result *see* outcome/result of (stage of) argumentative discussion
Reynolds tobacco case 20–21, 47–50
rhetor 40, 52, 59, 66, 70, 74, 77, 180–181
rhetorical aim/goal/objective 42, 44–46, 49, 58, 86, 96, 98, 159, 199, 231, 243, 260, 263–264, 273
rhetoric(al analysis) 2–3, 22, 31, 42–47, 49, 51–55, 58, 66–98, 101–102, 104, 107, 112–113, 115, 121–126, 133, 148, 153, 159, 179–183, 185, 188, 190, 199–200, 207–209, 231, 233–234, 239–240, 243, 252, 256–260, 262–264, 266–267, 269–270, 272–273
rhetorical criticism 78
rhetorical deductive syllogims *see* enthymeme
rhetorical dimension/perspective 42, 44, 51–53, 72, 76–81, 90–93, 97, 101, 133, 148, 179, 182, 188, 190, 233, 239, 263, 266
rhetorical evocation 86
rhetorical figure *see* figures of speech and thought
rhetorical inductive syllogism *see* example
rhetorical power 234
rhetorical question 121, 207–209
risk of non-persuasion 231
Roman-Hellenistic rhetoric 70
route *see* dialectical route
rule for critical discussion 6–7, 23, 32, 34, 43, 50, 89, 147, 191, 193–201, 204–205, 210–212, 217, 255–256, 258, 260, 264, 267–268
rule of communication 200

S

scenario 145, 186, 205
scholarly communication/domain 143, 206
Science Forum 30
scientific debate *see* debate
scientific/scholarly paper 143, 206
scope of conclusiveness 100
scrabble case 204–205
script 126
Searlean speech act theory 36, 96, 120, 225
secondary audience *see* audience
second order condition 156
selection function 104
semantic device 121
semantic tableaux 61
semi-conventional validity *see* conventional validity
set of commitments *see* commitment set
Shell case 143, 165–178, 182–183, 185–186, 209–212
shift of burden of proof *see* burden of proof
shift of initiative 215
sign argumentation *see* symptomatic argumentation/relation
sincerity condition 38–39, 236
single argumentation (structure) 216
situation
    argumentative 18, 42, 63, 91, 111–112, 115–116, 163–165, 168, 178–179, 182–183, 185, 221, 227, 229, 264, 272

Index of terms

dialectical 100, 112, 179–180, 182, 221–222, 247
rhetorical 179–182
socialization 6, 27–28, 108, 136, 144, 206, 213
  primary 144, 206
  secondary 144, 206
Socratic *elenchus see* elenchus
sophia 68
sophism/sophistry 60, 86, 188
sophist(ic tradition) 53, 67–68, 70, 86–87, 102, 188
soundness condition 75, 202–203, 244, 249, 251, 267–268
soundness criteria 197, 202, 204–206, 244, 264, 268
  general/context-independent 197, 202, 204, 206, 268
  specific/context-dependent 75, 202, 204–206, 267–268
speech act 2, 6–7, 9–11, 14–17, 27–28, 32–33, 36–37, 39–40, 74, 77, 79, 93, 96, 108, 111–112, 116, 120, 124, 133, 154, 178, 191, 193, 197, 207–208, 214, 216, 220, 223, 225–230, 236, 245, 254–255
  complex 6, 16, 27–29, 36, 39–40
  elementary 16
speech event 18, 87, 133–135, 138, 140, 142–143, 145, 147, 149, 153, 159, 197
sphere *see* communicative sphere
stage of critical discussion 6–7, 43–45, 97, 100, 112, 179, 254, 268, 272
standard approach *see* pragma-dialectical approach/method/theory
Standard Definition 189, 199
Standard Objection 64–65, 218
Standard Treatment 23, 187, 189–191, 193–194, 199
standpoint 1–8, 10–16, 19–21, 26, 28–29, 31, 33, 37–40, 42–50, 55–62, 76, 80, 89, 94, 99–100, 103–104, 109, 113, 120–122, 148, 150–151, 155–157, 161–162, 164–165, 169, 173, 175, 177–179, 182, 184–185, 191, 193–196, 201–202, 207–209, 211–215, 217–219, 221–224, 228–229, 233, 236–240, 242, 258, 260, 266–267

descriptive 2, 15, 39, 237, 240, 267
evaluative 2, 16, 235–237, 240
inciting *see* standpoint prescriptive
nature of *see* standpoint type of
negative 164, 184, 221–222, 232
positive 164, 221–222
practical, *see* standpoint prescriptive
prescriptive 2, 5, 16, 20, 39, 47, 235–236, 239, 267
type of 2, 100
Standpoint Rule 7
starting point/premise 5, 7, 9, 11–15, 18, 20, 26–27, 29, 31–34, 39, 44–46, 48, 56, 62, 64, 70–71, 76, 84, 94, 97, 99–100, 102–107, 110, 112–113, 115–116, 119, 121, 130, 146–153, 157, 164, 169, 172–173, 177, 179, 181, 185, 190–192, 194, 201–202, 204–205, 208–209, 214–217, 219, 221, 226–228, 231–232, 241–244, 246–251, 253, 256, 264, 267, 269, 273
  explicit 216
  implicit 216
  material 11, 13, 44–45, 94, 97, 100, 113, 147, 150–152, 169, 179, 185, 231–232, 241–242, 247–248, 251
  procedural 44, 99, 228–244, 247–248, 251, 253, 256, 260–261, 268, 270–271, 273
Starting Point Rule 7, 208
starting profile 99
stasis doctrine *see* status doctrine
status
  coniecturalis 153
  definitivus 153
  doctrine 70, 102, 105, 108, 153
  qualitatis 153
  quo 219, 226–230, 233, 271
    cognitive *see* status quo
    epistemic 226–227
    pragmatic 226–230, 233
  translativus 153
status topoi 100
stock issue 79, 102, 153

strategic function 23, 45, 93, 120, 160–165, 168, 174, 176, 178–179, 183, 185, 263–264, 267, 272
strategic maneuver(ing) 22–23, 25, 39–51, 55, 58, 72, 78–81, 84, 86–90, 92, 93–101, 104, 107–108, 110–113, 115, 118–122, 125, 129–131, 142, 144, 146, 148, 152–157, 159–166, 168–171, 173–183, 185–187, 196, 198–211, 213, 218, 230–234, 239–241, 243–244, 247–249, 251, 253, 256–274
  coordinative 47
  multiple 47
  notion of 39–45, 93–127
  result *see* outcome/result of (stage of) argumentative discussion
  subordinative 47
  triangle 93–96
strategy 41, 45–47, 49, 56–58, 63, 67, 74, 79, 90, 101–103, 123, 125, 153, 157–158, 198, 210, 211, 240, 257, 268, 271–272
strategy of certification 210
strategy of circumvention 211
strategy of creating a smokescreen 46
strategy of humanization 210
strategy of humptydumptying 46
strategy of making the audience bite the bullet 47
strategy of rubbing in the facts 210
straw man fallacy *see* fallacy of the straw man
stylistic device 95
sub-discussion 162, 242, 260, 261
subordinative argumentation (structure) 169
subordinative strategic maneuvers 47
substitution (transformation) 14–15
summoning 140, 143, 147, 206
superaddressee 117–118
syllogism 69
system of dialogue rules 63, 132
symptomatic argumentation/relation 12, 177, 202, 217
syntactic device 121

T

tact(ical) 41, 198
tasks of the orator 96, 98, 102, 107
techne 57, 69
technique 32, 41, 46, 57, 74, 76, 103, 119, 122, 165, 196, 203, 206, 231, 243–244
television debate *see* debate
tenability 31, 55, 60, 213, 221–222, 233, 260
testing procedure *see* intersubjective testing procedure
theoretical component research program 5–6, 8
thesis 63, 188
third order condition 35
third party (audience) 109, 148, 207
topic (topics) *see* topos (topoi)
topical choice/potential/repertoire/selection 93–98, 100–101, 107–108, 112, 125, 153–154, 161–162, 164–165, 168, 171, 185, 207, 261, 263, 267, 270
topic-shifting strategic maneuvering 274
topoi koinoi see *topos (topoi)*
topos (topoi) 48, 52, 56–57, 59, 70–71, 81, 84, 95–96, 98, 100–108, 124–125, 188, 256

dialectical 103
formal 102
general 102
material 102
rhetorical 96, 98
special 102
specific 103
topos of causality 104
Toulmin model 64, 101
transformation 14–16
reconstruction 15
triadic argument 109
trope 121, 124, 274
Trouw case 235–240
Trudeau case 252–253
truth finding/preservation 1, 2, 221
tu quoque see argumentum ad hominem tu quoque
typology of modes of strategic maneuvering 165, 267
types of strategic maneuvering 165, 267
classification of 165, 267

U

unexpressed premise 7, 12, 18, 26, 172, 194, 209
Unexpressed Premise Rule 7, 194

unified theory of the fallacies 192
universal audience 32, 76, 116–118
usage declarative 11, 195
utalitarian(ism) 34
negative 34

V

validity (norm) 32, 193, 237
Validity Rule 8, 57
value (hierarchy) 2, 216, 236
vertical convergence/coordination 47
vir bonus 71
virtual standpoint 100

W

white rhetoric 86
Woods-Walton treatment of the fallacies 190–192, 203, 206

Z

Zeno's dialectical reasoning 55, 58–59
zone of agreement 46, 100